2003

COACH OF THE YEAR CLINICS
FOOTBALL MANUAL

Edited by Earl Browning

COACHES CHOICE™

www.coacheschoice.com

ISBN: 1-58518-856-5
Library of Congress Control Number: 2003103855

Transcription: Tom Cheaney
Diagrams: Steve Haag
Book layout: Jennifer Bokelmann
Cover design: Kerry Hartjen

Cover photo: courtesy of The Ohio State University
Back cover photo of Jim Tressel: courtesy of The Ohio State University
Back cover photo of Darrell K Royal: courtesy of the University of Texas

> *Special thanks to the Nike clinic managers for having the lectures taped, and to Greg Aylsworth and The Ohio State University Sports Information and Graphics Departments.*

Coaches Choice
P.O. Box 1828
Monterey, CA 93942
www.coacheschoice.com

Contents

Contents

THE HURRY-UP, NO-HUDDLE OFFENSE

Clemson University

Let me assure you I had a hard time convincing my wife that I had to speak here on Friday night, Valentine's Day. Are any of you here tonight married? Let's see a show of hands. Well, you were married. You will be sleeping on the sofa when you get home Sunday, I will promise you that. Being here on Valentine's Day is a tough act. I have spoken at this clinic before. I was a former assistant at Kentucky and I knew you took football very seriously. We have always had a good crowd when I lecture here.

I want to go over the shotgun offense. When I first started using the shotgun in 1988 I was an assistant at Alabama. I was working with Homer Smith who had been in coaching a long time. Since that time I have always been involved with some aspect of the shotgun.

When I went to Tulane to be the head coach, we played in the Superdome. We did not have a lot of good players. We knew we had Astroturf and we knew we would have a fast track for our games. We wanted to be able to win some games and win with big scores. We favored the high scoring games over the close, defensive games. I have just finished my sixth year with this offense.

I have just finished my fourth year at Clemson. A lot of high schools have gone to this offense. Lou Holtz went to South Carolina the same time I went to Clemson. He was an I-formation and I-over type team. He had used the option game when he was at Notre Dame. After that first year we had some success with the shotgun at Clemson. In the second year South Carolina started running some of the shotgun. So we had both big state schools of South Carolina using the shotgun offense. A lot of the high schools around the state of South Carolina started using the shotgun offense.

Some of the things we try to do with the shotgun offense are similar to what most offensive teams want to do. First of all, we want to be able to run the football. It is our priority. Every time we go to the line of scrimmage we would like to run the ball. In the six years as a head coach, we have gained over 2,000 yards a year in five of those six years running the ball. This past year was the first year we did not run for 2,000 yards. A lot of people think the shotgun offense is a passing offense, but we consider it a running offense.

You do not need a big back to run the ball out of the shotgun. The first two years I was at Tulane we had Shawn King as our quarterback. He set the record in the NCAA for passing efficiency. He was only 6'1" and played quarterback for us. When I went to Clemson, the quarterback was about 5'10". His name was Woodrow Dantzler. He made it as a running back with the Dallas Cowboys. In the 2001 season, Woodrow Dantzler was the only player in NCAA history to pass for 2,000 yards and run for 1,000. I think the Iowa quarterback may have broken that record this past year.

I know the high schools are limited in personnel. You have to take what comes to you in your school. But most of the time coaches take their best athlete and put him at quarterback. If you only have one player that has speed and agility, you can still have success with this type of offense.

We move the pocket to give our quarterbacks a better view on the plays. We move the pocket for the short players so they can see the field. So, you do not need a 6'3" quarterback to run this offense. With Kentucky running the shotgun, many of you are familiar with the shotgun offense.

The first place I want to start in talking about the shotgun offense is with communications. If you have run this offense you know you must signal plays in by hand. The opponents will be able to pick up your signals. I want to give you some ideas that will help you when teams do get your signals on the offense.

I will cover some of the problems we have encountered over the last few years. If the opponents get the signals, what do you do? First is the snap count. We like a rhythmic cadence. We also go on a silent rhythm with our quarterback. We will change the rhythm to draw the defense offsides.

Several years ago we taught our center to make a soft, dead-floating snap to the quarterback in the shotgun. If it was a bad snap the ball would not go very far. If the snap was off center it would not be too hard to handle when it's the soft floating snap. This was back in 1988, which was some 14 years ago.

I think Jim Kelly of the Buffalo Bills was one of the first to take advantage of the shotgun attack. He had a lot of success in the shotgun.

We wanted that soft, dead-floating snap to come back between the waist and the top of the numbers inside the quarterback's body frame. Now, after 14 years in the shotgun, I know it is dangerous to float the ball back to the quarterback. Those players on the end will time it and come hard at the quarterback and get their about the time that floating snap gets back to him. So we have tried to speed up the snap now from the center to the quarterback. Now we want a loose, but somewhat tight spiral on the ball. You may want to know what a loose but somewhat tight spiral snap is. It has a little zip on it but it is not a hard snap like a punt or extra point snap. The ball has a little rotation on it.

If you are going to start the shotgun as a new formation, I would start with the dead floater. This will give your center more confidence and it will allow the deep back to handle any snap that is off center.

Here is our communication on the shotgun. The center will get over the ball and look between his legs. He looks at the quarterback. Our quarterback will raise his foot to indicate to the center when to snap the ball. By using the foot we hope to keep the signal from the safety. Hopefully, the foot will be low enough so the deep defenders will not see it. The center will snap the ball on the movement of the foot of the center or he will wait until the quarterback raises his head.

Another way to get the center to snap the ball is to have the quarterback lift his foot, then raise his head, and then have the center silently count to himself, "One thousand one, one thousand two." It is on a silent count.

The guards do not have a problem with this because they can sit there and see the snap. Some teams will hold hands on the snap. We do not hold hands. Most linemen can see the snaps out of the corner of their eyes. If you run this a lot of the time the linemen will get the feel of it and it will not be a problem.

Next I want to cover the communications from the sideline. Remember we do not huddle with this offense. We have not huddled in six years. We do not have a huddle in our notebook. We just do not huddle. We communicate to the offense when we want to milk the clock, short yardage, and goal line offense. It may be a key play in the game. Everything is done at the line of scrimmage.

We take the person that is going to send the signals to the offense and put him on the sideline. We are going to signal in the formation or the play. We signal this information to the quarterback. The players responsible for reading the signal include the wideouts, the backs, the tight end, and the quarterback. The quarterback does not have to communicate the information to the other receivers. They must get the information on their own.

The fat guys, or the offensive line, they just waddle up to the line of scrimmage and sit. They do not want to exert any more energy than they have to. We do not flip-flop our line. We go right and left with our line. As soon as we run a play the center will address the ball after the official marks it ready for play. The center takes his stance and the guards and tackles line up on him. They just sit there looking straight ahead.

All of the skilled players must read the signal from the sideline. The play may come down from the box to the person that is to signal the information to the offense. We signal the formation and the play. We signal the play to the quarterback. Once the quarterback sees the play he goes to the line and tells them the play. Let me give you an example. We signal in the 37 zone play to the left side. The quarterback calls out 37, 37 to the line. Everyone knows the play is going to be 37 zone to the left side. The quarterback drops back to his regular position in the shotgun.

Before he raises his foot he looks at the sideline at the signaler. We give him another signal. We tell him to stay with the play called or we will change the play based on numbers, or alignment, or what we are trying to do for that game.

The question is how much time do we have to do all of this communicating to the offense? If you watch the officials between downs you will see you have a lot of time. Some of those big fat officials do not move very swiftly. They walk up to the ball and make it. They go over to the chain gang and tell them to move the chains. There is a lot of time between the downs and the official marking the ball ready for play.

If you will time the play out, you will be surprised at the amount of time it takes to do all of this. From the time we signal in the formation and the play, and the time it takes the quarterback to go to the line and call out the play, and then drop to his set position, then look to the sideline to get the *stay* signal, a total of 17 seconds will be left on the 25-second clock. I can assure you of this because we have been running this system since 1988.

You can get the play off quicker than the 17 seconds left on the clock. I will show you some plays you can run quicker than the 17 seconds. They are plays that do not involve calls with the line. You can get the play off very fast if you do not want to add a lot of information to the play.

If you do change the play then you are talking about more time coming off the 25-second clock. Some of our plays that are changed go down to three or four seconds left on the 25-second clock.

You will be surprised at the amount of time between plays and the time you need to signal in the plays. You have a lot of time to discuss the situation with your coordinators or other coaches between plays. You can get a lot of information from the coaches up in the press box in that amount of time. We do not huddle and that is how the communication goes.

I want to show you some film just on the snap. If you have any questions about the snap ask them now.

(Question from audience) If you want to run the 37 play again, how do you keep the defense from knowing the play when you do call it a second time?

The defense will eventually get the call. But you can mix it up so they have a hard time figuring out what you are doing. For example, instead of calling the 37 left, we could call out 37 Louie, 37 Louie. This would tell our line we are going to the left. We would make up an L-word and an R-word to indicate left and right. Against teams that scout us several times forces us to change the name of the plays. I will show you some of the things we do to combat that situation.

(Film)

In our last game of the year we played South Carolina. We went on the snap with the quarterback lifting his foot. Last season we opened up the season with Georgia. They had three months to study our cadence. All of a sudden the quarterback lifts his foot but the center did not snap the ball. The center lifts his head and then snaps the ball. We drew them offsides seven times in that first game. I suggest you change your cadence to keep the defense honest. We have the center freeze just a minute on the snap and the defense will jump offsides.

The first thing you want to do is to get into a rhythm with the snap count. Then you work on being non-rhythmic. It is all done with silent signals.

After the defense starts stemming on us we change the cadence. The quarterback looks at the defense, and as soon as he lifts his foot he sees the defense move or stem to another position. The quarterback will lift his foot, and freeze. If the defense does move the quarterback will call a play we have set up in our game plan. We want him to pause with about seven seconds left on the clock. We change the play after movement by the defense.

Against Florida State we had to check off because of the blitz. The quarterback looked over to the sideline and we gave him the signal. We had a run play called. We see man coverage and a blitz coming. The quarterback looks over one more time and we signal a blitz check. We change the play to a pass play. We change the protection and call a pass play. All of the receivers are looking to the sideline for the signal. The quarterback does not have to tell them anything.

The quarterback will call 70 left, 70 left. That tells the line the protection is 70 and the tight end is going to block on the play. We try to hit a take-off route to the field side. That is all we are doing on the play. We have changed the play at the line of scrimmage from a run to a pass.

The question everyone wants to know is this: What happens when the defense knows your signals? We know some teams will get all the information on us from their scouting report. We can tell when the other teams get our signals. We can still run the play against them even if they do know where the play is going. That is not good, but we will change it up enough to keep them honest.

After we are aware the teams know our signals, we will change the plays. If you call the plays at the line of scrimmage they are going to get your signals. But you can change things around to keep teams honest. We will change from left to Louis or some other L-words.

When we go with the quarterback under the center we go to a verbal cadence. Anytime we are in the I formation with the quarterback under the center we will use the verbal count and we go on rhythm, or we can go on non-rhythm snap counts.

The next point I want to cover is our *dummy signaler*. We will put them on the sideline and they will give out a bunch of signals.

If we see the linebackers reading their wristbands, we know what they are doing. They are reading the blitz calls from the sideline. When we see them reading the wristbands we know it is going to be a blitz of some type. You can pick that up if you will look for it.

Anytime I ask for volunteers to give the dummy signals, I get about eight people that want to give them. They are all good at it. I will take a couple of guys and make one of them live the first quarter and the other man will be dead for that quarter. You can get the third-string quarterback or the freshman quarterback to signal in the dummy plays. You can have a live players and a dummy player calling the signals. It is easy to give signals. If we feel someone is getting our signals at the line, we use two people to signal the plays in. Our running back coach and wide receiver coach happens to be our signal people for us. They will exchange being live and being the dummy on the signals.

I want to talk about critical goal line check on the signals. We are not huddling and we are going in for the score. We are under center and we check off to an option play. We still do not huddle in those situations. We call the play accordingly.

The next situation is when we want to milk the clock. We want to run the clock down as much as we can. We try to get the ball snapped with only three seconds left on the 25-second clock. We make the team aware of the clock situations and we do not want to start the cadence before we are read. We will let the clock run down before we start our snap count. You can see what we do in those situations. I have some film where we ran the clock down that I want you to see so you can see what we do in those situations.

(Film)

I just wanted to show you that you can get the job done in the no-huddle offense. You can use it when the crowd noise is against you, and you can use it to milk the clock the same as you do with the huddle.

The question has been raised about the pros who cover their mouths when the coaches on the sideline are calling the plays to the quarterbacks on the headsets. The question is this: Do teams hire lip readers to try to get the plays from the coaches to the quarterbacks? I am not sure about that, but I guess they could. I think they are lip reading most of the time when they can do it. I guess the coaches do not want the defenses to read their lips. That is about the only thing I can think is the reason they cover their mouth when they talk with the quarterback.

I want to go over some plays that you can run fast out of the no-huddle offense. We want to snap the ball as soon as the umpire gets off the ball and the referee marks it ready for play. We have 25 seconds to put the ball into play.

If you are going to go on a fast count you cannot have the offensive line make blocking calls. The same is true with the protection. You do not have time to make those calls. I want to show you a couple of plays that do not involve a call at the line of scrimmage. I will show you a run that does not involve a call and I will show you a couple of protections you can use that does not require a call at the line. If you only have six plays you can run this offense. All you have to do is to complete one pass over 10 yards to keep the drive going.

First you can run the sprint-out pass with gap protection or slide protection depending on what you want to call the protection. We do not need a call to run this play. Everyone is going to step to the outside to block on the play. You can run the jailbreak screen pass without making a call. The linemen can go downfield on the play because you are throwing the ball behind the line of scrimmage. You can run a zone run play to the right or to the left. You can run the three-step drop passing game without making calls on the line.

I will show you a couple of plays that I feel the quarterback can execute without a lot of difficulty. The first play is a high-percentage play that is easy to execute. I will show you the play from a couple of formations. We want the slot man on the inside to be lined up on the hash marks. The wide man is lined up outside on the numbers. It is a long way outside. The wide man is between the sideline and the hash mark. This is our sprint play to the right side [Diagram 1].

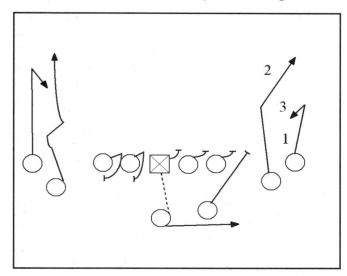

Diagram 1. Sprint play to the right side

The wide receiver runs a five-yard route and comes back to the football. The slot man runs a 10-yard flag route behind the wide receiver. We want the quarterback to throw the ball on his fifth step. That is his first read. If the receiver is open he will hit him with the pass.

My father went from playing football into college coaching. Had my dad gone on to coach in high school, I probably would have been a high school coach. He taught me this next point. If you have a booster club member's son on your team that does not pay a lot this will help you. The booster club member would give you more money if his son played more. This offense is suited for this type of move. You can take that booster club member's son and put him on the outside on the backside of the pattern. You can put him in the game on certain plays that will not hurt the offense. You can let him run the hitch route and then sprint away from him [Diagram 2].

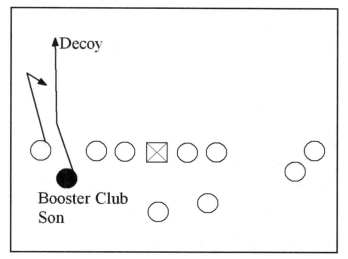

Diagram 2. Hitch route

As the season goes along, the son of the booster club member catches on to what you are doing with him. He lets you know that he thinks he can beat the defense deep. You tell him to go to the wide receiver position and to go deep. You sprint out away from him and throw the hitch to the sprint side. The son runs the deep route and keeps the defense honest and everyone is happy. We do not want to throw him the ball on the backside.

You can take the center and quarterback out on the field and have them practice this play from the different positions on the field. He can start on the left hash mark. The center snaps the ball to the quarterback and he sprints out to his right and throws the hitch route. Then you move the ball to the middle of the field. Now the quarterback can spring either way and throw the hitch route. Then the ball is placed on the right hash mark and the quarterback takes the snap and sprints to the left side. All you need for the drill is one center and two wide receivers with the quarterback. You can get five reps to the right and five to the left before practice starts.

I want to show you one additional formation with the same type of routes involved. We go from a trips formation. We want the outside receiver to run the deep route. The inside slot man runs a hitch route just beyond the area where the wide receiver lined up. The second back runs a 10-yard out route. It turns out to be a high-low route [Diagram 3]. We sprint to the outside on the play. Again we are throwing on the fifth step.

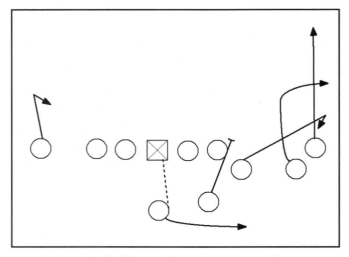

Diagram 3. High-low route

If you are looking for good plays that you can run coming out of your own end zone, you can use these two plays. They are safe plays. They are good coming-out patterns. The slant passes inside are dangerous plays. If we want a little more protection on the pass plays you can use these two plays.

If you play us, we are going to throw the ball coming off the goal line. We will throw the deep post, and the takeoff that is similar to the post. We will run the out route as well. The ball is going outside or it is going down the field. It is just like a punt if the defense intercepts the ball.

Here is a running play you can use when you want to go on the quick count. We like to run the sweep from the trips formation look [Diagram 4]. You do not need to make any calls on the play.

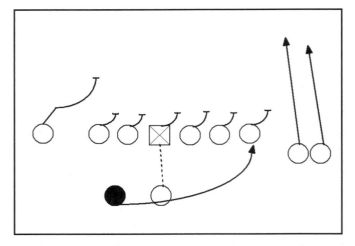

Diagram 4. Sweep from the trips formation

To keep the defense from keying on the sweep we have what we call *tendency breakers*. If the defense keys the tailback on the sweep each time he is lined up on the weakside, we run a tendency breaker. We line up in the same formation. Now we fake the sweep and have the quarterback keep the ball and break it over the backside [Diagram 5].

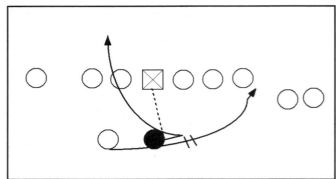

Diagram 5. Tendency breaker

I want you to know you can develop tendencies on offense. That is why we like to self-scout our offense to see if we are developing certain tendencies. If you are looking for fast plays where you can sprint out, you can run the zone plays. We do not need to make calls on these plays.

Here is another play you can use without making calls at the line. We spread the two ends on the play. It is a high-percentage throw [Diagram 6]. We can run the three-step drop game and block the gaps. We can throw the hitch, slants, takeoffs, and out routes from this set. I like hitches over outs.

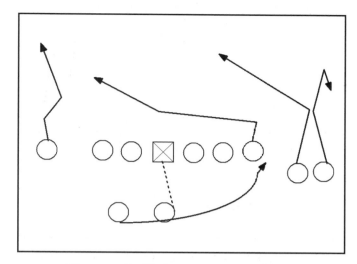

Diagram 6. High-percentage throw

If you are going to gap protect you can put the back to the opposite side. You can block the gaps with the line and have the back pick up the C gap on the backside.

If it is a short throw, the quarterback wants his hands in the proper position on the laces of the football. He may not get the laces the way he wants them. On a short throw it will not hurt the quarterback, but on a long throw he needs to get the laces turned properly in his hand.

When the quarterback gets the ball there is not a drop involved in the play. It is a matter of catch-and-throw on the play. It is like a shortstop in baseball. It is like a second baseman in baseball. He catches the ball and gets the ball off as soon as he can. It is the same with the quarterback. If the quarterback is under center he does take a one, two, three steps and then he throws. From the shotgun it is catch-and-throw on this route.

There is no call on our jailbreak screen play [Diagram 7]. If you want the blocking on the play, drop me a note and I will send you the blocking. Basically we are going to send the uncovered linemen out to block on the play. This is just another play that does not involve call for your linemen.

The question is asked about the line splits between the guard and tackle. Here is our rule. It is in its most generic form because we will split to take advantage of the defense. We tell the guard to split

one-and-a-half feet from the center. The tackle is going to split two feet. The tight end splits three feet if he is in position. We will play around with the splits against certain fronts.

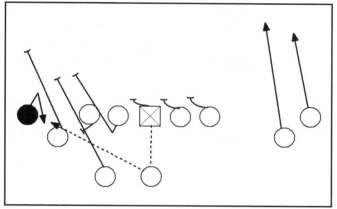

Diagram 7. Jailbreak screen play

The next play I want to talk about has been the number one play in our offense the last six years. However, we do not run it fast and it does involve a call by the line. We have the backside tackle pull on the play. We try to run the play out of trips set [Diagram 8].

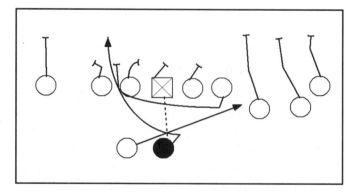

Diagram 8. Backside tackle pulls out of trips set

We can have the tailback run the ball instead of the quarterback. We counter the play and give the ball to the tailback on the cutback [Diagram 9].

A good play to run against the teams that try to send their defensive end with the pulling take is the quarterback keep play to the area where the tackle pulled [Diagram 10]. The quarterback reads the defensive end. If the defensive end goes with our pulling tackle, the quarterback reads him and runs the ball to the open area where the end left. The offense does not need to know the quarterback is keeping the ball on the play.

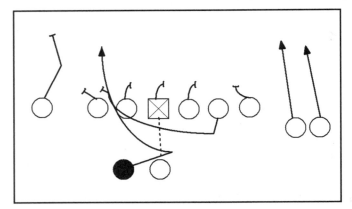

Diagram 9. Tailback on the cutback

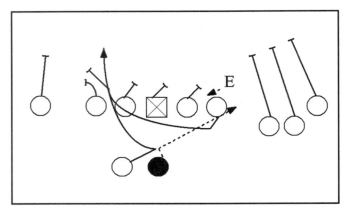

Diagram 10. Quarterback keep

The question asked about the quick plays is: How do you know when to run the quick plays? We use an indicator to let the team know we are going to use our fast offense. We have the quarterback come to the line and call the play. He may call out, "80 – 80." He may call out, "85 – 85." To us the 80 is the sprint-out protection and the 5 is the route. We use 80 to the right and 90 to the left. The 5 in the 85 is a pass-route package. It is a mirrored passing route [Diagram 11].

To get the team in the fast mode, Rich Rodriguez of WVU has the quarterback call out, "Indy – Indy," indicating the Indianapolis 500. He may have the quarterback call out, "Daytona – Daytona."

Our 83 package is a vertical pass route. The 80 is the spring out to the right side. The 3 is the vertical route for us.

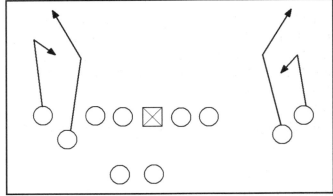

Diagram 11. Quick play

When the players hear those calls they sprint back to the line of scrimmage to line up. We use a live work to let the team know we are going to run the quick plays.

I learned a lot from Homer Smith when we worked together at Alabama. Homer had a military background. He would use words that were military words that were used in the heat of battle. For example the words *Tango, Niner, Alpha, Foxtrot,* and *Charlie* are used by the military. Homer was very smart. The words he used made a lot of sense.

A question is asked about our protection from the I formation. We call it 69 man protection. We have five linemen blocking plus one back. That is our 69 man protection. If we call 89 we spring to the play. If we call 69 it is a dropback play.

I will close here. You are welcome to come to see us at Clemson. I appreciate your attention. Thank you.

SECONDARY COVERAGE AND ZONE DOGS

University of Kentucky

It is a pleasure to be here representing the University of Kentucky. The last two months have been a blur for me. I was given the opportunity to take the head coaching position at Kentucky at the first of the year. I had to assemble an entire staff in a short amount of time. I have to get the recruiting started and try to hang on to the recruits that had already committed to Kentucky.

We also had to get the off-season program started. We are finishing up recruiting and getting our playbooks together.

I am extremely excited about the opportunity to coach at the University of Kentucky. I think Coach Morris did a great job there last year. The facilities at Kentucky were much better than I had envisioned them being. With their practice facilities, indoor practice facility, and the new football offices, there is no reason for our school not to be competitive. They expanded the football stadium in 1999 to a capacity of 68,000 and have sold it out for the past three years when the team went 2-9, 2-9, and 7-5.

The support is there and the facilities are there. We have to get some continuity in the staff so we can add to the good players that are already there. When we get that done, all we have to do is coach them. That is the good news about the Kentucky program. The bad news is everyone else in the SEC has those types of facilities and stadiums. It is a tough league in which to play.

I was able to assemble an outstanding staff of assistant coaches. I added Ron Hudson from Kansas State as my offensive coordinator. Ron brought Paul Dunn from Kansas State with him to coach the offensive line. Ron Caragher will coach the running backs. Joker Phillips is going to be our receivers' coach and recruiting coordinator. Steve Ortmayer will coach or tight ends and special teams.

On the defensive side I hired Steve Brown to coach the defensive secondary. Michael Gray will coach the defensive line. Ron McBride is going to coach our linebackers. For the past 13 years he was the head coach at the University of Utah. Finally Mike Archer, the former head coach at LSU and most recently the linebacker coach with the Pittsburgh Steelers the last seven years, is going to be our defensive coordinator.

I am overwhelmed that we were able to assemble a staff as experienced and talented as these guys are. They are not only good coaches, but good people. I told them we were going to roll up our sleeves and go out on the field and kick some butt, and we were going to have a good time doing it. If you don't have fun coaching, you are in it for the wrong reasons. It has to be fun. To me one of the best challenges is taking over a situation and making it better.

Coaching is teaching. Teaching is seeing people getting better at what they are doing. I am a defensive coach, but I'm going to talk a little about what we are going to run offensively at Kentucky. After that I'll get into my topic that is the zone-blitz package.

Offensively we are going to a balanced offense that can run and throw. We will adjust our offensive thinking around the personnel we have. Eventually we want mobile quarterbacks who can run a little bit as well as throw it. This year with the quarterback we have at Kentucky, we will take advantage of the skills he has. He is an excellent passer but not a real nifty runner. We will emphasize that part of the offense as we make the transition into the offense we want to run.

Defensively we are going to do some different things this year. Last year Kentucky played a 4-2-5 defensive alignment. In analyzing the defensive talent, we have two ways to go. We are going to play a 4-3 defense or the 3-4 defense. What we are initially thinking is we will play the 3-4 defense. Coach Archer has had a lot of experience with it and I coached it at Oregon for about six of the 18 years I was there.

One of the things I believe in as a coaching axiom is that you have to *run a system that your players can execute*. The worst thing a coach can do is force a system on players who can't be successful in that system. Do not put players in a system in which it is hard for them to be successful. Obviously it is hard to be successful no matter what you do, if you don't have enough talent to play the game.

If I am going to play man-to-man coverage, with a 4.8 corner, I am going to be in trouble. Most receivers are 4.5 or better. If the offense knows I am in man coverage it will be a disaster. The corner has a bigger problem, because I have put him into a situation where he can't be successful. There are times when I am going to ask that corner to cover man-to-man, but the offense is not going to know when that is. We will adjust his technique so he can be successful.

I have coached at all levels of football, at all positions, and on both sides of the ball. I have seen coaches absolutely chew out and ridicule players because they can't execute what they've been asked to do. Some of the times they are asking their players to do things they can't do. I have been around some schemes that I would say are unsound. If you have good enough players, you can do unsound things and beat people with it.

In my opinion you must look at your players and adjust what you are doing to fit what they can do. I think you have to adjust it week to week depending on which team they have to align against. If you want to throw the ball and have no one who can throw it, you better think of some other way to move the ball.

At the college level we have a better opportunity to keep the system the same from year to year. We can recruit players that fit the system we run. But even at the college level we end up in some years with players that don't fit our system.

I am going to be on the opposite side of the lecture you just heard. Coach Friedgen talked about training the quarterback to attack the defense. I think this will be a pretty good comparison. Coach Friedgen talked about teaching the quarterback a pre-snap read. That is where my teaching starts. You can't tell the offense what the coverage you are in by alignment. It is a chess game to decide who is going to play the game the best.

When I went to the Falcons, I was the last guy hired on the defensive side by Dan Reeves. He had hired the defensive secondary, linebacker, and line coaches before I was hired as the defensive coordinator. We analyzed our players and decided what we were going to run on defense. We ended up putting in the college 4-3 defense with the defensive end outside and the Sam linebacker inside on the tight end. We put in a lot of secondary coverage along with the front package. The front we ended up playing about 70 percent of the time for the next two years wasn't even in our playbook. When we got through training camp we decided our people couldn't do what we were asking them to do.

We ended up playing a bastardized 4-3 defense. We lined up with the defensive end to the tight end side in a 7 technique. The Sam linebacker was outside and off the ball to that side. The defensive tackles were in a 3 technique to the strongside and a 2i technique to the weakside. The Mike linebacker aligned in a strong shade on the center at linebacker depth and the Will linebacker was in a 40 technique to the weakside. We aligned our safeties at 10 yards on the tight end and weakside offensive tackle. The corners were aligned at seven yards on the outside receivers.

We were going to play cover 2 and cover 1 in the secondary. But we ended up playing cover 4 about 70 percent of the time. If we didn't play cover 4, we played a variation of it with quarter-quarter-half coverage. We ended up rolling the secondary to our corners more than we wanted to. One of our corners was Ronnie Bradford. He couldn't play corner in the NFL. He wasn't fast enough and shouldn't have been there, but he was the best we had. He was smart and he understood he was slow so he made adjustments to his techniques. We didn't want expose him so we rolled the coverage a lot his way.

The biggest key to the entire defense was the alignment of the safeties. They had to align the same way every time. On occasion we brought our corners up into a press position and still play the same coverage's. We tried to disguise the look in the secondary to confuse the quarterback.

The year before we came to the Falcons, they ranked at or near the bottom of the league in all defensive statistics. Within two years we went to second in rushing defense, first in turnovers, second in sacks, and eighth in total defense with a defense that wasn't even in our playbooks when we started putting the defense together.

We had a bunch of guys who played hard. The secondary was smart and they understood what they could not show the quarterback in a pre-snap read. Playing this philosophy, we really had nine men in the box. Both our safeties were going to be run-support guys and had gap responsibility. If the offense ran the ball in a gap, they were responsible for it and it was alright if they gained three yards. That was the thing we had to convince them on. We didn't expect the safety to make a play in his gap for less than three yards. The thing you have to explain to your players was the strengths and the weaknesses of the defense. In certain defenses you can stop some plays better than others.

In this defense the defensive end to the tight end played a C gap responsibility [Diagram 1]. The defensive tackle toward the tight end had the B gap. The backside tackle played the A gap and the backside end played the C gap. The linebackers played their gaps according to the flow of the offensive backs. If the flow attacked the C gap strong, the Mike linebacker voided the strongside A gap and filled in the C gap. If they doubled down on the tackle and kicked out the end, the Mike linebacker met the play in the hole. If they tried to block the Mike linebacker, he spilled the play to the outside and the Sam linebacker was unblocked and made the tackle.

The weakness of this defense on the run to the strong C gap is the playside A gap. If the play started off-tackle and broke back up the middle, the Will linebacker had to get across into the strongside A gap. The weak safety was responsible for the backside B gap. He did that from a depth of 10 yards. If the ball started off-tackle to the tight end and bent all the way back to the weakside B gap, we expected the weak safety to make the play for no more than a three-yard gain.

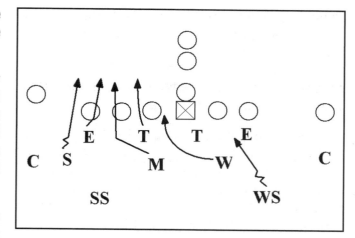

Diagram 1. 4-3 versus strongside flow

If we got flow to the weakside, the Will linebacker scraped outside the defensive end [Diagram 2]. The Mike linebacker was flowing to the weakside and scraped into the B gap. The strongside A gap is the toughest gap to cover on this type of flow. We held the Sam linebacker back and filled the A gap with the strong safety. He was coming from 10 yards deep and we didn't expect him to make a play for less than a four-yard gain.

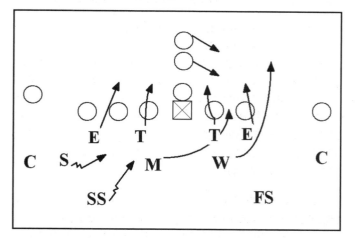

Diagram 2. 4-3 versus weakside flow

Once people found out who was filling the A gap [Diagram 3], they began to turn out of the defensive end with the offensive tackle and fold the tight end up into the hole to block the safety. The adjustment we used to handle that scheme was to move the end outside and the Sam linebacker inside. We switched the responsibility of the strong safety and the Sam linebacker.

To start with, let's put up a two-back offense in an I formation. With any two-back set our defensive secondary aligns with the corners at seven yards and the safeties at 10 yards. I'll go over the coverage we call cover 4 [Diagram 4]. I'll put a three-man front in this defensive set with four linebackers. This is probably the set we will start spring practice with. The defensive ends will be in a 4 or 5 technique and the noseguard will be in a 0 technique. We have a Will and Sam linebacker outside and two inside linebackers. In this defense we are going to bring four players all the time on the pass rush. The additional rusher will come from the outside or inside linebackers.

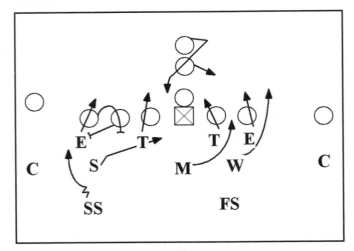

Diagram 3. Tight end fold block

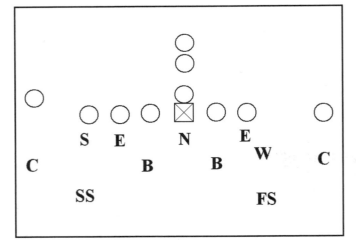

Diagram 4. 3-4 defense

In cover 4, the receivers are numbered from the sideline coming in to the formation. The flanker in this set is number one and the tight end is number two. Toward the weakside, the split end is number one and the second receiver is in the backfield. To the strongside, the corner and strong safety are reading number two, who is the tight end. The corner has

outside leverage on the flanker. He is aligned with his inside shoulder on the receiver's outside shoulder. He maintains that position on the flanker until he finds out what number two is doing.

If the tight end releases to the flat or across the field on a drag, the corner knows the safety is going to help him. He knows he has to keep outside leverage on the flanker. If the flanker runs an out pattern, the corner should be all over the out. If the flanker pushes the corner out and curls back inside at 12 yards, the safety has the play on the curl. As the safety reads number two going to the flat, he turns his attention to receiver number one. The safety makes any play coming inside by the number one receiver. The corner should not react to the inside move by number one. If the number one receiver runs a post, the corner will come over the top of the safety. The safety wheels on the post and comes underneath the pattern. The corner is over the top and the safety wheels and comes underneath. If the tight end runs something shallow or runs across, we end up in double coverage on the flanker.

If the number two receiver goes vertical, the corner knows he is not going to get help from the safety. He has to transfer his outside alignment on the split end to an inside alignment. I don't expect the corner to stop the out pattern from an inside alignment. I do expect him to make the tackle and not let the play advance up the field.

The under coverage of cover 4 is a three-under scheme. One of the linebackers is coming on a blitz [Diagram 5]. In this case we will bring the Will linebacker on the blitz. The weak safety and the inside linebacker are reading number two. If number two goes to the flat, the inside linebacker takes him in the flat, and the weak safety and corner double the split end. If number two runs across the field, the inside linebacker takes him. If the number two receiver goes vertical, the inside linebacker plays him inside out and walls him off up to 10 to 12 yards. The weak safety reads the vertical release by number two.

If the number two receiver hooks at 10 to 12 or runs across the field at that level, the inside linebacker has him. The weak safety stays on top of the number two receiver with a four-yard cushion reading the quarterback. He has to remain inside and deep to give a present inside to help the corner on a post cut by the split end. If the ball is thrown to the number two receiver, the safety can break down on him and make the tackle if the inside linebacker can't break up the pass.

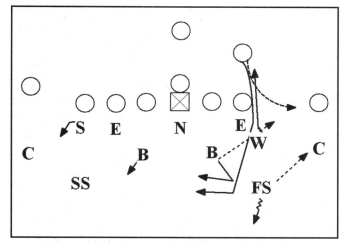

Diagram 5. Cover 4 number two vertical

The next thing we can go to from this same cover is quarter-quarter-half [Diagram 6]. On this play we will rush the Sam linebacker. The safeties cannot cheat their alignments. If they start to widen their alignment, the quarterback can see it. We are going to roll weak with the corner taking the weak flat area and the weak safety playing half the field behind the corner. On the snap of the ball the weak corner backpedals slightly to disguise the coverage. He is rolling up and wants to engage the split end. You can do this one or two ways. The corner can funnel the receiver inside or kick him outside. If we are playing a team that likes to option into the boundary, we want the corner kicking the receiver outside. That gives him inside position in run support instead of outside position against a possible block from the wide receiver.

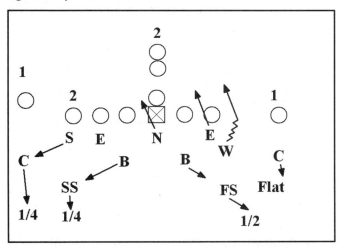

Diagram 6. Quarter-quarter-half

If the receiver is forced to the boundary he has only one way to go on the safety. If the receiver is funneled inside, the safety has to square up on the receiver because he has to play him on the post and the post corner. We can do it both ways depending on what type of offense we are running against or the ability of the safety [Diagram 7]. The Will linebacker drops into the weakside hook zone. The weak inside linebacker drops to the middle-hook zone and the strongside linebacker has to get on his horse to cover the tight end in the flat. If that gets to be a problem, we put the Sam linebacker into the flat and blitz the inside linebacker.

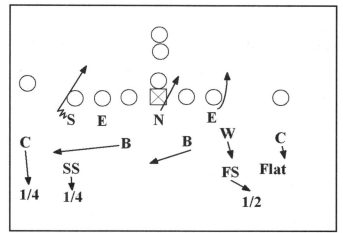

Diagram 7. Under cover

The strongside corner and safety are playing quarter-quarter cover 4 and applying their rules as before. They are both keying the tight end. If the tight end releases vertical it is just like the other coverage. The only problem is if the tight end releases to the flat. That makes a long run for the inside linebacker.

The worst thing I see in college football today is a receiver running down the field totally unmolested. I don't want to play in the secondary if no one is going to knock those receivers around.

Let's get into what I call cover 35 [Diagram 8]. Cover 35 is my concept of a three-deep zone. We added the number five to the cover to get the run support down to the most immediate run threat. If we established the right side of our defense as the strongside, on the snap of the ball the strong safety is rolling down into the box and the weak safety is rotating into the middle of the field. The Sam linebacker is coming for solid support to that side. The corners are playing the outside one-thirds of the field with an outside leverage. The outside leverage carries all the way up to seven yards from the sideline. If the receiver gets that close to the sideline, the defensive back moves back inside of the receiver. We adjust the corner inside or outside based on how close the receiver gets to the sideline. If the strength changed through a shift, we would rotate the other way. We use a simple call to change the direction. We call *Lou* for left and *Rose* for right.

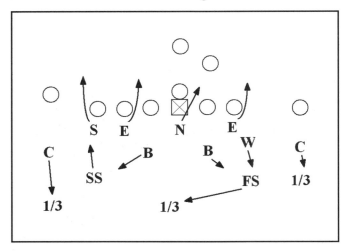

Diagram 8. Cover 35

If a team lined up in an I formation and showed no strong- or weak-back set, we make our calls from a scouting report. If the offense favored the tight end side, we call *Lou* and rotate strong. If a team likes to run the weakside lead play, we call *Rose* and rotate weak. That brings the weak safety into the box, the Will linebacker on the solid support, and the strong safety into the middle of the field. The remaining linebackers rotate accordingly. The linebacker gives a *Rip* or *Liz* call to let the Sam and Will linebacker know who is going and who is dropping. The *Rip* and *Liz* calls go to the front and the *Lou* and *Rose* calls go with the secondary.

Another thing we do from this concept is play cover 1 that is man coverage with a free safety [Diagram 9]. We start in the same alignment as we do on every play. The weakside safety is the free safety. I'll show you a different front on this defense also. We will play a reduction front to the tight end. The defensive ends are in a 3 technique weak and a 5 technique strong. The noseguard is in a strongside shade on the center. The Will linebacker is in a 5 technique to the weakside and the Sam linebacker is in a 9 technique strong on the tight end. The corners

take the outside receivers man-to-man aligning in outside leverage. They align in outside leverage positions because they are going to have help down the middle. The strong safety has the tight end man-to-man. The Will linebacker is rushing and the Sam linebacker is dropping. The inside linebacker and the Sam linebacker are responsible for the back or tight end depending on what he does. If the tight end breaks outside quickly, the Sam linebacker takes him. If he breaks inside and shallow, the inside linebacker takes him.

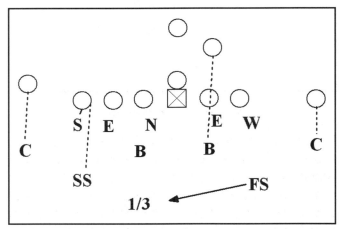

Diagram 9. Cover 1

If that happens, the strong safety becomes free and plays a robber technique. That gives the strong safety time to get down into his coverage. He does not have to cover the tight end if he runs away from him shallow. If the tight end releases upfield, the strong safety takes him. The strong safety, Sam linebacker, and inside linebacker are playing a 3-on-2 scheme with the tight end and the third receiver in the backfield to the strongside. Whoever takes the tight end, the other two defenders play inside and outside on the remaining back coming out of the backfield. If the tight end runs up the field and the back runs to the flat, the strong safety takes the tight end and the Sam linebacker takes the back. The inside linebacker is free and we probably would assign him to double on the tight end with the strong safety.

If the tight end released to the flat and the back ran a crossing route, the Sam linebacker takes the tight end and the inside linebacker takes the back [Diagram 10]. The strong safety is free to play robber or double someone. If the tight end released up the field and the back ran a crossing route, the strong safety takes the tight end, the inside linebacker takes the back, and the Sam linebacker is free to play robber or double.

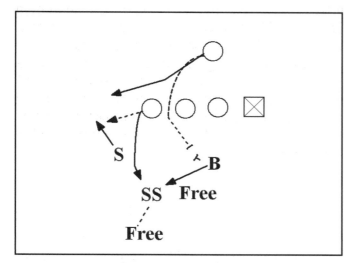

Diagram 10. Double coverage cover 1

If a team has a good tight end we simply call *cover 1, double Y*. That means the strong safety, Sam linebacker, or the inside linebacker is going to double on the tight end. The double man will be the linebacker or safety who is not covering the back. We could do the same thing on the flanker by calling *cover 1, double Z*. The key to the coverage is not letting the offense know what you are going to do until they snap the ball.

Too many times we overcoached the free safety. We wanted him deep in the middle where he doesn't get beat by anyone. The problem was he got so deep that it was almost like we were playing with 10 men and he was not in on any plays. If you have a good corner, you can play lock coverage. That means the corner is going to have his receiver man-to-man with no help. He gets in an inside leverage position and takes him without any help deep. We told the free safety to play shallower and to favor the strongside. The free safety is in position to make a play on the dig route or the shallow post.

Another thing we could do from the cover 1 coverage was to make a *jump* call [Diagram 11]. If we get a one-back and four wide receiver set, cover 1 is hard to play. The offense wants to run crossing routes on man coverage. If we get motion or a tight split by one of the split receivers, we have to make some adjustments. The shallow cross can hang a corner out to dry because he is aligned outside already. If the wide receiver jumps inside and runs the shallow cross, the corner cannot catch up. The free

safety in the middle of the field makes a call to the corner to alert him. The call tells the corner if the receiver runs the shallow cross, the safety will take him and the corner replaces the safety in the deep middle. That gives the defense a faster player into the middle and gets a player in better position to sift through the traffic to cover the shallow cross. We can do this to both sides of the set.

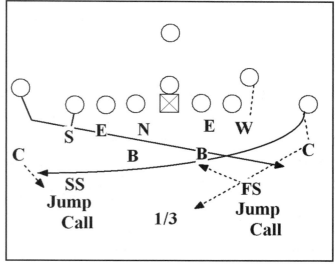

Diagram 11. Jump

I want to get into our *zone dog* coverage's. These types of defenses are happening more and more and it really screws up the quarterback's read. In this diagram I'll flip-flop the formation and run the stunt from the reduced front. This stunt has taken college and pro football by storm. We call *it 93 steam* or *storm* [Diagram 12]. The nine is our zone dog defense and the three is the coverage we are running. What we are going to do is make the quarterback think he has a hot route to his tight end. We align in the reduced front to the tight end. We bring the Sam linebacker from the outside. The defensive end slants into the B gap and the inside linebacker blitzes into the C gap. The noseguard slants across the center's face into the weakside A gap. The backside defensive end takes a wide power charge to the outside through the offensive tackle.

When the quarterback sees both the inside and Sam linebackers coming, he thinks he has the hot route to the tight end. The weakside inside linebacker jumps the tight end and the Will linebacker plays the backside hook and/or flat area. All he is doing is backing up and playing football to whatever comes his way.

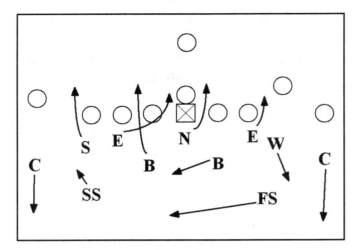

Diagram 12. Steam or storm

You can run the stunt any number of ways [Diagram 13]. Instead of dropping the Will linebacker, you can rush the Will linebacker and drop the noseguard into the backside hook zone. If you bring the Will linebacker, you can bring him behind the outside rush of the defensive end. You can also rush the noseguard and drop the defensive end into the backside hook.

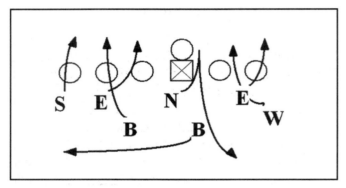

Diagram 13. Noseguard drop

These types of defenses screw up the concepts that Coach Friedgen said he was teaching his quarterback. That is why you see interceptions that look like the quarterback is throwing it to the defender.

We substitute according to what personnel package is on the field. If we get three wide receivers on the field, we take a linebacker out and replace him with a corner. If we get a four wide receiver package in the game, two linebackers are coming out and two corners will be in the game. We are not going to have a linebacker split out on wide receivers. When a team goes to four wideouts we will always have four defensive linemen down, even if we are in a 3-4

defensive scheme. The nickel and dime corners are going to be no deeper than five yards regardless of what coverage we are playing. The safeties are slightly wider and in position to play a lot of different coverage's from this set.

We call this stunt *tank* [Diagram 14]. The nickel and dime corners are blitzing outside. The defensive ends are taking one step upfield and driving inside on the offensive tackles trying to draw their blocks. The tackle and nose guard are taking one step into the offensive guards and dropping out into a hook zone on their side. The Mike linebacker is constantly moving up and back on the center so the quarterback doesn't know whether he is going to blitz. Sometimes we blitzed him and sometimes we dropped him into coverage as well. If we felt comfortable with our coverage we blitz him. If we were a bit nervous we dropped him to the deep middle to give us that security blanket.

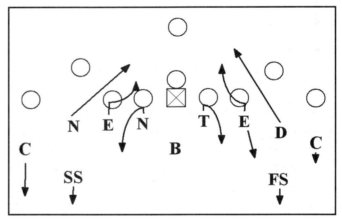

Diagram 14. Tank

The safeties and corners play what we call a *two-read coverage*. They are reading the number two receiver to their side. If the number two receiver runs an out pattern, the safety plays over the top corner as he rolled. If the number two receiver ran across or went vertical, the safety and corner played man-to-man on their receivers. That is a zone concept with man-to-man principles played from an off-man position. We do that to both sides. We have tackles making interceptions and we got a ton of sacks from this defense. One of the outside blitzers should come free. When the quarterback sees the blitz, he tries to throw hot. The nickel and dime backs have to be alert to that possibility so they can get up and knock the ball down.

Let me show you the same thing against two tight ends [Diagram 15]. This worked very, very well for us. We brought both the Sam and Will linebackers. We widen them a little and let them come off the edge. The defensive ends slant hard into the B gaps. The noseguard rushes right over the center. The inside linebacker jockeys up and back on the guards. When the ball is snapped they drop outside and wall off the tight ends from the inside. We play the same coverage.

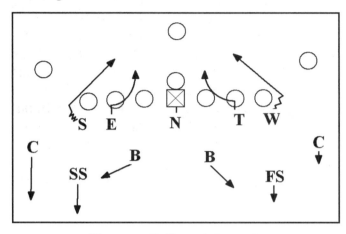

Diagram 15. Two tight ends

The safeties and corners are keying the tight ends. If either of them block, we get a double by the corner and safety on the outside. If the tight end goes to the inside, the inside linebacker walls him off and takes him and we get the double on the outside. If the tight end goes outside, the corner rolls up and the safety goes over the top. This was really a good zone dog against two tight ends.

If the offense did a lot of dropback passing out of this set, this scheme worked well against it. If they tried to maximum protect and kept one or both the tight ends in to block, we ran this stunt. We called it *guts* [Diagram 16]. We slanted the noseguard into the weakside A gap. We blitzed the linebacker from that side across the center into a strongside tight B gap. The frontside linebacker came off the butt of the other linebacker and blitzed over the center. The defensive ends power rush through the outside shoulders of the offensive tackles. The Sam and Will

linebacker dropped to the inside of the tight end to wall them off if they tried to release across or up the field. We played the corners and safeties in the *two-read coverage* and reacted to the reads on the number two receivers.

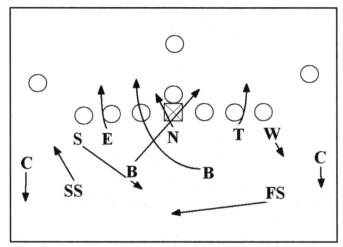

Diagram 16. Guts

We got tremendous pressure up the middle on this stunt and it really affected the quarterback. He had to get rid of the ball in a hurry.

If we face a twin set, I like to match personnel. I bring both the corners to the two-receiver side. The Will linebacker will walk off on the inside receiver and take an inside position about four yards off him. The strong safety goes to the tight end side and the free safety is on the twin side. If we had a cover 4 called, both corners are reading the inside receiver. The Will linebacker is taking the inside route of the inside receiver and the two corners are taking the outside receiver. The weak safety is almost like a free safety in the slot formation.

Fellows, it is a pleasure for me to be here. I played for Tommy Prothro at Oregon State and later coached with him at UCLA and the Rams. He said the best time in a coach's life is the time between the day he's hired and the day he plays his first game — you haven't done a hell of a lot wrong in that time. I am enjoying this time. Until we play Louisville, this is not a bad job. Thank you for your patience and your attendance.

USC BASE-UNDER DEFENSE

University of Southern California

It is always a pleasure to speak for Nike and the Coach of the Year Clinic. I'm pleased to be here. When I was in the NFL, we didn't talk to anyone about what we were doing or shared anything with anyone.

Nike has done a fantastic job of giving us the opportunity to speak at these clinics. It is a lot of fun to visit with high school coaches. I know you guys are coming to these clinics to try to find ways to get better. We are doing the same thing. We are talking football and trying to find ways to get better.

I have been asked to talk about *defense*. I'm going to start off with some general things. I am really excited about being at USC and I'm really excited about our team. I grew up in Southern California. I was captured by the style and the special atmosphere that surrounded USC. To come back after all these years and get a chance to coach there is really thrilling.

I am so excited about the environment that I'm in. Being in the college setting and working with kids is so much fun. There is a growing ball of enthusiasm about the USC football program.

It took us two years to get the program in shape. We had a tremendous run to end the season this past year. When I took the job last year it was too late to get the program to where I thought it should be. But this year we got things going in the right direction. I thought we could make some noise this year and maybe get into the top 10 in the country. I am thrilled with the results.

In our first year we started out 1-4 and were struggling. We kept losing games on the last play or last drive of a ball game. We were so close to winning game within our conference, but we were playing lousy football. We always found some way to lose the game instead of win it. We knew if we could get on a roll and take care of our own business, we could win some of those close games.

We finally got going and started to build on some of the humbling things that were happening. We didn't do anything too well, but started to play good defense. When we did that, it was hard to get us. We won some games at the end of the season that set us up for this year.

As I looked at our schedule for this past year I realized how difficult it was. I didn't feel we were ready for that kind of schedule. What that schedule did was to set a challenge for our football team. If we didn't play well, the next season we were going to get embarrassed. That was our theme for the entire winter program.

We felt if we weren't physically and mentally ready for the upcoming season, we were going to get murdered. It set the tone for our program. We talked about finishing well in our games. Because we were so weak in finishing games the year before, it became the central theme for our players.

This year, the later in the game it got, the better we played. I can never remember being on a team where it was so clearly obvious that we were a better team in the fourth quarter than we were at any other time in the game. It was such a great thing to happen to our football team. We were executing better and putting people away.

They were doing all the things that a good football team was supposed to do. The only thing I can attribute that attitude to was we were scared to death. We were scared we weren't going to be able to stand up to the people we were going to play against. In our strength and conditioning program this summer, we keep driving home the idea of having to perform to compete against the people we were going to play.

That kind of stuff doesn't happen without players. Paul Hackett did an outstanding job of recruiting these kids into SC. Our players are making some noise at the NFL combines and will make good NFL players. Our quarterback, Carson Palmer, had a fantastic season and won the Heisman Trophy. It was so much fun to see that happen. But that goes to show you it wasn't all coaching. We had some good players.

It has been a great year and we are excited about it. The challenge is to come back next season and do it again. If you can have a good season year after year, you know you have turned the corner. Any time you do well as a team it is because you have good coaches. We have a great staff of assistant coaches. Norm Chow was chosen the National Assistant Coach of the Year. That was recognition for all of us at Southern California.

I want to talk a little philosophy to give you a feel about how we run our approach to the defense. After that, I'll work my way into some defensive schemes.

After all these years of coaching, I continue to look for better ways to do things and improve. I found that after all these years I'm seeing things clearer than I used to. I am able to benefit for all the mistakes, screw ups, bad ideas, and bad game plans.

My role as the head coach is very simple. I have to orchestrate the performance of our players on game day. When you realize all that you have to do, it can be overwhelming. If I can get game-day performance to its height and get our players playing well, then I can blend together the things I need to do to get that mix.

Some of these things are so basic, but you have to do a lot of things right. If you don't, you will find there are areas within your football team that are going backwards. We don't want to give our opponents an advantage anywhere.

If there are things in our program that we would like to do, but we don't execute them well, we don't do them. We have to have all our schemes, clock management, and game plan in order. If we don't have them in order, we don't attempt to do them on game day. I have found over the years that the more you try to do, the thinner you spread yourself. The thinner you spread yourself, the more apt you are to make mistakes and errors. To be a good football team you have to be hard to beat. That means you are not beating yourself with mistakes and turnovers.

To do those things you have to have a clear vision of what you want your team to look like. You have to know that so well that you can convince your players and coaches of what they should see when they watch films of your team. If they can't do that, they are still misguided in their vision.

My philosophy is real simple. I want to play with a football team that plays with *great effort* in all phases of the game. Players have to play with *great enthusiasm*. That type of play energizes your team, staff, and everyone in the stadium.

The thing that I believe in is *playing smart*. This has to do with everything we do. It is what the coaches ask the players to do, and how the coaches handle the game itself. It is the solid techniques they teach, the game they call, and the system they use. It is also our players on game day as to the way they handle the game. I want our players to be prepared for every situation that may arise in a game so they can make the proper decision. I want them to have confidence and to play like they have been there before.

If we play with great effort, are enthusiastic, and play smart, we have a chance to play well. Philosophy is a like a railroad track. If you are off the tracks, you have a bumpy road to travel. You know something is wrong, but you don't know how to fix it. The philosophy is the guideline that puts you back on the track. My philosophy about our football team is really simple. It is all about the *ball*. In all areas of the football game, if you don't have the football, you are nothing.

On offense, we want to take care of the football for as long as we can until we score. That doesn't sound like there is much to that statement. Every phase of our offense has to be geared to taking care of the ball. Obviously I'm talking about not turning the ball over. We want to keep on making first downs and keep the ball until we score. We want to guard the ball with our lives. If you can do that as an offensive coach, you have a chance.

We want to constantly remind the team of possessing the ball. When your players are standing around with a ball in their hands, a coach will walk over and try to knock the ball out of his hands. We do it on the sidelines at a game, in practice, or anywhere to remind them how important it is. That has to become the consciousness of taking care of the ball.

Defensively we try to do a lot of things, but we play defense not to stop people. We don't play to make the offense go three and out. We don't play defense to shut out people. We play defense to *get the football*. Every time the ball is snapped, the defense tries to get the ball. If the defense can take the ball away from the offense, they are going to give it to an offense that is going to keep it until they score.

The offense cannot score without the football. For that matter, the defense can score if they get possession of the football. A philosophy will only work if all of your players totally agree with it and will play to it.

Our first year at SC we were plus 14 in turnovers. The year before I arrived there, they were a minus 36 in turnovers. This year we were plus 18 in turnovers. Over a two-year period that makes us plus 32 and there is no one in the country that can touch that. What I'm trying to show you about philosophy is the fact you should get what you emphasize.

Whether we can continue to improve in that area is a mystery, but that is how we do it. The first year we ended up 6-6 and were a sloppy football team. But this year we did more things right, got ourselves into position to win, took care of the football, and had a hell of a season.

If you don't have a philosophy, you better be coaching from the middle of your heart. If you are not doing that, you will screw everything up, because you won't emphasize what you are doing enough. If you don't emphasize things enough, you are not going to get what you want.

There is another thing about philosophy that I'm not quite sure how to say it. Football is a *collection* of a lot of little philosophies. I don't quite know how to describe it, but there are little philosophies in everything that you do. It goes from holding on to the football to coaching stances or to getting after the football on defense.

When coaches have a strong belief in something, you tend to form your philosophy. When you believe in something strongly, you emphasize that and it becomes a part of your coaching philosophy. If you are sketchy on what you believe and how you do things on offense and defense, you will be a sketchy football team.

I have really been fortunate in my coaching career. When I started out I spent three years a graduate assistance. No one would hire me or even send me a rejection letter. A good friend of mine told me there was a graduate assistant's job open at the University of Arkansas. That was the year Lou Holtz went there as the head coach. I got it and that was the best thing that ever happened to me.

I got to work on Monte Kiffin's staff. He had been at Nebraska before he came to Arkansas. I think he is the best football coach in the United States. He is just an unbelievable coach. He ran the under defense at Nebraska and they had won a couple of national championships. He brought that to Arkansas. I have been running that defense since 1977 when I learned it from him.

I have used a variation of this defense my entire career. I stayed with that principle through all these years of coaching. I have a real strong belief in that defense. I know the defense and the adjustments so well that my belief system is strong and rock solid.

During the course of my career, I have played some other defenses, which have been great for my exposure to the game. It has added to my knowledge of the game, but it is not the defense I want to run. If you have changed your philosophy, there is a chance there are some areas within your system that can cause you some problems. You are trying to work out the problems and you are experimenting with the system. That is natural, but sometimes you have to find a system and just live with it.

There is no offensive play or defensive scheme that is going to win championships for you. It is how you can adapt and adjust to make the schemes work. The only way you can do that is to have a strong belief. If you can't say what your philosophy is or tell others what you believe in, you don't have a philosophy.

Once you come up with the belief and the philosophy, you add on to it. You make adjustments to it and tweak it and fix it to reflect your beliefs. When the road gets bumpy you can get yourself back on track.

The most important thing that we do as head coaches is *practice and preparation*. You play like you practice. If you practice badly, that is the way you play. You have to design your practice for the players to get out of them what you want. Coaches have to envision how they want their practices to be and make it happen. If you come to one of our practices, you will see wall-to-wall enthusiasm. You will see and hear our players and our coaches really into what we are doing. They will be smoking for an hour and 45 minutes, with competition coming from every drill.

Any phase of practice that I can get players to compete against one another, I'm doing it. They stay on task for every drill we do. I want our practices to be uplifting, challenging, and physical. I want something at stake on every snap. If something isn't at stake, he is not going to do his best. We never want our players to play a game when they are not trying to do their best. So why would you every have a practice where the players are not trying to do their best.

At practice, if you are teaching something and everyone is standing around, most likely you are wasting someone's time. Don't have your players standing around on the practice field listening to someone talk. Sit them down before you go on the field and tell them what is going to happen in practice. Do all your teaching in meetings with the group, so when you hit the field you are doing things and not standing. When they get on the field the players are running, working, hitting, and are enthusiastic.

Somewhere in the middle of practice, we stop the activity and take a break. That is what happens at halftime of a game. During the break you give your instructions and do some coaching. After the break you have to get them going again. You can't come back after halftime of a game and be flat. Teach them to handle that during practices. Make sure you always finish your practices hard and not slacking off. That is the way you want to finish a game.

The players have to want to practice that way. The assistant coaches have to carry the message. When the players go from one drill to the other, there has to be the same intensity and same message coming from every coach on the field. It is the mentality of the guys running the drills that make the practice go. I had been coaching a long time before I really realized how important that was.

What I am trying to get done with our staff, our team, and our individual players, is to get to game day with a *tremendous level of confidence*. I want them to know we can do a lot of things right. I want them to know through their practice they are ready to give the kind of effort it is going to take to win. We are not going to ask them to do a thing in the game they have not accomplished in practice. Nothing should ever happen in a game a situation that you have not covered in practice. If that does happen, it is your fault as the coach.

You want them in a frame of mind so they don't worry about anything. You want your team to come on the field and be confident regardless of who you are playing, whether the game is home or away, or whether it is raining or snowing.

When you get that from your players, they know they are going to win. The feeling that goes with knowing you are going to win is an exciting thing. If you don't know what you are trying to get done, you will be lucky if it ever does happen.

I want to talk some football and show you some techniques. We play our *base defense* about 50 snaps a year. That sounds like a small amount to play the base defense. What we play are the adjustments off the base most of the time.

This defense has stood the test of time. This front and secondary concept is the same one Monte Kiffin brought to Arkansas in 1977. This is the same defense we adapted at the Minnesota Vikings with Floyd Peters. We have run this defense so long and tweaked it so well that it is simple and simple to adjust. It is a good defense for stopping the run and can give you an aggressive pass rush.

The front of the defense is called *under*. We use *cover 1* with this front, which is man-to-man coverage. We use the word *flex*. It is a term that we use in reference to the split end side of the offensive set. We refer to the tight end side as the *solid* side.

This front is called *under-cover 1-flex* [Diagram 1]. The flex call means the free safety is going to the split end side of the offense. From this front you get a gap-control type of play. When you put a defensive lineman in a gap and tell him he has to control that gap, he can play very aggressively. He can aggressively attack the line of scrimmage.

The more attacking-oriented the defense is, the better off it will be. Obviously when you come off the ball, sometimes it is run and sometimes it is pass. We like to be in the mode of attacking the line of scrimmage, so when it is pass, we will get pressure on the quarterback.

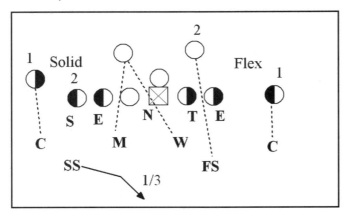

Diagram 1. Under-cover 1-flex front

There are eight players in the box area of this defense. We are going to stop the run with this defense. In this defense we outnumber the offense. The defense has more players at the line than they can block.

The Sam linebacker plays the tight end man-to-man using outside leverage in a loose 9 technique. The Sam linebacker cannot get hooked because he is playing outside leverage on all blocks.

The free safety is playing down to the line of scrimmage and is responsible for the number two receiver to the weakside of the formation. He plays the receiver with outside leverage. That is easy for him. It should allow him to play really aggressive in the running game, because the running back cannot beat the free safety coming out of the backfield. The Will and Mike linebackers are bracketed on the other running back playing him in and out with outside leverage. The corners are matched up on the wide receivers man-to-man.

The thing that is challenging is the Mike linebacker playing the play-action. However, he knows he has help and can overplay to where he is vulnerable.

No matter what man-to-man coverage you are playing, you have to convince your players to win on their leverage side. If the coach tells a player to play outside leverage and complains when a receiver catches a ball to his inside, the coach is wrong. When we give them a leverage side, we are telling them to at least do something right.

Let's take this one step further. From the NFL to the college level, if you tell your corners to stop the out route, you better have someone playing over the top of them. There is not a corner in the world that can play out routes and stop the deep ball. You have to be realistic as to what your players can do. If you tell the corner he has to play the out route and the deep ball, he will hang on the deep ball because he doesn't want to get beat deep. If you get beat deep, you can't play football. You have to go to the sideline.

We tell our corner to play inside leverage on the wide receivers. How can the corner make a play on the out route? The only way the corner can make a play on the out route is if the offense screws up; the quarterback makes a bad throw or the receiver runs a bad route. If you don't understand that, you are going to ask the corner to do something he can't do.

The flexside end is playing on the outside shoulder of the tackle and can be a pass-rushing fool. The only thing he cannot do is get hooked. He can really play aggressive. He can play pass first and run second and still be effective.

The key to this defense is not getting hooked. If the solidside defensive end is aligned in the C gap, he can't get hooked. He has to control that gap. The strong safety in this defense is going to the middle third.

If the offense comes out in a one-back set, everyone plays the same except the free safety [Diagram 2]. He is still playing the number two receiver to the flexside, but he has to move outside to cover him.

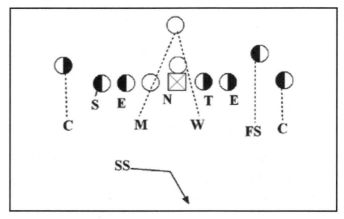

Diagram 2. One-back set doubles

If we get a trips set, we handle that adjust with our two safeties [Diagram 3]. No one changes except the safeties. The strong safety moves out to cover the number two receiver to his side. The Sam linebacker is still on the tight end. The corner has the number one receiver and the free safety rotates to the middle.

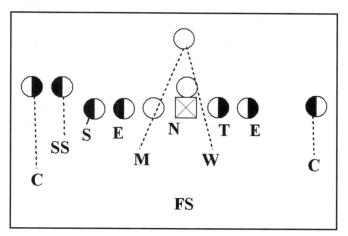

Diagram 3. Trips set

To stay out of mismatches, the corner can take the wide receivers and match up with them [Diagram 4]. If both wide receivers come to the same side, we can put both corner on them and cover with the safety on the remaining receiver. If the corners are into the boundary, the free safety is in the middle. If the corners are into the wideside of the field, the strong safety is in the middle.

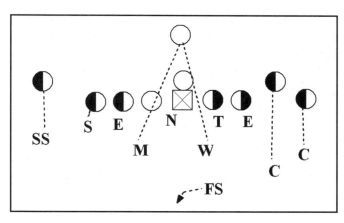

Diagram 4. Twin doubles

The other one-back set is the one-back and two tight ends set [Diagram 5]. We put the free safety up on the second tight end. That gives you a problem with run support, but we can play it that way. Everything in the defense is the same.

If the offense comes out and gives the defense a two-back set with two tight ends, nothing changes for the defense [Diagram 6]. The corner comes inside and plays man-to-man on the second tight end. Everyone else has the same match ups they had with any two-back sets.

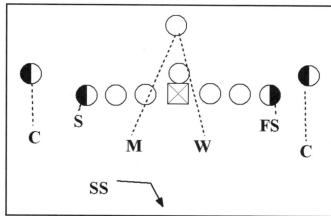

Diagram 5. One-back and two tight ends set

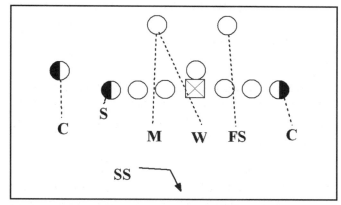

Diagram 6. Two-back set with two tight ends

I want to show you how we react to the run, so when you see the film you will know what we are doing [Diagram 7]. Our defensive ends are aligned in 5 techniques. The noseguard is in the A gap to the solidside. The flexside tackle is in a 3 technique to the flexside. The Will linebacker has the A gap responsibility to the flexside, but on plays run to the solidside he has to get over the center's block quickly. He cheats somewhat to the solidside.

Everyone in the defense is turning everything inside. No one can get hooked. The Mike linebacker has the solidside B gap. If he is attacking in the B gap, he meets the block and turns it back inside. He plays with his head and outside arm free taking the block on with his inside shoulder. The free safety is our backside player. If the ball breaks back to the flexside A gap, he makes the play there. If there is a reverse run back the other way, he also makes that play. He does not cross the center to make any plays.

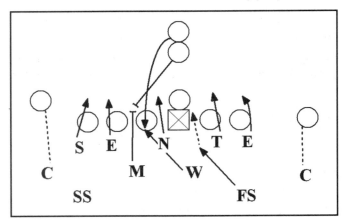

Diagram 7. Solidside run responsibility

On the solidside with the offense in an I formation, they have four blockers. The defense has four defenders with the Will linebacker fast flowing to that side. Everyone on the defense is knocking the ball back inside to the Will linebacker.

If the ball is run to the flexside, the Mike linebacker becomes the backside run player [Diagram 8]. He does not have to cross the center to make plays. If he needs to run through the backside B gap on plays away from him, he can. The free safety can do the same thing on plays away from him. If you ask the Mike linebacker to play the cutback and get over the top, he is not going to aggressive.

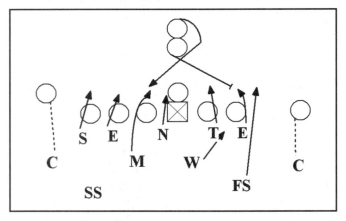

Diagram 8. Flexside run responsibility

To the solidside, everyone plays with their outside arm free [Diagram 9]. If the Sam linebacker gets a down block from the tight end, he rides him down and looks into the backfield for the next block coming to him. On that block we ask him to wrong arm

that block and bounce the ball outside. With that type of play we get what we call *backer force*. The Mike linebacker sees the power play going off-tackle. He knows the Sam linebacker is going to bounce the play. He comes over the top and plays the ball with the strong safety coming up late to play the ball from the outside. Outside of that situation, everyone plays with their outside arm free.

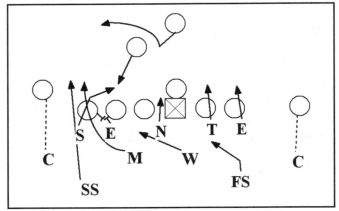

Diagram 9. Backer force

There are some adjustments we can make with our noseguard. We can move him over to head-up the guard into what we call a *G position*. What we normally do with that alignment is slant back to where we came from. As long as the defender keeps the ball on his inside shoulder he can play as fast as he wants to.

We use our alignment to show overload to one side and slant everyone back to the other side. That is the flexibility of the defense.

There is a lot of flexibility for changing the force in this defensive scheme [Diagram 10]. If you believe in what you are doing, then you can do other things to complement what you are doing. If the offense knows the free safety is your flexside force man, they can develop schemes to make it hard on him. All we do is change the force from free safety force to *corner force*.

We change the force by slanting the defensive 3 and 5 techniques inside and scraping the Will linebacker outside. We bring the corner off his wideout and make him the force man. He is playing the number two receiver out of the backfield and is the force man on the run to him. The free safety rolls over the top of the corner into the deep half field. If you don't want to play man-to-man, you can play zone. With this kind of force change, you can play quarter coverage to the solidside and half coverage to the flexside.

I'm going back to the film and show you some different kinds of force and talk about the technique used in that type of force. I think it is important that your players in the secondary know how to play the force. The style of technique is important to them. If the safety man is up in force and has minimum pass coverage responsibility, he can be extremely aggressive. Minimum coverage would be taking a running back out of the backfield or flat-to-curl zone coverage. I let them get all the way in the backfield on play-action passes even if they are wrong. They are taught if they get caught, they can punch their inside foot and get depth to their area very quickly. What I get from this action is a very aggressive hard-ass play from the safeties.

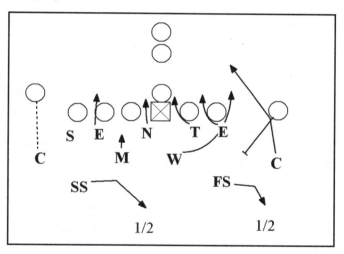

Diagram 10. Corner force

They want to take everything on with the inside shoulder with their inside leg up. The outside arm and leg are to be kept free. They have to be prepared to bounce to the outside, but they must squeeze to the inside as hard as they can. We are not asking the force man to make the tackle. We are asking him to squeeze the space down and the next man coming from the inside will make the tackle.

The idea is to be really simple. Don't give him too many things to do so he can be really aggressive. As long as he keeps the football on his inside shoulder,

he can chase the football all the way across the formation. It will almost look like he is blitzing.

If the wide receiver cracks on the free safety, we teach the free safety to attack the crack-back block as aggressively as he can. That makes it easy for the corner to see what is going on and to get outside for the force.

When the Sam linebacker forces, he has to keep the relative spacing between himself and the defensive end. He can't allow the ball to get between him and the defensive end. He has to keep his shoulders square and shuffle down the line of scrimmage. If the ball bounces, he can pursue the ball outside easily.

Ninety-nine percent of the time we play our corners in press coverage. Against some spread offenses we will back them off. The more option the offense runs the less man-to-man coverage we play. We want to get the defensive backs eyes on the football. I think option football is the worst thing that could happen to the defense. We will never schedule Air Force because it is too hard to defense that stuff.

The *deep safety* is something that is really dear to my heart. That is where I played. The deep safety has to play two routes. He has to play the *seam route* and the *post route*. That is all I ask him to play. He has to find the seam route from the number two receiver. If there are two of them, he has to get in the middle and play them both. On the post route he has to stay on top of that route. That is easy to do, but it becomes hard because they want to do more than that.

Once in awhile the deep safety may run into a deep crossing route. We don't coach our guys to do that, but every once in awhile they may see it.

We flip-flop our defense. The Sam linebacker goes to the tight end. We have a rush-and-drop end. The rush goes with the Sam linebacker and the drop goes with the Will linebacker. The Mike linebacker aligns to the Sam linebacker side. The corners match up with wide receivers and the safeties flip-flop to passing strength and running strength.

Guys, thanks for your attention.

APPLYING PRESSURE ON THE QUARTERBACK

University of Dayton

I was able to see Coach Don Houser of Youngstown State at the end of his lecture. I saw he had his PowerPoint slides going. Guys, you will have to remember I am coaching at a poor Catholic University. We do not have all of that fancy equipment. You will see my overhead diagrams.

My topic is about *pressuring the quarterback*. Regardless of the level you are coaching on, that seems to be a topic everyone is talking about. The biggest challenge to defenses today is pressuring the quarterback. This is because of the number of teams that are passing the football today. The passing game has really evolved through the years with all of the different offensive sets. With the liberal rules on pass protection and offenses sending out four and five receivers, it becomes very difficult to pressure the quarterback and still have good sound defensive coverages. It is amazing how the officials have allowed the pass protection to progress. Offensive line coaches may be calling it protection, but I call it grab and hold. They call it protection.

Each year we have an official come speak to our team about the new rules. We ask them questions about holding and this is what they tell us. "Guy, don't come up to the officials complaining about the offense holding." The point is the officials are not going to call it. If it is not a blatant hold that impedes the defender's path to the quarterback, they are not going to call it. It is that plain and simple. As a result, we have to come up with some different ways to get pressure on the quarterback. That is what I want to share with you here today. I want to talk about how Dayton University gets pressure on the quarterback.

I want to start with a quote I found a couple of years ago. It is not by a football player. Of all things it was by a basketball player. The basketball player was Bill Russell, the Hall of Fame Boston Celtic. He was not known for his offense, but he was known for his

defense. Bill Russell said, "Defense is a science and not a helter-skelter thing that you just luck into." Defensive coaches will prepare for the upcoming game if they take that approach. You must look at defense as a teaching situation and as a classroom situation. You must organize your defensive scheme to counter the offense.

When I saw that statement, I felt it fit in very well with our defensive philosophy at the University of Dayton. At Dayton we are not a big believer in man-to-man defense. We love to play *zone coverage*. We like to play the two-deep zone and the three-deep zone. We are not going to apply pressure on the quarterback by blitzing. We are not a blitzing-man coverage defense. We are must apply pressure with our front four defenders. We must figure out a way to get pressure on the quarterback by twisting with the front four men.

We have been very successful with this philosophy over the years and especially in the last couple of years. The reason we play zone coverage is because we feel we can play the run much better. Our defenders are not turning their backs and they are not running out of the lanes.

In 2001 we had 31 interceptions. In 2002 we had 28 interceptions. A big reason for those interceptions was because of our pass rush. The majority of the time we were running some type of twist with those four down linemen. We do not want to guess on defense. We like to know what we are doing and how we are going to stop a play.

When we were looking at our defensive scheme, we had to look at the *strength* of our defense. The thing we do best relates to *speed*. This is what we do best on defense. We recruit the type of players with speed. We do not get the big, strong individual players at Dayton.

When it comes to the pass rush from the front four down linemen, it becomes difficult to rush the quarterback with more than four defenders running. If you leave a passing lane open, the good quarterback will find that passing lane. We had to come up with something that would allow us to put pressure on the quarterback and to allow us to take advantage of what we had as far as our personnel.

There are *three types of defensive players* that we look at when putting our defense together. First is the player who *watches things happen.* This is the worst type of defensive player. As a defensive coach this is something you cannot stand for. When we are looking at recruits on film and we see a player that stands and watches the play, we are not going to recruit that kid. I am sure if you see that on your game tape you are going to get after the player and let him know you are not going to stand for that in a game. Our defensive players do not stand and watch. We are not going to have players that watch things happen.

In practice, if we feel the defense is not getting to the ball fast enough, we will go to our *double-whistle drill.* The first whistle stops the play. Then a second whistle blows and we want all 11 players swarming to the ball. It does not matter if it is a pass or a run; we want all 11 players around the ball. If an individual defensive man does not get to the ball, the defensive staff will point that out to them. So we use the double whistle to get the defense to the football when they are not hustling to the ball.

The second type of defensive player that we look at is the defensive player who *wonders what happened.* The play is run and the player is blocked and he has no idea what happened on the play. You cannot play with that type of player. You must have a defender that knows what is going on when he is on defense.

The third type of player is the one who *makes things happen.* That is the type of individual that you want on defense. The offense can have any type of players they want. But on defense, we want players who make things happen. Some coaches will tell you their linebackers or safeties make things happen. We want *all* of our defensive players to make things happen. When it comes to pass rush, it better be those four front men on the rush who make things happen.

There are two basic fronts that we run. We use these two fronts the majority of the time. The first front is what we call our *kickdown front* [Diagram 1]. Some teams call it an eagle look, and some teams call it shade. We call it a kickdown front.

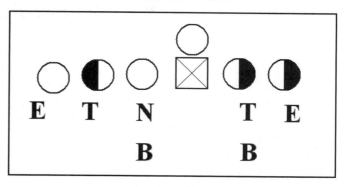

Diagram 1. Kickdown front

It is a five-man front. We have kicked down to the tight end side. In our numbering system, we number each lineman 1, 2, and 3. We call them in a 1, 2, or 3 — and inside, heads up, or outside shoulder. The defensive end is in a 9 technique. The strong tackle is in a 5 technique and the nose is shaded to the tight end side of the center. The weakside tackle is in a 3 technique and the backside defensive end is in a 5 technique. We can move the noseguard to a head-up position at times to give the offense a different look.

The other front we work out of is our nickel front and we call it our *box front* [Diagram 2]. We have two tackles in a 1 and a 3 technique in the middle. We have the ends on the outside in 5 techniques. We bring in an extra back when we run this defense. The four players up front could be two tackles and two ends. They could be three tackles and one end. What we are looking for on the front line are the four best passrushers on our defense.

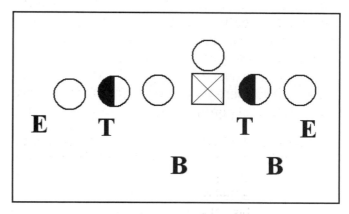

Diagram 2. Box front

We do not flip-flop our linemen. Our players know if they are playing a 1 technique or a 3 technique they have to play it on that side of the line. We do not get into moving the players from side to side. We are a 52 defense, but rarely are we in an odd front. We are going to be in the knockdown or the nickel package.

Out of these two fronts we run our *twist*. Our basic philosophy on the twist has three parts. First, we want to *execute on the offensive side of the ball*. If you do the twist on your side of the ball, the offensive blockers will pass the lineman off to the next man and they will block you. Once the ball is snapped, the offensive linemen want to keep separation from the defensive linemen. So our philosophy is to execute on the offensive side of the ball. We want to work upfield before we do anything. This makes it much tougher for them to pick up their blocks. They can knock each other off and that will allow one of our linemen to come free.

Second, we want to *do our twist on both sides of our line*. The reason for this is because the offense can help to one side, and if you only twist to one side of the line the offense can block your defense. Remember we are only sending four rushers. The offense can have someone to pick up the twist. To counter this we always run the twist to both sides of the line. Now we have a good chance of having someone come free. We should get some type of 1-on-1 where they cannot double-team you and close off a gap. When I show you our film you will see that we run it to both sides of the ball.

Third, we want to *time the defensive moves*. We can only get better with practice reps. If you are going to run the twist you must practice the moves. Our defensive staff will take prepractice time and they will take time during two-a-days to work on the timing the twists. We are making these moves on the run. The defenders must get a feeling for each other. They have to know how fast a teammate is on a play. If we play a team that is going to be throwing the ball a lot, we work on the twist on Tuesday and Wednesday. We must get the timing down. That is the only thing you can get better running this defense. When we fist start running these stunts, we run into each other a lot running the twist. We want to make sure we give them a lot of reps.

Our final point on our philosophy is *dogs and rabbits*. When you rush four defenders, it seems there is always a lane open. We have four rushers busting their butts trying to get to the quarterback. As the quarterback steps up he finds the passing lane. This is the analogy that I give to our players. How many of you go hunting? Do you ever go rabbit hunting? You take a beagle dog with you, right? What do you use the beagle for? You use the dog to bring that rabbit to you, right? You send the dog to the brush to flush the rabbit out to the hunter. The hunter is standing outside the brush ready to shoot the rabbit. This is the same philosophy we use with the twist on defense.

We are going to turn someone loose to *flush the quarterback out*. We are always going to have someone ready to make the kill on the quarterback. When he steps up in the pocket, we want our man ready to take him down. This has been a big part of our philosophy over the last few years. We want the dog to chase the rabbit out in the open to the hunter. The hunter will take care of the rabbit.

What type of twist are we talking about here? The first twist I want to cover is what we call *Tom* [Diagram 3]. It is a Tom stunt. When we call Tom, the tackle goes first on the stunt. This makes it easy for the defensive men to remember the stunt.

We can tag any coverage with our twist. We call 80 Tom and run the Tom twist. This keeps it simple for our defensive team. We can run the *box* defense and call a *jet* and run the stunts. We can play a two deep or a three deep with the call and keep the twist on.

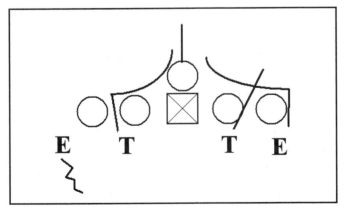

Diagram 3. Knockdown – Tom

We do not give the defensive linemen a specific alignment on the twist. We do a lot of moving with our defensive front. However, we tell the tackle he is going to be head-up to a shade 3 technique. The tackle goes first and the defensive end goes second. The alignment for the stunt is as follows. Again, the defensive tackle is head-up to outside shoulder of the offensive guard. The defensive end is wide outside.

The defensive tackle drives up through the gap and contains. The offensive guard and offensive tackle have their hips together, so we must get outside of the offensive tackle with a spin or swim technique.

The defensive end must drive upfield, then go under the defensive tackle [Diagram 4]. We do not want any contact with the offensive tackle. He may rush in any gap but he does not want to cross the nose of the center. He can anticipate a second move on the offensive guard or by a running back.

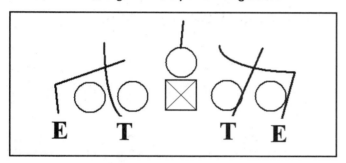

Diagram 4. Nickel – Tom

One problem we are concerned with is spacing. We do not want the two defenders making contact with each other. They must widen their stance.

We run a jet with the defensive end going first and the tackle going second. It is a tackle and end stunt. The defensive tackle is head-up to the inside shoulder of the offensive guard. The defensive end is the same as it is in a Tom stunt [Diagram 5]. The defensive end is responsible to get upfield and then get inside the offensive tackle. Again, we do not want contact with the offensive tackle. The end wants to use a rip or a swim move.

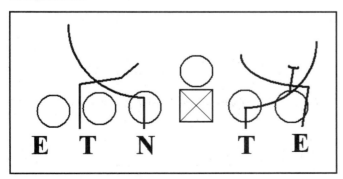

Diagram 5. Knockdown – jet

The defensive tackle must punch the offensive guard [Diagram 6]. He loops around the defensive end but he wants to make sure he does not get too wide.

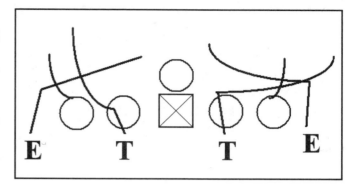

Diagram 6. Nickel – jet

Here is a coaching point for the ends. They are the guys who are coming inside. They do not want to make contact with that tackle. Remember our strength is our speed. We do not want to lock up with the tackle. We have to constantly remind our ends of this fact.

On the jet move, we leave it up to the individuals as to the move they want to use. One player may use the swim move and another may use a rip move. The other point we must stress is for them not to get too wide on the rush. They must not forget they are still pass rushers.

Our last stunt is what we call a *flash* move. It is a twist move called to only a certain side. We call the side we want the stunt to be run to. We said we liked to run the stunts to both sides of the line, but the flash is run to only one side. It is a stunt that we only use in our box or nickel package. It could be run to the strongside, weakside, or any other tendency we may find in our scouting report.

This is how the flash works [Diagram 7]. The linebacker will make a call. He may say we are going to the wideside of the field or we are going to the two-receiver side. Let's look at a flash right.

The defensive end lines up on the called side. He runs a jet stunt. The defensive tackle is on the called side. He aligns in a 3 technique. He punches the offensive guard then loops around the defensive end. He must keep his shoulders square to the line of scrimmage.

The defensive end away from the call uses a bull rush. He takes a couple of steps upfield. He turns his shoulders perpendicular to the line. He forces the offensive tackle back down the line. Again, we only run the flash from our box or nickel package.

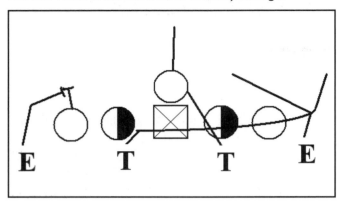

Diagram 7. Flash right

A twisting stunt we have developed over the last few years is what we call an *automatic*. An automatic is a line twist that is run without calling one. The defensive tackle and defensive end will only run this twist if they get a pass read. This is helpful on those run/pass situations.

We usually run this twist only on one side and it is either a Tom or a jet. The side will be determined by the defensive tackles' alignment and the twist we want to use that week.

Let me give you an example. Say this week we want our automatic to be a Tom stunt on the 3 technique side. When our defensive end and defensive tackle on the 3 technique side read pass, they run the Tom stunt [Diagram 8]. The other defensive tackle and defensive end will have a normal pass-rush lane.

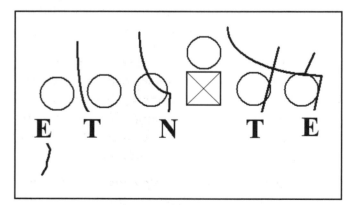

Diagram 8. Kickdown – automatic Tom

This is something you must practice to make sure everyone knows what they are doing. If the defense gets a normal running play, they continue to play the run. If they read a pass, we have two men running a twist stunt. We tell the noseguard to work upfield and then work to the B gap [Diagram 9].

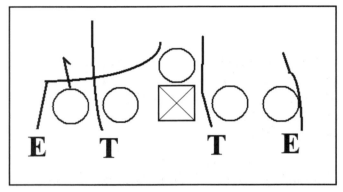

Diagram 9. Nickel – automatic Tom

The question is asked if this will take too long to develop if we are reading the pass. It will not take that long if you rep the play.

The next question that comes up is that the offense will know every time they run a pass, the defense is going to run a twist. During the course of the game we will tell our front no automatic twist for the next few downs. This tells the defensive line they must go back to their normal pass-rush lanes without the twist. We will change it throughout the game along with running the called twist. We feel this will keep the offensive line off balance in their protection.

This phase of the defense has been very good to us. Again, utilizing what we do best, and that is speed. That is why we have put these automatic calls in our defensive plan. We vary the calls from week to week using what we think is best each week. It is a very simple thing to teach the defensive line and they can learn the techniques with a lot of reps.

I want to show you the film of the twist in game situations. Thank you for your attention.

MULTIPLE FRONTS VERSUS THE SPREAD OFFENSE

University of Tennessee

It is truly a pleasure to be here. I feel honored to be asked to speak. My talk today is about Tennessee's *multiple fronts*. When we went to this defensive package, we wanted to make sure we were in it for the long haul.

It had gotten to the point where defensive coordinators didn't stay at Tennessee too long. Tennessee was known as an offensive-based school. We were known as *wide receiver U.* The offense was doing a good job of scoring a lot of points, but we weren't stopping anybody. In 1995, when Coach Fulmer promoted me to defensive coordinator, we decided to go to a package we could play and adjust from year to year.

We wanted to establish a philosophy and a build a foundation on that philosophy. We wanted to sell our players on those ideas. I think that is important. Over the last couple of years people have complimented me on how hard our kids play. What one gentleman said stuck out in my mind. He said it was like *magic* the way our kids played. The magic is not in the scheme and the X's and O's, it is the *effort*.

If we get that kind of effort from our players, we are going to be successful. We sell our players on that and communicate it to them. I think the time you spend with your players letting them know what is expected of them is just as important as the time you spend talking to them about the scheme. Our players did a tremendous job of buying into what we had to say. That is the reason we have had success at Tennessee.

Our head coach and our offensive coordinator want the ball. If they loose it, they want it back. They want the defense to get the ball back and do it in a hurry. As one of our offensive goals, we want to go *three and out* seven times within a football game. That gets the ball back in a hurry for our offense. The quickest way to get the ball back is through *turnovers*.

We have a statement on our bulletin board that our kids read every day. It states: "*You are judged by your team's performance, not by the victory itself.*" Our number one goal is to win the football game, but we want to make sure we have great individual performances.

We have some priorities that we set for our football team. The first priority is to *play with unbelievable effort*. When you come in to grade the film after Saturday's game, you want to see plays in that film that amaze you. We grade our players on technique, alignment, and effort. The first thing the players want to know is how they did on effort. If we play with the kind of effort we expect, we will win the football game.

We strive hard to *get the best 11 players on the field.* To do that your players must be unselfish. Our third priority is *always put the team first.*

In 23 years of coaching I have never been around a great football team that was not unselfish. When you have players on your team that care more about what happens to them than what happens on the team, your chances for having a good team are not very good.

We want to *play an aggressive, attacking scheme*. We are very multiple in our fronts. That is the topic of my lecture. We have simplicity in our techniques. We don't ask our players to learn a lot of different techniques. We are going to have movement and be multiple with our schemes. We are always going to be on the attacking edge. We are not going to sit back and let things come to us. Our players take a lot of pride in being a pressure defense.

We coach our players to *play one play at a time.* They can not do anything about the play they just played. That one is over. The only play that matters is the one that is coming next. If our players need a blow, all they need to do is tap their helmet and we will substitute for them. But while they are on the field we want them playing as hard as they possibly can. We want them playing with unbelievable effort.

The biggest thing a defensive team can do is *force turnovers*. We work a turnover circuit at least twice a week. In those circuits we actually work on stripping the football and taking the football away.

I think it is very important for the defense to *force teams into making mistakes.* Our pressure defense starts with making people make mistakes. We do a good job of charting production on first and third downs. Any time you play the first down very well, your production on third down is very good. The games where we struggle as a defensive team are the ones in which we don't play first down very well. When the defense is always facing a second-and-two to go, those are difficult downs to make defensive calls.

Great defensive teams have great *tacklers* on them. We spend a tremendous amount of time working on our tackling techniques from a defensive standpoint. There is not a day that our defensive team does not spend some time on tackling. It doesn't matter whether we are in shorts or full gear; we are going to do some kind of tackling.

We want to try to *score on defense.* In 1998 when we won the National Championship against Florida State, scoring on defense was an important part of that game. Florida State had a great football team. Our offensive team got on the board first. The next series our defense was able to pick off a pass and take it back for a score. That put Florida State in a situation where they had to come from behind if they were going to win the game. It is easier to play when you are 14 points ahead than it is when you are 14 points behind. That kind of momentum will really turn games around.

There are a lot of things that the players have to do to accomplish our priorities. They have to be in *excellent playing condition.* We have a tremendous strength coaching staff, but I think the players have to take the responsibility to be in great playing condition. They have to understand what it takes to get into great shape. We expect them to do that and we are going to push them to get into that kind of shape.

We have to *eliminate mistakes* if we are going to be a great team. We talked about that earlier, but it is extremely important. We want daily improvement. We have to be better tomorrow than we were today if we are to achieve our goals.

For a defense to play well they must have great *executions and second effort.* That will show up on game films. You will be able to grade that part of a player's game and show them where they are. You have to take the time to sit down and talk to players about giving second effort. If they know what you want they will take a great deal of pride in their effort.

One of the biggest plays that happen in a college football game is a player losing his cool and getting an unnecessary penalty. We have to maintain *poise and confidence* at all times. I can give you a lot of examples of that accomplishment. I have been a part of five SEC championships and one national championship team. There was something special about all those teams.

The story that comes to mind was the game we had with Arkansas. Defensively we had not played very well. In fact we had given up 21 points in the first half. We were down 21-3 going into the second half. We played a lot better the second half and had an opportunity to go ahead with a minute and 30 seconds to go in the game. We were down by four points but our offense was driving. The drive stalled and 107,000 people in the stadium thought the game was over and started to leave.

As our offense came off the field, we had a defensive tackle tell the quarterback to keep his helmet on, because the defense was not going to be on the field very long. He lined up over the guard. On the snap of the ball he got a great takeoff, knocked the guard back into the quarterback, and caused a fumbled. We recovered and eight plays later we scored to win the game. That showed poise and confidence and that is what you have to have in that situation. You have to have a little luck but you have to believe. There was no doubt in that defensive tackle's mind that we were going to get the ball back.

Any football player who expects to win has to have love and respect for their teammates. They have to play for one another. Our players don't give up on each other. They believe in each other. To have a team, you have to have love and respect for each other. We have another sign that we post in our locker room. I believe in this statement with all my heart. It states that *winners have won because of their commitment to each other.*

That is our philosophy. You can put anything down on paper, but if you cannot get your players to buy into it you are not going to win. We have been very fortunate to have players that have bought into our philosophy.

The thing that we emphasize with our defense is *pursuit*. I don't know of anything more important to a defensive football team. Unbelievable effort is the theme that runs through our pursuit training. We talk to our players about it and it becomes something we hang our hats on. Pursuit is a mental process. If you want to pursue the ball you can. All that it takes to run and pursue the football is effort. It doesn't take talent or skill. It takes unbelievable effort. If a player doesn't have that kind of effort, he will not play for Tennessee.

To pursue the football you have to be fast and in good shape. When we go out to recruit, speed is one of the things we look for. Great pursuit eliminates long-yardage plays. Going into this season we didn't know how good we would be. We lost nine starters last year and most of them went to the NFL. We lost our entire front four. All four of them were drafted into the NFL and three of them were starters as rookies for their teams.

We didn't know how much success we would have, but we had a very productive year. We finished fifth in the nation in total defense. We were fourth in the nation in pass defense. However, our rushing defense dropped to 28th in the nation. That is the worst we have done in the last seven years. We had a good defensive year because we didn't give up big plays and long touchdowns. Another thing that does is discourage your opponent. After some of our games, opposing team coaches have asked me what we do to get our kids to play that hard. Playing hard helps cover up mistakes. We sell our players on the idea that *the magic is not in the scheme, it is in the effort.*

Effort helps make us a great defensive football. Effort also helps make us a great gang-tackling football team. When you gang tackle it helps create turnovers.

We are a 4-3 defense [Diagram 1]. Teams that we play will tell you that we never line up in 4-3 defense.

That is the defense we base all our fronts from and where we start to teach our scheme.

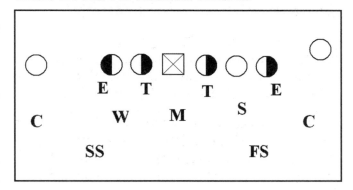

Diagram 1. 4-3 defense

We are going to play the defensive end in a 9 technique. He is going to play a loose technique with his inside hand down on the ground. We are going to have his inside hand aligned on the outside foot of the tight end. His inside foot is going to be back in his stagger and his alignment will be tilted slightly inside. The defensive tackle to the tight end side is in a 3 technique with his inside hand down and his inside leg back. His stance is staggered about two to four inches.

The defensive tackle to the weakside is going to be in an inside-shade technique on the offensive guard, which we call a 2i technique. He will have his outside hand down on the ground. His stagger is going to be about two to four inches. His outside foot is back. The weakside defensive end is in a loose 5 technique on the offensive tackle.

Our Sam and Will linebackers are going to align in a 50 techniques. They are going to have their heels at five yards. They are going to split the stance of the offensive tackle. The Mike linebacker aligns in a 10 technique, which is going to be the strongside half of the offensive center. That is where we start to teach our scheme.

We use a lot of movement in our defensive front, because until the last two or three years, we couldn't stay in a base front and stop people from running the ball. Until two years ago we were simply not good enough to play a base defense and stop people. We had to move and stunt to be effective.

The first stunt we use is a defensive front called our *aim* [Diagram 2]. It is a four-man movement slanting away from the strongside. The 9 technique end slants across the face of the tight end and is slanting all the way to the hip of the offensive tackle. His defensive key is the offensive tackle and he wants to make sure he penetrates through the hip of the tackle.

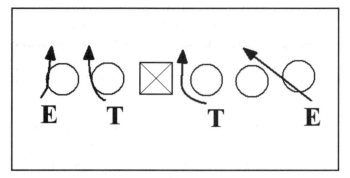

Diagram 2. Aim stunt

The 3 technique tackle is going to slant across the face of the guard and is keying the center. His movement is slightly different. As he slants across the face of the guard, he wants to get up into the gap of the center and guard. The weakside tackle is running the same type of slant keying the offensive tackle.

The weakside defensive end is going to run a skin technique since he has no offensive lineman outside of him. He is going to step with his outside foot and get penetration off the edge upfield.

Offensive coaches will tell you that you can't slant across offensive linemen faces from that distance, but we have been very successful doing it. We work on our slanting techniques extremely hard. The first thing the defender has to do is to transfer 90 percent of his weight onto his outside foot. He narrows his stance slightly so he can get his hips inside on the movement. He has to keep his shoulders down as he starts his slant. On the inside slant, the lineman wants to turn his shoulders and keep them down so he can rip across the face of the offensive blocker.

If the tight end gets his head in front of the slanting defender, we take the tight end and fill the gap with his body. We are going to make the tight end become part of our stunt.

When we make a *toy* call, we are talking to the two tackles [Diagram 3]. This stunt is a slant to the strongside by the defensive tackles. The 3 technique is already in a shade technique and he uses what we refer to as an away move. He slants hard into the B gap. He leaves his shoulder alignment and penetrates the gap.

Diagram 3. Toy stunt

The weakside tackle is in an inside shade on the guard. On his movement, he is going to slant and attack the center's backside shoulder.

The *tango* is just like the aim stunt [Diagram 4]. It is a four-man movement slanting towards the strongside. The weakside defensive end slants across the offensive tackle's face into the B gap. The weakside tackle slants across the face of the center into the strongside A gap. The 3 technique tackle slants into the C gap and the 9 technique end skins outside and upfield.

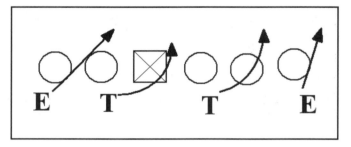

Diagram 4. Tango stunt

We can become multiple with this stunt. If we want to add to the tango stunt, we simple say *Will-tango* [Diagram 5]. We bring the Will linebacker on a blitz outside the offensive tackle to his side. That gives us a five-man pressure package.

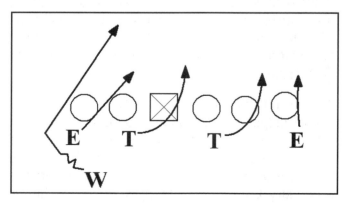

Diagram 5. Will-tango stunt

When we add tags to the stunts we have to coordinate the movement of the linebackers. If we are going to send the Will linebacker on the tango stunt, we kick the free safety down into the box [Diagram 6]. On the strongside we are playing quarter coverage and to the weakside we are playing man-to-man. The weakside corner is playing man-to-man on the wide receiver and the free safety is playing man on the number two receiver to the weakside. The Mike and Sam linebackers are playing quarter coverage to the strongside.

We can run the Will-tango, and change up the coverage. All we have to do is move the Sam linebackers a half step to the strongside and play man- free coverage. The Sam linebacker takes the number two strong and the strong safety rolls into the middle and plays free.

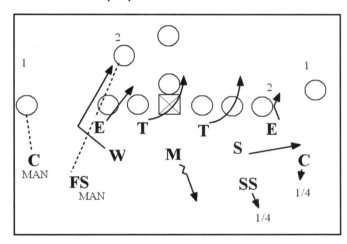

Diagram 6. Half-man/quarter coverage

We can do the same thing to the strongside by simply saying *Sam-tango.* In the secondary we can rock the strong safety down into the box and play man coverage to the strongside and quarter coverage to the weakside, or play man-free coverage with the free safety becoming the middle player. There is no difference in coverage in the Will- and Sam-tangos. The coverage is simple reversed from weakside to strongside.

We run two types of zone blitzes. One of the blitzes helps us in the running game and the other helps us in the passing game. I'll show you a spread formation with a one-back set. Everything we do should look like a quarter-quarter shell in the secondary. Our whole philosophy is to play the run with numbers and the pass with speed.

We are going to run the Will-tango stunt. The free safety is rolling down into the box. He is going to become a seam to flat defender. The corner to the free safety is going to play the outside third. The Sam linebacker is our seam to flat players on the strongside. The corner to his side plays the outside third. The Mike linebacker is the middle hook player and the strong safety is the middle third player. We are in a three-under, three-deep, *zone-blitz coverage* [Diagram 7].

Our philosophy in the zone-blitz coverage is to take the quick pass away. We expect the free safety and Sam linebacker to take the quick throws to the number two receiver on their sides. Even though we are in three-deep coverage, we get our corners up in press coverage on the wide receivers.

The next front we play quite a bit is our *eagle front* [Diagram 8]. Eagle to us is a strongside call. The defensive end to the tight end side will be in a 5 technique on the offensive tackle. The 3 technique tackle moves to a strong shade on the center. The weakside tackle and end are in a 3 technique and a 5 technique. The Sam linebacker aligns on the tight end in a 9 technique. The Mike and Will linebacker are going to align in a 30 technique on the outside shoulders of the guards.

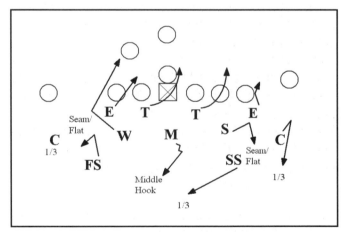

Diagram 7. Zone-blitz coverage

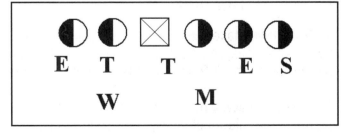

Diagram 8. Eagle front

When we ran our aim slant, we ended up in the same places as when we are aligned in the eagle. It creates a different situation for the offense. We have the ability to be a multiple front from the eagle. We can call the adjustments a number of ways. The eagle can be a formation, field, boundary, or half-call for us.

We play some split defense and it has been a good defense for us. When we start talking about the split package all we are talking about is the eagle. Instead of the tight eagle front, it is the split eagle front. We don't have to do any additional teaching. The split eagle is shifted away from the split and toward the tight end. We tell our defensive end, any time he is away from the call and has a tight end his way, he moves to a 6 technique. If the Sam linebacker gets a trips formation to his side in the eagle defense, he has to walk out on the split receiver.

We can run our stunt from the eagle front as well. If we want to call our *toy eagle*, it sends both tackles toward the tight end [Diagram 9]. The stunt is slightly different because of the tackles alignment. The shade tackle has to get across the face of the guard and into the B gap. That becomes more of a loop instead of a slant. The weakside tackle has a slant across the face of the guard into the A gap.

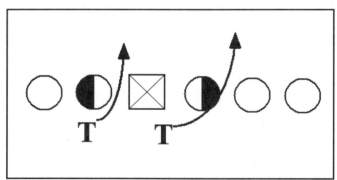

Diagram 9. Toy eagle

A lot of people got out of running the eagle defense a few years ago because of the cutback lanes created in the zone play. Since defenses have begun to involve their safeties in the cutback running defense, the eagle front has become popular again. We really like this next stunt. We call it *change* [Diagram 10]. It is a run stunt that is good because it is run on the backside of a formation. It stops the cutback running that has become the trend. The 3 technique goes first and slants hard into the offensive tackle working outside for contain. The

defensive end comes underneath the charge of the tackle and blitzes hard into the A gap.

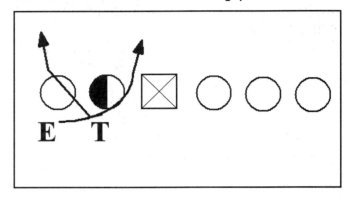

Diagram 10. Change stunt

When we give a *gap* call it is usually a weakside stunt. The gap call brings the defensive end from a 5 technique on the offensive tackle to a 4 technique charge through the B gap. It is a one man stunt. If we want the gap call run to the strongside we simply say *strong gap* [Diagram 11]. This helps you defense against teams that want to run at the bubbles created by the linebackers being off the line of scrimmage.

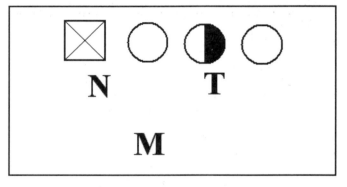

Diagram 11. Strong gap

This next call has been good for us. I think everyone in the country is running this stunt. It is a field call stunt. We call it *smokey* [Diagram 12]. It doesn't matter what formation the offense sets. We are going to run it from the field. The 5 technique end to the field runs a gap technique. The Mike linebacker blitzes off his tail and the Sam linebacker is blitzing from the outside. In the twin set he is walked off on the slot receiver. He comes off his alignment and blitzes off the edge.

The coverage we play is zone-blitz principles. The strong safety is the seam/flat defender. The Will linebacker becomes a middle hook player. The weakside end reads and drops into the seam/flat area. The corners and free safety are covering in a three-deep mode. We play this coverage with our end into the boundary, that way he doesn't have a lot of ground to cover.

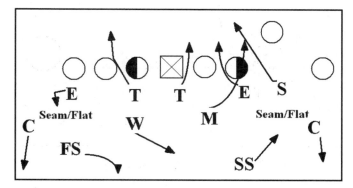

Diagram 12. Smokey stunt

If the offense gives us some set that makes the defensive end play seam/flat on a receiver that is outside of him, we call a *gut check* [Diagram 13]. That switches assignments between the defensive end and Will linebacker. The Will linebacker plays the seam/flat area and the defensive end drops into the middle hook zone and plays the third receiver out to either side.

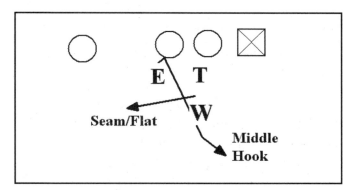

Diagram 13. Gut check

In our defense we have a *slide* call [Diagram 14]. On this call we are changing the responsibility and alignment with the Sam linebacker and the defensive end. We are going to slide the defensive end from a 9 technique to a 6 technique and step the Sam linebacker outside in a 90 alignment. It is another way to get into an eight-man front and we don't have to do a lot of teaching.

We can use the safeties down in the box and create some stack positions for our Mike and Will linebackers. We can play cover 1 or 3 from this alignment and we haven't changed anything for the

guys up front. We keep it simple for them. We have found out through the years that it works really well. The only people who have to make an adjustment are the linebackers. They have to know where their support is when we drop the safety into coverage. The linebackers know that any play toward the support, they are going to play slow. That means they have to slow down because of the cutback lane. They are steering everything to the support and not allowing the football to cut back.

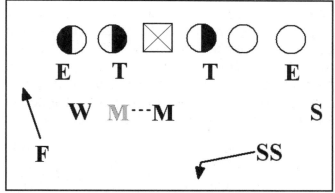

Diagram 14. Slide

If the play is run away from the support call, the linebackers can play fast. They know the rolled down safety is playing the cutback lane and they can pursue the ball rapidly. On this defense if the formation is a two tight end formation we balance up the defense. The defensive end away from the call can't play a 5 technique with a tight end outside of him. He slides to a 6 technique and the weakside shade tackle slides to a 3 technique to balance up the defense.

In the secondary we align every time in a quarter shell with four-defensive backs aligned straight across the formation. Just before the ball is snapped we move to whatever coverage we have called. We want to disguise the coverage until the last second. There are some formations that won't let allow us to use as much disguise as we want, but we want to disguise whenever possible.

Because we play a lot of eight-man front principles, we are going to put our best cover linebacker at the Sam linebacker position. We are going to put our best blitz linebacker at the Will linebacker position. I have talked to a lot of people that play the 4-3 scheme and we are probably one of the few teams that do it that way. When you break our defense down in terms of personnel, the free safety and the Sam linebacker are going to be very similar players. The strong safety is really a free safety type of player. We play our free safety in the box more times than not. He is going to be the run-support player and a seam to flat player most of the time. We put our best cover safety at the strong safety position because he is going to be in the middle of the field a lot more. We put both the safeties in the box at times, but when we start developing our personnel, we play a little differently than most 4-3 teams. The Mike linebacker is a traditional linebacker.

The last thing I want to show you before we get to the film is the *bear package* [Diagram 15]. We do a lot of things out of this front. We kick the strong defensive end out into a loose 9 technique. The Sam linebacker gets on the line of scrimmage in a 7 technique on the tight end. The strong tackle and weakside defensive end aligns in 3 techniques and the weakside tackle is in a 0 technique head up the center. The Will linebacker is going to be on the line of scrimmage and an outside rusher from the weakside. The Mike linebacker and strong safety are in stack 30 techniques behind the defensive end and tackle.

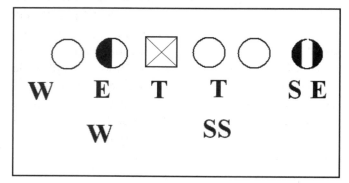

Diagram 15. Bear package

We play this front a little differently than a lot of people. Most people put their defensive tackles on the same side. We don't do that because we want to have the ability to drop in and out of this front. We want to be able to stem into the front or line up in the front and stem out of it without making people get up to change their alignments. We want to be able to slide people up and down the line of scrimmage.

The nose tackle is playing a two-gap principle, but he is playing out the backdoor on everything. We don't care if he gets reached because he is playing from the backside A gap and pushing the center to the playside. We are not going to ask the tackle to cross

the face of the center. We play a lot of bear package but very little of it will be straight defense.

We change our stunts from week to week. We don't go into any game and run the same stunts. We also have the ability to run zone blitzes out of our bear package. We package our stunts from week to week. We run these stunts to take away what the offense does well. We run a three-man stunt game to both sides. In one group we have the nose tackle, defensive end, and Mike linebacker. We do the same thing with the strong tackle, Sam linebacker, and strong safety. We call this stunt *X-Mike* [Diagram 16]. The defensive end and nose tackle are going to run an X stunt. The defensive end goes first and runs a gap stunt inside. The nose tackle comes second across the face of the weakside offensive guard into the B gap. The Mike linebacker goes third into the weakside A gap.

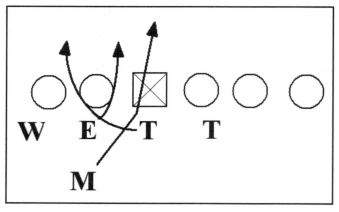

Diagram 16. X-Mike stunt

If we want a tackle-tackle combination, we would call *bear-twist-Mike* [Diagram 17]. That gives us a twist stunt by the two tackles with the Mike linebacker coming into the strongside A gap. The nose tackle goes first into the strongside A gap. The strongside tackle comes second across the center's face into the weakside A gap. The Mike linebacker comes next into the strongside.

We can group the weakside defensive end, Will linebacker, and Mike linebacker together and run a group of stunts. You can see the numbers of stunts that are possible are numerous. That is where we really become multiple with what we can do. All you have to have is imagination and soundness. What I would like to do is show you some of these things on film and then we will take a break.

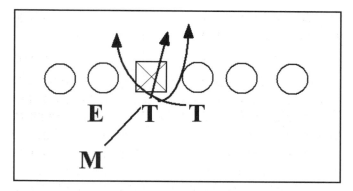

Diagram 17. Bear-twist-Mike stunt

(Film)

Next I am going to talk about *defending the spread offense*. In our league, 90 percent of the teams we are playing want to spread the field and throw the ball. I look at it as being basketball on grass. It is basketball fast break on grass.

The biggest thing about the spread offense is match ups and the advantages you can create off the match ups. We are going to stop the run with numbers. We are going to put more men in the box than the offense can block. We are going to rush the passer with speed. A big part of having success against the spread offense is being able to rush the passer.

I'm going to talk about the pass rush first and later I'll talk about schemes. In the spread game, the offense wants to get their best receiver on your worst defender in a 1-on-1 situation. You have to be conscious of that as you are putting together a game plan.

We feel like stopping the run game makes it easier to play pass defense. If you want to stop the run by loading up the box, you have to be able to play man-to-man in the secondary. That is our whole philosophy when we recruit. We want to recruit corners who can play man-to-man. If you can't play press-man coverage, it is going to be very difficult to play in our scheme.

To play against the spread offense, you have to get the right players on the field. We call our nickel and dime package *mustang.* We want to get our best six defensive backs on the field. Last year we played 300 snaps with six defensive backs on the field. That plays a big part when you start looking at recruiting.

Everything we do is geared around speed. The first thing we talk to our defensive ends about is *get off.* We want the defensive end to beat the offensive tackle to a point one-yard outside and two-yards deep behind the offensive tackle's alignment. The offensive tackles in the league are good athletes, but they are not going to be the athlete our defensive ends are.

We want to get speed on the pass rush so the offensive tackles have to move. We want to make the offensive tackle respect the speed of the defensive end. After we get the tackle set up for the outside move, we want to bring the defensive end underneath the offensive tackle.

We do the same thing with the defensive tackles working on the offensive guard. We want to attack the guards on their outside shoulder to begin with. We want to make the guards work and set and be a good enough athletes to block us. When we add movement it will help us attack those blockers.

When we start running games we want to identify which way the offense is turning the center. We also want to identify which one of the two offensive linemen is the *soft-set* player. If we think the tackle is the soft-set player, we want to attack him. We are going to run an inside stunt at him [Diagram 18]. We want to run the stunt to the side opposite the center's turn. The defensive tackle attacks the inside hip of the offensive tackle. He wants to make sure he gets our helmet behind the hip of the tackle. The defensive end sets up the move by stepping up the field and then comes inside behind the defensive tackle and attacks the guard.

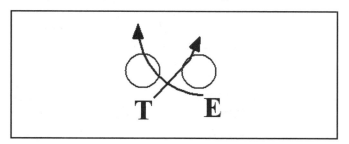

Diagram 18. Soft set

If the tackle gets his helmet behind the hip of the offensive tackle, he will come free if the offensive linemen attempt to zone the stunt. The offensive tackle can't make the block on the defensive tackle. If the protection is man protection, there is no way the tackle can get to defensive end. It doesn't matter whether the offensive uses a man or zone scheme, one of the defenders is coming free on the rush.

When the defense looks at the spread offense from a scheme standpoint, they are going to have to decide what to do. You have to decide whether you are going to pressure the passer or load the secondary and cover. You have to make a commitment to one of those areas. We are going to pressure the passer. We want to keep a safety in the middle of the field. We are going to be able to keep the safety in the middle by overloading a side on the offense.

We are going into a nickel and dime defense with an odd front. We have the ability to bring four people from either side. We are going to drop the free safety down and be able to play zone, man-free, and zone-blitz coverage. We can drop the strong safety down to the other side and run the same coverage. If we drop the free safety down, we are rolling the secondary toward him and just the opposite if we drop the strong safety down. We also play some double zone, but I'll talk about that later.

If we want to blitz the strongside, we roll the strong safety down and he becomes the seam to flat player [Diagram 19]. The left defensive end gets a speed rush off the edge of the offensive tackle. The Will linebacker blitzes the left B gap. The shade noseguard crosses the center's face into the backside A gap. The Mike linebacker blitzes the strongside A gap. The right defensive tackle rushes through the offensive tackle working for contain on that side. The nickel back drops in seam to curl coverage. The corners are playing the outside thirds and the free safety is going to the middle of the field. The dime back takes the middle hook area.

We are going to pressure by overloading, but we are also going to take away the quick throw. When we play our seam/flat technique, it is going to look like man-to-man coverage. If the seam/flat defender gets an inside cut, he is going to zone off the play. If there is an outside break by the receiver, it will look like man-to-man coverage.

We have to be aware of the match ups in a nickel and dime front. We can't have linebackers on the field in bad match-up situations with wide receivers. We call this defense *mustang Willie* [Diagram 20]. On this defense we are going to run an end and tackle twist and an end and linebacker stunt. We are going to involve the Will linebacker in the stunt. We get four-man pressure on the quarterback. The best cover linebacker is in coverage. We have our nickel and dime corners on the slots and the corners on the wideouts. The strong and free safeties are on the hashes. We can play any coverage we want. We can lock down the coverage in base man coverage or we can bring one more man and play the same coverage. We can play cover 2, which is our double-zone coverage.

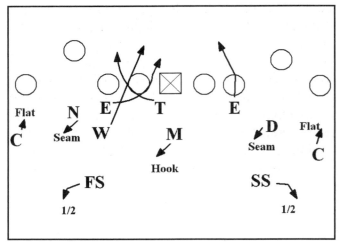

Diagram 20. Mustang Willie

If we are in the cover 2, there is a couple of ways we can play the defense. We can key the corner and free safety on the number two receiver. That gives the strong safety the responsibility for the number two receiver going vertical, with the corner hanging on the vertical by the number one receiver. In this type of coverage we can play the nickel, dime, and linebacker in their zone drop or we can play a hard corner. With that type of coverage we roll the corners up into the flat area. The free safety plays over the top for the vertical route by the number one

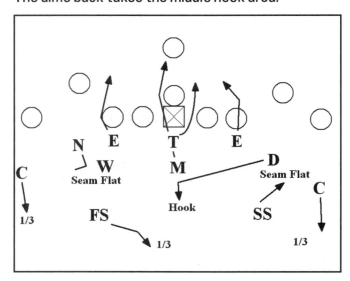

Diagram 19. Strongside blitz

receiver. If the number two receiver goes vertical, the dime back takes him. We can play the same coverage to both sides.

We play some quarter coverage, but not much. We could play quarter coverage with this scheme, but we realize we must create as much pressure as we can, because that is the type of game we are going to play.

If we get a four wide receiver package we can go to what we call *0 (Zero) pressure* [Diagram 21]. The defensive ends are in 5 techniques with no tight ends. The tackles are in a center shade strong and a 3 technique weak. The 3 technique tackle runs a gap stunt and the Sam linebacker comes right behind him in the B gap. The Will linebacker shoots the B gap on the other side. That gives us six-man pressure.

If the offense goes into an empty formation, we have one blitz that we are going to run. We get into a bear front. Our weakside defensive end and tackle are in a 5 technique and 3 technique, and the shade 3 technique tackle slides over to a head-up position on the center. The defensive end to the strongside is in a 3 technique. The Sam linebacker is aligned in a 5 technique on the outside shoulder of the offensive tackle. The Will linebacker is in coverage on the trips set. The Mike linebacker is aligned in the strongside A gap behind the nose tackle. We would like to get a nickel back into the game for the Will linebacker so we can match up against an empty formation. The corners safeties and the Will linebacker or the nickel back have the coverage on the number five receiver.

We are going to take the weakside defensive end and bring him up the field hard [Diagram 22]. The nose tackle slants into the strongside A gap and the Mike linebacker blitzes the weakside A gap. The 3 techniques are coming hard off the edge of the offensive guards. The Sam linebacker is coming hard off the edge. The offensive line will try to slide protect one way or the other. Normally when they use that type of protection, the offense will turn one of the outside defenders loose.

When they use that kind of protection, we are going to take our shot and go after the quarterback. This is an exception for us because we don't play a lot of 0 coverage. If we have a 0 blitz call and the offense comes out in an empty set, we are going to check out of the blitz unless we have it in our game plan to run the blitz. The players we are going to keep in coverage are the strong safety, free safety, and the Sam linebacker. If we run a 0 cover, about 90 percent of the time we will have a nickel back in for the Will linebacker.

Offenses that get into four wide receiver sets put their best receivers at the slot positions. They are hoping to get matched up on linebackers. When we play against a four wide receiver set, we want to get our nickel and dime package on the field. That puts our four best corners on their receivers.

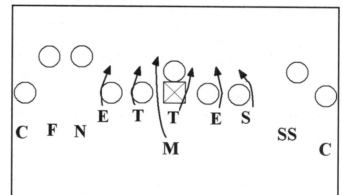

Diagram 22. Bear blitz

Let me show the film of what we have just covered. If you have questions let me know.

(Film)

Men, I have enjoyed your attention. Thank you very much.

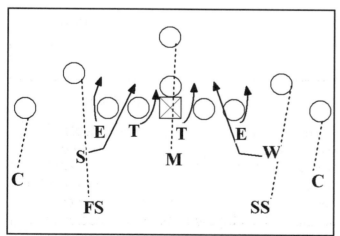

Diagram 21. 0 pressure

THE OPTION GAME VS. 7- AND 8-MAN FRONTS

Air Force Academy

It is a distinct pleasure to be here today representing the Air Force Academy. Last football season was an exciting one for us. We have a number of things on which we base our foundation. At the Academy we have a family concept that we live by. Every day when we go to practice, we have a routine. We tell our players to grab your brother's hand and let's go to practice. We are going to compete hard against each other in practice. But when practice is all over we are on the same team and committed to the same purpose. We do that every day and talk about it every day with our players.

I learned a long time ago, growing up in a little country town, if you got into a fight and whipped somebody's brother, you were going to have to fight his brother, too. That is the attitude we want our players to have. Brothers are hard to beat.

We ask the players in our program to do what is *right*. Players today know what is right and what is wrong. Last year I had to suspend 12 players at the end of the season from the last game. They didn't do the right thing and I didn't have any choice but to suspend them. It really hurt me because some of our seniors didn't get to play in their last college game in Falcon stadium. But I think we did the right thing and we tried to impress upon them that the team comes first. I think it made an impression on those 12 players.

The players need to take *pride* in their work ethics and play hard. Any time a recruit comes into my office or we go into his home, the one thing that I can promise him is we are going to work his butt off. I don't know of any shortcut other than just hard work to succeed. I believe we will never lose a game at Air Force. We didn't lose a game last year; time just ran out on us. It ran out on us in the last two ball games. We have to find a way to finish games. That will be one of our focal points going into next year.

In our last two games last year, we ended up on the three-yard line and the four-yard line. Your players have to understand when you are that close you have to find a way to get the ball in the end zone.

We have to win the *four critical areas*. There are four critical areas in every football game that we have to win consistently to be a winning football program. The number one thing is the *turnover margin*. That determines the outcome of games more than any other factor in the world. We have to win the turnover battle every ball game. We must have fewer turnovers than our opponent. We are going to be in the top 10 in the nation in that area. If you are in the top 10, you are going to have a very successful football program.

We are extremely tough on that area in practice. If a player turns the ball over, he is not going to practice or play. If he is a competitor, there is nothing that hurts more. I feel it is important for them to understand that is what we have to do.

The second critical area is the *kicking game*. We have to win the kicking game. We keep a lot of statistics and make our players conscious of field position, net punting averages, and big plays. To me, the biggest play in football is the blocked kick. That can determine the outcome and complexion of a football game. It really has an impact on the attitude of the players in the game. In the 1990s, we were second in the nation behind Virginia Tech in blocked kicks.

We played them in the bowl game this year and neither one of us blocked a kick. But the bottom line is, we have won a lot of games as they have by blocking kicks. We don't give lip service to kick blocking; we spend a lot of time working on that aspect of the game. We try to impress upon our players that the kicking game is the most important thing we do. We win championships with defense and the kicking game. I am talking about offense tonight, but you win with defense and the kicking game.

We work on our kicking game early in practice so the players know it is important in our plan of things. We put our starting players on our special teams. When we are asked to list our starting players, we put our offensive starters, our defensive starters, and our special team starters on the sheet. That makes them feel special.

Penalties in a football game will beat you quicker than your opponent. We are going to be number one in the conference every year as the least-penalized team. That is something we work extremely hard at in practice and talk about every day. We use officials in our practice sessions. We eliminate pre-snap penalties in practice. If a player gets a pre-snap penalty in practice, he does some punishment running. There is never anything said. The players know they have to do the running and get back in line before his group runs another play.

The last of the critical points is to win the *possession game.* That means the number of plays your offense runs in a game as well as the amount of time you control the football. I believe your offense can ultimately be your best defense. If you can run more plays in a game than your opponent, you have enhanced your chance of winning the game.

If you keep a good offensive football team sitting on the sideline waiting to get on the field, you can frustrate them. That is something that is important to us and something we give a lot of credence to. The offense can't score if they don't have the football.

There are a number of reasons we run the *option.* I believe it suits the type of personnel we are able to get at the Academy. It is a unique offense and a tough offense to prepare for. It is a run-oriented offense. Teams that can consistently run the football are the teams that have been successful.

I remember something that Lou Holtz said at a lecture. He said he had studied the top 20 rushing football teams in America and 19 of them had winning football seasons and not one head coach got fired. When he looked at the top 20 passing teams in the country, 14 of them had losing seasons and four head coaches got fired. That made an impression on me. If

you can minimize your errors, I think we have a chance to win. You can do it in the running game then you can do it in the passing game. The team that makes the fewest mistakes is the team that wins the game. I also believe you have to throw the football to have a successful running game. During the regular season we led the nation in yards per catch in the passing game. We do a lot of play-action passing. When you throw those types of passes, you can anticipate some big plays.

We prefer the option attack because it is fun. Option football creates assignment football for the defense. If the defense makes a mistake in assignment football, the results are usually big plays.

We see very few blitzes by the defense. I like an offense that gets a lead blocker ahead of the ballcarrier. It is an offense that goes north and south in the open field. That is what we try to get when we are designing our plays.

The option is a *quick-hitting offense*, which doesn't require the offensive linemen to create huge running lanes. All we are looking for in offensive blocking is a tie with the defense. Our fullback can run through some of the arm tackles that come from getting a tie with the defender on the offensive block.

We run the *triple and double option* to get the ball on the corner into some seams, which have big-play potential. I believe that reading the defense equalizes and neutralizes the opponent to a certain extent. In the triple option, we do not block two of the defense's best football players. We do that every play. When you can play 11 men against 9 defenders, then that gives us more of a chance to win the game. When we played Virginia Tech in the bowl game, they were an eight-man front. They brought their 7i technique players, inside every play, and took the fullback on the dive. It was a tough night for our fullback, but we eliminated two of their best football players every time.

The triple and double option is a unique offense. It is hard to prepare for that type of offense in the three to four days the defense has to prepare for it. Most of the time defenses have been playing against a passing offense in the weeks before they play us. It is tough to shift gears and get ready to cover the type of scheme we present. It is hard to find a scout team quarterback who can give an accurate picture of what the defense is going to face. When the defense is playing assignment football, it gives them a greater liability as far as making a mistake is concerned.

The option creates toughness within your football team. It teaches a physical approach to the game. We all want our teams to be tough. Football is a tough and physical game. The size of a player doesn't have anything to do with his physical toughness.

We have some things that we do in practice every day. We call them *every day drills*. One thing we do every day is to come off the ball and work against a seven-man sled. We are going to be synchronized, have a great punch, move the sled, and exercise a great offense.

This offense is designed to hit the defense in the mouth. It is not a dropback offense. We are coming off the ball in an attack mode as far as our offense is concerned. Gaining four yards is an excellent football play as far as we are concerned. It is important for our defense to have to defend this in practice. That lets them practice against the toughness it takes to run this offense.

Option football is a *balanced offense*. Our quarterback has to be able to count defenders on each side of the ball. If the defense overshifts to the wideside of the field, 60 to 70 percent of our offense is designed to go into the boundary. If the defense has the rover and shade noseguard to the same side, that tells our quarterback there are six people to that side of the defense. We are never going to run into a six-man side of the defense. If that is the situation, the quarterback is going to audible and run to the other side.

We are looking for a five-and-a-half man to five-and-a- half man ratio. When we get those kinds of numbers we have to out execute the defense. The option is a balanced attack that forces defenses to stay honest against it. We execute better if we know where the defense is going to be. Our quarterback does have to audible quite a bit.

The offense is a *ball-control offense*. If we can keep the ball and run more plays than the opponent, it increases our chances of winning the game. That is particularly true if the clock doesn't stop. The offense might be the best defense. That is important to us. The offense suits the player we have at the

Academy. We take pride in discipline at the Academy. It has a discipline approach to education as you know. They take pride in doing the little things because doing the little things makes the big things happen.

We have a *quick and solidside in our offense*. The reason we do that is to minimize teaching, and increase practice opportunities and repetitions. When you run the option, the most important thing is to find ways to get repetitions. We designate our halfbacks as slots and wings. Our slot backs do most of the blocking and the wings do most of the ball carrying. We think that helps a lot and suits the players.

This offense is the same offense from *goal line to goal line*. When a passing team gets inside the red zone, their passing zones tighten up and scoring becomes more difficult. This past year we were second in the nation is red zone productivity. We take great pride in the way we execute in the red zone. We scored 56 out of 60 times in the red zone this year. There is not a lot of change in the offense we run outside the red zone. The pressure may get heavier and the zones get tighter, but we see the same defense in the red zone that we see outside the red zone. We think that is important and is a definite advantage for us. You can execute from the minus one to the plus 10, but if you don't get the ball in the end zone, you aren't going to win many.

That doesn't mean we don't practice in the red zone. We paint our football field. Everything from the 20-yard line to the goal line is painted red. That means the sidelines, hash marks, numbers, and yard marks are painted red. The reason we do that is to impress upon our player when they get into that area it is time to get the job done. They need to concentrate more and execute better. We want to make that important to them from that standpoint.

Our players believe in what we are doing. To me that is the most important statement about our program. If I went back to the Academy and told our players that we were going to change our offense, I think we would have a revolt on our hands. They truly believe that we are going to be successful in what we do. They have confidence in what we are doing and believe we can score against anybody.

The option has a lot of critics. They say the biggest drawback in the option scheme is the inability to pass when they need to and the inability to play from behind. I refute that. I believe if you practice enough you can develop into a very potent attack. We can move the football at the end of the game or at the end of the half, just like a passing team. In the last two games, we moved the football the length of the field to inside the 10-yard line but didn't score.

A few years ago we played BYU. We were on our half-yard line and drove the ball 99 yards to score in one minute and 12 seconds. We ran a lot of option into the boundary, but we scored on the last play of the game on a pass play. We went for two on the conversion and won the game 39-38.

Our best passes are *play-action passes*. We think the best down to throw the football is first down. We are like any passing team; we don't have much luck throwing the ball on third-and-long yardage. In 13 football games we had only five sacks. We work extremely hard every day in team pass protection. I think it better to work in team pass protection than it is to work in skeleton pass protection. It lets the linemen and quarterback develop the feel for the passing game.

The theory in our offense is to use wide-line splits to spread out the defense. In the triple option, the quarterback doesn't know what he is going to do with the ball until the defense makes a commitment. We have to be able to execute whenever the defense makes a commitment. If we execute, the defense can't be right. I don't think the option game will work unless the quarterback is reading. When the offensive line splits are as wide as they are, it forces the defense to commit quicker.

From the guards to the center, the split is three feet [Diagram 1]. From the guards to the tackles, the split is five feet. From the tackle to the tight end, we are split four to five feet. That makes the defense cover a lot of ground. It makes the defense show what their responsibilities are. The greater the distance between the handoff key and the quarterback, the easier it is to read. There are some plays in our offense that require us to tighten our splits down, but all triple-option plays are run with wide splits.

The fullback is going to align with his hands six feet from the heels of the quarterback. We are looking for a fullback who has tremendous

acceleration. The quarterback and fullback are the main men in what we are trying to do. If you are not good at those two positions, you are not going to be very good. We have been blessed to have talented guys in those positions.

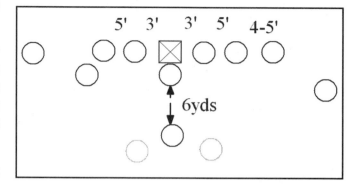

Diagram 1. Splits and alignments

The option we run depends on the defense we are facing. If there is a lineman or linebacker playing a 0 technique, we are going to run a zone scheme. On the zone scheme, we are going to outside release with our offensive tackle. If it is a 4-3 defense, he will release inside. If he has a defensive tackle aligned on him he releases outside.

If there is no 0 technique player, we are looking at an eight-man front. If that is the situation we are going to veer release our offensive linemen. That is the theory of the two schemes we are trying to run with our triple option. Our option is predicated on whether the defense is a seven-man front or an eight-man front. Defensive recognition of the front and its balance is the key. The quarterback is the one who will determine what he is seeing.

In our quarterback, we are looking for a halfback who can play quarterback. He has to have very quick feet. He has to be able to make good decisions. He has to have quick hands also.

That reminds me of a story about quick thinking. There was a clerk working in the produce department in a grocery store. One day a lady came in and requested a half a head of lettuce. He told her he couldn't sell her a half a head. She would have to buy the whole head of lettuce. She demanded to be sold a half a head of lettuce. He told her he would go ask the manager. He went back to ask the manager, unaware the lady had followed him back to where the manager was working.

When the manager asked the clerk what the problem was, the clerk told him "There is a dumb blond up front that wants to buy a half a head of lettuce." As he turned around the lady was standing right behind him. Thinking quickly, he said; "And this beautiful young lady would like to buy the other half."

The manager was impressed with his quick thinking. He asked the clerk where he was from. The clerk told him he was from the great state of Minnesota. He told the manager we have the best football players in America, but the women are the ugliest in the world. The store manager said his wife was from Minnesota. With that, the clerk asked him what position she played.

Sometimes you have to think very quickly.

One of the qualities we are looking for at fullback is *great acceleration*. He can align in a three- or four-point stance. He has to have enormous strength in his legs and has to be a tough son-of-a-gun. He is going to get hit every play. He very seldom gets hit with a face-up tackle, but he is going to take a lot of hits. He gets hit at an angle but he can absorb most of those hits with his pads.

We want our quarterback in a *good football stance*. We want a good bend in his ankles and knees. We want his tail down and his arms relaxed. When the quarterback takes the snap and presents the ball to the fullback, he never looks at the fullback. He is looking at the handoff key. He sinks his elbow into his side and steps at four o'clock toward the fullback.

When the quarterback presents the ball the fullback opens his pocket. The quarterback puts the ball in the pocket. We don't tell him to pressure the ball or when to leave the ball or pull it out of the pocket. It becomes a *feel* thing between the quarterback and the fullback. It comes from long hours of repetition on the ride. The next step is his gather step. After that step he rides the ball in the fullback's pocket. We don't know who is going to get the ball until the defense makes us commit.

When we drill this in practice, we paint the fullback's path on the ground with white paint. The quarterback is not looking at the fullback's pocket. He is reading the handoff key. The fullback has to run the same track over and over again. He cannot deviate from that path.

The quarterback is going to read the first man outside the offensive guard on the triple option. He is looking for the jersey numbers of the handoff key. If he can read the numbers of the handoff key, he gives the ball to the fullback. If he sees the handoff key closing on the fullback, he pulls the ball and looks for the next option key. We have a number of ways to get the pitchman into the scheme. We can align him in the formation or motion him into position. We use motion and counter motion. Counter motion is starting one way, reversing the motion, and going the other way.

If we have a 4-3 look on the line of scrimmage, the offensive tackle is releasing inside and combination blocking with the guard on the 3 technique tackle [[Diagram 2]. The fullback's aiming point is the inside hip of the guard. Against this defense the quarterback is reading the 7 technique end. The tight end is releasing upfield and blocking the Sam linebacker. The slot back is coming off on the corner. If the quarterback pulls the ball, he continues down the line looking for the support. He is going to keep or pitch off the strong safety.

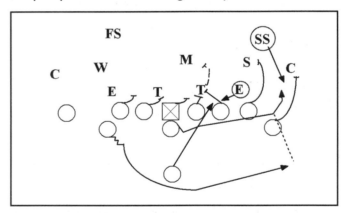

Diagram 2. Triple option

If we have a nose tackle and the offensive tackle is covered, we block this defense slightly different [Diagram 3]. The fundamentals of the play remain the same and the aiming point of the fullback is always the same track. We don't feel the offensive tackle can veer release across the face of the defensive lineman. We take an outside release and go for the linebacker on the second level. Everything else is the same. We are still reading the first man outside the guard and pitching off the support.

Our midline play is called *24/25* [Diagram #4]. On this play the quarterback is reading the 3 technique.

He has to clear the center because the fullback is coming almost directly over the center. The offensive tackle turns out on the 5 technique. The tight end is arcing on the Sam linebacker to try to get him to widen. The center is blocking back on the backside shade. The backside guard is pulling through the hole looking for the backside linebacker.

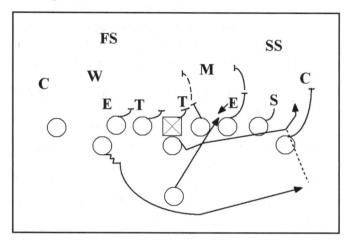

Diagram 3. Triple option versus odd

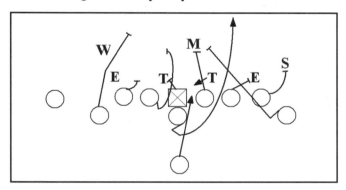

Diagram 4. Midline 24/25

The quarterback is reading the 3 technique. If the 3 technique takes the fullback, the quarterback pulls the ball, steps around the 3 technique, and explodes upfield inside the offensive tackle's block. On this play the slot back comes back inside on the linebacker. This blocking scheme has been very good for us.

This next play has been very good for us. We can run the play a number of different ways. The play is the off-tackle *belly play* [Diagram 5]. On this play the fullback's aiming point is the inside foot of the tight end. We are going to pull the onside guard and kick out on the first man outside of the tackle. The fullback has to key the offensive guard and see what the guard is seeing. The backside is zone stepping to the playside. The playside offensive tackle blocks back

for the pulling guard. The quarterback reverses out and hands the ball to the fullback. There is no option read on this play.

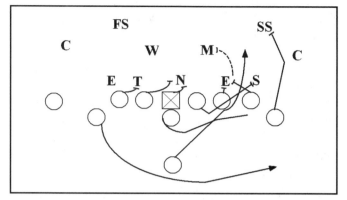

Diagram 5. Belly play

The tight end and offensive tackle have a number of things that could happen to them. A lot depends on your personnel as to how you block this play. If the guard is uncovered, the tackle more than likely will have someone aligned on him. If the center can handle a shade noseguard to the playside, the tackle doubles with the tight end on the defender. The tight end and tackle are running a combo block with someone coming off for the Mike linebacker. If you have a good blocking tight end, the tackle can come down the line and help the center by chipping the shade noseguard onto the center's block. The tackle continues to the backside to block the weakside linebacker. If the guard is covered the tackle has to come down on that block.

The pulling guard comes around the tackles block looking to kick out on the defensive end or Sam linebacker. If he can't get inside to kick out the defender, he logs the defender inside and the fullback takes the ball outside. If the strong safety is hanging inside the slot back has to block him. If he is on the way up to support, the slot by passes him and blocks the free safety.

When the defenders start playing the fullback belly play, we run the *belly option* [Diagram 6]. The belly option looks like the belly play except we get an additional blocker at the point of attack. Everything else is the same except for the pulling guard and fullback. The fullback is running the same track, taking the fake, and logging the defender outside the tackle's block. The pulling guard is going to pull outside the log block of the fullback looking back inside for the Mike linebacker. The slot back by passes the support and goes for the corner. The quarterback rides the fullback, pulls the ball, and options off the support.

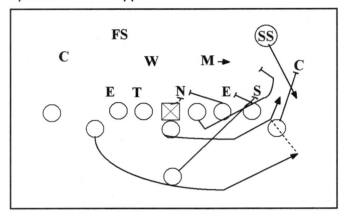

Diagram 6. Belly option

We can run these plays without a tight end in the game [Diagram 7]. If we run this play to the splitside, everything else is the same except the blocks of the guard and fullback. If we have a split end to that side the tackle will be covered. The Sam linebacker will walk out on the slot back and he will become the pitch key. The pulling guard will pull around and log on the defensive end. That block is easier for the guard than the fullback. The fullback takes the fake and continues to the second level to block the Mike linebacker. The split receiver blocks the corner and the slot back arc blocks on the strong safety.

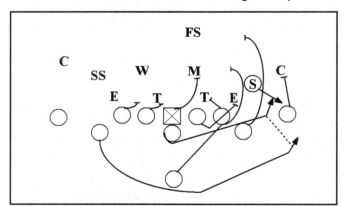

Diagram 7. Belly option split

The quarterback does the same thing and is pitching off the Sam linebacker. The Sam linebacker will be closer to the line of scrimmage, so the decision to pitch or keep will come earlier for the quarterback. The quarterback must force the hand of the Sam linebacker at the same time gain width to create vertical seams in the pursuit.

We use motion with our double-slot set to confuse the defense or gain leverage on a defender [Diagram 8]. When we find the defense reacting to the direction of our motion, we then use counter motion. We motion our slot backs so they can get into a pitch relationship with the quarterback. But we don't always run in the direction of the motion or we use counter motion to confuse a defensive call or check. The midline play times out better for the slot backs. We can run this play without motion and get them into a proper pitch relationship.

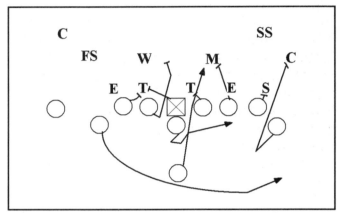

Diagram 8. Midline/motion

The quarterback is not moving away from the slot back on the midline like he is on the triple option. That gives him time to get into the proper position on his pitch path.

I want to get to the film and show you some of the things I've been talking about. Before I do that let me show you a couple of our play-action passes.

When the defense is reacting to an offense like we run at the Air Force Academy, the safeties have to get involved with the support package. When they get too involved is when we hit them with our play-action passes.

The places we feel the defense is weak are down the seams of the field. Since we are reading defenders at the line of scrimmage, that means we are gaining blockers to the point of attack. If the defense has four defenders to one side of the ball and the offense has four blockers to that side of the ball, we actually outnumber the defense because we are not going to block one of those defenders. The defense has to get someone else into the box to stop the run and match up with our blockers. That puts a tremendous amount of pressure on the secondary to read the play properly every time.

The defense is playing assignment defense. Everyone has an assignment they have to carry out. The play-action pass puts those defensive backs in limbo. If they don't fill the ally the quarterback is running free. We try to attack the defense with skinny posts and wheel routes.

We have play-action passes to go with all our best running plays. From the midline scheme we run a quick slant from the split end and a seam route by the slot back [Diagram 9]. The slot takes a path to block on the corner. He is waiting for the split end to break inside. As the split end breaks inside, the slot trails him up the seam. We feel the strong safety will react to the pattern of the split end and we can get behind him and up the seam. We have position on the corner and the free safety is too far away to make a play on this pattern.

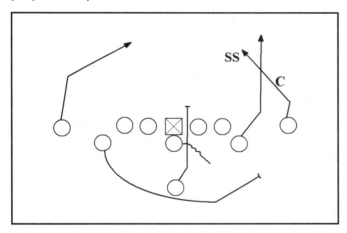

Diagram 9. Midline pass

The next pattern is similar to the other pattern, but the action comes off the triple option [Diagram 10]. The threat of the quarterback running really pulls defenders to him. On this pattern the split end is trying to get behind the strong safety. He is running a post cut keying the free safety. The slot starts his path on the corner, but this time he continues outside the corner and up the sideline.

We motion the slot back to give the appearance of the triple option being run. The fullback runs his path and sets up to block, if he is not tackled. The slot back comes around the pitch path and to the line of scrimmage as a blocker. The quarterback rides the fullback, pulls the ball, and runs three steps down the

line of scrimmage before retreating into his drop to throw the ball.

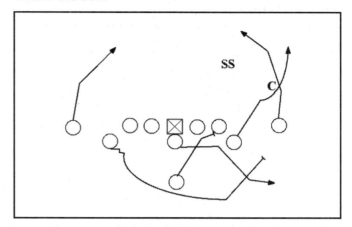

Diagram 10. Wheel pass

Let's watch the film and you can see what I have been talking about. (Film)

Let me say in closing that you and your staff are welcome at the Air Force Academy. If you would like to come up and view our campus and visit with us you are certainly welcome. Usually about the third week in April we have a bunch of high school staffs come visit us. I think they learn a heck of a lot more from each other than they do from us. They have unbelievable clinic sessions among those staffs.

The successes in coaching are not always related to the X's and O's. The real success sometimes is the Johnny and Jody in your program. I know you are in coaching to help young people. I think today our players want to know how much we care about them than how much we know.

Research tells us the most popular guy in any community is the coach. I am very proud to be called a coach. To me that is an awesome responsibility. There are three things I know young people want. I know they want *positive role models*. I know they want *family stability*. And I know they want *discipline*. I know for a fact they can get all of those things in football and the athletic arena. We all have a strong responsibility to protect and defend our game, which I think and I know you agree is the greatest game of them all.

It has been a real pleasure being with you. I hope you got something from my lecture. If you got one idea you can incorporate into what you are doing, then our time was worthwhile. It has been my pleasure. Thank you very much.

THE EAGLE PACKAGE AND GOAL LINE DEFENSE

Kansas State University

It is a great honor for me to speak to you guys. At Kansas State we have had good defensive teams. I don't pretend to have all the answers as far as defenses go. Bill Snyder has built a program at Kansas State. He built the program from scratch in a place that you wouldn't believe you could build a program. Coach Snyder has done a great job.

I think a lot of that has to do with the history, tradition, and continuity that Coach Snyder has had at Kansas State. The defensive tradition goes way back into the early 1990s with Bob Stoops. He turned it over to Mike Stoops, who is now with his brother at Oklahoma. After that, Phil Bennett became the defensive coordinator and he is now the head coach at SMU. After Phil left, I got the chance to be the defensive coordinator.

The key thread through all the coordinators is that the philosophy of Bill Snyder never changed. The things he was exposed to at Iowa under Hayden Frye never changed when he came to Kansas State.

As the defense went from coordinator to coordinator, there was the understanding the base philosophy would always remain the same. When I got a chance to come to Kansas State, there was no question that we were going to do the same things they had done before on defense. There may have been some additions and tweaking, but the base fundamentals of the eagle defense have stayed the same.

At Kansas State we are an eagle-front defense based on 4-3 personnel. We are going to be a five-man front almost exclusively. We will play some 4-3 package on rare occasions. We are going to be good at a few things and accomplish that through repetition. We are not as multiple, fancy, or creative as you might see in some other teams, but we are going to be good at what we do. One of the things that has been a tradition at Kansas State is press tight, man-to-man coverage. The front that I'm going to talk about tonight is the *eagle front with man-free coverage.* Although we do some other things with it, that is the base we work from.

We have had excellent defensive backs over the years at Kansas State. The Kansas State defense is always going to be built on speed. Of course 40-yard dash times are not all we are looking for. We want someone who can play fast. We want someone who can transfer what they see into movement rapidly. *Playing fast* is a lot more than just being fast. We pride ourselves on being able to play fast. That has to do with the simplicity of the system and the repetition we do.

What you see from the Kansas State defense is a lot of safeties down in the box with an *eight- and nine-man pressure system.* We are going to stop the run by outnumbering the offense in the box. We play more eight-man front with a free safety than anything else. We are going to play run defense first. When the offense goes to the passing game, we are going to play that with pressure. Generally Kansas State was known for its man-to-man coverage and an all out rush. This year we played more five-man pressure with a free safety and some zone blitzes.

On defense we try to *score or set up scores.* We did a good job of that this year. On defense we want to deny consistent movement on the ground. *Three and out* is a big part of our terminology. We keep track of the number of times we accomplish that goal.

We want to *take away the offense's best plays and match ups.* Match ups in college are fast becoming just as important as they are in the pros. In a man scheme, match ups are more important. Offenses want to use formations to match up linebackers on receivers and get safeties in a bad situation.

We want to *deny the big play.* If we are going to be an aggressive team, that becomes difficult sometimes. Because of the style of defense we play we have to keep those plays to an absolute minimum.

The defense wants to *create turnovers and minus yardage plays*. We have always been good at that goal and we were again this past season.

We want to *rise up in critical situations*. When there is a big third down play inside the 20-yard line or a goal line play, we want to win in those situations. The defensive focus of our group is to get off the field. Very seldom do we practice first-down defense. We are always practicing defense in a down-and-distance situation. You have to practice that way, so when you have those situations on Saturday, you will know how to handle them.

We practice with a chain crew on the field. We practice all the yardage situations during the week. We practice short yardage and goal line on Tuesdays. On Wednesday we practice the medium-yardage plays. Our players get use to that routine and become comfortable in those situations.

We have some principles and strategies we adhere to no matter what we are doing with our scheme. The first thing we want to do is *play our game and let the offense adjust to us.* It is important that we establish the tempo of the game and make the offense react to what we are doing.

In our defensive scheme, we want to *attack and move*. We are not a slant-and-angle team. Although we do cross face some and turn our front on occasion, we are attacking the line of scrimmage. We want to get off the ball and make the offensive block us on the move. We want to beat the offensive blocks across the line of scrimmage. We read hats and blocking schemes, but we do it on the run. If the offense is going to block us they have to hit a moving target. We are going to disrupt the offense scheme. If we play a team that uses man-blocking schemes, we are going to cross face them and make them do something else.

Disguise is important to us. We want to make sure we are disguising our secondary coverages and disguising the fronts or the movement we are using. When I talk about disguise in the front, we will align in one front and stem to another one. Disguise in the secondary is to keep the quarterback unsure of the coverage until he snaps the ball.

To play defense against today's offenses, the defense has to be *flexible*. We have to adjust to different styles of offenses. We are going to see teams that empty out the backfield or play three backs in the backfield. In college and high school football, the defense is presented with a wide variety of offensive scheme. We see ground-base option teams and spread-passing teams. In pro football, they see primarily the same offense every week. In college you have to be flexible to play Nebraska one week and Iowa State the next.

Consistency is very important to us. That has been true at Kansas State. We don't want to be a defense that makes a big play by intercepting a pass and the next series gives up a long touchdown pass. We want to be consistent during the course of the game and the course of the season. Consistency comes from soundness in our scheme, simplicity, and repetition.

I listened to a pro coach the other day. He said when Sunday's game is over they get out the big eraser. They erase everything they had on the grease board and start all over for next week's game. We can't do that in college. We don't have those guys for an unlimited amount of time. We have them for maybe three hours a day. If you don't have simplicity and repetition, you don't have a chance to be consistent.

We don't change what we do from week to week. You have to have continuity in your program. We have a base system that we use. We use game planning, but we don't go overboard on preparation. We put in our package in training camp and pick from that package from week to week. We don't add adjustments, we use the adjustments we already have in the package. We do not have major changes from year to year

Everything we do within our program is based upon *effort*. One thing about a Kansas State defense, we will play hard. We play hard through the entire game. Those are the principles we believe in at Kansas State.

We have 10 strategies that we employ and make sure we do them weekly. We are going to *account for the run defense first*. We want to make sure we are never outnumbered or out-gapped. In the next hour you are going to hear me talk about *run fits* about 500 times. Run fits are part of our terminology at Kansas State. We are constantly talking about our fits to particular offensive schemes. You never want to be outflanked and always be option sound.

In the secondary we want to *play tight coverage.* We want to force receivers off their route and destroy their timing. We want to disrupt the receivers and force them out of their rhythm. We do that with tight press coverage.

We want to *disrupt the offense* on early downs and force the offense into long-yardage plays on second and third downs. We want the offense in a predictable situation. That means we want to use our fire zones and blitz pressure on first and second down as much as we can.

We want to *adjust to formations and situations based on our ability to execute.* If we have an adjustment to make, I want to do what our players know how to do and not what I saw Nebraska do. I'm not looking for adjustments that look good on the blackboard. I want adjustments that we can make and our players know how to play it. I have two ways to adjust to everything, even if you don't you become predictable. I am not interested in more than two adjustments per situation.

We want to have a *change-up off of every look* we have. The change-ups may be very slight or small movements but they serve the purpose for what we are trying to do.

Your *base defenses must hold up* to all situations. Coach Snyder dictates what the defense is allowed to do in a scrimmage. That makes us play a base defense. The idea is to give the offense confidence, but in reality it makes the defense play base and win with it.

We *study personnel* and plan accordingly. To me, my personnel are more important than the offense's personnel. The personnel that we have to conceal, hide, or compensate for is more important than what is on the other side of the ball. We do look at coverage match-ups in our coverage schemes. The front is more difficult to adjust.

We *want to plan a fast start for every game and every second half.* That is one thing that you can't always guarantee. Sometimes your team doesn't come to play and there is nothing you can do about it. One of the things I've learned over the course of time

about players is you can make them play. In pregame warm-up, if you notice your defense dull and not into the game, there is something you should try. When the game starts, begin blitzing even if you make a mistake. That type of activity may bring them out of their funk. By blitzing you increase their aggressiveness.

As a defense you *should look at your defense through the eyes of the offense.* That means we should scout ourselves and see what the offense sees. We want to ask our offensive coaches what they see in our defense. They can give you hints and clues as to how you are tipping a coverage or movement or how we are becoming predictable in some adjustment.

The last thing is *only motivated players can make the game plan work.* It doesn't matter who you are playing or what type of team they have, if your players are not ready to play, it will be a long afternoon.

I listened to a sport psychologist talk. Some of the things he said were really interesting. He said it was important for the players on the field to think in order. They should have a *progression* of things they do.

I learned this next thought as a player at the University of Iowa. I have used it every day in my coaching career. If the player can think in a systematic fashion, everything that goes on around him won't matter. All the distractions, the crowd, television cameras, and things like that won't matter because the player is focusing on the moment. This is how we teach our players the coverage and front.

The first element is *call.* Make sure you get the entire call on defense. The second element is *align.* Make sure to recognize formations, communicate calls, and line up properly. The third element is *stance.* It is important in every position to get into a good stance. If you start out in a bad stance, everything goes downhill from there. The fourth element is *key.* Everybody on every play has a key. No one is watching the football. If the defensive player doesn't know where his eyes are supposed to be, he can't read run/pass or the type of blocking scheme that is coming at him. The next element is *execution.* The fifth element is *responsibility.* The player must execute his responsibility with proper technique and finish the play. What all that says is *C-A-S-K-E-R,* and that equals consistency.

I'm going to talk about our eagle package and our goal line defense. Our goal line defense is an extension of our eagle package. We don't sub on the goal line. We play our base personnel down there. We believe while we are practicing short-yardage defense, we are also practicing goal line defense.

Our terminology for our eagle front and man-free coverage is *eagle-brown* [Diagram 1]. We base our defense out of a four-man front with a stand-up Sam linebacker. We have a Mike and Will as our inside linebackers. That is a 50 defense. When we were at Iowa, we called it a 3-4 defense. We had three down linemen, two stand-up outside linebackers, and two inside linebackers.

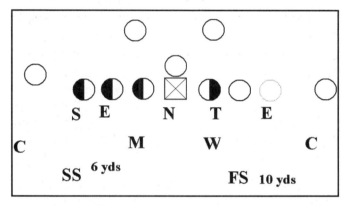

Diagram 1. Eagle brown

We align the Sam linebacker in a 9 technique. The defensive end to the tight end side is in a wide 5 technique. We have a strongside shade by the nose tackle. The weakside tackle is in a wide 3 technique and the defensive end is in a ghost 6 technique.

With the size of offensive lineman and the holding that goes on in our game, we can't play head-up techniques or tight shades and expect to hold our gap. We take wide alignments and attack. Because of the size of the linemen and their ability to pull the defense down, I think that is the only way to play aggressive any more.

To us, a wide alignment is a *shoe-to-shoe alignment*. The inside shoe of the 9 technique will be on the outside shoe of the tight end. The 5 technique is a shoe-to-shoe alignment. The nose tackle is shoe-to-shoe on the center and sometimes he is in a 2i on the offensive guard. The 3 technique is a shoe-to-shoe alignment. The ghost end aligns in a 6 technique on a tight end if he were there. That alignment is wider than a shoe-to-shoe alignment.

Our linebackers are off the ball four-and-a-half yards in a 30 technique. I tell them to align two-and-a-half yards from the feet of the defensive down linemen.

If you look at the strong safety, he is down in the box. I believe if you are going to play down safeties and make them responsible for a gap, you have to play them low enough to beat the block. The strong safety and free safety, when they are involved in run support, are going to be at six yards or closer.

Our Sam linebacker, when we start him off, is in a cocked 9 technique. His aiming point is the V of the neck of the tight end. If the tight end blocks down, the 9 technique attacks the next block coming his way with an aggressive charge. We wrong arm and spill everything outside.

The down four linemen are going to align in a stance that puts their up foot in their stance into their gap-control responsible. Since all of our alignments are outside shades, the linemen's outside foot should be up in his stance. The reason for that is the first step, which is a six-inch step. The second step is the step that we use to control the gap.

The stance is a heel-to-toe stagger with the feet shoulder- width apart. The butt will be slightly higher than the head. When we line up we want our hand behind the ball and our head six-inches behind our hand.

We do not flip-flop our down linemen. We have a left and right side of the defensive line. We feel when the defense takes a block on or reads a scheme, it is important that they see it from the same side all the time. That means you are getting only those repetitions. The second reason is the way offenses are attacking defenses these days.

So much of the running game is being directed at the nose and 3 technique players. Coaches want to run the midline at the 3 technique or they always run toward the nose shade if they are going to block down. Our 3 technique can be a noseguard and the noseguard can be a 3 technique. We stem those two guys back and forth on certain plays. Because we do that, we have become a team that people don't trap too much on.

The linebackers are going to take a parallel stance. We want them to bend at their knees and not their waist. We want our players in a comfortable stance with their hands slightly on the thigh-boards.

We have talked about the first step for our down linemen. We described that step as a short jab step. When we make the first step, we are getting our hand ready to shoot them at the V of the neck of the offensive blocker. On the second step, we are shooting the hands and getting control of the gap in which we are assigned.

The visual key for the down five linemen is the gapside shoulder pad of the offensive linemen they are lined up on. That is what they are seeing with their eyes. Obviously the linemen on the interior can see the ball also. They are looking at the ball using their wide vision. They are not looking directly at the ball, they are watching the shoulder pad, but they can still see that movement of the ball.

The *pressure key* comes from the adjacent offensive lineman. In the case of the 5 technique end, his pressure key would be the tight end. In the case of the noseguard it would be the guard, and for the 3 technique tackle it would be the offensive tackle. After the pressure key the linemen read blocking schemes. They read the down block and look for the next blocker. Those types of schemes are the things that are drilled with repetition in practice.

The Sam linebacker is going to key much like the defensive down linemen. He is going to key the tight end and move from there to the backfield action. He is reading backfield-blocking schemes, much like the other down linemen. However, the inside linebackers are different. We have a *bubble* linebacker and a *covered* linebacker. The Mike linebacker is playing a 30 alignment on an uncovered guard. He is the bubble linebacker. The Will linebacker is stacked behind the 3 technique tackle and is a covered linebacker, but in some situations that could change.

The covered linebacker is going to *key the flow of the backs* exclusively. He is a backfield reader. We are reading full-flow strong and weak and split flow. He is going to see those flows in two speeds. *Fast-flow* is action by the backs parallel to the line of scrimmage. *Slow-flow* is action by the offensive backs at the line of scrimmage. He has to know if it is split or full-flow and the angle the backs are attacking the line of scrimmage.

All those things happen at once. Good linebackers, through repetition in practice, can read all those things

immediately. He is seeing the flow of the backs, but he must feel the pulls of the offensive linemen. The pulls are going to take him to all the counter and power plays that he needs to play as a linebacker.

The Mike linebacker is seeing the first step of the guard and than seeing the backfield action. He has to see the first step of the uncovered guard because he is looking for a zone scheme. That lets him attack the zone blocker coming up the line of scrimmage for him. He can also see the pull scheme start to develop.

Playing the twins set from a man-to-man scheme has become fairly simple because of the way we play our corners [Diagram 2]. When the offensive team gives us a *twin set*, we flip both corners to the same side to cover the twin receivers. The tight end represents the run strength of the offense. That side of the defense has not changed, regardless of where the corners are aligned. The safeties are in the same position to fit the run game regardless of where the corners are aligned. I don't want a corner trying to read the tight end and fitting into the run game. If the safety didn't have a gap responsibility it wouldn't matter. But since the safeties have an assigned responsibility in the run scheme, we want them in the same positions.

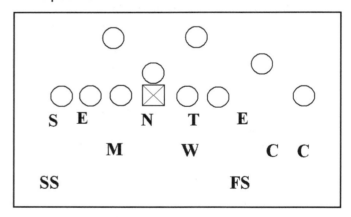

Diagram 2. Twin set

Let's talk about some base adjustments we make for different formations. When we play against *22 personnel*, the adjustments on the backside of the eagle defense can be handled two different ways [Diagram 3]. Twenty-two personnel to us is two tight ends and two backs and one wide receiver. We can move the defensive end into a 6 technique on the second tight end. The corner aligns two-yards outside the tight end and two-yards deep. He is keying and playing like the Sam linebacker on the other side. In essence he is the 9 technique to the weakside. He has a D gap responsibility. The 6 technique defensive end has C gap responsibility. We can play the safety high or low depending upon the coverage.

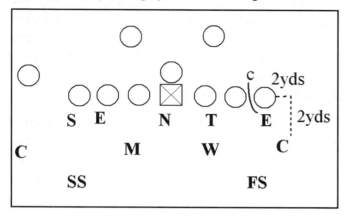

Diagram 3. 22 corner down

The second adjustment we can make is called *eagle wide* [Diagram 4]. We move the 3 technique tackle into a 4i on the offensive tackle. When he gets into that position he has to reverse his stance and get his inside foot up in his stance. The defensive end moves outside to a 9 technique on the tight end. The corner gets into what we call an *overhang position*. That is basically a stack position for the corner on the defensive end.

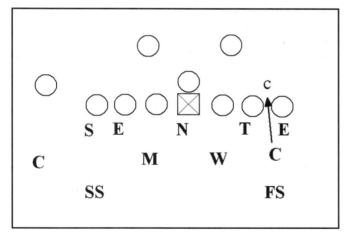

Diagram 4. Eagle Wide

We use the wide adjustments against teams that like to run the option to the backside. They want to scoop block on the 6 technique and get up on the linebacker. The corner plays essentially the same man-to-man pass responsibilities on the tight end in both adjustments. In the run game, his run fit is different. The corner reads the tight ends block and fits the C gap on a running play when he is playing in

the wide eagle. The defensive end fits into the D gap. The corner and defensive end has exchanged run responsibilities they played in the first adjustment.

If we get into a situation where the *tight end flexes*, we want to make sure the offense doesn't take us out of our run fits [Diagram 5]. The strong safety goes out to cover the flexed tight end. The Sam linebacker moves to a two-by-two-yard alignment behind the defensive end. From that position he assumes the run fit responsibility of the strong safety.

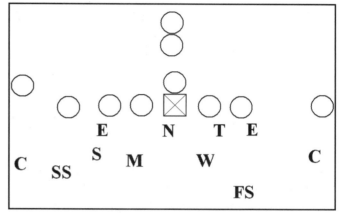

Diagram 5. Flexed tight end

If the offense gives us what we call a *queen* or *weak halfback set* in the backfield, we can get the free safety down in coverage. We do this by game planning. It is not an automatic adjustment to our defense. We did it against Southern Cal and sometimes it is a check and sometimes it is a call. When we bring the free safety down, he takes the tailback out of the backfield, the strong safety becomes free in the middle of the field, and the Sam linebacker takes the tight end man-to-man. It is basically a one- back adjustment to a two-back set.

If the offense went to a *one-back set* by motioning a back out of the backfield, the safeties will make the adjust [Diagram 6]. One of the safeties will leave the box to cover the motion. If that happens, one safety takes the motion and the other becomes the free middle field safety. The Sam linebacker has the tight end man-to-man. The corners have the wide receivers in man coverage. The Mike and Will linebackers are locked on the remaining back in the backfield. If the back comes out of the backfield, the linebacker to that side picks him up and the other linebacker plays the hole in the short middle.

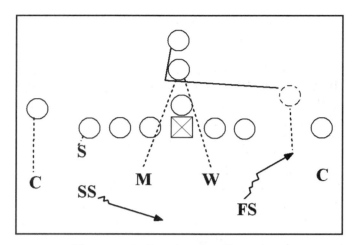

Diagram 6. One-back adjustment

We tie our safeties into our run fits. There is going to be a low safety on one side of the formation all the times. In some cases we will have both safeties down, but generally we have a high and low safety. The strong safety needs to communicate with the Mike and Will linebackers. The strong safety makes a call to the Mike linebacker to let him know he is down. He comes down to a depth of six yards [Diagram 7]. That tells the Mike linebacker a number of things. If the offense brings a lead play at him, he wrong arms the play and spills the ball outside to the safety. The Will linebacker is playing slow and has the cutback lane. If the ball is a full- flow play away from the Mike linebacker, the Mike linebacker can play fast- flow to the ball because he has a cutback player behind him.

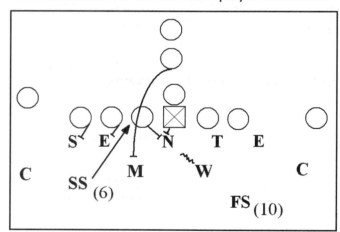

Diagram 7. Strong safety down

If the strong safety did not give a call to the Mike linebacker, on the flow at him he takes the block on with his outside shoulder and spills the ball inside to the Will linebacker and nose tackle. On the flow away from the Mike linebacker, he has to play slow and stop

behind the double-team to make sure there is no cutback before he can pursue the ball.

If the tight end engages the Sam linebacker and then releases, the Sam linebacker takes him. Once the tight end blocks our Sam linebacker and engages him with his hands, the Sam linebacker has him man-to-man. If that doesn't happen we can't ask the strong safety to fill a gap. If he has to sit back and wait to find out what the tight end is doing, he cannot fill a gap.

If the free safety reads a scoop block by the offensive tackle, he becomes what we call a *fence-line player*. He stays lateral in his pursuit. He doesn't attack downhill. He is playing down the middle of the field watching for a play-action pass or the ball breaking loose.

If we get the *isolation play* to the weakside, the Will linebacker is going to spill the play to the outside even though he doesn't have a safety down [Diagram 8]. The Mike linebacker is fast-flowing to the weakside and becomes the over-the-top player. He plays over the top of the Will linebacker to the outside.

We cannot get the free safety too involved in the running game to the weakside. He is keying the uncovered linemen for a high or low hat. If we tell him to key the hat of the tackle, he is going to bail out to the middle on a high hat and the offense will be running an isolation draw play. That is why we let the Mike linebacker play over the top of the Will linebacker. The down linemen have to squeeze their holes as much as possible. If they have an outside gap responsibility they have to keep those gaps from getting so wide the linebackers can fill them.

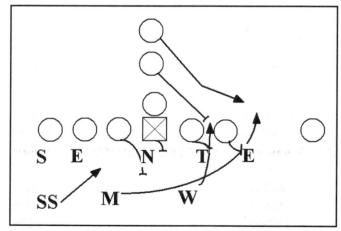

Diagram 8. Weakside isolation

The strong safety fit depends on the block of the tight end. If the tight end blocks out on the Sam linebacker, the strong safety fits inside the D gap. If the tight end blocks down, the strong safety becomes an outside scraper.

The free safety is keying the offensive tackle. If you are going to involve him in all runs, you may as well put him in the box. I am going to give the free safety two to three keys that will bring him up on the run. I let him attack on an option to the weakside or a down block by the offensive tackle. Other than that, he does not react up to any other running play.

The next running play that everyone is running is some kind of *power or counter* [Diagram 9]. When the Sam linebacker reads the down block of the tight end, he is coming down off the hip of the tight end looking for the next block. He is going to wrong arm all blocks coming at him. We don't ask him to spill the blocks of an onside guard or tackle. We don't think he can get under them. We fit on the outside of the near guards and tackles. We ask him to spill the pulls of backside guards and tackles. The defense depends on the play of the Sam linebacker. If he gets washed out of the play, the gap becomes too wide for the linebackers to play. He has to make a pile and hold his ground.

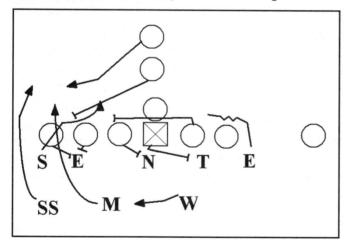

Diagram 9. Power play

When the strong safety sees the tight end block down, he scrapes outside, gets outside any blocker on this play, and turns the play back inside. The Mike linebacker sees the flow but he reads the down-block scheme and flows outside and fits inside the next blocker. He can't fill outside the blocker, because the safety is already out there. The key to the play is the placement of the strong safety head. He has to have

his head outside the last blocker and the Mike linebacker has to have his head inside that blocker.

The Will linebacker sees the flow, but he also sees the guard pull. When the guard pulls the cutback goes to the nose and backside tackle. There is no cutback and he has to get across the ball as quick as he can. The guards pull to take him out of the slow read.

The backside defensive end shuffles down the line of scrimmage square. I guess we are old school in that technique. We don't turn and chase the ball down the line like a lot of teams. Our defensive end has to play the bootleg and reverses.

When we spill the play, we tell our defender if he throws his body into the pulling guard and gets washed out, it doesn't help us. We want him to take the blocker on the inside half, fire through him, and get upfield to knock down the second block. If he doesn't take two players out, the offense still has an answer for our defense. Every set we deal with has to be met with power aggressiveness and downhill movement.

If the offense runs the power or counter to the split side, we spill the play to the outside [Diagram 10]. The defensive end spills the play to the outside. The Will linebacker scrapes and puts his head inside the next blocker. The Mike linebacker is playing over the top of the Will linebacker. The free safety has to read this block by the offensive tackle. When he reads that aggressive down block by the offensive tackle, the free safety has to come up. If the ball is bounced sideways the free safety may have to run it down. That is a long way to come, but he has to do it. He is coming from a depth of 10 yards.

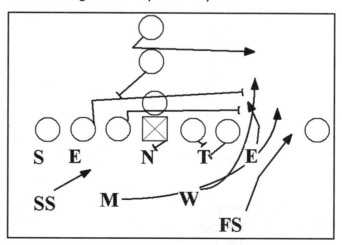

Diagram 10. Weakside counter

If we are having trouble with this kind of support, we can make a *cloud call*. That brings the corner to support and plays the free safety over the top of the corner.

The play that has frustrated me is the *split back zone play* [Diagram 11]. This is an inside zone play, except the offense blocks the fullback on the backside end. It is almost like a second tight end, which creates an additional gap for the defense. There are two ways to defense the play. The Mike linebacker sees the play coming at him, but he also sees split flow. The split flow tells the Mike linebacker to rock back. The Will linebacker sees the split flow and that tells him to rock back. The defensive end sees the fullback block coming and gets under the block. The Will linebacker is coming outside of the defensive end. The Mike linebacker rocks back and then fits into the weakside A gap. The strong safety has the frontside B gap alone.

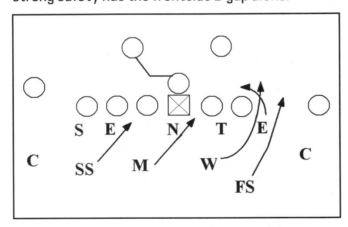

Diagram 11. Split back zone play

The *lead zone play* is a different play [Diagram 12]. I consider the lead zone a toss play. The fits for the lead zone play and the toss sweep are the *exact fits*. The strong safety fits on the outside shoulder of the lead blocker. Everyone else plays their gap responsibility. Where the lead blocker goes, the strong safety is going to fit on his inside or outside. The strong safety fits either inside or outside of the Sam linebacker depending on where the lead blocker goes.

A lot of people don't think they can get the 5 technique hooked. They bring the tight end down on the 5 technique and fold the tackle around on the Sam linebacker. We tell the Sam linebacker it is more important to drive the tackle back than it is not to get hooked. We don't ask the Sam linebacker not to get hooked, we as him to drive the tackle back. It is

important for the Sam linebacker not to run away from that block. If he stays in there and fights the block, the Mike linebacker and strong safety will make the play.

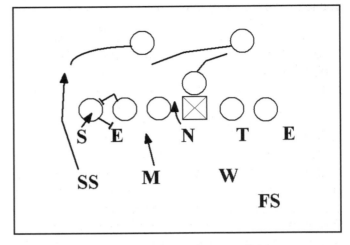

Diagram 12. Lead zone play

The linebackers are reading full-flow parallel to the line of scrimmage. That means they are in a fast-flow read. The Will linebacker is pursuing the ball from the backside, but he is coming in a hurry.

This is a lesson I learned the hard way. Kansas State taught me this when I was at Iowa State. The strong safety's run support responsibility was the pitch on the option. He had to play the lead back and the pitchman. That was well and good on the blackboard. Because of the nature of the run-support fit of the strong safety, he can't get licked.

If you are a secondary player playing an arc block, you better get plenty of width. If the secondary player comes up the field at the arc blocker, he will cut the safety down. That's what happened to me against Kansas State. They knock my players down like they were bowling pins.

At Kansas State we play the pitch at the line of scrimmage. On the *lead option* the Sam linebacker is the one who plays the pitch [Diagram 13]. The strong safety has the outside half of the quarterback. He fits himself under all blockers. The outside half of the quarterback has to be outside the blockers. The Mike linebacker has to get over the combination block from the tight end and tackle and fit on the inside half of the quarterback. If the tight end is tapping the 5 technique and getting up on the Mike linebacker, the 5 technique will get on the inside half of the quarterback. Either the 5 technique or the Mike linebacker has to get on the inside half of the quarterback. The outside half player is also the ally runner. The Will linebacker should be coming too, because he is reading fast-flow.

On the weakside, that is one of the actions the free safety has to be responsible for. The Will linebacker scrapes outside and has the outside half of the quarterback and the inside half of the pitch.

One of the schemes that is making a comeback in college is the *veer option*. That was the rage a few years ago. People got away from it and now we are starting to see it again. That is something your linebackers have to practice against. The back is coming at them in their gap and they want to step up. What they have to see is the block of the tackle coming down on them with a veer block. They have to be able to slip that block and help on the option outside

The Sam linebacker has the pitch. The strong safety has the outside half of the quarterback, but he has to get over an arc block. The arc blocker is the tight end. The strong safety also has to play him on a pass. The Mike linebacker exchanges responsibility with the defensive end. The defensive end takes the dive, Mike takes the quarterback and the Will linebacker is over the top.

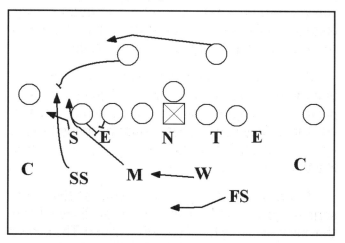

Diagram 13. Lead option.

This offensive scheme in college football is really difficult to play. It makes it difficult on the strong safety to become a force player and still cover the tight end.

When we are playing a base two-back team, our base coverage is *man free* with a linebacker playing in the middle underneath free. Sometimes that player is our strong safety. We have a four-man pass rush

with the linebackers providing secondary containment against a sprint-out pass. The lead blockers on the sprint-out pass are generally the backs aligned in the backfield. The linebackers who are covering those running backs are running up into the face of the quarterback.

Our philosophy for our secondary is to play *tight coverage* on wide receivers and backs with security deep in the middle. We always have a free linebacker as a low-hole player in the underneath coverage. He plays crosses, quarterback scrambles, and screens.

In zone coverage, the linebackers are dropping out in coverage at a depth of 10 to 12 yards. The defense is playing great coverage so the quarterback can't throw the ball. He pulls the ball down and scrambles out of the pocket for seven or eight yards and makes the first down. The advantage is you are always going to have someone in the middle that can react quickly to quarterback scrambles.

Within our system, the linebacker passes off the crossing routes. In the running game we have run fits. In the passing game we have *pattern matches*. We are going to have a pass-off system for crossing routes and picks, which generally refers to the backs and tight end. We are not going ask our linebacker to run with the crossing route run by wide receivers. That is what the offense is looking for. That is the type of mismatches they want to get the defense involved with.

We talked about alignment, stance, and keys with the front earlier. Now I'm will talk about alignment, stance, and keys with the secondary.

At Kansas State we are known for our *press corners*. That is not all we play. We also play an *off-position* on the receivers in the backpedal with our corners. We teach both types of coverages and I don't discourage the use of the off coverage. I don't tell the corners what to play. When I coach the coverage I tell them what is best for certain situations.

As a general rule our corners will line up in *press coverage*. They are going to have a slight inside-to-out shade depending on the split of the wide receiver. We are in a *parallel stance*. If we are in pedal-man coverage, we are off the receiver five to seven yards. We will be in an inside or outside shade based on the split of the receiver. In the press coverage I want the corners in a parallel stance with their wrists cocked but not up. They are ready to punch, but they don't have their hands up.

In the backpedal position I want a large stagger in their feet with a flat back. I want a good bend in the knees. I prefer their outside foot up and their inside foot back in their stance.

The strong safety is aligned about six-yards off the ball. He is aligned in an outside shade on the tight in a parallel linebacker stance. The free safety is at 12 yards, aligned on the outside shoulder of the weakside offensive tackle. His stance is also parallel. On movement our safeties remain flatfooted. We don't shuffle back. The free safety has to play a little taller than the strong safety. He has to see the line movement as part of his key. He kind of clears his cleats and bounces a little to get ready to run. The safeties and corners are the same type of personnel.

When I coach the cornerback, I tell him that he has no inside help on his receiver. Now technically he does with the free safety helping him on the post route, but he does not have skinny post or slant help, and he only has underneath help when he gets to the low-hole player. The outside corner has to take an inside leverage position.

In the twin set, the inside corner or slot player can take an outside leverage position, because he closer to the low-hole player and the inside post help. From that position there is no skinny-post route for the receiver. We play our defensive backs off at different levels. It is important for the defensive backs not to get on the same level so they don't get picked off. The general rule is the defensive back who is covering the man on the line of scrimmage is in press coverage. The defensive back covering the slot receiver is in off coverage. Since the receiver is not on the line of scrimmage, the defender cannot press him.

If the offense reverses the receivers in the twin set and backs the outside receiver off the ball and puts the slot receiver on the ball, the corner reverses their position. The outside corner becomes the off player and the inside corner is the press player.

There are a number of ways to play press coverage. The defensive back can slide to make the contact or he can use his hands. We also see defensive backs who motor off the ball, try to catch the receiver, and press him that way. If we were to

play that technique, it would put us in a position to get picked and rubbed out of the coverage.

We are going to use the slide technique and punch down the line of scrimmage. The shade is going to be a foot-to-crotch relationship. It is not going to be a full shade. If you shade all the way inside, that gives the receiver the fade route. We want to make sure we have a chance to slide and get a good fade relationship. We use the near hand as the shock hand and the outside hand as the control hand.

This is our base coverage against *21 personnel*. That is two backs, one tight, end and two wide receivers. The two-back set in the passing game without some kind of motion doesn't happen anymore. We put this tape together with a whole season of eagle-brown coverage on it. We played 25 snaps in the season against this kind of set.

They ran the football from this set, but if they were going to throw the football they used motion or some other formation. They were not going to let us play this coverage all that much.

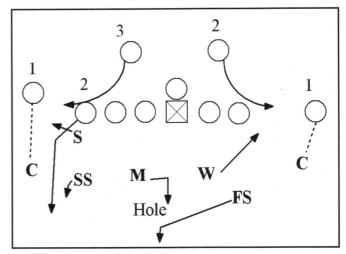

Diagram 14. Pattern matches

I want to talk about our *pattern matches* in brown coverage [Diagram 14]. From the split backs set, the strong safety has the tight end on all vertical routes over the depth of the Mike linebacker. The Sam linebacker has the first receiver to the flat. The Will linebacker has the first to the flat on the other side. The Mike linebacker becomes the hole player in the middle. The Mike linebacker matches the third receiver. The third receiver will be any back to the two-receiver side. The Mike linebacker is going to match three and five to six-yards deep and sit in the hole. He is not going to take a zone drop that puts him out of the play if the quarterback scrambles with the ball.

The free safety goes to the middle of the field. The strong safety has the tight end and the corner has the wide receiver. Hopefully the low-hole player can give underneath help on crossing route and inside moves. The best thing he can do is knock down the receivers who are trying to get through his area.

Here is another *split-flow pattern match* [Diagram 15]. The Sam linebacker takes the first receiver to the flat, who is the tight end. The Mike linebacker stacks over the third receiver. The Will linebacker stacks over number two to his side and takes the first to the flat. The low-hole player becomes the strong safety. His job is to look for the dig route by the wide receivers.

If the tight end runs a drag across the formation, the Mike linebacker picks him up man-to-man [Diagram 16]. The Mike linebacker is stacked over the third receiver in the backfield. If the third receiver goes to the flat, the Mike linebacker opens to take him to the flat, but encounters the tight end coming on the drag. He takes the tight end and lets the back go to the flat. The Sam linebacker has the first receiver to the flat. Since the tight end went inside, he picks up the third receiver coming to the flat. The strong safety is taking the tight end on all verticals over the Mike linebacker. When the tight end went to the inside, he becomes the hole player.

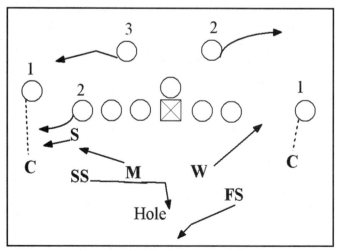

Diagram 15. Pattern matches two

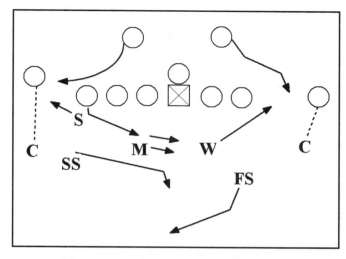

Diagram 16. Pattern matches three

We are not passing off route by the wideouts, but we are passing off combinations of patterns by the tight end and the backs. The Mike linebacker has to go through a progression to find his receiver. He is taking the third receiver, but he has to readjust to pick up the crossing pattern. Really, this is a *zone-under coverage*, which is a good way to do that. The strong safety, tight end, and Mike linebacker do a good job of communicating on these combinations.

The *power pass* is a hard pass for the Mike linebacker to cover. If he gets too committed up into the line and is late taking the third receiver to the flat, we think he can force a perfect throw by the quarterback to get the completion. He has to run hard to get under the receiver and make the quarterback deliver a perfect ball. We stack the linebackers over the split backs and tell them they should have a three-yard cushion on them.

I'm out of time. I hope you got something out of this. If you are ever in Manhattan, Kansas, drop in and say hello to us. Thank you.

DEFENSIVE CONCEPTS EMPHASIZING DEFENSIVE LINE

Western Kentucky University

It is a pleasure to be here representing Coach Jack Harbaugh and the Division I-AA National Champs, Western Kentucky. I would like to thank Nike, Earl Browning, and his staff for inviting me back to the clinic. It is a real thrill to speak at this clinic and a pleasure to talk about our defense.

It has been a busy week for us. We went to Frankfort to the state capital early in the week and were honored by the General Assembly for winning the National Championship. I would like to thank the coaches who helped us with recruiting this year. We felt we had a good signing class. We are extremely happy with the kids we signed. I know we missed some people this season because we couldn't get out to all the schools. We didn't finish our playoff games until December 20. That really put us behind the eight ball in our recruiting. However, we got the kids we wanted.

I am grateful to be here and I hope there is something I can give you that will help you down the line as a young coach. I am still a young coach. The head coach at Western Kentucky is Jack Harbaugh. He is a great coach from the old school. He is from Michigan and has two sons that play in the NFL. One of his sons played for the Philadelphia Eagles and the other played for the Oakland Raiders. We were hoping the two would meet in the Super Bowl, but it didn't happen.

I want to share some things with you about our defense. Our defense was number one in our conference this year. We run the 3-4 defense and it has been very good for us. We play in the Gateway Conference. We lead the conference in rushing and scoring defense and were number one in total defense. In the national ranking, we were 27th in rushing defense, 11th in scoring defense, and 23rd in total defense. The team just ahead of us was McNeese State. We played them twice last year. We played them during the regular season and in the National Championship finals.

We accomplished a lot for the University this year. It was the first National Championship ever won by the school. We finished the year 12-3 and were ranked first in all three national polls. We shared the Gateway Conference Championship with Western Illinois. We played them during the regular season and they beat us on our home field. We played them in the playoffs and beat them on their home field. We won 10 straight games to finish the season. That was the longest winning streak in the history of the school. Our record against ranked opponents this year was 6-1. The American Football Coaches Association honored Coach Jack Harbaugh as the Coach of the Year in Division I-AA. We had four players earn All-American honors. We had thirteen players make the all-conference team. Two of the players named to the all-conference team were defensive linemen. We were ranked in the top 10 nationally in rushing for the twelfth consecutive year. We set a school record for points and total yards for a season.

I want to give you a quick summary of our defense. In my first year at Western we had a big thick playbook. I wasn't very happy with it because there were some things in there that we didn't use. I believe less is better. The more reps your players can do the better they become. This year we decided to condense our playbook and make it a thin copy. All our players have a copy of it and bring it to all team meetings. I wanted to make them responsible for the playbook. If our players don't bring their playbook and a note pad to meetings, they get fined. Our fine is running after practice. I want the defensive line to have the section of the playbook that relates to them. They don't need the secondary section of the book.

You always need a defensive philosophy. In our playbook we have our philosophies for the offensive team, defensive team, and the special teams. When you form your philosophy make sure it is sound, basic, and easy for your players to understand. Our defensive philosophy is: *attack-confuse-attack*. I'll talk more about that later.

We have team goals we emphasize with our defense. We develop weekly goals for our defense. They are very simple but necessary in getting our players to focus on some specifics for each game.

The first goal is to *win* the game. We all want to win and that is the place to begin to build. We feel if we can *hold our opponents to 13 points or less*, we have a chance to win the game. We want to *create three or more turnovers*. That is probably the biggest goal we have. This past season we had 15 fumble recoveries and 20 interceptions. During the course of the game, we want to *force the offense into a critical mistake*. To get your defense off the field you have to be proficient on third-down plays. We want to *stop the opponent on 30 percent of their third-down plays*. We want to prevent the offense from getting big plays on the defense. We want *nothing over 12 yards in the running game and nothing over 18 yards in the passing game*. When our offense turns the ball over on a fumble or interception, we want our defense to come in and stop the other team's offense. We call that sudden change. We *want a 100-percent stop in the sudden change* category.

We post our weekly goals in our locker room and fill in the ones that we complete. We want our players to see what they accomplished and where they fall short. They can see from the goal sheet what it takes to win a game.

The next section is important, but I am going to go through it quickly. These are principles that are important in playing great defense. It is extremely important to be able to communicate with your players. You have to talk to your players. Let them know that you love and care about them. If there are problems they want to talk about, make sure they know you are available to counsel them or simply be someone who will listen to them. Let them know you care about their welfare and not just about their football ability.

To play in the defensive line, a player has to improve and master the techniques it takes to play the game. The player has to become a *technician*. I feel this is my biggest asset as a coach. I want to think I do a very good job working on individual techniques for each player.

If a defensive football player wants to be successful, he must have tremendous effort. I want my players to understand it is important to give a 110-percent effort when they step on the field. All I ask from my players during a game is an honest effort. Running to the football is nothing more than effort. The game of football has gotten very sophisticated. We are requiring more out of our players in making adjustments and reading offenses. Players have to be smart to play the game today. The intelligence part of the game is important. They don't have to be brilliant to play the game, but they must have a good football IQ. I guess that is what we call *functional intelligence*. They have to play the game smart and think on the field.

The game of football requires players to have *emotional stability*. That keeps them from overreacting to situations that arise in the heat of battle. That keeps a player from getting the killer, dumb penalty when you can least afford it. He has to be able to handle the winning as well as the losing. Every game is filled with small individual battles between players. A player has to play with a calm demeanor and at the same time be aggressive. He has to play the game with *harnessed aggression*.

You have to coach good practice habits and stress to the players to always finish the play. It is not enough to simply do your job; you have to complete every play. Running to the ball and getting in on the play is a finish to the technique the defender played to get off a block. We have a slogan at Western that deals with pursuit. We took it from a movie, but it reflects what we want them to do. When we talk about running to the ball we tell our players to *get in the gun line*. We want everyone on the defense to be within five yards of the ball when the whistle blows. If our players are not *in the gun line*, they get shot and have to run after practice. It really showed in our team this year. We had people swarming to the football. We want people breaking up passes, turning and running to the ball, playing violent, and becoming a ballistic missile out on the field.

We post signs in our locker room to get our players to focus on what is important. One of the signs we hang in our locker room is: *Think like a Winner*. They see the sign coming into and going out of the building. We talk about it in our drills and emphasize it during practice. The biggest thing we work on in coaching defense is *pursuit*. Getting in the gun line has become our faith and motto. That phrase has become synonymous with pursuit at Western Kentucky.

We have a practice-and-players policy sheet we go over with our players. That gives our players a guide to what they should expect from our practices. The player policy lets them know what is expected of them at practice and all other activities they may be involved in. That is a part of our ongoing attempt to communicate with our players.

The biggest defensive skill a defender has to master is *tackling*. The defensive team that can't tackle won't win many games. You have to define what you expect from your players. Give them the objectives you hope to accomplish in your team tackling. You have to teach them the techniques that go with tackling. If you watched our championship game, I think you would have been impressed by the way we tackled. We did not miss a tackle in the championship game. We work on tackling every day. Each position coach has tackling drills every day we practice. The progression we teach in tackling is the *approach*, *contact*, and the *finish*.

When your offense turns the ball over to the opposing team it creates a sudden-change situation in the game. The attitude we try to get over to our kids is a happy occasion. We want the challenge of trying to go out and stop the offense. We have a word we use in this situation. The word is *mana*. It is a Hawaiian word that means *power within a person*. Before the defense goes on the field, they gather around the coach and have a mini-pep rally.

We break the field into zones to describe the type of effort we want from our defense. The first zone is called the *gut zone*. We describe the gut zone as the area between the opponent's goal line and the opponent's 25-yard line. When the opponent has the ball in the gut zone, we want to hold them in that zone and not let them out. We want the opponent to kick from a backed up position.

The second zone is called the *normal zone*. That zone extends from the 26-yard line to the opposite 26-yard line. In that zone we want to attack on first down. In the third-down situation we will blitz on occasion if it is long yardage.

The *red zone* is the area between our 25-yard line and the five-yard line. In that zone the defense wants to be in attack mode and mix in some man coverage.

The last zone is the *goal line zone*. That zone stretches from the four-yard line to the goal line. In that zone we are in goal line defense most of the time.

The offense has a two-minute offense for the last two minutes of the game or a half. We have to do the same thing on defense. We must have a plan to defend during the last minutes of a half because most teams are going to be in a no-huddle offense. We have to be prepared to play without a huddle and get into a proper alignment.

Each of our coaches has a sign posted on their door, which relates to the playing habits of playing the game. It states that *every day and every play there are things to be done*. There is a list of items on each sign. They are broken into pre-snap and post-snap responsibilities. In the pre-snap situation the players have to consider alignment, stance, field position, and responsibility. In the post-snap situation there is read, react, execute, delivery a blow, get off the block, and tackle. These are things that they have to do as they line up and get ready to play.

We have *three nevers* that we teach all the time. They are to *never* get knocked down, *never* get knocked off the ball, and *never* run around a block. These *nevers* are also posted on our doors in our coach's office. These are situations we want to constantly reinforce to our players.

Next is our *scouting report*. Each coach has a responsibility to make up his part of the playbook and the scouting report. Our graduate assistant has responsibility for the front cover of the scouting report. He has to come up with a thought for the week to go on the front of that report. For our scouting report on McNeese State in the championship game he came up with: *Those Who Stay Will Become National Champions!*

As you walk into our facility, our head coach has that slogan posted on his door. It is ironic to think about that now. I never thought we would get that far. We just played our butts off in those final games and came away with the championship.

The next page of the scouting report is a breakdown of personnel, formations, top runs, and top passes. Our defensive coordinator puts this part of the report together. The first thing you see on this sheet is *overall record*. Since we were playing McNeese State in the last game, the first thing they saw was the 13-1 record. The next thing is the name of the team, their national ranking, and the games that were used to scout them. In this case we used the last five games. We list the opponents and the final score of each game.

We are a very personnel-oriented team. We like to know who the top personnel are and what they do in the game. That helps us make our calls. We list the top personnel by numbers and the percentage of time they run or throw the ball. For instance, McNeese State's top personnel's grouping was what we refer to as 21. That means they have two wide receivers and one tight end in the game. From that set they ran the ball 70 percent of the time and passed it 30 percent of the time. We list their top formation, top runs, and top passes. We list their top formation with their top personnel [Diagram 1].

Top Personnel	
21 – 70/30	20 – 30/70
11 – 65/42	22 – 100/0
32 – 100/0	

Diagram 1. Top personnel chart

McNeese State's top formations from their 21 personnel package was pro and slot. In each formation we list the percentage of times they ran the ball as opposed to the times they threw it [Diagram 2].

The defensive linemen love the next sheet on the report. That is where we get our tendencies and techniques. We test our team on the scouting report. Most of the material comes from that sheet. The first year I was at Western we had a huge scouting report for each game. We have taken all the verbiage out of the report and condensed it to a four- or five-page report. We get all the scouting report to the team on Tuesday afternoon. Each of our defensive coaches is in charge of one section of the scouting

report. The outside linebacker coach is in charge of the section called *field zone run/pass percentage*. That section of the report lists the field broken down into zones [Diagram 3]. This chart breaks the field down and gives us the percentage of times they run the ball or throw it in each zone.

Top Formations	
Flex	Pro
Slot	Slot hip
Top Runs	
Belly	Toss
Iso	Power
Draw	Jet sweep
Top Passes	
2 Spot	QK – 2332/2322
Flex – BJ get open	Shallow crossers
Curl/flat	I slot – P43 058B3

Diagram 2. Top formations and plays chart

Field Zone Run/Pass Percentage 60/40	
-1 to +10	100/0
-11 to −39	53/47
−40 to +40	54/46
+39 to +26	63/37
+25 to +5	77/23
+4 to +1	68/32

Diagram 3. Field zone run/pass percentage chart

I am in charge of the short-yardage section of the report. As you can see, this tells us what they like to run in the short-yardage situations in the game [Diagram 4].

Short Yardage

I pro – 52/53 belly

I slot – 43 lead

I flex – 52/53 belly-fake pitch

Diagram 4. Short-yardage chart

McNeese State's favorite sets in the short-yardage situation were I-pro, I-slot, and I-flex. From the pro set they like to run what we call 52/53 belly. From the slot set they ran the 43-lead play. From the flex set they ran the 52/53 belly fake pitch.

In the goal line situation, I don't have to tell the defensive line what they run. It is the same series they use in short yardage. The difference is the formation in which they are aligned. Most of their formations are tight formations with two or more tight ends [Diagram 5].

Goal Line

1 tight – 53 belly

PQA/M to tight – 45 blast

11 run to slot hip – 53 belly F/P

Diagram 5. Goal line situation chart

Each coach has a responsibility to break down the red zone situations. I'll show you an example of our red zone breakdown [Diagram 6].

Our scouting report showed us that McNeese was in the red zone 70 times in those five games that we scouted. They ran the ball 80 percent of the time and threw it 20 percent of the time. From their 21-personnel grouping they ran the I-pro/slot. From those formations they ran 52/53 belly, 44 lead, 48 G-sweep, two reverses, and one trick play. We break each personnel grouping down in similar manner.

I am also in charge of doing the section that deals with the backs set. I list each back set and show the number times the ball is run or passed from that set [Diagram 7]. From the ace set, McNeese State ran the ball 58 percent of the time and threw it 42 percent of the time.

Red Zone – 70 x – 80/20

<u>21 – 79/21</u> = 1 pros/slot – 52 B/53 B/44 L/48 G – 2 reverses, 1 trick

<u>20 – 58/42</u> = 1 flex = run – belly/43 LO/AGS Detroit hip = pass

<u>22 – 9 runs</u> – 1 tight – 44 L/49 G/53 B/48 G

11 – 4 runs

32 – 1 run

Diagram 6. Red zone situation chart

We played McNeese during the regular season at their place. They beat us in that game. They were a very good team. It was a nasty and hostile atmosphere and a difficult environment in which to play a game. After the first game one of my defensive linemen was really down about the defeat. I told him we had just gotten our tails kicked but we would meet those guys again down the road. In the championship game we played them in Chattanooga. We were ready for McNeese in the Division I-AA Championship Game.

Back Set	Run/Pass
I	75/25
Ace	58/42
SG	16/84
QN	36/64
AGS	15/85
KG	0/100

Diagram 7. Backs set chart

The final section on this page is the run/pass tendencies. We list them by percentages. McNeese ran the ball 60 percent of the time and threw it 40 percent of the time. We list the tendencies by down-and-distance situations. We break our down-and-distances into 12 categories [Diagram 8].

We have first-and-ten, fourth-and-one to two yards, and fourth-and-three yards plus. In the second- and third-down situations we use long, medium, and short yardage to classify what they are doing.

The next sheet of the scouting report is a two-deep listing of personnel. That lets us know who is playing in the game. We list the players by name with their height and weight. Next we list several sheets with the plays they run. We draw each play they like to run from their personnel groups and show how they block the plays. I am in charge of the pass- protection sheet. We show how they are protecting in each formation. We show the formations they like to throw from and the protection that goes with each formation.

Run/Pass Tendencies (60/40)	
1st +10	73/27
2nd +L	50/50
2nd +LL	54/46
2nd +M	74/26
2nd +S	82/18
3rd +L	18/85
3rd +LL	28/72
3rd +M	18/82
3rd +S	100/0
3rd +3	50/50
4th 1-2	7 runs
4th and 3+	1 pass

Diagram 8. Run/pass tendencies

We also give our defensive players a tip sheet. The first section on this sheet is *alignment*. We give them tips about stance whether it is heavy or light. We watch the splits of the linemen and what they like to do from a tight or wide split. We give them the opponent's snap count and what they use for their hard count.

Each coach is responsible for giving his position group a quiz on the scouting report. It is a 10-question quiz about the information in the scouting report [Diagram 9]. My

sheet starts out with some goals listed at the top of the sheet. For McNeese State I listed: *play with mana, play with power,* and *play with quickness.* I followed that with a statement to challenge them. For McNeese it was: *Those who play and pour out their hearts will become champions tonight.* After that comes the quiz.

Hilltopper Linemen Quiz Versus McNeese

1) I-back means? _____

2) What type of alignment will they show us?

_____

3) How will they block us up front?

_____

4) Anytime we're in a 3 technique we must be ready for what?

_____

5) We must get or come off line of scrimmage and also need to be the _____ .

6) What is their favorite outside run play?

_____

7) What do they like to do in the red zone?

_____

8) What is their passing formation in the red zone? _____ .

9) What kind of offense is McNeese State?

_____

10) What do we need to accomplish this week? _____ .

Diagram 9. Scouting report quiz

I conclude the sheet with a mission statement. It stated: *Magnify Your Stewardship and Finish!* I told my players the day we played McNeese State that everyone would be watching them on TV. I told them they needed to play hard and show everyone what our program was all about. I told them this game could open some doors for those who had dreams about the next level. If they played well people would follow them. These guys played their butts off that day and we became champions.

After each game the coaches grade the film. We grade our players on production. Each production has a point value assigned to it [Diagram 10].

Hilltopper Production Chart		
ITEMS	PTS.	GAMES>>>>
Tackle	2	
Assists	1	
Tackle for loss	3	
Kickoff tackle (-20)	5	
QB harass	3	
Sack	5	
Big Hit	3	
Exceptional play	3	
Caused fumble	5	
Recovered fumble	5	
Onside kick recovery	7	
Pass breakup	4	
Interception	7	
Blocked kick	6	
Score on defense	8	
Gun line	-1	
Missed assignment	-3	
Missed tackles	-2	
Special Comments		
PLAYS		
TOTAL PLAYS		
TOTAL POINTS		
RATIO		

Diagram 10. Production chart

If a person makes a tackle he receives two points. If he gets an assist he gets one point. You can see the point value and how we rate the players. In addition to the positive scores there are negative scores. If you fail to *get in the gun line*, that is a minus one. A missed assignment is minus three, and a missed tackle is minus two points.

We total the plays each player is involved in, add up his total points, and compute the player's ratio. We divide the number of plays into his number of points. That gives us a ratio for the number of plays that a player was productive. If the players ratio figures out to 1.2 to 1.5 score, that is good. That means he is making a productive play almost every play.

We do the production chart on Sunday night and have it posted on the production board in the locker room on Monday. That is the first place the players go. They want to see how they did. We also give them a percentage score on their play in the game. The rating sheet is divided into five columns with the headings of play, player, (+ or -), production, and assignment/technique comment [Diagram 11].

Hilltopper Grade Sheet				
PLAY	PL. #	+ OR -	PROD.	COMMENTS
#1	LDE			
	RDE			
	NT			
#2				

Diagram 11. Grade sheet

Coming down the page there are three line divisions for each play. This means for each play run the three defensive linemen are graded. Each player gets a percentage grade from the number of pluses he has, divided by the number of plays he played. What you don't want to see are players with high-percentage grades and low-production ratios. That means his assignment and technique is good but he is not making any plays.

As a coach at Western Kentucky, you have to be involved with some kind of special team. My area is the extra point and field goal block team. When we start practice we start with five minutes of field goal blocking. We blocked four field goals this year and one of them was in the championship game. The first block is called *MC Hammer* [Diagram 12], which stands for middle block. We don't change any personnel on our block team. Whoever is in the game stays in the game and aligns on the block team. The left and right corners play their side. The Mike linebacker goes to the left side and the Will linebacker goes to the right. We have a nickel and a linebacker in the game and they deploy with the nickel to the left C gap and the in the right B gap. The defensive ends are in the left B gap and the right A gap. The nose tackle is in the left A gap. In the middle of the formation we have what we call our leapers. Those are the players that are going to jump and block low kicks. These are safety positions, but we want our highest jumpers in those positions.

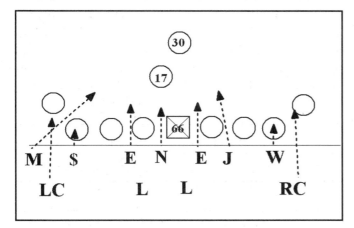

Diagram 12. MC Hammer (middle block)

If the ball is on the left hash mark, we call hammer right [Diagram 13]. Nothing changes for anyone on their alignments. The only assignments that have changed are the right end and joker. They become the blockers. The Mike linebacker has to make sure the kick is off. If the ball is blocked, he may have a chance to scoop it and score. If there is a bad snap and the kicking team makes a fire call, he has the kicker. Everyone else has a man on the play. The joker and left defensive end are blocking the left offensive guard off the line of scrimmage. We are trying to get the leaper through or at least get him deeper in the backfield.

If the ball is on the right hash mark we call hammer left [Diagram 14]. The alignments are the same. The nose tackle and defensive left end are the blockers. The linemen are in a power charge. They lead with their helmet hard and low. The linemen

should extend the hands into the offensive lineman like an incline press. They need to get their pads under the pads of the offensive lineman and work upward. They should bench press the lineman and keep coming hard with their legs moving and their arms extended.

They need to get vertical as well as horizontal push. The left leaper has to adjust his path and everything else is the same as the hammer right.

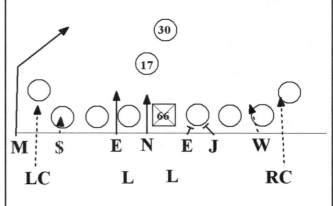

Diagram 13. Hammer right

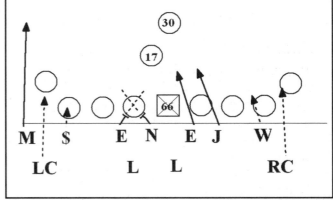

Diagram 14. Hammer left.

If we want to try and block the ball coming off the edge, I call that an H&R block [Diagram 15]. We give a Liz or Ricky call to tell us which side is coming. The best kick blocker on the team should be put to the side the block is coming from. We cover man-to-man on the receivers with the Mike and Will linebackers having the tight ends. The free and strong safeties have the wingbacks. If we are coming from the left, our best blocker is coming from outside the wing. We align him in a cocked position to the inside. We want his outside foot back. He aligns wide enough to get a good close angle to the spot four-and-a-half yards in front of the ball. On his first step he takes his outside foot across the line of scrimmage. On the second step he steps with his inside foot. The third step is a drive step to the inside to adjust his course. On the fourth step he takes off and lays out with his arms extended. We want his eyes open so he can move his hands to the ball. The next rusher is coming inside the wing to draw his block. That gives the blocker a chance to get on the right angle to the ball. If we make a Ricky call, the block comes from the right side. Everything remains the same as far as responsibility, except the blockers go to the right side.

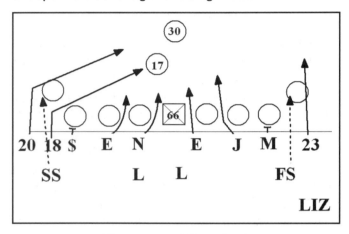

Diagram 15. H&R block

Let's talk about defense real quick before I run out of time. We are a 3-4 defense. We coach our players to attack what is attacking them. We want to attack the offensive linemen. We want to penetrate, not read. I spent some time with the Philadelphia Eagles last year doing an internship in a fellowship program. They really emphasized a wide base with good knee bend for their defensive lineman. They spend a tremendous amount of time working on get off.

When I talk about the target area, you need to know about *vision point*. The defensive linemen have to see and read the hips of the offensive lineman as they slant. The defensive lineman in his stance comes off with a 45-degree step. He is looking at the hip of the offensive guard. If the hip goes down on a down block, the defensive lineman comes inside off his hip. If the hip comes toward him, his hands shoot out and he makes his move off the block. Another vision point we use is the *V* of the neck. On the snap of the ball we get great takeoff and attack the *V* of the neck.

To play defense, the lineman has to play with his eyes. He has to see what is happening. We attack off the line and read on the run. We have to see which way the offensive linemen are going. If we have a fill call we attack the V of the neck. The course of the lineman is changed. He wants to come flatter to the scrimmage. If his vision point is the hip, his charge is more upfield with penetration and vertical push. I want them to see the blockers and cross face every chance they get. If the defender is getting a reach or a zone block on a fill call, he is going flat down the line and has to redirect when he reads the reach. On a pass protection or fan-out block the defensive lineman has to cross face.

When the defensive lineman takes on a block, there are three elements he has to consider. They are *my body*, *his body*, and *eyes*. I got this from the Philadelphia Eagles. You attack with your body, use the offensive blocker's body as a shield, and play with your eyes. In the 3-4 defense, the defensive end is playing in a 4 technique. On some of our defensive calls he has to use a loop step. He is going to loop outside on the tight end and play the C gap. He has to see the alignment of the tight end. If the split of the tight end is tight, he takes a small step to get to the inside shoulder of the tight end or 7 technique. If the tight end has a wide split, he has to take a larger step to get into position. He is taking a lateral step and controlling the C gap. If the tackle is trying to reach him, he gets his hands on the tackle and stays inside the C gap.

The alignment of our nose tackle is head-up on the center. He is getting as close to the ball as he can. Our defensive ends are in 4 techniques head-up on the tackles. They are backed off the ball 18 inches. We want them to have a little clearance off the ball. We are a slanting defense about 70 percent of the time. The other 30 percent, we are an eagle, over, or under front. When we are playing what we call a 70 front, our defensive ends are using a jam technique on the offensive tackle [Diagram 16]. That is another term for a bull rush on the tackles working their way upfield. The nose tackle is aligned on the center and doing the same thing. The Mike and Will linebackers have A gap responsibility. The joker linebacker is dropping into coverage and the nickel linebacker is rushing. We are playing cover 2 in the secondary.

When we call 72 [Diagram 17], it tells our players the defensive line is slanting to the right. The right defensive end has a loop technique if he has a tight end to his side. If he is to the openside of the set, he has a jam technique and contains outside. The nose tackle doesn't worry about the block of the center. He is slanting at the offensive guard and reading his hip. If the hip goes outside, he attacks the hip because the play is going outside. The nose tackle is the core of the defense. He is the heart and soul of the defense. He cannot get blocked by the center. He has to tilt his hip and get on the guard. The left defensive end is slanting inside and reading the hip of the offensive guard. If the guard is down blocking, zone blocking, or pulling, the defensive end attacks his hip. If the defensive end has a fill technique, he is coming flat to the line of scrimmage. If the center tries to block back on him, he wants to go cross face as quickly as he can. The nickel linebacker knows he has containment, but he is slanting too. The Mike and Will linebacker are scraping over the top on flow. The joker is dropping and has the curl zone to the flat area.

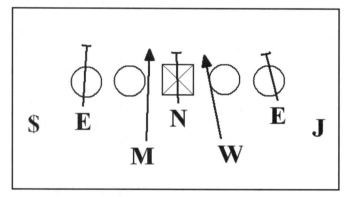

Diagram 16. 70 front jam technique

The 73 call is the opposite slant. The defensive front is slanting left. The left defensive end has to read the split of the tight end. If he has a tight split, he takes the small loop step into the C gap. If the tight end's split is wider, he has to take a longer loop step. Everyone else is playing the defense the same. If the defensive call is 74I, that tells the nose tackle to shade the center.

If we make a *reduction call* that means we are going to reduce away from the call. We are going to reduce away from the tight end or the split end. The reduction call moves our defensive line to shade techniques away from the call. If the call is to the defensive right side, the right defensive end moves from a 4 technique to a 3 technique, and the left defensive end moves from a 4 technique to a 5 technique away from the call.

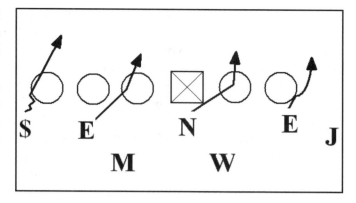

Diagram 17. 72 call

The nose tackle moves to a shade on the guard away from the call. If we make a *bonzai* call, that changes the direction of our slant from one side to the other side. If we have a split-fill call [Diagram 18], the front is going away from the split end. If the tight end comes out to the left and the split end is right, our angle charge would be toward the tight end. However, if the tight end shifted to the other side before the ball was snapped, that would reverse our call. The Mike linebacker would call *bonzai* and change the angle from left to right. The defensive front is slanting using a fill technique as their charge course. That means their angles are flatter to the line of scrimmage. They are redirecting on blocks at them and cross facing on blocks going the other way.

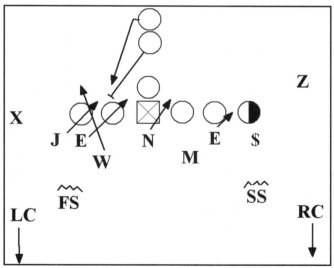

Diagram 18. Split-fill call

If we run a tight fill, it is the opposite of the split fill. The front is slanting away from the tight end. If the tight end changes sides, we get the bonzai call, which changes our direction on our slant. Behind both of these fill defenses we are playing cover 3. This is very simple for our kids to learn.

We also have a double fill [Diagram 19]. Any time the defensive line hears *double* they know they are coming inside. This is a pinching defense. Both sides of the defense are coming inside. The nose tackle is playing a jam technique on the center. The defensive ends are slanting hard inside keying the offensive guards. The joker and nickel linebackers are slanting inside also. We use this defense in our goal line defense. Ninety percent of our short-yardage defense is our base defense. The Mike and Will linebackers are keying the backs. If it is a run, they are shooting their gaps. The Mike linebacker on flow toward him is scraping outside. On flow away he is scrapping inside. The Will linebacker is doing the same thing. On pass the linebackers have the backs coming their way.

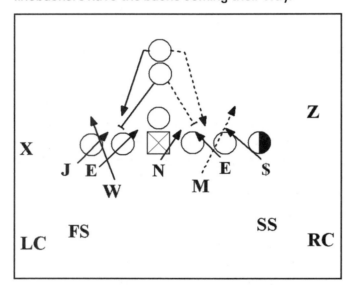

Diagram 19. Double-fill call

In our Okie fronts we have four defenses we run. We run what we call *south, west, southwest,* and *freeze.* I'll talk about them in a minute. We play four basic coverages. We have *black coverage,* which is a cover 1. The *blue coverage* is our cover 2. Our *green coverage* is cover 3 and the *silver* is our cover 6, which is our quarter-quarter-half coverage. Our blitz and move calls are southwest twist, wham, magic, and 33. We can also blitz with the nickel package. That is called *snack-nickel.* If we want a blitz coming from the secondary, we call *snake-safety.*

The first Okie front I want to show you is our *west* [Diagram 20]. In this defense the angle is coming

from the weakside. The joker has an inside slant and is coming outside. If a back releases toward him he takes him in coverage. The defensive end is slanting inside, attacking the guard, and getting across the face of the offensive guard. The nose tackle is slanting at the V of the offensive guard's neck and getting upfield, looking for penetration. The Will linebacker is taking a tight path off the defensive end tail and blitzing the B gap. The defensive end to the strongside has containment responsibility. The nickel linebacker is dropping into coverage. The Mike linebacker has the middle-hook zone on pass.

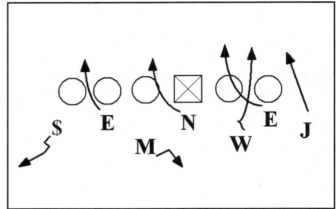

Diagram 20. West defense

The second Okie front is called *south* [Diagram 21]. It is the mirror opposite of the west defense. The only difference in this stunt is the blitz is coming from the strongside with the Mike linebacker doing the blitzing.

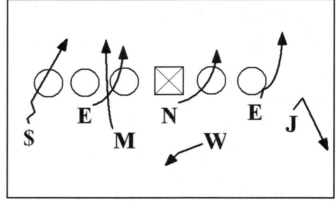

Diagram 21. South defense

The next Okie front is called *southwest* [Diagram 22]. This is a combination stunt. We have everyone coming. Both sides are pinching to the inside. The Will linebacker is blitzing the B gap behind the slant of the defensive end. The Mike linebacker is blitzing the

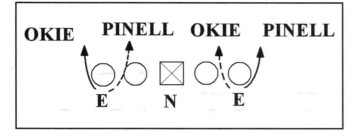

Diagram 19. Pinch

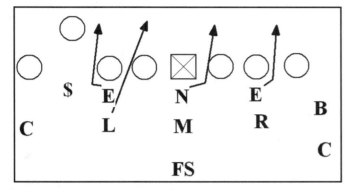

Diagram 20

If we want to bring the Mike linebacker as part of the four-man pressure, we call *plug*. That brings the Mike linebacker in the A gap. If the Mike linebacker is blitzing the weakside A gap, the noseguard takes the opposite A gap [Diagram 21].

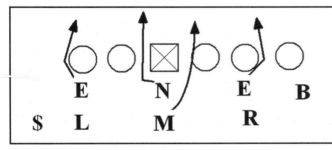

Diagram 21. Plug

We can bring the bandit and spur on a blitz. It is really simple because that is their responsibility in the slant-and-angle defense. The difference is we bring a strong safety that can run. I really like that. That gives us some real speed coming off the edge.

We have the ability to bring five-man pressure. We don't like to play man coverage. We will play three deep in behind the five-man pressure working some inside-outside brackets with our bandit or spur and Mike linebacker. We walk the Lou and Rob linebackers up on the line of scrimmage and bring them off the edge. We call this blitz *sting-3* [Diagram 22].

You can invent all kinds of five-man pressure stunts. We call this stunt *lightning* [Diagram 23]. We slant both defensive ends to the inside B gap. We bring Lou through the strongside C gap and the bandit outside of him. The noseguard takes a wide outside charge through the weakside C gap. We adjust the coverage to cover for the blitzing linebackers. This is a boundary stunt because we are blitzing the bandit. We like to make our calls as to where the offense aligns, but we can make our call to the boundary or field.

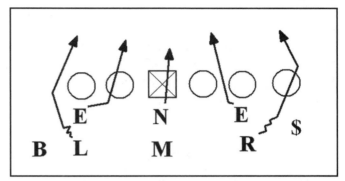

Diagram 22. Sting-3 blitz

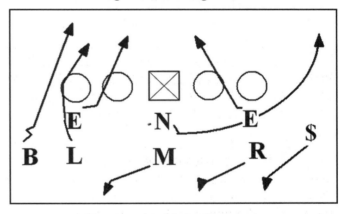

Diagram 23. Lightning stunt

I rushed at the end, but I do want you to know if you come to Winston Salem, we will spend all the time with you that you would like. We love to have people visit. My coaches enjoy having guys come down to visit. We have an open door at our place. We'll let you watch as much film as you like and visit with every coach we have. I don't know if anything I talked about helped you, but it has been good for us. The message I want to leave for you today is to play a scheme that your kids can be successful in. I want to thank Nike for giving us the chance to speak and thank you guys for sticking it out with the weather. Thank you so much.

DEVELOPING THE YOUNG QUARTERBACK

University of Pittsburgh

I want to start by talking about Coach John Majors. Early in my career he gave me a chance to become an offensive coordinator for the first time. He was very good to me. Before I joined Coach Majors at Tennessee, I had worked for Coach Mike White at the University of Illinois. We had produced two first round draft choices at quarterback. Then Coach Majors offered me the job of offensive coordinator. I went to Coach White and talked to him about moving. He told me, "I do not think you are ready to be coordinator." That was the wrong thing to say to me because I wanted to prove to him that I was ready. That was a great experience at the University of Tennessee.

I went back to the University of the Pacific in California, which is my alma mater. The school has produced some outstanding coaches. I left there and went to the New York Jets. I coaches there for three years. Everyone knows how tough it is to stay very long in the NFL. After three years in the NFL, I lucked out and ended up going to Ohio State. We were able to recruit a few good players. We were able to win 11 games in a row at Ohio State. We defeated Arizona State in the Rose Bowl. That was a great time for us in that 1996 season and 1997 Rose Bowl. We took a drive down the field in the last 40 seconds and beat Arizona State. Bruce Snyder was the coach at Arizona State and they were only one drive away from being the National Champs. Two years later he gets fired. It makes you wonder a little about this profession. I think it is a great game. Most of the time administrators get very involved and that is the sad part of it. We owe a lot to the game of football. As I go into high schools recruiting today, just talking to the principals, I can tell they know how important the football team is to the morale of the school.

I appreciate you being here today. Hopefully you will get something out of this lecture. I think we are in a great game. It is an unselfish game and it is a challenging game. Every year it is different. We had a real good football team last year. We were only one score away from winning in our four losses. We did resurrect the program at Pitt that had won only 15 games in the five previous years. Coach Majors was a great coach but they did not give him the things you need to be successful. But our A.D. did some great things to help us. He gave us a chance to be somebody.

We have led the Big East in passing for the last six years. I can't wait until we are referred to as *tailback-U* instead of *wide receiver-U*. That would mean we would be getting the job done the way you need to get it done. I say this even though the Oakland Raiders may think differently. By the way, Jon Gruden was my G.A. for three years at Tennessee. He was the first coach that I hired as an assistant when I went to the University of the Pacific. He earns everything he can get. He sees a lot of things that you and I do not see. He never blinks at situations. It was a great victory for Jon Gruden and his staff.

My topic is *developing the young high school quarterbacks*. There are a lot of ways to do this. When I was coaching in high school football, I coached defense. I may not be able to help you a lot in that respect, but I do not believe it is any different in high school as it is in college. I think it a great position. I coach the position and call the plays. I coach a position because I do not want to be a head coach who just walks around and blows the whistle. I like to coach. I call the plays on offense. That way the offensive coordinator does not have to answer the media. The newspaper people come to me on any questions about our offense. All in all it makes my job harder because I still have head coaching responsibilities.

I like to coach. Coaching the quarterback is the most challenging position of them all. Why? Because every time the quarterback touches the football something good or bad happens. They touch it every down. You cannot win without a real good quarterback.

The first phase of developing the quarterback is to *have a plan*. The mental approach is very important to developing consistent quarterback play. You must be able to help the quarterback handle the mental aspects of the game. It is a hard position to play quarterback.

The quarterback must master the proper passing techniques and develop the fundamentals of quarterback. As the coach of the quarterback, you must make sure he creates the proper habits.

First, to execute the game plan we must start from the beginning. Here are the considerations you must consider in working with the quarterback. What is the role of the quarterback? The best thing I ever did when I worked for coach John Majors at Tennessee was to ask him what he expected out of the quarterback position. I think it is important for you to find out from the head coach what he wants from the position. Make the head coach declare himself. Then the quarterback coach must declare himself to the quarterback. He must understand if he is not doing what you want him to do as quarterback; no one has to get upset. If he is not doing what you expect, he is not going to be playing quarterback.

The big factor in the game today is *turnovers*. We play in the Big East and it is one of the best conferences in the country today. The Big E does not stand for the *Big Easy* anymore. Two years ago we had 18 turnovers in our first six games. We were getting our butts beat. We decided to change the situation. We had too many players who were thinking about their stats and their careers in the NFL. I quit being the good guy and decided to make a change in our approach to the game. In the last six games that year we only had seven turnovers. We won all six of those games.

Turnovers are the name of the game. If you do not win the turnover battle you are not going to win many games. You must commit the football team to protecting the football. We work hard to prevent the turnovers. Our quarterbacks, receivers, and backs do not switch the football. Once we put the ball away we do not switch the ball. It is too risky. So we do not switch the ball once we have in our possession. It

may not be the best in all situations, but our running back coach really did an outstanding job in that area.

The player I coached fumbled seven times. It is also exciting for the assistant coaches for the head coach to be a position coach. A lot of the times the head coach will walk around and tell the assistant coaches they need to do this and they need to do that, it makes a difference if he is also coaching a position. So the player I coached had seven turnovers. Unfortunately I could not take him out of the game. If you can make the player better by sitting him on the bench when he turns the ball over, then you need to do that if you have someone capable of replacing him. I could not do that because our quarterback was so good in other areas. I cannot tell you enough about turnovers.

You must talk with the quarterback about *field position*. Also, you must talk about *momentum* with the quarterback. You must include those situations in the game plan. It does not matter the level of the game you are playing at, momentum is a big part of the game. I believe every game has highs and lows. One of the great ways to prevent the lows is to prevent the turnovers. If you can do that you will have a lot less highs and lows.

It is important to understand the impact of the quarterback position in winning. I grew up on the West Coast and I was always a San Francisco 49'ers fan. I am a big Bill Walsh disciple. Why? I love to run the football, but the hardest part of coaching is to get good linemen. Linemen win championships and they are hard to get. We try to control the ball with the forward pass. We have gotten better at running the football. Anytime we can run the ball we are going to be hard to beat.

My point on all of this is the fact the quarterback must be able to dump the football. He has to understand what it is like to be a *high-percentage passer*. I talk to him all of the time about making high-percentage throws. Their job is to get the ball into the end zone. They must move the stakes and they must move the clock. We want to keep our defense off the field. That was the best thing we did this past year. We got beat out by five seconds on leading in the total time of possession in our conference this year. We were second in that stat behind West Virginia University. We were second in time of possession in that aspect. We were not close in rushing offense, but we really held the ball in the time of possession area. That helped our defense. Our defense was ranked number 10 nationally in total defense. To do this you must be able to control the football.

We work on the center-quarterback exchange every day. Once a week we run the *wet ball drill*. When you have to take the ball from the center, you never know how the weather is going to be like. We will be using the Nike football this coming year. I feel certain it will be just as good as the other balls we have used in the past. I know it will be good because Nike is outstanding and that is the reason I am here speaking. (Ha, Ha!)

Each day we work between 5 and 10 minutes on what we call *T and A*. This is *timing and assignment* with the running backs and quarterback on the exchange. We go full speed on this. You cannot practice half speed on drill. Those two exchanges, between the quarterback and center, and between the quarterback and running backs, will get you beat if you do not work on them full speed in practice.

We talk to the quarterback about getting on the ground after he gets the first down. We want our quarterback to be able to get on the ground on the dive or to slide after the first down.

Let me move to the interception phase of the game. There has never been an interception that was okay. The only possible exception would be at the end of the half or end of the game. Quarterbacks hate it if they have to throw an interception then. That is part of the game. There is no reason for fumbles or interceptions.

I think it is very important for the quarterback to have discipline. He must take care of the football. I have coached the quarterback position for a long time and it does not change. You try to be nice, and try to be positive, and you try to build them up, but the bottom is that they must take care of the ball. I hope you have enough competition at quarterback so if they are undisciplined they do not play.

We feel simplicity of the offense is important in helping the quarterback. We seem to be fairly complex in our system, but we're not really. It just means a quarterback cannot play early and do a good job. We are simple in staying within our concepts. Our

basic concept on the pass is this: *If it is tight getting the ball to a receiver, dump the ball off.* If the back is not open in the flat, we tell the quarterback to run the ball. To me, you must get the ball down the field. If the pass is open, then fine, but running is part of the game.

The quarterback must understand the pass offense. You can have a lot of routes, but if the quarterback does not understand what he is trying to do it is not going to work. Running routes against man-to-man coverage is not that difficult, but still the quarterback should know where he is going with the football. Against zone coverage he must understand how you are trying to attack the zones.

We have our concepts for attacking *zone-coverage defenses*. We have four concepts we work on against the zones. Basically, they are very simple. Most all teams use these concepts.

If we have a hook route, we will have someone come outside. It will be run with an inside receiver and an outside receiver. We run a simple *curl-flat route* [Diagram 1].

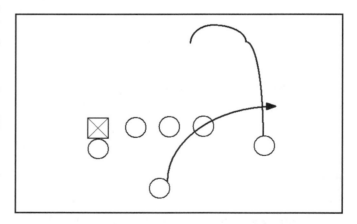

Diagram 1. Curl-flat route

The next route we use is a *high-low route* [Diagram 2]. Against the cover 2 look, we will have the outside receiver run an out release and the back will swing out in the flat area. The quarterback reads the corner on the play. That route is a high-low route. We love throwing the ball to the backs.

Another concept that we use is called a *triangle-read route* [Diagram 3]. When we run a crossing route we have three receivers involved. We use two receivers and a back on the routes. We run a lot of the post-cross routes. The reason we run the post is because we are looking at the angles of the drop of the linebacker. We are looking for the hole. On our crossing routes we will hook. If the ball is not there we will continue to sit. We do not like to run the play against the zone defense. We sit against the zone and run away from defenders in the man-to-man. That is our triangle read or *3-on-2 concept*.

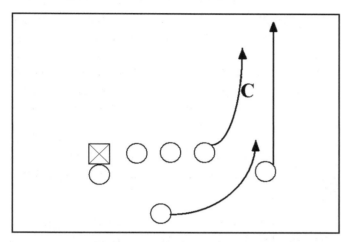

Diagram 2. High-low route

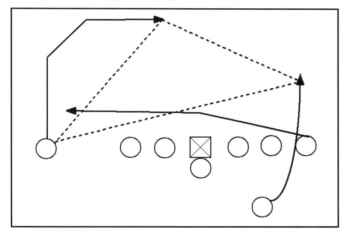

Diagram 3. Triangle-read route (3-on-2)

The last concept is what we call the *three-level pass* [Diagram 4]. Sometimes this play is hard to run. The play can be good for the fast tight end. He is going to run an out route at 10 to 12 yards deep to the outside. The wide receiver is going to take off deep. He must be a legitimate threat deep. The back is going to swing to the outside. You must get the corner defender out of the area.

Those are the concepts we use to attach zone defenses. They are simple plays but you must work on them a great deal so everyone is on the same page.

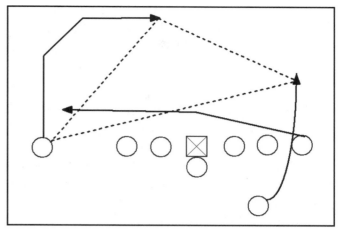

Diagram 4. Three-level pass

The quarterback needs to understand how the pass patterns work and what his *progressions* are versus various coverages. A lot of the time our progression will change based on the coverage. They will change and the players must understand this. It all goes back to the mental approach.

We tell our quarterback he must be able to recognize the various pass defensive coverages. We expect him to know the coverage after he takes one step on his drop. We teach him to read through the goalpost. He will also understand the keys on the linebackers. The linebackers are going to drop back, move outside, or they are going to blitz and come after the quarterback. They will tell the quarterback a lot of what the defense is going to do on a play.

The quarterback is going to look at middle of the field to see how many safeties are there. If there is no one in the middle of the field, it is what we call *cover 0*. If the defense has two safeties in the middle of the field, it is *cover 2*, or it may be a defense with a middle safety and they may rotate. We are going to go away from rotation, so the quarterback has to be able to read the coverage. He has to be able to recognize *man-to-man coverage*.

If the quarterback reads a two-deep coverage, he has one man to throw to. If the man is not open, then the quarterback is going to do something different. We are not going to throw the ball to the back if there is a linebacker running with him.

The quarterback must be able to understand under coverage. He must understand the strengths and weaknesses of the defenses. We have plays that we call *cover-beater plays.* We have a cover 2 beater. If we do not see the cover 2 look, it is the job of the quarterback to get us some type of completion. It is the *save-the-day* pass so to speak. Otherwise, I would be afraid to call the cover 2 beater play. If we do not get a completion, I will not be able to trust the quarterback on the play.

We grade the quarterbacks on every play. We have an end zone view and a side view of every play in practice. I coach the quarterbacks so I grade the practices for the quarterbacks. It is a written grade. I may be tough on them, but I am going to do everything I can to get them ready to play. I want to give them all the help I can so they will know what to do in a game.

We talk about *practice field approach.* When the quarterbacks come to the practice field we want them ready to go. That does not mean they cannot be relaxed and be able to have fun, but they must be focused. When they come to practice they must come with a purpose. They must learn that we cannot let one quarterback take every snap. This is especially true for the second-team quarterback. He is not going to get every rep. If the starting quarterback needs reps, then the second-team quarterback is going to get less and less reps. If the first-string quarterback is a quick learner, the second quarterback may get more snaps. We do not try to get more than two quarterbacks ready for a game. We will run the first quarterback four plays and the second quarterback two plays. It is very important to stress they will play like they practice. The players should be tired after practice. Why? Because they must concentrate mentally while on the field. As I said before, I believe strongly in mental reps.

Now I want to talk about the basic techniques and fundamentals of *throwing the football.* The first approach to this area is to determine why we have techniques, which are covered in the following reasons.

The first fundamental reason for throwing techniques the quarterback must focus on is *accuracy.* A quarterback can improve his passing accuracy. Steve Young of the 49'ers was a good example of a quarterback improving his accuracy. When he was with Tampa Bay he was not very good. But when he went to San Francisco he improved a

great deal. Why? Obviously the system had a great deal to this. He went to a much better system. He was older and he had been cut so his eyes were open more. His focus was a lot better. He became very good at putting the ball in a spot. He learned to hit the receiver where he wanted the ball to go. He was not just getting the ball to the receiver, but he was getting it to a spot where the receiver could catch the ball. I like to say we want to *hit the receiver in the eyeball with the ball.* If we throw the ball at his eye, the receiver should have great hand-eye coordination and he can see the ball. He should be able to catch the ball in that area.

Quickness of decision is another fundamental to consider when working with quarterbacks. When I was working with Jeff Blake with the Jets, he used a phrase that I liked: *Process it quickly.* The faster you can go through the progression and get the ball out, the better you are going to be at throwing the ball.

The way I like to help the quarterback with this process is to have him drop back to pass. It is amazing how much the whole process speeds up when he is dropping back.

Quickness of the release is another fundamental to consider when discussing techniques for the quarterback. *Arm strength* is another part of it. *Movement in the pocket* is another factor to consider. *Being able to scramble* is very important in the techniques for a quarterback. When we have to scramble on a play, I tell the quarterback I want those plays to be the highest percentage of plays for the whole day. Why? Because most of the time we can give the quarterback the looks he is going to see or what we expect to see in a game. But when the quarterback is outside scrambling right or left he will see his teammates and the defenders in all different areas. He must make sure what he does with the ball in those situations is correct. We want a very high-percentage rate of success when we are scrambling on a play. He must understand why he is scrambling in the first place. He is scrambling because someone else made a mistake. It may be a missed block or a missed route. But the quarterback must write a check for the entire football program and make the play right. We want him to be very sure of what he does when he scrambles. I tell him to make something positive happen. To us a positive play is a throw away.

We have 11 coaching points or proper techniques and fundamentals in working with the quarterback. I would *never* coach all 11 of these with a player. We call it *paralysis by analysis*. Hopefully when you pick your quarterback he will have some ability to throw the football. It is best if you do not have too much to change as far as his habits. You must analyze what your player must do in order to improve his skill. That is your challenge as a coach. Even though we can recruit, we still have to talk to our quarterbacks about their throwing technique.

The first technique relates to the *feet*. It all starts with the quarterback's feet. This means he must get into the proper angles to throw the football to be consistent. He must get his body aligned to make the best throw and it all starts with his feet. You cannot just have a tall player at quarterback, especially if he's slow. He will have problems against a quick defensive team because he will not be able to get his body aligned to throw the ball with defenders around him. Do not fall into the trap of playing a guy that looks like he can throw the ball but he can't move. If you do have a kid that can throw the ball it is your job to get him to be a lot better. Things we do to help the quarterbacks improve their speed are to jump rope and do the wave drill.

We use this *tennis ball drill* to help the quarterbacks [Diagram 5]. You have them start by facing the coach. Take a shoebox and place it near a line. The quarterback starts out and shuffles 10 yards to a second line and comes back to the shoebox. He picks up a tennis ball out of the shoebox and shuffles 10 yards gain. He picks up a total of three tennis balls out of the shoebox on at a time. A time of 12.2 seconds is really good. This teaches the quarterback to accelerate and get going.

As I mentioned, the *wave drill* is another good drill to help quarterbacks improve their speed [Diagram 6]. The drill is set up with two receivers and the quarterback. The coach is in front of the quarterback. The quarterback takes his drop and the coach yells, "Now!" Then one of the receivers will hold his hands up with both hands open. The other receiver will hold up his hands but they will be crossed. The quarterback must pick out the receiver with the open hands.

When the quarterback drops back to set up, I will direct him on the wave drill. We call a play and he must

execute the play. When I call out, "Now!" the quarterback must hit the receiver with the open hands. I will tell the receivers what I want them to do before the quarterback makes his drop.

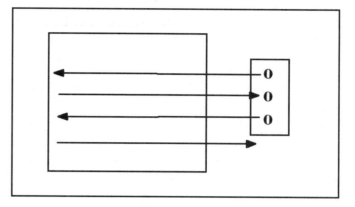

Diagram 5. Tennis ball drill

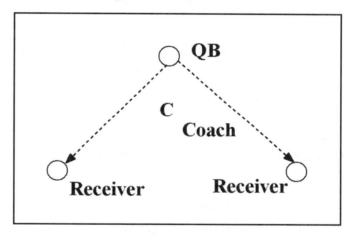

Diagram 6. Wave drill

Again, the wave drill is based on accuracy. We want him to throw the ball quick but we want him to make the throw accurate. However, the focus of this drill is to improve the mobility of the quarterback in the pocket.

The next drill helps the young quarterback find the safe spot in the pocket. We call this drill the *avoid drill* [Diagram 7]. This drill is used in the spring practice or early in the year. We take four receivers and line them up and down the field at a set distance. We have the quarterback take his drop for the play called. We have four defenders that are going to rush him, one at a time. The fist defender will go to the area where the quarterback will be setting up. We want the quarterback to climb in the pocket and not just flush out of the pocket. As soon as the first defense gets halfway to the top of the pocket the second defender is going to be on his way toward the quarterback. When the second defender is halfway to the quarterback the third defender is going to come. Now the quarterback must move over in the pocket. As soon as the third man gets halfway to the quarterback the fourth rusher goes toward the quarterback. Again, the quarterback has to move over in the pocket. Any time during the drill I can call the word, "Now!" and the quarterback must come up to see if he can find the open receiver with his hands up. He must try to throw the ball with the defender's hands in his face. He must try to get rid of the ball and throw it accurately to the receiver with his hands open. It is a good drill for the quarterbacks to get the *feel of the pocket.*

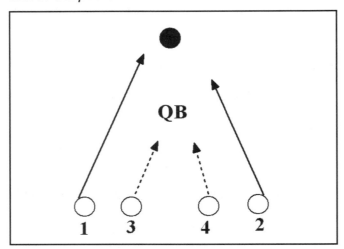

Diagram 7. Avoid drill

We can change the avoid drill and have the defenders run straight at the quarterback. We can change the order of the pass rushers so he has to flush to one side of the pocket or the other, or he must scramble to one side or the other. You can teach a lot of escape techniques in this drill.

You can have the inside defenders rush first and force the quarterback to go sideways to avoid the rush. So, any four of the defenders can flush the quarterback. You control the drill and you can mix it up from day to day. If you point at one defender he can run straight at the quarterback. Now he must work on his escape against that man. We run the avoid drill about three-quarter speed.

Our next coaching point is *alignment.* First we talked about the feet. Now we must talk about the shoulders. I am talking about right-handed quarterbacks

for this lecture. We always talk to the quarterbacks about having their shoulder pointed toward the target. We refer to their shoulder as a *radar gun.* It becomes a problem when you are throwing the ball outside. We try to get our quarterbacks to align to the target.

We do a simple *shift drill* to help the quarterbacks work on their alignment [Diagram 8]. We have the quarterback set up at 10 yards from two receivers on the line. We will move the two receivers from one side to the other as much as 20 yards from the original spot they line up in. The quarterback must move or shift to the side the receiver has moved to and make the throw.

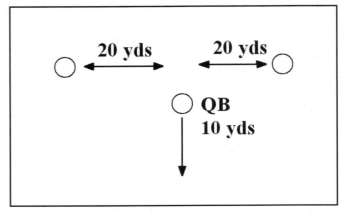

Diagram 8. Shift drill

We stress two hands on the ball on the quarterback's dropback. I do not want him to set up and sit in the pocket patting the ball with his off hand. This is just a bad habit. They see this on TV and think it is a good technique. I tell them, "When you make it to the NFL, you can pat the ball all you want." Until they make it to the NFL, I do not want to see the pat-pat on the ball.

To add to the drill we will put four receivers in. Then the quarterback has to shift to find the receiver we want him to throw the ball to. Keep in mind that you should not emphasize too many things at the same time on a drill. To be fair to the players you should work on one fundamental at a time and coach that fundamental. If the player learns the fundamental but does something else that is not perfect, do not criticize him for that aspect of the play. If he did what you wanted him to, compliment him on that aspect of the drill. Again, it is very difficult to change bad habits, but you must always work on them.

The shoulders come into play on throws like the out route and on comeback routes. If the quarterback is a right-handed passer, the out route and the comeback route to his left side becomes a problem. There are a couple of different ways to run the play. One way is for the quarterback to come back four steps and to kick on the fifth step. The quarterback gets a little wider to make the throw when he does that, but I also think he gets so much momentum that he ends up falling off the throw. Most of those throws are then low and away.

What I like to teach them is this: If we are going to throw to the left side, I want the quarterback to *step to the right* when he is throwing to his left. He takes the four steps and on the fifth step he swings himself outside and is aligned to the target. Another coaching point is the quarterback should be a little deeper from the defensive end who has his hands up in the air. If the quarterback is not going to throw to the number one receiver, he will be more in an area where the offensive line expects him to be.

When the right-handed quarterback is throwing the out route to the right side, it is a hard throw to make. If the defender intercepts the ball there is nothing out there except a lot of green grass. It is a dangerous throw but a lot of teams on defense will give you that throw. How do you take the out route if they are giving it to you?

We try to get the quarterback aligned to the target. We have thrown the ball off the plant step and now we are throwing it off the hitch step. This has helped us on the play. We think we can be more accurate on the out route although we do not throw a lot of out routes.

The next area to consider for the quarterback is his *legs*. Whenever possible he wants to get his legs into the throw. The reason for this is because most guys are not strong enough to throw the ball with their arm. As quarterbacks get older and stronger they can throw the ball with their arm. Dan Marino and Brett Favre are upper-body throwers. With young quarterbacks, they need to get their legs into the throw. Most of the throws should come off the hitch. If we are taking a five-step drop, we come back and plant the foot, hitch it up, and let the ball go to the primary receiver. Most of our plays are timed out at 10 to 12 yards in depth on a five-step drop. This times it up pretty good for us.

We will run the plant step when we run the straight vertical routes and when we are coming right back down the pass-route stem. It is a form of the out route, but we do not have the receiver break to the outside. That throw we will throw off the plant step. The quarterback is moving backwards and he must stop, change his momentum, and get his legs into the throw. This is very difficult. To help our quarterback on the play we tell him to chop and try to stop on the fourth step. He will probably stop on the fifth step and plant his foot. His body will be in a position where he can straighten his leg and make the throw. If his weight is on his back foot as he gets to the fourth step, he will have to wait until he can get his balance before he can make the throw. Or, he will throw the ball out of the hole and he will not get much on the ball. That is a dangerous throw because it is out in the flat. He needs to plant his foot and then make the throw. We throw the plant route off the plant step.

We do the same things off the seven-step drop and call it the turn route, which is at 16 yards. On most of our drops we try to throw the ball off the first hitch and try to get the quarterback to get his legs into the throw.

The plant drill has the quarterback dropping back and throwing the ball off his plant step [Diagram 9]. We do not want him to exaggerate the throw, but we do want to know if he exaggerates getting his body into the throw. We want to know if he gets his legs into the throw. We are not concerned about the kind of throw it was. If he is not getting his legs and body into the throw this is what we must work on.

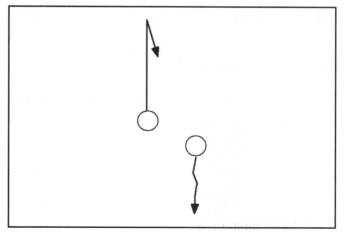

Diagram 9. Plant drill

As I told you earlier, there are 11 fundamentals that we work on with quarterbacks. You are only going to get him to work on one, two, or three of these techniques at any given time, and he may only need one or two of these to improve his game.

The next fundamental to work on is *weight shift*. The goal for the quarterback is to shift his weight so he can throw the ball from a bent front knee. He should not lock his knee out. He can get a lot of power if he can get his weight over the front knee. A lot of kids will straighten their knee to get more torque on the ball. They will straighten their left knee to get more whip or snap into the throw and it will lock the knee out. That used to be a five-hour surgery. It does not take that long now, but when the quarterback gets hit with his legs locked he is in big-time trouble. Do not let them throw the ball with a straight front knee. They need to have a bent front knee.

We will go back over these fundamentals with the quarterbacks in the spring. I will tell the quarterbacks they must be able to coach themselves. They must get a video and watch the film. They must learn what it feels like on these drills. I do not worry a lot about the fundamentals during practice. I am working on the reads. He must work on the individual techniques in the early spring and on his own time. The fundamentals do not get as much attention as the decisions do once the season gets underway.

We always make the quarterback take the steps he will take in a game in working on the fundamentals. Always have them drop back on the drills. Make it realistic for them.

We stress accuracy in our drills. When we are working on the passing drills, we want the receiver to give the quarterback a target just before he lets the ball go. We are going to be good at what we emphasize.

The next coaching point is the *draw back*. We are talking about drawing the football back in the passing motion. We have two hands on the football and we want the ball up under the chin on the chest. We do not want it down low or up high. We talk to the quarterbacks about drawing the ball back. We tell them to get it back, cock it, and throw it.

Pro football is not good for younger quarterbacks. The young kids see the NFL quarterbacks and the bad habits they have. One of the reasons for the bad habits of the pros is that the offensive coordinator is coaching the quarterbacks. He is not coaching

techniques very much. The coordinator is coaching the system and expecting the individual player to work on his techniques. He cannot do that. That is why we coach the techniques. Now most pro teams are getting quarterback coaches.

The next fundamental is the *quick release*. The quickest release in football was that of Dan Marino. Dan did drop the ball down on his dropback, but his muscles were so developed that he could do that. You can explain to you quarterbacks that they are not in pro football so they need to adhere to the basic fundamentals you are teaching them.

The next point is that we want a *slight tilt of the shoulders*. It is important to get the ball over the tips of the defenders' shoulders on the pass rush. I do not want the quarterback with the ball up high and his shoulders flat. If this happens it slows down the release of the ball. Do not let him get the ball up over his head.

If the quarterback has his shoulders squared up with the turf before he throws the ball, and then tilts his shoulders forward just as he is ready to release the ball, it forces the tip of the ball to come up. What happens then is the quarterback gets the ball up but he does not have the ball behind his head. The slight tilt of his shoulders gets the ball out higher. The ball is alongside his body and not behind his head. He must not overtilt to the point where he is off balance.

There is a theory that goes something like this: If the quarterback can get the ball up with the tilt of his shoulders, he will get in a groove where he can throw the ball with consistency. It is a lot like the golf swing. If you can get the swing down where you are in a groove, it makes the swing a lot more consistent. Golfers want the same swing and we want the same throw. We want the same motion all of the time.

The next fundamental we stress is to *lead with the elbow*. We want the quarterback to lead with his elbow so he is in the groove and every throw is the same, unless he is under stress and he throws the ball sidearm like Rich Gannon does. We want every throw the same with the elbow leading.

Next we want to *pronate the wrist at the top of the release*. This helps with the spiral on the ball. With a tight spiral the quarterback really pronates the wrist at the top of his throw.

This is the last of the techniques for the quarterback. As the ball comes off his hand, the quarterback wants to put his *right thumb in his left pocket*. Some quarterbacks will stop their thumb at their midsection. We like to see the quarterback turn his hand to get his thumb down inside and turned toward his left pocket. This is the way to get a nice tight spiral on the ball.

I want to wind this down with a few general comments. There are a couple of important points I want to talk about. We stress *key habits*. We want two hands on the ball in the pocket. We stress *rhythm* and being on time with the ball. The difference between a college passer and an NFL passer is when the quarterback lets the ball go on the release. In the NFL they let the ball go early. That is because the corners in the NFL are so good and they never play zone defense. They will play a combination of man and zone coverage.

A drill I like to use that develops confidence in the quarterback's accuracy is called the *confidence drill* [Diagram 10]. The best way for him to gain confidence is to develop accuracy. We place a coach, another player, or another quarterback five-yards apart. We want the quarterback to throw the ball to another man and throw at his numbers. We have him to throw five passes in a row to where we designate.

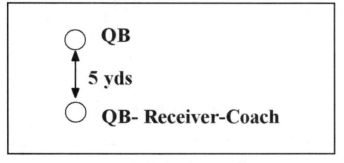

Diagram 10. Confidence drill

Next the quarterback takes a step back and throws the ball five more times to where we designate. We want him to develop some confidence in his accuracy. The off-season is the time to work on the techniques and fundamentals. We want our quarterbacks to work on these before they get into 7-on-7 drills and team drills.

We ask him to step back each time after he hits five passes in a row accurately. We work until he gets 15 yards from the receiver. We want him to start thinking he is more accurate. If he does not throw five accurate passes in a row, then we move him back five yards and do it again. It is all about developing the quarterback's confidence.

We can use different targets on the body. We can have him throw at the receiver's hands. We do not want him to aim his toe toward the target. We want him to aim his foot toward the target and the toe will aim slightly to the right of his target.

I want to end with a film clip so you can see the quarterback fundamentals and techniques I have talked about. I have a second tape on quarterbacks that I will share with you. I will stress the coaching points we have discussed here today.

Men, I am going to be here a while longer. Hopefully you did get something from this lecture.

Finally, we are going to be expanding our recruiting territory. If you have a quarterback that is interested in playing for us let me know. I have coached 13 players that have had a chance to go to NFL camps. We have had seven first-round draft choices in the NFL. If you have any other players you think we may be interested in give us a call. You will not be disappointed with the facilities we have and the program we run. Thank you very much.

DEFENSIVE LINE TECHNIQUES AND DRILLS

Ohio State University

After listening to that introduction, the only thing that was important about it was the fact I have worked with a lot of good coaches. One of my best stops in college coaching was at the University of Washington. I worked with Don James there and he taught me as much about defensive line play and coaching that area as anyone I've ever been associated with. I was lucky to work with John Cooper at Ohio State and even luckier after Coach Cooper left to work for Jim Tressel. I feel fortunate to work for a man like him.

The first thing I want do is talk about the *philosophy of defensive line play* and then get into some of our drill work and techniques. If I have time at the end I'll show you some of the things we are trying to do with the spread offense. In our first six games this year we only saw 10 plays by teams in a two-back offense. The Wisconsin game was the first team that ran a two-back offense. The spread offense is the trend in college football offense today.

There are two areas where Coach Tressel did an unbelievable job with our football team. The first area was vision and the second area was focus. When he talked about vision, he put a picture of the Fiesta Bowl on the wall. I guess he knew back then that we were destined for something big. That is when the team got the vision of the goal and started working in that direction.

The second area I believe he talked about today was the topic *focus on the moment*. It was unbelievable the focus of this football team. I think we had a good defensive line this year. I think we played *lights out* against Miami, but that is the way we played all year long. There were a couple of reasons they were able to do that. We emphasized a couple of things to them. The first thing we stressed was *team*. We decided that everybody was going to be a positive member of this football team. The team is more important than the individual. That is a hard concept to get over to your team. Everyone seems to want to know who the next Lombardi winner is going to be. They all want to know who the Heisman Trophy winner is going to be. Everyone is talking about individuality. We got our defensive line together and told them from the start we were going to be a team. It is amazing what you can accomplish when they believe that.

The second thing we stressed is *attack*. We wanted to be an attacking front. We wanted to have a relentless mentality for 60 minutes. We wanted to get off on the ball and make something happen and be consistent with it.

We wanted to stress *activity*. I had some great defensive fronts when I coached at Washington. We had a bunch of first-round draft choices in the NFL and some great players. But I have never coached a defensive front that was as active as this group. We as a coaching staff were expecting this group to make plays. The day of just keeping the linebacker free to make all the plays is over. The defensive line has to make plays for us to win games. We moved our defensive ends into inside positions. They had never played in there before. What we were trying to do was create mismatches and move more speed onto the field. The defensive end we moved inside made two sacks in the Fiesta Bowl. We took inside linebackers and moved them to defensive end positions. The reason we did this was to make plays in the defensive line.

We told our players they had to *improve* as the year went along. Their last football game should be their best game of the year. That is the coach's responsibility. If your kids are not improving as the season goes along, the coaches are not doing a good job of coaching. Your kids have to get better daily. When I think back to my early coaching jobs, when my players weren't playing well it was because I was trying to do too much scheme work. If we played a bad game I changed defenses.

Good coaches use *repetition* to improve their players. They decide what they are going to do and use repetition to perfect it. The repetition of techniques is the best learning process we have. Repetition eliminates mistakes in a football game. If you have players making mistakes, it is generally because you have not had enough repetitions at that technique. Remember what you see on film is a reflection of what you are teaching. If your players are making mistakes, it is your fault.

I think this year our coaching staff did a good job of *adjusting* at halftime. Our second-half statistics were outstanding. Our fourth- quarter statistics were tremendous. In the second half of our games this year, we had only three second-half rushing touchdowns against us. Our players did a good job of adjusting their play in the second half.

Your *assignments* have to be flawless. If we cannot do it by Thursday, we have to get rid of it. Never go into a game with some flawed piece of a game plan. If the defense doesn't know what they are doing, the only thing that can happen is bad.

If things don't go the way you like, that is called *adversity*. As a team we got focused and turned the intensity up a notch. Against Purdue, we had a fourth-and-one from their 31-yard line and threw a touchdown pass to win the game. There were games this year when adversity kept setting in, but our team kept fighting and stayed in the game.

We have a team *policy*. We don't have many rules for our players to follow. We have some team rules, but we don't have time for distractions. We don't have time to have team meetings about rules and policies. We tell them the team policies and if they don't do them they are not going to play. That is the end of that conversation. We expect them to take care of business on and off the field. If they are going to create problems, they are not going to play.

The last thing in our philosophy is to *expect to win*. If we expect excellence we have to push our players some times to get them to perform. The reason we are getting after them is to make them better players. If they can't understand that, then we have a problem. If the players want to be the best they can be, then they are on the same page as the coaching staff.

I give our defensive linemen a checklist. These are things I believe are important. The first and most important thing is to *defeat the blocker*. I say that at least a hundred times a practice session. If I am a defensive lineman, someone on the offensive line is going to block me every play. If the offensive lineman blocks the defensive lineman, the defensive lineman is not going to be a factor in the play and the offensive lineman wins. If the offensive lineman can't block the defensive lineman, the defensive lineman will be a factor in the play and the defense wins. When the play starts, the defensive lineman is not thinking about anything except defeating the blocker. All he is thinking about is knocking the face off the offensive lineman.

Defeating the block is just like boxing. If I am boxing a fighter, but I am looking at the corner man, I'm going to get my head knocked off. You can't look at the quarterback when you start rushing him. The defensive lineman must give 100 percent of his concentration on defeating the blocker before he can think about sacking the quarterback. Before the defensive lineman can make a play, he has to defeat the blocker. I still believe football is a tough game played by tough people. I think mental and physical toughness is something you have to have in the defensive line. We are going to hit, be physical, and be tough.

Attitude and effort affect performance more than anything. You have to have great attitude to play in the defensive line.

I'm spending too much time talking about these things. I'll put them up for you to see and we'll move along. We have already talked about repetition. Defensive linemen must rise to the occasion and make plays. The last thing is *defensive line pride*. We were able to control the tempo of the game and we created great pressure from our front four.

We coached pre-snap preparation this year. I taught more this year at Ohio State then I ever had before. At Ohio State we do a lot of moving and zone pressures. That requires us to have a stance that allows us to accomplish what we are trying to do. We are more balanced in our stance then we have been in the past. I am pretty old school when it comes to stance. You won't see us in the sprinter stances you see in the NFL. We are still pretty much in a heel-to-toe relationship in our stance. We went to a zone-pressure scheme because we ran out of all-American cornerbacks. We went to Oklahoma to fine-tune our defense. Oklahoma had gone through the same situation as we had. That is where we installed our zone-pressure package. That allowed us to rush five guys and still play three under and three deep, or four under and two-deep zones in the secondary.

Alignment and assignment are still important pre-snap preparations. The ultimate key to victory is the team that executes their assignments. We really stressed that this year. If you look at the big plays that were against you, it was probably because someone made a mental mistake. You have to eliminate mental mistakes if you are going to be successful.

This next part is the part that I tried to emphasize this year. I had never done that in my coaching career. I gave a lot of lip service to it but never really emphasized it. These are the variables in the football game that the defensive linemen had to deal with.

Defensive linemen have to know what is *going on* in the game. They have to have *awareness* on the field. They need to know the down-and-distance, special plays, personnel, sets, field position, score, time on the clock, and the weather. We really worked on that in practice this year. We talked about it and made them aware of all the things that are going on in the game.

We are a *gap-assignment team* [Diagram 1]. Someone is responsible for every gap on the line of scrimmage. We assign letters to each gap on either side of the ball. Our gaps run from A to E on each side of the ball. In our defensive scheme the defensive linemen have to be aware of the gaps they play and the ones they are responsible for.

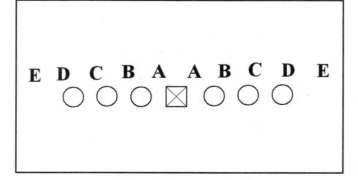

Diagram 1. Gap assignments

The trend in college football today is the *spread offense*. We have to make sure we understand our theory on rush lanes to play against this offense. Most everyone is in some kind of spread with the quarterback in the shotgun set. I don't think containment is a big a factor as it used to be. The way to get great pressure on the quarterback is to come underneath the offensive tackles. The key to stopping the success of the shotgun is getting in the face of the quarterback. I'll talk about that a little more in a minute.

Let me get into some of the drills we do. We break our drills down into segments from the time the ball is snapped until the tackle is made. The first things we work on are *stance*, *alignment*, and *assignment*. When we talk about defending the run, the first thing we have to do is perfect our *get off*. That is probably the most important thing we do. A defensive lineman has to react to the football. Every drill we do is started with the movement of the football.

The second thing we drill is *delivering a blow*. When we strike a blow, we want our thumbs under the arm pits of the offensive lineman with our elbows in tight to our body. We are a standard old school in this type of teaching. We want our eyes to see the V of the neck. We tell our players that the low man will always win. We want our pads under their pads.

The next thing we drill is *separation*. Holding by the offensive line is bad in college, but I know it is getting bad in high school, too. That is why these drills are tremendously important. We teach locking out on the offensive lineman with our hands and arms. From separation drills we go to *disengage, pursuit*, and *tackling drills*.

That is the way we step up our drills. Each day we do one drill that includes one of those skills. That is what I mean by breaking our drills down into segments of teaching. We go through the progression from start to finish.

We do the same thing when practicing the pass rush. The first type of drill we teach relating to the pass rush is the *get- off drill*. From there we go to what I call *set-up drill*. I listen to offensive line coaches talk about their techniques. The one thing they all talk about is staying balanced. In our set-up drill, we work on getting the offensive linemen off balance. We stutter step and fake to make the offensive linemen move. We reach with our left hand and make the move right. If we can make them lean left, we have a chance to get by them on the right side. If we get them to lean any direction, we have a chance to get by them.

We work on our *pass-rush technique* in drill work. If you do the same thing every time the offensive lineman will block you. In our pass-rush technique, for every move we use we have to have a *counter move*. In addition to teaching the techniques of pass rushing, we teach counters off each move in drill work. The last type of drills we work on is the actual *sack* of the quarterback.

I'll put this drill film on and run through it really quick. But there is one statement I want to make before I do that. One of the best things I do is done during our agility period. It is probably the most fun too. When I look back on my career there are so many things in my coaching career that I screwed up on. But my agility period has become a series of drills to make sure I cover every type of skill we could possibly use during the course of the year.

We work a *low-block drill* every day in our agility period. When I was at Washington we played Southern California. Rodney Peete was their quarterback at the time. Southern Cal really liked to chop the defensive linemen when they ran their plays. I spent the entire week of practice before the S.C. game working against the low block. In the game on Saturday they cut us down like a bunch of trees. I told Coach James that I had spent the week working on that block. He told me I needed to spend the whole year working on them. Work on all the skills you could possibly need before you need them. Don't wait until the game before to teach your players a skill they need. Teach it year round and all you will need to do is refresh the skill on which you have already been working.

One drill we work on daily is throwing the far arm at the quarterback on the pass rush. If I am a defensive end rushing the quarterback from the left side, as I beat the blocker and get to the quarterback, I throw my outside arm toward the quarterback. If I reach with my inside arm, I go right on by the quarterback as he steps up into the pocket. If I throw my outside arm, it turns my butt toward the sideline and steers me into the quarterback, not by him. We drill that every day for that simple reason. In the bowl

game we had a 3 technique that beat his block, threw his far arm, and caused a fumble by the quarterback.

In the first drill we are teaching two or three things. I am teaching foot movement, agility, and playing a low block [Diagram 2]. We are stepping over a gauntlet of three dummies to work on our foot movement and agility. At the end of the dummies, I have two managers rolling big balls at the players. The players chop step over three dummies, and low-play the two balls that are rolled at them. They punch down on the ball and keep their feet moving. They punch the ball away from them.

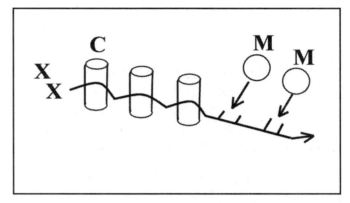

Diagram 2. Dummy/ball drill

If you want to add something to the drill, have someone throw a ball on the ground as they come off the low blocks. We do this drill every day. If you don't have those big balls, use hand dummies to throw at them. Make them be an athlete and not a clumsy lineman.

We put them in a chute and make them bend their knees [Diagram 3]. We turn them sideways and make them shuffle down the chute. As they come out of the chute we roll more balls or throw dummies at their feet.

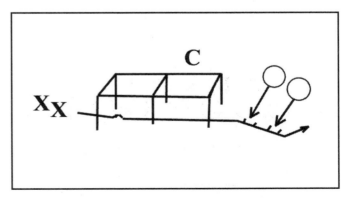

Diagram 3. Chute/ball drill

We do another similar drill, but instead of rolling balls at them we work on throwing the far arm [Diagram 4]. We place a stand-up dummy at the end of the chute and a stand-up dummy that represents the quarterback in his pass set. The lineman shuffles through the chute, clubs the dummy at the end, rips through and attacks the quarterback with his far arm.

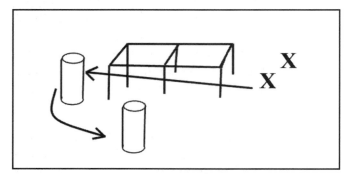

Diagram 4. Chute/far-arm drill

When we do these drills we want the defensive linemen going full speed. We want them to go as quick as they can. I like to show our linemen why we do certain drills. When I show them a drill tape, I always tack on some game footage that shows the skills we drill in practice.

Another dummy drill we use is a *pass-rush gauntlet drill* [Diagram 5]. We space three stand-up dummies in a line. We put another dummy in the drill to represent the quarterback. A defensive lineman starts at the first dummy. He has to use a set-up move and a pass-rush move on that dummy. He does the same thing on the second dummy, except he uses a counter move. He does the same thing to the third dummy. He starts with an outside move, followed by an inside move and another outside move. As he comes around the last dummy, he turns inside and rushes the quarterback dummy, attacking it with his far arm.

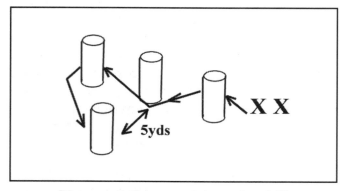

Diagram 5. Pass-rush gauntlet drill

We use a simple *get-off drill* to teach that same skill. I line up two linemen facing the coach. He is moving a ball and watching the initial step of the linemen. The coach has the ball on a stick. The ball on a stick is nothing more than a football attached to a broom stick. It allows the coach the freedom to stand and watch his players and move a ball to trigger their start. When we teach get off, we want the players to take a short six-inch step. I don't want them to take a long stride. I feel when they overstride it makes their pads come up. I want them low and driving out, not high. We are working on a good balanced base with our feet nice and wide. We work the get-off drill into the chute also.

The next drill we work on in our progression is *delivering a blow*. We start teaching that on the sled. We start in a six-point stance. A six-point stance is a kneeling position in front of the sled pad. The idea is to punch the dummy with the hands. We move the ball and watch the technique of the lineman. We are watching the punch and hand placement. We watch for the hips sinking and the thrust forward. We want to see the eyes go into the V of the neck.

From the six-point stance we go to the three-point stance and do the same thing. It is a progression of teaching that breaks down each move. If you watch these two guys on the tape, I'll show you when you know they are into the drill. They strike the sled, lock out with their hands, and get off the sled. After they complete the drill they go to the end of the line and head butt each other. When they get that excited about a drill, you know you are on the right track.

After we get off the sled, we go into a *1-on-1 drill*. We are in close quarters and go half speed so no one gets hurt. It teaches the technique of get off, strike, and lock out. We watch the same techniques we saw on the sled. The punch, hand position, short first step, eyes in the V of the neck, sinking of the hips, and locking-out techniques are all displayed in this drill. The last thing we look at is to make sure their feet are continuously moving. We don't want our players to stop their feet. We want them to chop them all the way through the drill.

This next drill we do involves a move we call the *dog technique*. We got this from the Tampa Bay Buccaneers. This is the way they play defense. They move on movement and attack the outside tip of the offensive blocker. We are reacting on the run to the blocking scheme. If we are playing a spread offense, we like to use this technique. We want to get off the ball and upfield for the pass rush.

We work all kinds of 1-on-1 drills to teach *separation and disengagement.* In one drill we tell the offensive lineman to throw his hips to the outside and try to get them around the defensive lineman. We teach the defensive guy to bench press the offensive lineman and lock out. We are looking for a good back and body angle, with a good wide base. After they lock out the block, they rip through with their inside arm and make a play on a ballcarrier. The players have to be violent with their arms and hands to play in the defensive line. The defensive lineman wants to use the offensive lineman like a door. He doesn't want to go around him; he wants to go through him. As he locks out he cannot loose ground. He locks out, twists his hips outside, pulls hard with his outside hand, and rips his inside arm past the offensive lineman.

We do this drill on the *Crowther sled.* We do it on this sled because it will spin in a circle if the drill is not done right. As the player comes off the ball and engages the sled pad with his hands, if his base is too narrow the sled will start to work in a circle. This teaches a good base and strong hands.

Before I quit I want to talk about the spread offense again. When we started out we were talking about stopping the spread offense. In the second phase we talked about slowing down the spread offense. Now we are talking about dealing with the spread offense. In our first game last year we played Texas Tech, which was one of the better teams in the country with the spread offense. We played Washington State, who did a great job with the spread offense. We played six teams last year that ran the spread offense.

We studied the heck out of the spread offense in the off-season because prior to this year we did not play it very well. The first thing we decided to do was to use different fronts against the spread offense. We used at least two different fronts. We went with a four-man front and a three-man front. Two years ago when we played South Carolina in the Outback Bowl, we stumbled upon the three-man front. We had gotten behind and didn't know what to do. We went to the 30 front as a stop-gap defense. We decided to

make that our second front. The good thing about that was we didn't have to change personnel. We used our rush and drop ends as part of the 30 package. By doing that we were able to stem at the line of scrimmage.

On the quarterback's pre-snap, we tried to disguise what the defense was doing. The quarterback in the spread offense was waiting for the coach on the sideline to call the play from what the coach in the press box saw on the field. We disguised the front by not changing personnel and stemming on the line of scrimmage. The whole idea was to confuse the quarterback so he wasn't quite sure what defense he was going to get.

The next thing we came upon was critical to our game play. We had to *stop the run.* We found out that people who ran the spread offense were successful if they could run the ball. The play we needed to stop was the *quarterback-follow play.* We wanted to make sure we got movement in the box and got after the run.

We wanted to get pressure on the quarterback and hit him. We had 158 hits on quarterbacks this year. That is in addition to all the sacks we got. I feel strongly our success in the fourth quarter came from the fact we were hitting the quarterback so much. By the fourth quarter the quarterback was throwing the ball early to get rid of it. We wanted to make the quarterback start running in the passing game.

The more I studied the spread offense, the more I felt we had to get someone into the inside throwing lanes. We talked to Coach Tressel about that idea and he told us to go ahead with our plan. We were going to get someone in the face of the quarterback at the risk of losing containment. We were not going to let the quarterback stand in the pocket and pick us apart. We were going to make him run for his life. We called this stunt *cover me* [Diagram 6]. We felt the best way to pressure the quarterback was to give the defensive end a two-way-go on the offensive tackle. We gave the defensive end a power rush inside the offensive tackle to get to inside the throwing lane. The tackle was going to power rush but he was working outside and was responsible for containment. If the quarterback broke containment, we chased him. We had good success against the teams we played.

We can also do it the way Tampa Bay does. They make the *cover-me-tackle* call [Diagram 7] and the 3 technique charges at the inside shoulder of the offensive tackle and power rushes upfield. The defensive end jammed the tackle and came under the charge of the 3 technique. That got quick pressure in the face of the quarterback. I know the quarterback from Washington State had a really low completion ratio when we had him on the run. When he was in the pocket, he was unbelievable.

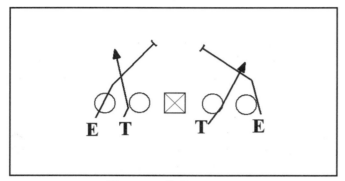

Diagram 6. Cover me

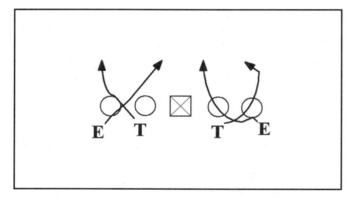

Diagram 7. Cover me tackle

You have to be physical with these types of teams. We turned up the heat in the fourth quarter. We rotated six defensive linemen into the game. I used a sophomore and freshmen in the rotation this year. They got game experience the whole year and are coming back next year. If anyone got hurt, you weren't replacing him with someone who had not played. It kept all six of the guys into the game plan. The night before a game, they were not playing around because they knew they were going to play the next day. We were great in the fourth quarter because we were fresh. The last four or five years we have not had a drop off in our defensive line's performance because we are rotating these underclassmen during the season and giving them experience.

We use a pattern in the rotation. We start off by rotating every three plays. We have a six-play max for the defensive linemen. As the year goes on, the better players played more plays. I'm not stupid enough to leave my best player on the bench too long. The thing we tried to do was stay fresh for the fourth quarter. In the bowl game against Miami we played first and second down with a strong run player and on third down we brought in a strong pass rusher.

Our goal against the spread offense was to not allow any big plays. We wanted to make them go the long field to score if they could. We had to play with great poise. There are great multitudes of things that go on during a football game. The offense is constantly changing personnel. They have a no-huddle scheme. It seems the pace of the game has increased and there is tension all over the field. You have to remain poised and calm to play against that type of offense.

The last thing we have to do to deal with in the spread offense is to *run to the ball*. That is one thing the defensive line did really well this year. We demand that they sprint all out from the start of the play until the whistle blows. If they are tired and didn't run to the ball, they knew they were coming out of the game. We preached that all the time. We went back and looked at one of our games this season and found five defensive plays that won the game for us. I told them they may pursue 50 times in a game and nothing happens, but the next game they may run to the ball once and cause a fumble. Every time they run to the ball it makes a difference.

That's all the time I have, but I'll stay around for a little bit. I appreciate your attention. The neat thing about coaching defensive line is you can control the game. You can control the tempo of a game. My guys will believe me because they watched the defensive front of Tampa Bay control the Super Bowl. Our defensive line is a great group to coach. I appreciate all you coming to hear this lecture. Any time you are in the Columbus area drop in and see us. You are always welcome at Ohio State.

ZONE BLITZ PACKAGE

Youngstown State University

It is a pleasure to be here as part of this clinic. I want to thank everyone involved with the Nike Coach of the Year Clinic. Youngstown State is honored to be a part of this clinic. Tonight I'm going to talk about the *zone-blitz package*. That package has become what Youngstown State's defense is all about. I want to cover a couple of ideas on how we run our package, the way we teach it, and why we run the package.

I want to talk about some of the keys that are important to having a successful defense. I want to show you some of our zone blitzes out of a base-front package. We are basically a *field defense* as far as our alignment is concerned. We align to the offensive passing strength or the wideside of the field.

I want to talk about our *30-front package*, which is becoming a big part of our defensive package. Within that package I'll talk about our *cyclone zone-blitz package*. I'm also going to touch on the bottom line of what we think is important at Youngstown State.

We like the zone blitz for a couple of reasons. It is conducive to our personnel. Our defense is not a man-to-man type of team. Our free safety this year was a little Italian guy who was 5'9" and weighed 165 pounds. Because he knew the defense, he was able to be successful in our scheme. By using the zone-blitz package, it takes some of the control away from the quarterbacks. Offensive coordinators and quarterbacks are getting smarter and better at reading defenses. The defense is not going to have much success if it allows the quarterback to read it and audible in a better play. I'm going to talk about some of the things we do to take the control away from the quarterback.

This next item comes directly from our defensive playbook: *It is the job of the defense to keep the offense from scoring.* But more important is the defense's ability to *take the ball away* from the offense.

Generally, interceptions are created by a zone defense in the secondary. The defense has to be aggressive and attack the offense. We are in the zone-blitz package about 75 to 80 percent of the time. If you take away goal line and red zone defenses, we are in it a higher percentage of the time. *Getting to the football* is the number one things we stress. We use the catch phrase, "*Fun is playing fast together.*" I want to overemphasize that point. We stress pursuit and getting to the football with some emotion. We start every practice off with a pursuit drill.

Knowing where your help is coming from is one of the keys to playing good defense. To run the zone-blitz package or any defensive scheme, the players have to know where they have support. The linebackers in the defense can attack downhill, if they know the ball is being turned into them.

A big thing that is often overlooked by the defense is the *vocabulary used to communicate* throughout the defense. We don't have a great system, but we try to give names to our defenses that create a picture for our players. We don't toss out words and tell them to memorize them. We want our terminology to give our players an idea of what is going to happen in the defense.

You have to have built-in adjustments to offensive formations. As we were preparing for our game against Indiana State, we had three or four chalkboards full of offensive formations they were running. That is the scheme of offenses today. Instead of running a lot of plays, they run a few plays from multiple formations, motions, and shifts. You have to have some built-in adjustments that are easy for your players to grasp and that keeps your defense sound.

The last key to success in the zone-blitz package is to have a secondary coverage that complements the whole package. There are no great secrets in football as far as the X's and O's are concerned. As long as your X's are faster than the offense's O's, you have a chance to be successful. *It is not the blitz; it is the blitzer.* If you are an offensive coordinator in a goal line situation, you are going to get the ball into the hands of your playmaker. The defensive coordinator in those critical situations is going to blitz the player who is going to get to the football.

In our base package we call *field falcon nite*. In this call, *field* is the call for the defensive front, *falcon* is the blitz that is being run, and *nite* is the secondary coverage. The corner to the wideside of the field gives a *Ram* or *Liz* call in the secondary. That obviously stands for left or right. The linebackers call *Lonnie.* That tells our front seven the wideside is left. *Falcon* is the blitz. It has been our number one blitz over the past two seasons [Diagram 1]. Our callside end is aligned in a 5 technique. He reads the playside guard's release. If the guard goes away, he follows his hip. If he comes to him, he rips upfield in the B gap.

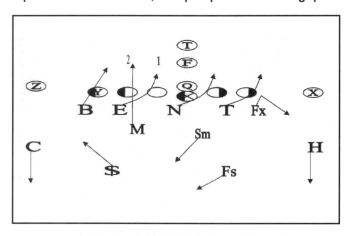

Diagram 1. Field falcon nite

The nose aligns in a fieldside shade on the center. He reads the backside guard. If the guard goes away, he follows his hip. If the guard comes toward him, he rips upfield in the offside B gap. The tackle takes the C gap opposite the front call. He is aligned in a 3 technique on the backside guard. The bandit has what we call a *pitch/peel* course. He has the *pitch man* on an option play. He also has to *peel off and cover* any back that crosses his face. He aligns on the number two receiver to his side. The fox is our zone dropper. He drops into coverage. The Mike linebacker blitzes on a path off the end's tail and goes under all blocks he meets on the way. If we can get the linebacker 1-on-1 with the running back, we have a shot to make a big play.

There are some adjustments we make off this defense. The Sam linebacker makes an *Indy* or an *Ohio* call every play. If the offense brings a second receiver to the weakside, the Sam linebacker makes an adjustment. The *Indy* call tells the fox end that the Sam linebacker is outside the box on a receiver and is dropping into his zone [Diagram 2]. The fox end knows his drop is inside into the hook zone and not the flat area. The *Ohio* call means the Sam linebacker is still in the box and dropping into his hook zone on a pass play.

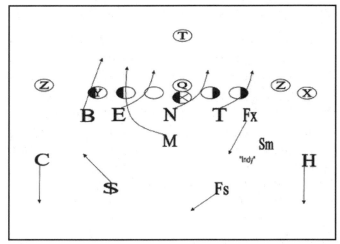

Diagram 2. Indy call

If we get a trey formation left we make a *switch* call. The bandit's alignment is always over the second receiver to his side and he has a seam drop on pass coverage [Diagram 3]. When he gets that far removed from his technique, we don't feel he can be a factor on a running play that way. We make the *switch* call and the Mike linebacker takes the bandits position on the outside and becomes the pitch/peel player. The Sam linebacker sneaks over from his position and becomes the blitzer.

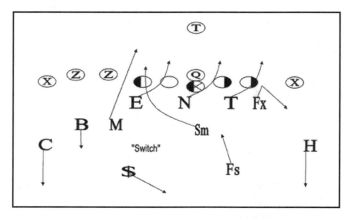

Diagram 3. Switch call

If the offense has a trey formation left using a tight end as the third receiver, we may not use a switch call. If we think the Sam linebacker can get under the number third receiver in the trey set, we let the bandit come and run the normal stunt.

If the offense came out in an empty set in the backfield, we make a *China* call. That means we call off the blitz and go to normal coverage. If you have experienced linebackers who understand the defense, you can stay with the blitz against the three-by-two receiver scheme and still stay sound.

A change-up we use is called *field eagle nite*. We tell our linebackers to play a cat-and-mouse game with the quarterback [Diagram 4]. They watch the 25-second clock and stem inside/outside and up/back in their position. We hope to confuse the quarterback as to what technique we are playing. When we run our eagle we want the linebacker to be in any position except the eagle position before the ball is snapped. If the linebacker is a B gap player, we don't want him lined up there. We want him jockeying around in some kind of outside or inside technique. The only difference between the *eagle* and *falcon* is which player goes first in the stunt. In the *eagle* stunt the Mike linebacker blitzes first inside the offensive tackle trying to get the attention of the offensive guard. The end comes second off the tail of the linebacker and should come home free. This is a good run stunt as well as a pass rush. This was an effective change-up because we ran the *falcon* so often.

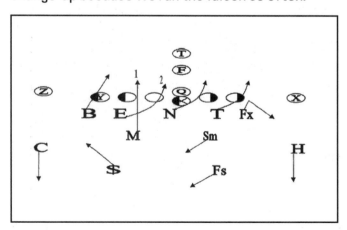

Diagram 4. Field eagle nite

If you have watched any college football games this year, you have seen this blitz or something like it. Ohio State ran this blitz in the National Championship game. This is a sound blitz verses the running game.

We call the stunt *field bozo flow*. The noseguard attacks across the playside guard's face into the B gap. The tackle takes the backside B gap. The Mike linebacker comes first into the offside A gap. The Sam linebacker comes second into the playside A gap. This stunt is really good against a five-step dropback pass [Diagram 5]. It seems to bust wide open when we run it. We told the second blitzer that his technique was like a middle linebacker in a 6-1 defense. This stunt takes time to run. As the second linebacker starts his blitz, if he sees an option pitch to his side, he can scrape outside. That allows him to play like a middle linebacker in a 6-1 defense. He can flow outside. This keeps the defense from losing both linebackers on a run off tackle or wide.

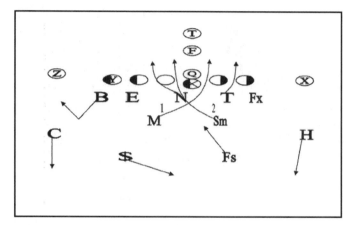

Diagram 5. Field bozo flow

We can run the stunt both ways by calling *bozo opposite*. In this case the stunt reverses with the nose going to the weakside B gap, the Sam linebacker going first into the playside A gap, and the Mike linebacker coming second into the weakside A gap. The Mike linebacker would be playing the 6-1 defense as he runs the stunt.

We like to get the safeties into the box verses the running game. We can set our front to the longside of the offense. That means we set our front to the three-man blocking side. It doesn't matter whether it is a tight end, guard, and tackle, or a guard and two tackles. We call *long thunder zone* [Diagram #6]. The thunder tells our defense we are stunting to the tight end side. If there are two tight ends, we blitz the fieldside. The safety and linebacker to the tight end side are the blitzers. If the strong safety is the blitzer, we will be in *nite* or three-deep coverage. The bandit and fox must play run first then pass. They have to keep everything inside of them. The tackle and end widen for contain. The nose takes the A gap opposite the front call. The Mike linebacker blitzes the A gap on his side and the strong safety blitzes the B gap.

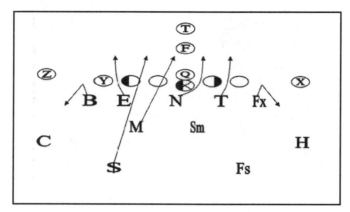

Diagram 6. Long thunder zone

If we had a twin set with the tight end opposite, we would call a *flash* [Diagram 7]. On the *flash* call the free safety would run the blitz along with the Sam linebacker. The noseguard runs through the callside A gap.

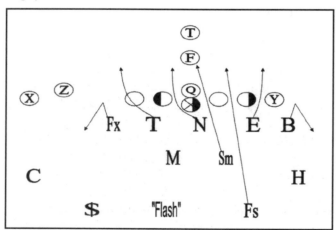

Diagram 7. Flash

We run the 30-front package because of the number of defensive linemen it requires to run this front. It is hard to find defensive linemen. This type of defense requires less depth in the defensive line than a four-man front. The bigger programs like Florida State and Ohio State are going to a 30 package because it allows them to have less depth in the defensive line. Another reason to run the 30 front is the way offenses are reading the defenses. Teams are running what we call the *attack series*. Northwestern runs the attack series. They align in a shotgun and spread formation with the tailback

beside the quarterback. They are running the zone series and reading the defensive ends. Teams are also getting the plays from the sidelines after they align down on the line of scrimmage.

Quarterbacks are getting more sophisticated in the way they call for the snap. They are using a fake hitch with their legs to try to get the defense to tip their stunts. They hitch their leg as if they are calling for the ball to be snapped. What they are really doing is trying to get the defense to tip the blitz so they can audible to another play. We had senior linebackers this past year that could play the cat-and-mouse game very well. They very seldom tipped their hand before the ball was snapped. However, if we got caught and the quarterback called an audible, we made our *China* call and got out of the stunt. Sometimes we made a dummy call to give the appearance we had gotten out of the stunt, when we actually hadn't. Never let the quarterback see where you are coming from before the play clock gets down below five seconds.

We call our 30 front *cyclone.* In our *cyclone* front, the end and tackles are aligned in a head-up position on the offensive tackles. The nose is in a 0 technique on the center [Diagram 8]. The bandit is in a 9 technique on the tight end. Instead of a fox end we have a dime back. If we run a *cyclone falcon nite*, this defensive call is the 30 front with a fieldside stunt, and a three-deep coverage behind it. The end angles flat across to the A gap. The nose takes the A gap opposite the front call. The bandit blitzes off of the corner and has the pitch/peel course. The Mike linebacker takes a tight path off the end's tail. He goes under any blocks thrown at him. The dime back is in a cover 3 into the boundary. He shows blitz to draw attention but is in the coverage. The strong safety works with the bandit and makes the proper adjustments to the formations. The Sam linebacker has the middle hook zone on passes.

The adjustments to the trey formation are like the falcon front. If the bandit is out on the second receiver, the Mike and Sam linebackers call *switch* and run the stunt. The adjustments are the same for both the base and 30 fronts.

If we want to run the eagle stunt, we call *cyclone eagle nite* [Diagram 9]. Everything is the same as the *falcon* except the Mike linebacker hits the B gap first

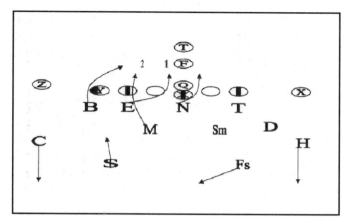

Diagram 8. Cyclone front

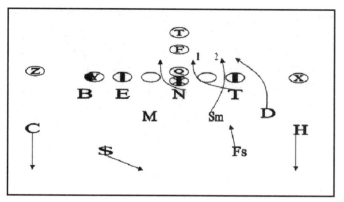

Diagram 10. Badger

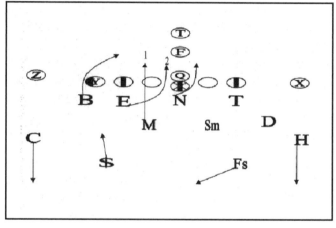

Diagram 9. Cyclone eagle nite

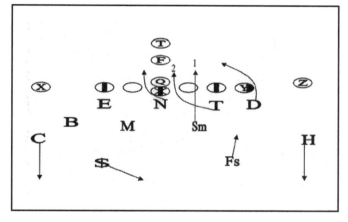

Diagram 11. Cyclone beaver flash

and the end comes second into the A gap. Everyone else on the defense plays the same.

If we want to run the stunt from the boundary we call it *badger*. Nothing changes in the mechanics of the stunt when you run it from the boundary [Diagram 10]. If we call *cyclone badger flash*, the tackle angles flat across to the A gap. The nose takes the A gap to the front call. The dime back blitzes off the corner and runs a pitch/peel course. The Sam linebacker takes a tight path off the tackle's tail and plays under all blocks thrown at him. The bandit plays cover 3 to his side. The free safety works with the dime back and adjusts to the formation. The Mike linebacker has the middle hook zone.

If we want to reverse the stunt for the tackle and linebacker, we call *cyclone beaver flash* [Diagram 11]. That gives us the eagle stunt into the boundary with the linebacker coming first and the tackle coming behind him. All responsibilities are the same with the exception of the linebacker and tackle.

A change-up we like from the *cyclone* front is what we call *cyclone beast flash/6* [Diagram 12]. This is a badger blitz except the tackle and dime back trade responsibilities. The tackle takes an outside rush and has the pitch/peel course. The dime back is cheating inside and blowing the B gap. The Sam linebacker fires the A gap while the nose takes the frontside A gap. The dime back aligns with depth even with a tight end to his side. He allows the blitz to develop by coming flat from the outside. In the secondary we play a cover flash or 6 according to the formation and situation.

We run *cyclone pinch 2-drop*. This is a simple stunt. We bring both the bandit and the dime back from the outside [Diagram 13]. The end and tackle take a B gap slant and rush hard up the field. The nose takes a flash step as if he is rushing and then drops into pass coverage looking for receivers on the crossing routes. That allows the Sam and Mike linebackers to get more width to the outside.

A coaching point that has to be emphasized with the tackles and ends in the 30-front package is their run *responsibility*. When the tackle and end are aligned in the head-up position of the 30 package, they are B gap players verses the run. However, if the play is a pass play, they are C gap players.

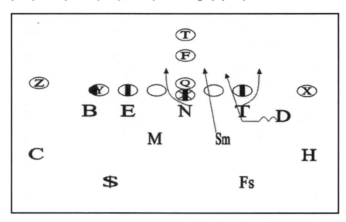

Diagram 12. Cyclone beast flash/6

We have a quote in our playbook we call our *bottom line*. Vince Lombardi was a big believer in clichés. It was a way you could take a big thought and put it down simply so people could remember it. This is one of the things I got from him. We believe in it and put it on the back page of our playbook.

"Imagine for a moment, if you can, a man running down the street carrying all your worldly possessions.

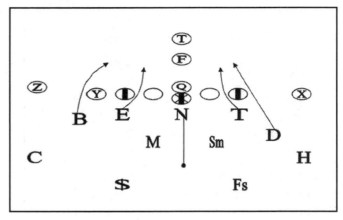

Diagram 13. Cyclone pinch 2-drop

Taking from you every person that you have ever loved and every thing that you hold dear. I guarantee you would find a way – by any means necessary – to stop that man. That, very simply put, is PURSUIT."

All the X's and O's will not help your players get to the football if they are not playing with emotion and heart.

Gentlemen, I appreciate your time. If you have any questions or would like to come visit us at Youngstown State, please feel free to call on us.

GETTING IT DONE IN THE TRENCHES

Ohio State University

Thank you. I appreciate the opportunity to be here today. We just had a whirlwind year at Ohio State. Going into the season I thought we were a very talented team on paper. But I wasn't sure if we were good enough to take the next step and compete for the National Championship. I think sometimes as coaches we get caught up in the amount of talent a team may have. We had some talent at Ohio State, but the thing that this team had was *great chemistry*. This team had those intangible qualities that come along once in a lifetime.

This season was a very humbling experience for the coaching staff. We are very fortunate to be at Ohio State. We don't want you to put us on a pedestal and think that we know it all. We are not the gurus of college football and we don't know every phase of the game. We are just like you guys sitting out there. We are trying to learn. This is my 20th year as the strength-and-conditioning coach and I'm still trying to learn. I don't have all the answers. Anyone who would say that is making a fool out of himself.

I want to start today by showing you this overhead. Sometimes I think the strength-and-conditioning coaches get stereotyped. People think that all we do is pump iron and get strong. Obviously we are trying to improve strength, but the bottom line in our field is *can they play the game.* Early in my career as a strength-and-conditioning coach, I had some athletes who were extremely strong. But they were limited in their lateral movement, flexibility, explosiveness, and quickness. They were very stiff athletes. Coaches have a tendency to get too caught up with strength. I'm not telling you that strength is not important. I am telling you that just being strong will not make you a better player. The key to playing football is lateral movement, being explosive, flexibility, and great quickness.

Our philosophy at Ohio State is to develop the *total athlete*. That thought is first and fore most in our thinking. We are trying to develop all the intangibles that go into developing an athlete. We want to develop *speed, explosion, flexibility, lateral movement, forward movement, short movement, power*, and *vertical jump*. I think the thing that we do at Ohio State is to develop the athlete not only from the neck down, but between the ears also. That goes for all nine assistant coaches, Coach Tressel, and our conditioning staff. The bottom line in our program is whether we can motivate our athletes to excel to the upper limits. The coach has to make sure his standards are higher for the athlete, then the standards the athlete sets for himself. If the coach doesn't do that he is destined to fail.

The biggest thing we have to fight at Ohio State is complacency. Last year we had a miniature bull's eye on our chests. After the National Championship game that sucker got huge. The expectations continue to rise with the success you have within a program. The bar has already been raised for next year. There are expectations of a repeat championship from everyone outside the program. The people within the program have to raise the standard expected of our athletes.

The place to begin your improvement is in the *trenches*. A football team has to be hard and aggressive in the trenches if they want to be successful. We have to push those athletes in the offensive and defensive lines to improve and get better. You have to keep telling them that good things happen to good people. If you work hard enough, we will have success. They have to believe in what you are doing. We won seven football games last year by a touchdown or less. If our kids did not believe, did not work hard, or were not intense, we would not have won those games. In each of those games our kids kept fighting and hoping for the best.

In our situation we want to develop a mindset to play 60-plus minutes a football game. I can go to downtown Cincinnati, find a drunk living in a cardboard box, and train him to play 45 minutes. That is not good enough. I want 60-plus minutes. Don't get down to the last minutes of the game and assume it is over. In our past season we had two overtime games. That requires your players to play 60-plus minutes. On our sidelines in those games there was no sense of chaos, disorganization, stress, or tension. Our players were calm on the sideline because they believed in each other. They knew that someone was going to make the play. They knew the coaches were going to call the right play. They knew they were going to get it done regardless of what was called. That is the sense of confidence that the coaching staff and players need to have.

At Ohio State we are the National Champions. The scary part about the Ohio State program is we are a work in progress. These kids in this program right now are nowhere close to their potential. We know we can get better. We have a long way to go in our program. I have offensive linemen who need to lose weight. I have defensive linemen who need to get bigger. There are always things that we can work on to make us a better team.

Let's look at the things we need to do to improve our offensive and defensive linemen. The first thing on our list is *planning. If you fail to plan; you plan to fail.* You have to sit down with each kid in your program individually and set some goals. You may not think you have time to do it. If you are motivated enough, you will find the time. We have a goal sheet that we sit down with each player and set goals within a time frame. The first set of goals is winter goals. The first thing we start with is their previous best effort. From there we decide where we want to go. You can use any area you want. We use *measurable* items. I take input from the athlete. I want to know what he thinks he needs to work on and I write down what I think he needs to work on. On each goal sheet we have a place for the player to sign a pledge. It states: *I agree to commit myself for the winter of 2003 to reach my goals and make myself, my teammates, and the team better through hard work and dedication.* He signs the pledge and I sign it. We give him a copy of it and I keep a copy of it. Each and every day he comes in to work out, the first thing he sees in his workout folder is his goal sheet.

The first thing we look at is the *body fat* of the linemen. The defensive linemen are the better athletes between the offensive and defensive lines. They can run, hit, and have a lot of power. Offensive linemen historically are bigger and slower. Ideally we want to keep the offensive lineman's body fat at 18 or 19 percent. Coach Heacock, who coaches our defensive line, has some deer on his squad. All his personnel are around the 12- to 13-percent level. These guys are smart about how they eat and how to take care of themselves.

You need to set up some kind of nutrition goals for your players. Come up with some recommendation to correct their unhealthy eating patterns. Kids don't have any idea about what is good for them and what is bad. It is like the guy who sued MacDonald's. He said he had been eating their food for 15 years and didn't know it would make him fat. They don't know. Give them some guidance into those facts.

The most important thing you do in your winter program is to *improve the football skills* of your athletes. They may look like Tarzan, but they may play like Jane. They may go out there and look like a bowling ball with legs and be the greatest thing since sliced bread. During the off-season program they need to improve their metabolic conditioning. Flexibility is tremendously important to the development of offensive and defensive linemen. We had a scholarship athlete who came to Ohio State five years ago as an offensive tackle. We grade all of our athletes as to their flexibility. This lineman graded out to be a negative 10. That is the worst I've ever seen on scholarship. He could hardly get down into a stance. The coaches didn't know what to think. They knew that whoever recruited him must have made a mistake. He couldn't play because he couldn't get into a stance.

This player's high school coaches never had their players stretch in their winter program. All they did was lift and run. I asked this player if he had any work habits at all. He told me he would do anything I asked. He played at Ohio State for five years. He went from a negative 10 as a freshman to a positive two as a fifth-year senior. That is a foot improvement in his flexibility. If I had not been there and done the measuring, I would not have believed he could improve that much. As a freshman he was 6'6" and 260 pounds. When he graduated he was 6'7" and 319 pounds. His 40-yard dash time went from 5.47 to 5.19 after he had gained 60 pounds. Of course he increased his strength in his legs and his power.

Flexibility is important. Make sure when you are finished with your strength training that you spend five to seven minutes in a stretching program. Whatever method you chose, make sure your players spend that time stretching. You can use partners to stretch each other. You can use the rubber band method they teach at Youngstown State. You can use a knotted rope to overstretch. Whatever you do will pay great dividends for you in the long run. Everyone is different and it may take some guys longer to improve, but it works. Basically fellows, we are used car salesmen. We are trying to sell these players on a car, but we are not allowing them to look under the hood. Little do they know there is no engine? The players are going to have to provide the power and strength and we are going to provide the vehicle. *Our number one job is motivation.*

The next thing you have to work on is their *work effort.* You have to constantly preach work effort and getting better. You can't have one team meeting and touch on all these things. You have to reinforce it on a daily basis. You have to make sure the head coach and all the assistant coaches are disciples of the same program. You have to constantly talk about all the goals you are trying to accomplish. Last year when Coach Tressel came in, I'm not sure all the seniors truly bought into everything we were doing. This year's senior class was entirely different. You could see the evolution of the program and their beliefs. You could see them getting excited. You could see the attitude about selfishness. They didn't care who got the credit as long as the goals were accomplished. In the end you could see the results of those beliefs.

You have to *improve mental toughness.* There is a fine line between creating mental toughness and harassment. You don't want to push your players away, but you have to create some sort of mental toughness. I'll talk more about that later. I've got a son who is a sophomore in high school. His school is one of the most affluent schools in the district. It is known as a soft school. You as the high school coach have your players for two to three hours daily. I hope you can teach mental toughness in the limited time

you have the player. He goes back to the environment he lives in for the remaining time. I hope the players become the product of his environment that you have him in and not the other way around. You have to bond with these kids.

In training the offensive and defensive linemen, you have to *improve speed and agility.* Offensive linemen's speed is short-space speed. The most overrated test for offensive linemen is a 40-yard dash. The defensive linemen need to run from sideline to sideline like a bunch of junkyard dogs. When you are developing drills for your linemen, use short-space speed and short-space agility drills.

The last thing on my list is *injury-prevention exercises.* This comes from muscle-balance training. If you have a trainer who works with your team, you should go to him once a week and inquire about your team's strengths and weakness. He can tell you that a player's arm strength on his left side is not good. He can tell you if a player is having trouble with his hamstrings or shoulder flexibility. He can give you clues as to what areas to strengthen to balance a player's muscles.

There are some things that I want to happen in my program daily. Before we begin our weight program, I want to do a *warm-up.* I don't care what type of warm-up you do or how limited with space you are, you have to do some kind of warm-up. If you have to do 15 jumping jacks and run in place for 30 seconds, then do it. It is a copout to say you don't have the space or budget for those kinds of things. Let me tell you one short story. When I was teaching at Northeast High School, I coached football too. One of the best athletes in the school could only lift in our after-school program two days a week. He had to go home and do chores on the farm the other days. He missed the activities bus one day and I gave him a ride home. As I drove up the winding dirt road to his house, I noticed some things in his yard. There were some tree stumps with boards lying across them. There were all kinds of automobile axles and bricks lying around. When I asked him what they were, he told me he used them to work out after he finished his chores. This kid was lying down on those boards and lifting those axles and bricks after he finished his chores at night. He would bench press some of the axles and squat the bigger one. He did dumb bell exercises with the bricks. This kid got the job done. He improvised and did what he had to do.

The core area of the body is the *abdominal and lower-back muscles*. That is the area of an athlete where all the power is generated. That is the area that gives an athlete the power to run, jump, block, and tackle. When you build an athlete, you start with the base and foundation. In our warm ups every day we work the core trunk of the body. We spend two to five minutes each day on the abdominal and lower-back muscles. At the end of the workout, we come back and stretch and work them again. In season this type of training is like everything else. *If you don't use it, you'll lose it.* In season we work the abdominal area three days a week. The players that travel with the team are with me three days a week. If the players are not on the traveling squad, they are with me four days a week.

In addition to the core area, we work the neck, hands, and wrist areas for strength every day. These are small muscle groups that recover fast. You can work them daily and not harm them or overwork them. Obviously we do the strength-training portion of the workout each day, but that is a different regiment.

Every workout we do with our players in the summer and off-season involves some kind of movement. It may be speed movements or agility movements. I've got a video to show you in a bit that shows these movements. These are skill drills for offensive and defensive linemen. I believe in movement drills every day. When I was a strength coach from 1982 to 1988, I wasn't as movement or flexibility oriented. I was strength and power oriented. I went to the Baltimore Orioles for three years. The hardest skill in the world is to hit a 90-mile–per-hour baseball coming right down the middle of the plate. This skill goes back to movement. To hit that ball you have to have good hands and foot movement. Strength without movement is almost useless. If you have a strong kid who is forceful with a great punch but is limited with his movement, he is going to be one-dimensional. If you don't spend time working on his foot speed and short-space running speed, you are defeating the purpose of having a strong player. Use rope jumping, 20-yard shuttle runs, dots, four-cone drills, or any of hundreds of other drills that create movement.

We briefly talked about *flexibility* earlier. We had the stiffest, tightest, very talented athletes that I had ever been around last year at Ohio State. In an ideal world I've got 45 minutes to teach flexibility. Most worlds are not ideal and the same thing is true at Ohio State. We have to incorporate our flexibility right into the training workout. If the athlete takes exercises through short arcs and doesn't take them through the full ranges of the motion, he is going to lose flexibility, range of motion, and movement skills. That means you are going to lose speed, quickness, and freedom of movement. Take every exercise you do and make sure they take the exercise through a full range of motion. If they don't and you lose flexibility, you have defeated the purpose of lifting weights. You have defeated the purpose of trying to enhance their movement skills. If you don't make them use the full range, they will look better, but their movement skills will be worse. After that you will develop a bunch of strained muscles.

I don't train our offensive and defensive linemen to be body builders. I train them to be athletes. That is the thing we loose sight of. I am not training them to be a better power lifter. If a kid comes to me and tells me he has finished his workout and wants to do something additional, I give him a jump rope. Strength is the easiest fitness component to develop. Why do kids spend so much time on weight training? It looks good. Just look in the mirror. They can see the pecs, the abs, the biceps, and the quads. The muscles that are used in the offensive and defensive line are not seen in a mirror. The hamstrings and lower back, the rotor cuff, and neck are things that help you in football. I've never seen an athlete in 20 years of training not want to know where the mirror is.

In your weight program you have to find a balance with what you are doing. What you need are ground-based activities. Try to do these activities with free weights if you can. There are some exercises like hamstring pulls that you can't do this way, but do as many as you can. When we do these exercises we are looking for triple extensions. *We want extensions in the hip, knee, and ankle.* If you can gain power and flexibility in those three areas you will be a better athlete. What exercises can you do to work on the triple extension? I am not trying to sell you on anything as far as a weight training regiment, but cleans squats, lunges, explosive step-ups, and box jumps are examples of triple-extension drills. You have to use what works for you.

The *ankle* is the most neglected area, which helps improve speed, change of direction, and quickness. You can work on that area and it only takes five minutes a day. All it takes is toe raisers on a weight plate or step. Rope or rubber band drills can also improve the flexibility in the heel cup.

Multiple joint exercises are essential. When you are doing an exercise, make sure it works more than one group of muscles. We want knees, ankles, butt, calves, and back involved in the same exercise. Make the bulk of your workouts multiple-joint exercises. If you take each joint movement to as many angles as you can, it will aid in injury prevention. Joints in a football game don't get stretched; only in the way you train do they get stretched. There are all kinds of awkward hits that occur in a game that cause severe injury. If you train that joint at all different angles it may help to prevent injuries.

Keep *variety* in your workouts. Change up what they are doing to keep them fresh in their approach to the workout. Keep records of their achievements to keep their interest peaked. Like I told you before, we are used car salesman. If you are timing them in a 40-yard dash, you have to know what to report. I had particular player that previously ran a 4.95 in the 40. He had worked extremely hard in our winter program to reduce his body fat by two percent, lose 15 pounds, and improve his flexibility by three inches. When he ran the forty after his improvement, his time turned out to be 4.99. When he asked me what he ran I told him 4.92. I want him to be motivated and believe that he can go to a level he has never been. I want him to believe his hard work has paid off.

One of the key things I am always striving to improve in our workouts is our *intensity*. I want them to be intense and work hard. I want them to achieve another level. I want them to say after four or five years at Ohio State that they can handle any adversity because of the training they had here. *The key to any program is consistency.* If they show up one day a week, your program is toast. You have to convince them they need to be there. There are kids who come in and work out for six weeks in your program, and if you took their pulse they would be lucky to have one. It is not enough to get them there.

You have to make them intense at what they are doing. Take a leader and pair him with three followers. Take a strong kid and put him with three weak ones. Work on their emotions. Tell the leader if his group doesn't get the job done, you are holding him accountable for his group. Or tell all four of them that they are accountable for the outcome of the workout. You've got to get them stimulated.

Here's a little tip for you: When we call our groups together, we always form a circle — we circle the wagons. I want my leaders on the inside of that circle. Some of the seniors who are not strong enough to lead stay on the outside of the circle. I want the senior who thinks he can lead and any one else on the team that thinks they have leadership quality to be on the inside of that circle. You would be surprised who you find on the inside of that circle. You may find one or two leaders that you never even thought about. But you may find some guys that have overrated their leadership ability and think they are better than they are. To get to the inside of the circle a player has to be motivated.

The next thing I want to talk about are *foot-movement drills*. It is amazing how many times you get a player that can't jump rope. It is essential to teach your players how to do that short-space drill. After they accomplish that skill, add something to it. Instead of having them jump rope in one place, have them jump rope and move five yards forward. That gives you two motor skills going on at the same time. Jump rope, dot drill, and speed ladder are examples of foot-movement drills. People don't have to buy a 75-dollar speed ladder. You can use tape on the floor or the ground to simulate ladder rungs every 12 to 15 inches. You can use a variety of drills in the speed ladder. They can use one foot in the each rung. They can put both feet in each rung. The drills are endless that go with this piece of equipment. All these drills are on one plane. We are shuffling, sliding, or backward running in a north/south or east/west direction. You can also use angles in this drill. Instead of going one direction, we go two. When you use angles you are going northeast or southwest instead of straight lines.

I'm going to show you this tape that has six drills on it. It lasts nine minutes. You will see some equipment in this tape that you can make and not spend a lot of money on. The first thing you are going to see is the *speed ladder*. Notice these guys have big rubber bands that are connected to each ankle. The length of the rubber band is the width we want their feet apart. It is a reminder for when the feet get too far apart or too close together. When we start our indoor program we go Tuesday and Thursday with post workout skill development. The first week we show the groups what we want them to do. The next week when we actually start the drill, I'll hand a senior leader a lamented card that has the first day three drills on one side of the card, and the second day three drills on the other side. Those seniors lead their group through the drills. All the strength coaches do is assist them if they are having some difficulty with the drill and to blow the whistle for drill changes. If you send us a blank tape I'll send you a copy of this tape.

This drill is called the *tennis ball stance-and-start*. This teaches first-step explosion. We have the offensive lineman get in a three-point stance. We line the player's hands up on the goal line. The coach stands at the three-yard line. He has a tennis ball extended to the side at shoulder's height. The object of the drill is for the players to catch the ball after it is dropped before it bounces twice. The first step is the most important thing you do as far as forward or lateral speed. The coach starts out at three yards and backs up to four and five yards. Michael Irvin did not have a great 40 time for Dallas Cowboys. He ran 4.6 for the 40-yard dash, but he could do this drill at seven yards. You will find a lot of your athletes can get the ball at four and five yards. If you want to get some competitiveness in the drill get two guys going at the same time. The coach can hold a ball in each hand and drop them at the same time. That lets the linemen compete against one another.

We do *big-ball drills* for hand movement. It is a good punching drill for offensive linemen. One player stands tall holding the big ball. The other player takes his stance. He breaks his stance and punches with both hands, recoils and punches again. We do a series of hand-punch movements. We punch with one hand and then alternate hands. We punch with both hands moving high to low on the ball. We alternate hands going high to low on the ball. After we hit the stationary target, the other player starts to move laterally with the ball. He goes right and left. We try not to develop any pattern in our change of direction.

We might move five yards right and two yards left. The offensive lineman has to move his feet and shuffle right and left while punching using the pattern we have designated.

You guys are the experts. Pick out any drill you want to do and do them. We work for 15 to 20 minutes two times a week. We are not trying to burn them out. We want them to keep their edge in football-related activities.

We have a lot of *hand-and-wrist strengthening drills*. The team that holds the best in most cases is going to win. We do wrist curls. We have a gripper machine we use. We take two 10-pound weight plates, place them back-to-back so the smooth side is out, and hold them for a certain length of time. We take dumbbells and do a farmers walk for 40, 50, or 100 yards. We use rice buckets for our defensive backs. The rice buckets are 16 to 18 inches high filled with rice or sand. We do four sets of 30 seconds with individual hands. They jam their hand into the rice bucket where they have to squeeze and release the rice or sand all the way to the bottom of the bucket. That develops great hand strength. Have your kids hold a 100-pound dumbbell and see who can hold them the longest. Have them carry a 45-pound weight plate for 100 yards. Those are things that develop grip strength.

The next thing I want to talk about is our *explosive movement in the weight room*. We do a hang cleans. I'm not a big proponent of power clean myself. I try to do everything from the knees up. I like doing combination movements. I like to do a hang clean into a front squat. Or do a hang clean into a push press. If you are limited with time and space, do the combination exercises to save time and space.

There are two things I want to do to improve our offensive and defensive line. I want to improve the player's *vertical and horizontal speed*. If I can do that, I can make them a better athlete. Little Johnny may be able to only jump vertically 14 inches, but if I can take him to 16 inches, he is a better athlete. That doesn't sound like much, but you have to work with the players you have. Helicopters don't come over and drop players out during two-a-days. It has taken me 20 years to figure out that *all the players we have are the players we have*. We have to work with what we have.

If it takes me two years to teach you a movement, I am not a very good coach and I've wasted a lot of time. We keep everything in our program simple. We do basic things in our program to produce power and strength. We use the bench, incline bench, back and front squats, forward and angle lunges in our program.

We work *speed and strength drills*. In your workout for offensive and defensive linemen, don't do slow, absolute strength movements in every workout. You are going to have those, but make sure you incorporate something explosive. An example would be to do a back squat followed by an explosive box jump. I go from a slow-twitch muscle fiber activity to a fast-twitch muscle fiber exercise.

The thing that we are starting to realize now is that kids don't know how to hop and jump. How many kids do you have that come from the middle school and can't do simple locomotive skills like hopping and skipping? I have some kids as sophomores who must have been locked in a barn. They can't jump rope. We are not just talking about hopping. We are talking about hopping and sticking the landing. That means we have balance when we come down. The good athletes have good balance. The athlete that jumps and lands has a good athletic position with good balance when he comes down.

We do a tremendous amount of *hopping, skipping, and jumping drills*. We do hip flexors, hip extenders, and swings. We do power push-ups. We have wooden blocks elevated off the floor. We get down between the blocks and push off the floor onto the tops of the blocks with our hands. This is an explosive movement off the floor to the top of the block. We walk our hands back to the floor and do it again. You don't have to use blocks. You can do the explosion push-up and clap your hands before you land back on them.

We use a med-ball drop. The player lies on his back with his hands in a cocked position. We stand over the player with a 10- to 12-pound medicine ball. I don't want the player to catch the ball and throw it back to me. I want him to get his hands in position, and as I drop the ball, I want him to punch and snap the ball back to me.

We work on drills that *prevent injuries*. We do shoulder-stabilization drills. One drill we use is what we call medicine ball push-ups. The players get down on two medicine balls and do push-ups. That develops tremendous stabilization and strength in the shoulder and scapular area. This prevents injury in the shoulders. We use medicine ball throws to improve the shoulder stabilization. These are simple chest passes, bounce passes, and over-the-head passes that are used in basketball. They have to absorb the throw and push the ball to get it back.

We have drills that work on the lower-back muscle. These are drills you don't need equipment for. We call the first one *superman*. The player lays face down on the ground. He extends his arm straight out in front of him and his legs straight behind him. The player pulls his arms and legs off the ground at the same time. He lifts his arms and legs five to seven inches, and holds them there for one to two counts at the top. The next thing we do is called *aquaman*. In this exercise the player lifts his opposite leg and opposite arm five to seven inches and holds them for one to two counts.

Another exercise is to lay face down and place a medicine ball behind the player's neck. He grabs the medicine ball and raises his upper torso off the ground five to seven inches. These are all lower-back exercises. The stronger the linemen can get in this region the better player he will be.

When we do our *post-workout flexibility*, we stress the ankle and hip areas. The areas we are concerned with at Ohio State are ankles, hips, lower back, hamstrings, quads, groins, and shoulders. Those are the areas we stress and want the most flexibility.

We use hurdles for hip mobility training. Get six hurdles from the track coach and stick them over in the corner until you are ready to use them. We use them to step over. When linemen go from their freshman year to their senior year, they will add weight and strength. As they eat right and get bigger, the area of concern for the coach is the loss of hip flexibility. We step over the hurdles going forward and sideways. Alternate the hurdles by putting one at the high-hurdle height and one and the low-hurdle height. Without bending from the torso, step through the high hurdle and over the low hurdle. We stagger the hurdles forward, so that the player steps through the high hurdle, steps forward with his next step, and over the low hurdle moving sideways. He steps forward for the next high hurdle and repeats the whole exercise going over three hurdles.

The type of conditioning we use for offensive and defensive linemen from January to March is a *general aerobic base*. If a lineman has to lose some weight, in addition to all the other things we are doing, the lineman owes me an extra 25 minutes of cardio-vascular training four to five days a week. It can be on a bike, a treadmill, or it can be any other type of aerobic exercise he wants to do. At this time of year and early in the summer you want to keep some things at a low impact. You don't want to beat them down with a lot of running on hard surfaces. If you do that they won't hold up when you start your intense summer sprinting. You have to be smart about those kinds of things. I want to make him a better athlete, not a better weightlifter.

Organize a basketball league on Saturday mornings. Make them play racquetball and other games, which will make them competitive. We do what is called *functional conditioning*. We put 1,000 pounds of sand bags or weight plates in one corner of a room. We divide our group into teams of three linemen. We compete to see who can move the sand bags from one corner of the room to the other corner in the shortest amount of time. This is physical labor. It is not all about bars and dumbbells.

We do very little conditioning from January through March. We only do agilities, aerobics, and functional conditioning. We do 15 minutes of speed drills daily, all kinds of movement drills daily, and skill-development drills on Tuesdays and Thursdays.

The last thing I want to cover is this aspect of *mental toughness*. This can be developed in the weight room. You have to hold them accountable and make them do the little things. They will become a product of their environment. It is a continual process, and it will not happen overnight. I have a couple of slug puppies that need to get tougher. I have to count on them in the future in our offensive line. They are young kids. They have to get better because they are not mentally tough enough yet. It is the little things that make them tougher. Don't let them quit and hang their heads. Always maintain a positive attitude toward them. I tell them we are only in the 38th minute of a 48-minute game. You have to get better. We need them in the last minute of the game. The question I need to ask is: "Are you going into the tank?" Do I need to get you out of the game? If I can't count on you in the 48th minute of the game, you are not the right man for the job. I love to take kids in the 1-on-1 atmosphere. I like to see what they are made of. I can go to the position coach after the winter program, and tell him which players are not tough enough. I want to find out about these players before they get to spring ball.

The foundation to achievement is intense desire. You players either have it or they don't. You have to give them positive reinforcement every day. It has to be real, because the players see right through the phoniness.

You have to set your own standards for the team. Team standards would be bowl games, Big Ten Championships, or National Championships. Set some standards in their weight training. My standards for a defensive lineman to be a national champion is to hang clean 385 pounds or squat 685. There is no such thing at Ohio State as a one-rep maximum. That is a joke. All our max lifts are three-reps maximum. The game of football is not a one-rep maximum. I want them to know that it is a series of repetitions. If you one-rep max on everything you do, what happens to the players on a 10-play drive? They start to wave the white flag and want out of the game. He is great for one play, but he is not in it for the long haul.

Here is a good question. A guy asked me if I am in favor of behind-the-neck press. I don't like to do anything that overextends a joint. If we do behind-the-neck press, we would not come down further than the back of the head. If we bring the weight down to the neck, the shoulder is going to be overextended and a stretching of the joint starts to develop. They get stronger, but a month or two down the road they will probably suffer a badly separated shoulder. The same thing is true of extremely heavy bench presses that drop the hands below the chest line. You are stretching the shoulder joint the wrong way. The same thing is true with lat pull downs. If they are pulling the bar down to their necks they are stretching the shoulder joint in a hyperextended way. It is especially hard on the quarterback. It is an unnatural resistance that stretches the shoulder capsule out. That causes him to loose control of the football as he throws. Instead of the shoulder capsule being tight where he can throw with accuracy, it is loose.

SPECIAL TEAM GOALS AND PUNT PROTECTION

Grand Valley State University

As the head coach at Grand Valley State, we were very fortunate to win the Division-II National Championship last year. All of you know there is more to winning a national championship than just offense and defense. As the head coach, offensive coordinator, and the quarterback coach, I can tell you a lot of our success is based on our ability to play great defense and play great on special teams. My talk today is not going to be only about special teams. I do not want to lose any more of you that are here tonight to the casino. I will try to keep you interested in what we are doing in our program.

An interesting side note came to me coming to the clinic. Only coaches have the ability to come to a clinic in a casino and think they are going to win. That tells me a lot about this group here tonight. Most people come to the casino resigned to the fact they are going to lose their money. I just talked to a coach before I walked into the lecture hall and he told me he was going to be the one that walked away from here with money in his pockets. Coaches are optimistic.

First, let me talk about *special teams*. It is like all other phases of the game in that you must have emphasis on special teams if you are to get that back from your players.

One of the things we want to do is to let the kids know there are areas where we can achieve certain goals on special teams. Clearly the skilled players want to be on the special teams. They want to touch the football. But the question is how do you draw the interest of the other players on the special team who do not get to touch the football? How do you keep the left tackle on the extra point team interested? We came up with an award for the special team player of the year based on a *point system*. We went out and got the largest trophy we could find. It is about three-feet high. We wanted to get the biggest and gaudiest trophy we could find. We wanted our players to see the trophy every day. The trophy cost

us about $100. The bang for our bucks came from the fact that we saw our kids change their attitude on how they could win the special teams player of the year. If you are going to emphasize something you must give the players a carrot, and we did that with the trophy.

In our team room we have three distinctive goals and the goals are displayed on banners. The banners are 12-feet wide by eight-feet tall. They are prominent in our team room. When you walk into our team room it is unmistakable that we have *special team goals*, *offensive team goals*, and defensive team goals. Let me go over our special team goals [Diagram 1].

- Win
- Better than average field position after kickoff than opponent
- Better net punt average than opponent
- Score or set up a score
- Give the offense the ball at least one time on the plus -50-yard line
- Never give the opponent the ball on our side of the 50-yard line
- Perfect execution on holds, snaps, and ball security
- Have at least one game breaker – score, block a punt, block a kick, recover an onside kick, cause a turnover, recover a turnover, down a punt inside the 10-yard line, 60 yards of field position change
- No penalties
- Win the hidden-yardage game - kickoff – kickoff return – punt - punt return

Diagram 1. GVSU special team goals

First is to *win*. That is our first goal. The reason we try to stay away from numbers on the net punt average is the fact there are so many obstacles that may not allow us to achieve these goals. If we get someone who kicks the ball in the end zone or there is a penalty after the kick, it can eschew the numbers relative to better kickoffs for the opponents. What we want is the average. The same thing is true with having a better punt return average than our opponents.

If you break down the film, you will find the special teams set up a lot of your scores. And a lot of the times the coaches do not even talk about that point. You do not build the creditability into your special teams. You tend to lose it in its perspective.

We want to give the ball to our offense at least one time on the plus 50-yard line. There are several ways to make this happen. It could be by a punt, pressure, or on any of our kickoffs. We want our kids to understand what we want in this respect. When we had all of the numbers as goals, such as getting the ball on the 25-yard line, or return the ball 25 yards, they do not remember those things.

On the other hand, we do not want to give our opponent the ball on our side of the ball. We want to have perfect execution on all special team plays. We want to have at least one *game breaker*. The one point here that we think is big is to down a punt inside he 10-yard line. To us, that is a game breaker. If you do the job on defense you will probably set up a score or get into a potential scoring situation.

All of these are great goals. But the one goal that we work on more than any other is the last goal: *win the hidden yardage game.* Let me categorize hidden yardage. Here we are talking about the kickoff, kickoff returns, punts, and punt returns. We use the 25-yard line on kickoff returns and 35-yards net on punts and calculate the yards. Let me give you an example. If we have a team that kicks the ball out of the end zone on us, it means we would start the ball in play from the 20-yard line. This means we are at a minus 5 yards in hidden yards against our opponents. Conversely, if we had a kickoff that we returned to the 50-yard line, we would have a plus 25 yards on the hidden yardage.

We do the same thing on punts. We use 35 as the magic number. If we had a punt that netted 50 yards,

we would be plus 15 yards in the hidden yardage. If you keep track of these hidden yards, you will find they make a difference in winning and losing. We have won 26 straight games and we have won 36 out of 37 games, and hidden yardage came into play in every one of those games.

In one of our playoff games we were plus 210 in hidden yards. Obviously we have turned over the field twice. Those numbers are going to come back to you better than some of the other numbers you may throw at your players when you put up your goals. You want to make sure when the players leave the meeting that they know what hidden yardage is. If you can get your players to understand hidden yardage, you are going to win a lot of battles.

We want to put some competitive goals into the special teams, so we came up with a *point production chart* [Diagram 2]. On the chart we have team points and individual points. We feel it is important if you are on a particular team to have a chance to get points on the special teams. Our long snapper came within four points of winning the award this year. Our left guard was in the top three for the special team award. So we have team points that we give out for punt and extra point as well as individual points. If you do not do this the skilled players will run away with the award.

GVSU Point Production Chart

TEAM POINTS – (10)

- Score
- Block a punt
- Block a kick
- Recover an onside kick
- Successful fake

TEAM POINTS (3)

- Stop a fake
- Down a punt inside 10-yard line
- Punt operation
- Field goal/PAT operation

												PLAYER			
												+10	SCORE	TEAM POINTS	SPECIAL TEAMS PRODUCTION
												+10	BLOCK A PUNT		
												+10	BLOCK A KICK		
												+10	RECOVER ONSIDE KICK		
												+10	SUCCESSFUL FAKE		
												+3	STOP A FAKE		
												+3	DOWNED PUNT INSIDE 10		
												+5	PUNT OPERATION		
												+3	FG/PAT OPERATION		
												+2	KOR OF 30+		
												+2	PUNT RETURN OF 10+		
												+10	CAUSE A TURNOVER	TEAM	TEAM
												+10	RECOVER A TURNOVER		
												+10	60 YRD FIELD POSITION CHANGE		
												+5	GAME WINNING FG		
												+5	INVOLVED IN 15 OR MORE PLAYS		INDIVIDUAL POINTS
												+3	DE-CLEATER		
												+3	TACKLE		
												+3	KEY BLOCK ON RETURN		
												+3	EXCEPTIONAL EFFORT		
												+3	4.0 HANG TIME ON KO OR TOUCHBACK		
												+3	4.5 HANG TIME ON PUNT OR 40 YD NET W/ FAIR CATCH		
												+2	ASSISTED TACKLE		
												+1	DOING JOB EVERY PLAY ON A SPECIFIC TEAM		
												+1	VICTORY AWARD		
												-5	PENALTY		
												-5	MISSED ASSIGNMENT		
													TOTAL POINTS		
												PLAYER			

Diagram 2. GVSU point production chart

TEAM POINTS (2)

- Kickoff return of plus 30 yards

- Punt return of plus 10 yards

INDIVIDUAL POINTS (10)

- Cause a turnover

- Recover a turnover

- 60-yard field position change

INDIVIDUAL POINTS (5)

- Game winning field goal

- Involved in 15 or more plays

INDIVIDUAL POINTS (3)

- De-cleater

- Tackle

- Key block on return

- Exceptional effort

- 4.0 hang time on kickoff or touchback

- 4.5 hand time on punt or 40-yards net with fair catch

INDIVIDUAL POINTS (2)

- Assisted tackle

INDIVIDUAL POINT (1)

- Doing your job on every play on a special team

- Victory award

The coach who is responsible for that particular team grades the film. There is some flexibility in the system and we do have minus points. If you get a penalty you get minus 5 points. On any missed assignment you receive minus 5 points. The kids are going to see the chart on Sunday. That is the first thing we talk about in our team meeting.

We have the chart in our team room. You can see how we chart the players each week. On the left-hand side of the chart we have all of the players listed. We grade the film and give the players the points they earn in each area. On the left side of the chart are the team points and on the right side of the chart are the individual points. Also on the right outside of the chart we have the players' total points for the last game.

I think it is important to have this information displayed in the locker room so the kids can see how they are being graded on the special teams. We are trying to build some ownership in this team. This chart will help you build your case for special teams.

We have another chart where we keep a running total of all the games. Each week the kids can see where they rate on the chart. They can come into our meeting knowing they earned a certain number of points from the last game or knowing they lost a certain number of points. We think the chart is good because the kids can see where they stand game by game.

I want to talk about the *punting game* because that is the area I coach on special teams. We have been lucky. In 14 games over the last two years we have only punted 84 times. That comes out to about three punts per game. We have not punted the ball a whole lot in the several games. We practice the punt team because we know how important this team is to our special teams. I do not believe there is any other play, other than a touchdown, that garners more momentum than a blocked punt. When a team blocks a punt, it gives them the confidence they need to win the game.

There are so many moving parts to the punting game that it requires the attention to detail that we all look for as coaches. We have the *snap*, *kick*, *protection*, *catch*, and the *coverage*. I take the responsibility for the punting game because I do not want to put that responsibility on an assistant coach. As the head coach I am going to put that load on my shoulders.

We run the *spread punt*. The spread punt is the easiest of the punts to teach. I have enough going on as the head coach and that was easiest for me to teach. We break our spread punt down into the following *five S's of the punt*:

- Split

- Stance

- Set

- Strike

- Sprint

If you can get those five things down, I think you can build your base for putting in the punting game. Here is more detail about the five S's:

- *Split*

  o Linemen split six inches. The wing must reach and touch the hip of the tackle.

  o Personal protector lines up six-yards deep behind the guard.

  o Gunners are 14 yards on the line of scrimmage (check with side or line judge).

- *Stance*

  o Linemen are lined up with their inside foot up. The heel-to-toe alignment is used. Their feet are shoulder-width apart. Their hands are on their thighs. We want them in a comfortable stance.

- *Set*

  o *Zone or man set* — it is a principle of taking three steps (*IOI* — inside, outside, inside) that keeps uniformity to the wall as well as possibly maintaining a consistent six-inch split relationship.

- *Strike*

  o When the enemy is in the strike zone don't overextend.

  o Strike the *hot zone* (torso of the body) with the hands (hot - hands on torso).

- *Sprint*

  o Center and gunners — go to the ball.

  o Slots — have containment.

  o Guards and tackles — stay in lanes keeping the ball on their inside shoulder.

  o Personal protector and punter are safeties. The personal protector goes to the ballside and the punter goes to the opposite side.

Our punter lines up 15-yards deep. You must have a snapper that can get the ball back to him. If we can get the snap and kick away in 1.9 seconds, I feel very good. If the kick is away in 2.0, we have done our job. We break that down on the snap at .8 and 1.1 for the kicker. It is difficult to block the kick if you can get the ball away in 2.0 seconds.

Let me give you the two rules for the center on our spread punt:

- The center blocks away from the punter or to the right or left call.

- If a man calls (3-3) he can release.

The personal protector is expected to count the defenders. He counts from our left to the right. He must declare which way he wants the center to block. Here are the rules for the personal protector on our spread punt:

- The personal protector is responsible for the overload player. The personal protector will always go away from the center on a 44 call.

- A *three* count is an automatic man.

- Only count those players whose feet are on the line of scrimmage with linemen or in a threatening position.

- The personal protector reads left to right.

- The personal protector scans if there is no man to pick up.

- The center is always counted.

The magic number is *eight men in the box*. You see all combinations of eight. We see the 4-4, 5-3, 3-5, and 6-2 look. This is an example of the call 44 [Diagram 3]. The personal protector calls out "44-44 left - left." We know eight is the number of possible rushers I the box. The number 44 is 4 rushers to the right and 4 to the left side. Left is the direction the center is to block on the play.

The center snaps the ball and then steps back to get big or wide to keep a seam from forming. Everyone still takes their zone steps and *IOI* to help the player to his inside. For example, the guards help the center, the tackles help the guards, and the slot helps the tackles. Once the wall is formed and secure, then you drive out on your primary defender. The left slot has the number one, left tackle has number two, the left guard has number three, and the center has number four to the left. The right guard has number three, the right tackle has number two, and the right slot has the number one man. The personal protector has the fourth man to the right side.

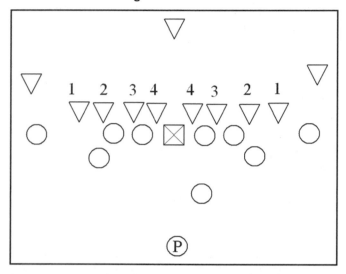

Diagram 3. Eight-man combinations (4-4, 5-3, 3-5, 6-2 possible fake)

If we call *three* it is automatic man blocking. If you are in a 33 protection you can release the center. You have them outnumbered. You are able to block them man-on-man but you never change your steps. It may be conceived as man protection, but you still take the zone steps. If the defense is running a three-man rush on one side, then they are going to try to run some type of game on the overloaded side. If we get a three-man, we communicate it from the guard outside to the tackle and to the slot back. When our blockers hear *three* they yell *twist alert*. Diagram 4 is an example of the *5-3 look*.

Again, *eight* is the call. It is *53-53-Left-Left*. We have five defenders to our left side. We have three defenders to the right side. Left tells the center to block to the left. The center snaps the ball then steps back to get width that keeps a seam from forming. Everybody still takes a zone step (IOI) to help the player to the inside. Once the wall is formed and secure, the blockers drive out on their primary defender. The left slot has number one. The left tackle has number two. The left guard has number three. The center will always have number five in an

overload situation. The personal protector has number four to the left. We only count the players who have their feet on the line of scrimmage. We do not count stacked outside linebackers.

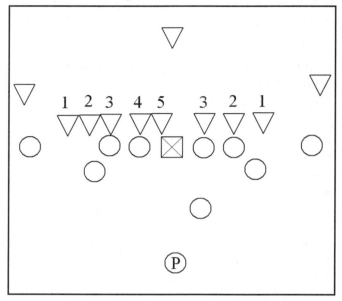

Diagram 4. 5-3 look

This is where zone and man protection come together. I have made it clear in our special teams meeting if you are on the punt team you had better get your three steps down. You handle yourself relative to the zone element. You must zone the area and stay square. You must use good three-step mechanics. Now, from there everyone is working together. If two defenders come at the blocker he is going to help inside with his hands before he works out to his primary man. The three steps help take the pressure off the man inside. After we take the three steps, then we set up to take on the primary rusher.

Most of the blockers tend to rush the block. Most of the time they want to go get their man. If they do that they leave the inside man on an island. If the slot man goes out after the number four man outside, he leaves the tackle on his own against the number three man. If the number four man comes inside, the tackle has to take on both number four and number three rushers. The tackle cannot let number three go because he has to help out inside. I try to overemphasize the zone steps before we talk about the man steps. If you talk about the man steps they'll want to one-step set and jump their man. It goes against the principles of the three-step set and keeping the shoulders square.

In any of the film I can tell the players their mistakes. "You did not get the third step down and you did not keep your shoulders square." I say this more than anything else. If they turn the shoulders they open up the voids. If they stay square and build the wall and then recognize their man they will have the protection concerns covered.

If a team puts six men on one side of the center and only two men on the other side, that is an *alert situation* for us. If we are ahead 60-0, we will bring a man over to block on the strongside after the snap. If we are not ahead 60-0, we will run the fake punt to the two-man side. We do not want to run the score up on anyone. If we do get the sixth man on one side we call *alert: Fan left – Fan left*. We fan the guard to the left side to pick up the sixth rusher.

Now let me review the coaching points and our concerns on the punt. Another situation we need to cover is when we have less than 15 yards to operate in for the punter. In the spread punt you are working off *geometry angles*. You do not have a block point from the outside because of the set you are in. In theory the punter is supposed to catch the snap and step and strike the ball at nine yards. If we take our three steps, they cannot block the punt at that block point. The rusher cannot bend it inside enough to get the block point at nine yards. If you change the distance, the punter is kicking the ball from a point farther back that allows a potentially straight-line block point. It is less than it would be if the punter was 15-yards deep.

The way we handle the punt when we are backed up on our goal line is with our *gunners*. We will bring our gunners inside to help block. We want to widen the angle out. We will call the gunners inside. They are still responsible to getting head-up on the football. We tell them to make sure they release through their man. That is all they need to do. If they will release through their man the defenders will not have enough time to get to the block point. So we bring the gunners inside if we have less than 15 yards for the punter to line up from the ball. That is how we adjust on the punt when we are backed up on our goal line.

Let me talk about the *center*. The center must block, but first he must snap the ball. This protection will not work unless we get a good snap by the center. I spend a lot of time working with the center, personal protector, and punter in discussing snap location. If we face a 53 look our steps for the punter will change a little. He will work slightly to his right with his first step. If the center pulls the snap a little to the punter's right, it is okay because we want him stepping in that direction. It is not a slide step. It is a directional step. We want the center to know where the overload is so he can make the proper snap. We get that done in drill work. We have our center snap until he hits the goalpost 25 times. We put him out by the goalpost after practice and have him work on the snaps. He snaps at the goalpost until he hits it 25 times. You can put a manager with them to help retrieve the balls. We want the center banging the post on the snaps. We realize this is a tight location but at least he has something he can aim at on the snap.

If you could pick out one thing that I could give you in regards to the long snappers, it would be this: *if they would keep their rear end down and keep the bend in their knees, they will be able to snap the ball on a good line*. This is what I work on more than anything else. If they can keep their back flat and keep the bend in their knees, they have a great chance to get the snap back successful. If their rear end is up high, I can tell them where the ball is going to go.

It is obvious that we all want *two-step punters*. Generally we get two-plus-step punters. The first step is what we call a zero step. That first step is difficult for a lot of young punters. It is hard for them to catch the ball and to take that step to get momentum at the same time. That is why I call it a zero step because most of the punters catch the ball and jab the step. So we talk about *no zero step*. If we can get this, we are going to have a chance to get the ball off in a good time.

Here is the problem I see in punting. Generally our punters are not scholarship players. They are not real gifted athletes. Most of the punters will start with their hands extended but they always want to bring their arms back inside. They either break their hands down and bring them inside and look at the ball and then bring them back up, or they let the ball come back into their body.

If the ball doesn't hit their hands like a receiver catching a pass with hands like shock absorbers, you are going to have a punter that takes that zero step. If you cannot get him to catch the ball and let his hands act as shock absorbers, he will take that extra step. If he does take that extra step, he is going to deliver the ball later than what you want.

You can get the punters out to kick and some of them have read the book. They look like a million bucks. They will have their arms locked out to receive the punt. You have to teach them to extend their hands so they can catch the ball and use their arms as shock absorbers. If the punter has to bring the ball inside, he is going to change the position of his feet. For most of the details on punting you need to send the punters to camp. But in terms of what you can work on, fielding the ball is one area you can help him with. Teach him to relax his hands just like the receivers do. Have him play pitch and catch with the receivers. Teach him to field the ball and to use the arms and hands as shock absorbers. If you can do that you are doing him a service to eliminate that extra step.

I want to leave you with some things you should keep your eyes on. The following are *six coaching points of concern* when punting:

- The most vulnerable area is between the wing and tackle. In 98 percent of the situations, the tackle is not sinking deep enough or quick enough.

- Drifting by linemen — they need to keep straight vertical set.

- Turning shoulders — they must keep their shoulders parallel to the line of scrimmage.

- If two defenders are on a gunner, he must watch for the inside man to become a screamer off the edge.

- Never follow a twister. We want to take a step back and look for another defender to come into the area.

- On any movement such as stemming by the defense, the personal protector will give a *right* or *left* call to communicate to the center and any possible overload.

If the defense lines up in a 44 and then shifts after we call the set, we just check the move and call *right* or *left*. We are telling the center the direction we want him to block. The communication is important when you have movement. If we are getting a lot of stemming or movement, we have a *red* call that sets our blocking. We get on the ball and everyone gets set. There is no verbal communication by the personal protector. The center snaps the ball right away and we block 44 protection. We just zone everything on the snap. We do not want to get into an *analysis paralysis*. If there is a lot of movement, we call red from the sideline. We run our punt team on the field and snap it on a quick count without any communication. We zone block and punt the football. This takes away the stemming and movement.

I would encourage you to build in an *award system* for your special teams. We call our punt team the *Bomb Squad.* We give them t-shirts with *Bomb Squad* on them. We like to build team pride. The other squads have their names for their teams. I think it is important to give an award to the player who accumulates the most points for the special team player of the year. The more gadgets you can put on the trophy the better. The players really want to win that trophy.

We feel it is important to post all of the grades on the charts. If you want special teams to take a special emphasize within your program, don't just give it lip service. I think goals and production charts will help make special teams *special.*

It is important for the players to understand the *hidden yardage.* If you can get that across to the players they will be able to understand how special teams win football games. This is especially true when the talent level is equal. When the talent level is equal, the hidden yardage is going to show itself in the games. The teams that understand this are the teams that win the close games.

Thank you for your patience. If you want to visit us at Grand Valley State, please give us a call. Thank you very much.

OFFENSIVE LINE TECHNIQUES AND DRILLS

University of South Carolina

On behalf of Coach Lou Holtz and the University of South Carolina, it is a pleasure to be here. I was a high school coach for 12 years in Florida and South Georgia. I like to talk X's and O's and learn more about that part of the game, but I believe *drill work* is where you improve your team. What I want to do today is talk about our techniques and drill work. I'm going to explain why we do the drills and what we are trying to accomplish from them. The drills have to relate to what you do offensively so they carry over to what you want to accomplish on the field.

I want to start out by talking a little about our *offensive line philosophy*. I was a high school coach and teacher for 12 years. Coaching and teaching are the same things. It doesn't matter if you are coaching on the NFL, college, high school, or junior high levels, coaching is teaching.

Coaching is all about what you are able to convey to your players and what they are able to handle. Coaching is not about telling players how to play; it is teaching them how to play. It is not what you know that counts; it is what they know. You have to get your players to do what you want them to do to improve.

When you have a meeting with your players, make sure you are organized in that meeting. If you are organized in your meetings, it will save lots of misdirection and wasted time. That thought really carries over to the practice field because being organized on the practice field is essential. If you are organized on the practice field you can avoid distractions and get more out of your players. That lets you work on work ethics and tempo on the practice field.

Coaching the small things will lead to player improvements. You have to be big on details. When I teach the first step to a lineman, you don't tell them the step is about six inches. The step is between four and six inches. Be specific on details when you teach

a skill or drill. If the eyes are supposed to be focused on the breastplate, make sure that is where the eyes are focused. Let them know that is important. Tell them exactly how much width you want between their hands.

Be demanding when you are coaching your players. Your players will respond to you if you ask them to do something. You don't have to berate them, they will respond to you if you demand that they do things a certain way. If you expect excellence from them, then they will give you excellence. Be demanding of your players on the field and in your meeting room.

We have instilled *accountability* into our players. As an offensive line coach, you have to teach accountability to the offensive linemen. If the ball is intercepted the offensive line should feel it is their fault. The quarterback didn't get to finish his read because of the pressure that was put upon him. He got hit as he was delivering the ball. He threw quickly because he had been knocked down three plays in a row.

The players have to understand their play is an *accumulative* thing. They are part of a unit. How the unit does depends on their individual efforts. They do not succeed as individuals. They succeed when their group does the job. This is a huge thing with the offensive line. They don't get a lot of recognition for the job they do until someone makes a mistake. When you succeed as an offensive line, it gives you and your group a good feeling. But when you fail as an offensive line, you have to be accountable.

The offensive line is the most important group of players on the field. The team wins or loses depending on how the offensive line plays. They are the biggest people on the field. They are the largest segment of players on the field. If you can get your five offensive linemen thinking the same way and winning together, that will spread throughout your entire team. They are the biggest bodies on the team and have the best work ethics. That in itself lends to building leadership within that group and on the team.

Players have to learn to accept *corrective criticism*. But the coach has to understand it is not what he says that is important, it is the way he says it. They have to know the coach cares about them getting better. Coaches need to correct the mistake, not belittle the players in doing it.

We tell our players this all the time: *Players play and the coaches coach*. Since they are the players, they are the ones who have to be coached and you have to coach him. Make sure everyone knows their role. When you are doing your corrective criticism, stay as positive as you can. When an offensive lineman gets beat on a pass-rush block, don't jump down his throat. Tell him, "You did a good job on your pass set and a great job on the first step. However, you need to work on your punch, staying square, and keeping that guy off the quarterback."

Stay positive whenever possible and praise him when he does something well. Outstanding play in the offensive line is all about the coach convincing the players that he cares about the lineman's improvement. Make sure your players understand that and you will have a lot more success teaching them.

When you are coaching your players, you must be honest with them. Don't tell them they are doing a good job when they are not. If they screw up give them something that will help them get better. Sometimes you have to bite your tongue and not say anything when your linemen screw up. He may be the best lineman you have. You just keep your mouth shut and go to the next play.

The offensive line coach has to have a passion for coaching. I really enjoy coming to work every day. I enjoy being in meetings with my players, being with them on the field, and being in the locker room with them. I have a passion for coaching and teaching. That can carry over to your players. If you have a good attitude about coming to work, your players will pick that up.

I'm going to talk about some fundamentals before I get into our drills. The first basic fundamental to an offensive lineman is the *stance*. We teach a *three-point stance* and a *two-point stance*. The center has to make some adjustments to his stance to perform certain skills. The stance needs to be adjusted to the system being coached.

If your team is a wishbone team, the offensive linemen don't need to be in a two- or three-point stance. They need to be in a four-point stance with a lot of weight forward. All they want to do is come off the ball hard and move straight ahead.

At South Carolina we are a one-back team and we are going to throw the ball about 50 percent of the time. In this system we need to be in a three-point stance as our run stance. In our situation we use the three-point stance for run blocking as well as pass blocking.

In second- and third-down situations where we have long yardage, we are going to screen, draw, and throw the ball down the field. In these situations our linemen may be in a two-point stance.

I know you have heard this before, but it is the truth. Every spring and fall when we start practice, we go back to our stance and make sure we do all the little things right.

We start with a *shoulder-width foot placement*. That seems to be the best position for the body to have balance and be able to move. If a player's girth is bigger, he may have to be slightly wider. We are in a right-handed stance on the right side of the ball and a left-handed stance on the left side of the ball. There are two reasons we do that. We do not flip-flop our line and it is easier to pass block with the outside foot back. The stagger in the stance is slight. I like to have a toe-to-instep relationship with the feet.

When the linemen start to go down in their stance, I tell them to put their forearms on their thighs and bend their knees. When they put their forearms on their thighs, I want their knees over their toes and their toes straight down the field. A lot of people teach the stance with the toes slightly outside. That makes the linemen get into a knock-kneed stance. You can teach it that way if you want because it is sound, however we don't teach it that way at South Carolina.

The thing we are checking as they go down is the *knee-over-the-toes relationship*. We don't want their knees outside or inside their toes. If their knees go outside it is usually because their feet are too close together. If their knees are inside too much, their feet are too far back or too wide. That is what we mean by teaching the details.

If they are in a right-handed stance, we tell them to drop their right hand down to the ground right below their right eye socket. They are in a *fingertip stance*. I never want more than 20 percent of their weight on their hand. If you ask the player to pick up his hand, he should tilt forward slightly but not very fast. The natural thing they want to do is get weight on their hands so they can come off the ball. The off hand in the three-point stance rests against the outside of the left thigh and knee. We don't cross it over our thigh.

The problem with the weight on the hand is coming out of the stance. In the stance I want the lineman to have all the cleats on his up foot in the ground. On the back foot I want all his cleats in the ground with the exception of his heel. If the weight is forward, the first step has to be a big step. In order to take short steps, you can't have too much weight on the hand. Defensive linemen are taught to look for tips from the offensive linemen in their stance. Our defensive linemen call them out when they see a heavy stance or light stance. We work hard on trying to keep 80 percent of our weight on our feet.

You have to work hard on those numbers with some of your lineman. They don't understand what 20 percent of their weight feels like. After we show them film work of themselves, they begin to understand what we are looking for. We have to really give them guidance in those areas.

We want our linemen in their stance to have a *flat back*. We don't want their tails too high or low. The center gets his tail down a little while he is calling our line blocking, but he always comes back to flat before he snaps the ball.

The head in the stance is *up*. We don't want it up so far that there is a bow in the neck. All they need to see is the defensive linemen and the bottom half of the linebackers.

The two-point stance has the same fundamentals as the three-point stance. On the stagger, we allow the tackle to drop his outside foot back a little more in his stagger. We want his back up straight with his chest out. We want his head and shoulders back. I want their hands up in a ready position and actually touching the numbers on their jersey.

The point of concentration in the two-point stance is the *bend in the thigh*. What we like is to have their thighs parallel with the ground. If they don't bend their knees, their stance is too high and their legs are too straight. That good knee bend allows them to come off the ball in a two-point stance and run block.

In the two-point stance, we don't normally put more weight on one foot than the other. We want a *balanced stance*. There are times when we mentally shift the weight on to one foot, but we don't want to tilt and tip the movement.

The guard could be in a three-point stance all the time. The tackle is the one who can take advantage of the two-point stance. He is the one who is being threatened by the rush of a defensive end coming off the edge with speed. He has to kick back quickly and get depth straight back off the line to change the angle of the speed rusher. Obviously if he is already up in his stance, it helps him retreat quicker. The guard does not face that hard speed rusher.

We are a big shotgun team. In his stance, the center will not have any weight on the ball. We do not want him to stagger his feet. We want his hips square so that the shotgun snap comes back straight. We want the tail of the center flat. If he gets his butt up, that causes him to snap the ball high. If his butt is down and flat, the ball will come out low and flat. I want the center to get the ball as far out in front of him as he can. I want him to be able to make a good snap, but I want the defensive front as far away from the offensive line as I can get them.

When the quarterback is under the center and taking a direct snap, it takes thousands of reps to get the snap down. The center, as he snaps the ball, is stepping into his block. The quarterback has to ride the center until he secures the ball. *The center has to put the ball in the same place every time.* He cannot put the ball to the side one time and down the middle the next. The center grips the ball with his thumb on the laces. We don't want the center to think about rotating the ball to give it to the quarterback. We tell him to snap it as fast and hard as he can. The natural rotation of his arm will put the laces of the ball right in the quarterback's hand.

We do the same with the *shotgun snap*. That way the center does not have to readjust the ball regardless of the quarterback being in the shotgun or under the center. The shotgun snap is nothing more than the pendulum swing with the arm without breaking the wrist. This has to be done with thousands of repetitions. An important thing about the shotgun snap is the center and quarterback being aligned properly. The center's stance has to be straight and square and the quarterback has to be directly behind the center.

I try to draw a line from the laces of the ball to the quarterback's belt. We have the center swing the ball down that line and away we go. The ball should come off the center's fingers and spiral just like a pass. He is really throwing a pass, but I don't want the center to think about throwing the ball. I want him to think about swinging the ball down the line. The ball should be in the same place every time. We want pace on the ball. We don't want the ball floating back to the quarterback. It has to come back with some speed to accomplish the purpose of being in the shotgun.

If there is a mistake made in the shotgun snap, I want it low not high. The thing the center has to be careful of is not to raise his hips before he lets the ball go. If he raises his hips and straightens his legs, the ball will go in orbit. If he flips his wrist it will go high. When you practice the snaps make the center step right and left as he is making the snap. Make sure the arm is not going right or left as the centers steps in that direction. That fact that he has to block someone helps keep his hips down. *The snap is critical in the passing and running game.* If the snap is low or high, it destroys the timing of the run and the pass.

One of the basic fundamentals in offensive line play is *alignment*. To be legally aligned on the line of scrimmage, the offensive guard's helmet must break the belt line of the offensive center. We align with our helmet between the bottom of the center's numbers and his belt line. In the two-point stance, since the lineman is upright, his feet have to be closer to the line of scrimmage. The tackle lines up on the center and not the guard.

We are as far off the football as we can legally get because we run the zone scheme and throw the ball quite a bit. We may cheat back further in some situations, but we never want to get a penalty for not being on the line of scrimmage.

We move up on the ball in certain situations. If we have a certain pass protection we move up on the ball. In some cases we want to cut down on the movement by the defensive line, so we move up on the ball to decrease the distance between the offensive line and the defenders. Getting closer to the ball helps the offensive line in preventing the defense from cross facing on blocks. In a short-yardage or goal line situations, we move up on the ball to cut down on penetration. We adjust the depth of our offensive linemen depending on the situation.

We get off the ball so that we can get our first step on the ground and the second step on the way to the ground before we make contact with the defender. If the defender hits the offensive linemen before he gets his first step in the ground, the offensive lineman loses power.

Our splits between our linemen are two feet. We measure two feet from the outside leg of the guard to the inside leg of the tackle. The split rule comes from trial and error. We found the two-foot split fits what we are doing in our offensive system best.

We adjust our splits slightly if we are in certain situations. If are trying to cut down on penetration, we tighten our splits. If we are going to run outside, we tighten down on the splits. If we are going to run inside, we may widen the split slightly. The split between the tight end and the offensive tackle is two-and-a-half to three feet.

Your splits have to fit your offensive plan. We adjust the splits to the play we are running and to the talent level of our offensive line. There are certain situations that require us to adjust our splits. Make sure you consider all the factors and do what is right for your individual situation.

There some basic fundamentals that must go with *run blocking*. The first thing you have to concentrate on is the first step. The quicker the offensive lineman can get his foot in the ground, the better off he is. We never want to be caught with both feet out of the ground. We never want to hop in anything we do. If the lineman steps underneath himself, he is defeated from the get-go. In the stance, I want all the cleats on the lineman's shoes *in the ground.* Every step the lineman takes he wants to have all his cleats in the ground. We never want to be on our toes. We want the weight on the balls of our feet.

When the lineman gets in a stance, he creates power angles in his ankles, knees, and hips. It is important to release all that power at the proper time. If you release the angles too early, you will be fully extended before the contact is made. We want to *release the power* through the surface of the block, not at the surface of the block. If we get fully extended at the surface of the contact and through the surface, we have maximized the power that has been created in those power angles.

As the lineman comes off the ball using short steps, he wants to keep his feet at shoulder width. If a lineman takes a step underneath his body, his feet are too close together. When that happens he loses his balance and control of the block. We want to *drive with each step* the lineman takes. When the first step is in the ground, the lineman drives out with his second step. When that step is in the ground, he drives out with the next step and continues to repeat the movement. If we can get the defender back on his heels, we have a chance to move him the way we want him to go.

It is important to keep your head up and your tail down. The body will go where the head goes. If the head is down, the body is going to go down. If the head goes down, the tail comes up and the only thing the lineman can do is to fall to the ground.

As the lineman punches out with his hands, he wants to make sure he gets his hands *inside the defender's hands.* The man that gets his hands inside usually wins the battle. If the offensive lineman has his hands inside the defender's, he can lift the defender's shoulder back and up. We want to shoot the hands under and inside the defender's hands with our thumbs up. Every defensive coach is going to coach his players to get their hands inside also. To get their hands inside, the offensive linemen have to work extremely hard at it.

When the powers angles are released, the linemen wants to hit on the rise, lift with his hands,

and roll his hips. We don't want his shoulders and chest behind his hips. We want a full extension of the hips when the blow is delivered. Once the offensive linemen get the defender playing back, he wants to climb up the defender and keep him high.

We want to play behind our pads and hit the *proper landmarks* with our face and hands simultaneously. We have four landmarks that we talk about and teach in our technique drills. The first landmark is right down the *middle of the defender.* The hands are shot underneath and up into the sternum. Make sure the linemen strike with the facemask and never with the top of the helmet.

The second landmark is the *breastplate.* The breastplate is located in the pectoral areas. I want to give my players a landmark they can see with their eyes. I want to try to hook the pads and gain control with my hands.

We use the *armpit* as a landmark. The armpit is wider than the breastplate. I want one hand on the sternum and the other on the shoulder. You don't have to coach those positions, because it is a natural movement with the hands.

The last landmark is the *outside shoulder.* That is the landmark we use for a wide-reach block. The linemen have to keep their eyes open and focus on the landmark. When the landmark starts to move, the offensive linemen will move with the landmark if they keep focused on it. It is important to see the landmark the entire way through the block.

To block anyone, the linemen must *maintain* his base and a good football position. At some point during the block, the offensive lineman and defender will reach a stalemate. However, the defender has to get away from the offensive lineman if he is to win the battle. If there is a stalemate, the offense wins. The defender has to disengage to get to the ball. That is what the offensive lineman is waiting for. When the defender tries to get separation, the offensive lineman accelerates his feet and finishes the block.

When the offensive lineman feels the release of pressure from the defender as he attempts to get off the block, he comes alive and drives with his feet as hard as he can to bury the defender. The offensive lineman uses the movement created by the attempt to release from the block to drive and gain ground with the defender. The defender may make the tackle, but it will not be a form tackle. As long as the offensive blocker stays on his landmark, the defender has to deal with the blocker.

When we teach our *pass-blocking techniques*, the first thing we cover is the *set position*. The set position is a football position. We want the hands up and the head and shoulders back. We want the elbows turned in and the thumbs up. We want a good balanced base with the feet staggered with the outside foot back. The guard's stagger is not a big as the tackles. The guard faces a different charge than the tackle and doesn't need as big of stagger. He doesn't have to get wide in his pass protection. The guard and center's job is more of a power step both ways. The tackle has to be able to kick back and stay inside-out on a defender. The most important thing for an offensive lineman to have is flexibility in his knees and ankles. If he has that quality, then he has a chance to be a pretty good athlete.

If the tackle has a man on his outside, he has to force from the inside-out. He has to kick back with his outside foot and slide with his inside foot. He does two *kick-slide movements* and can give a little ground after the kick slides. The weight has to be on his inside foot. He never wants to have his feet very far off the ground. The inside foot is always going to be on the ground.

The kick by the tackle depends on the width and speed of the pass rusher. If the defender is extremely wide or fast, the kick-slide is deeper and faster. Conversely, the tighter the rusher is the less depth the tackle has to get. The rule is the farther away the lineman's pass blocking responsibility, the deeper and faster he sets.

We never want to hop in football. If the defender changes direction, and the offensive lineman has both feet off the ground, he has to come down before he can change direction. If he has his weight on his inside foot and is sliding, he simply steps off on his inside foot and seals the move of the pass rusher.

The other step is the *power step*. That is an inside move by the pass rusher. The power step is a short, quick step inside parallel to the line of scrimmage. After the inside step the lineman is sliding. The center

and guards get the power rush inside and outside. They block it with the same technique. If for some reason the center or guard is getting a wide rush, they can use the kick-slide method

In the passing game, the offensive line has to *maintain the pocket integrity*. The tackles are responsibility for the width of the pocket. They have to stop the speed rushers from the outside from collapsing the pocket. The center and guards are responsibility for the depth of the pocket. They have to stop the power rushers from pushing the pocket back into the quarterback's lap. That is their job to maintain a pocket for the quarterback to throw from.

Work your players in the set position. Have them set in that position for 15 seconds. Do it daily and increase the time each day until you have worked your way up to one minute. When you get to a minute, you will have some strong, confident legs in the set position. It is hard to hold that position for any length of time. That is why we have so many false starts unless they are trained to hold in that position for a long time.

The offensive lineman wants to mirror the defender and keep his eyes on the inside breastplate landmark. He needs to keep a knee-to-crotch relationship at all times.

When the offensive lineman is pass blocking, he has to keep his head out of the block and get his hands inside the defender's hands. If the offensive lineman tries to use his head to butt a defender, all he does is destroy his balance. He has to keep his head back to maintain his balance. He punches with his hands and presses the defender away from him. He tries to keep his hands on him if possible.

If you convey this next point to your offensive linemen the way I describe it, they will remember it. Quarterbacks are prima donnas, and like to have their picture in the papers. Linemen are grunts; they never get their picture in the papers. They are the ones taking the pictures. We tell our linemen in pass protection to imagine they have a camera inserted in their anal cavity. It is important they keep their camera pointed at the quarterback so they can take his picture. That is an important point. They have to keep their butts pointed at the quarterback, which means *staying square to the line of scrimmage*.

Drill your players on the defender's *rush moves*. The rips, bull rush, swim, and pull-and-grab are moves you have to work on. You have to teach counter to all those moves. The *punch-and-press* is one move to counter change of direction and spin moves. The punch-and-press technique is alternating hands on the defender. If you have both hands on the defender and he spins, you have nothing to stop him. We punch with one hand and press or ride the defender with the other hand.

There are some *variation blocks* that I want to cover briefly. There are two types of pulls that we use in the run game. The first type of pull is called *kick*. It is a trap-type pull. If the guard is going to trap a gap on the line of scrimmage, he pulls into the line. He rips his elbow and twists his hips and runs on an inside out path to kick out a defensive end or trap a 3 technique. On this pull if the defender runs out of the play, we don't chase him. We turn up in the hole and block the next thing that shows.

The second pull we use is called the *man-eye* pull. That is the type of pull you would use on a toss sweep. With that pull, the lineman takes a deep bucket step to get depth out of the line of scrimmage. The offensive lineman is looking for a linebacker to block. We call it a *man-eye* pull because he has to eyeball the linebacker and mirror his path. The hips are running toward the outside, but the shoulders and head are parallel with the line of scrimmage.

Linebackers are coached to pursue through gaps. The lineman has to watch the linebacker. If he drops his eyes to look for a gap to turn into, he will lose the linebacker. When the linebacker turns into the line of scrimmage, the lineman mirrors that move and goes into the hole to block him. If the guard pulls and the linebacker blitzes the gap on a delayed blitz, he stops his pull comes back to block the linebacker. The depth pull allows him to do that.

On the counter trey, the guard has a trap pull on the defensive end. The pulling tackle has a man-eye pull and is looking for the linebacker as he turns up. Anytime we are pulling to get to the second level, we treat that as a man-eye pull.

We are a *zone team*. On the inside zone, we are using the breastplate as the landmark. We are going to give some ground at the beginning of the play, but

we are working to get on our landmark. Once we get to the landmark we are not going to continue east and west. We are going to work north and south and get downfield.

If I have to use a wide-shoulder landmark, I may have to cross over to get to the point. But once I get to the landmark, I am going to work north and south. If the defender keeps going to the outside, I take him where he wants to go.

The *inside zone play* is a slow developing play. If the playside guard blocks the 3 technique to his side, his first step is over and up looking for the outside breastplate. He does not cross over on his second step. He is going for the breasts plate and drive blocks up the field. If the 3 technique widens, the guard stays on him and the ball breaks back inside of him.

On the *outside zone play*, the guard takes a lead step and a crossover step to get on the outside-shoulder landmark. After he gets to his landmark, he drives north and south.

If the guard is uncovered and the center has a shade on him, the guard is taking one step keying the shaded nose. If the nose does not cross the center's face by the time the guard takes his step, the guard is going north and south looking to cut off linebackers.

If we think there is a slant coming from an outside man, the offensive lineman is reading knees. If the knee comes toward the lineman, it is a inside slant. If the knee moves away, the slant is not coming.

In the isolation play, you want to seal the backside and expand the playside. If I am running a weakside isolation play against a reduced 3 technique and a 5 technique, I want to reach both those defenders. I increase my splits and go for the reach block. If the defenders widen, they expand the hole for the linebacker. If they come inside, you bounce the play to the outside.

Those are just some ideas that might help you with a running scheme. I'm running out of time quick, but I want to show you this drill tape.

Let me answer this last question and than we have to go to the film. There are two theories on pass protection and we use both of them. You start with *man-blocking rules* and make zone adjustments to them, or start with *zone-blocking rules* and make man adjustments to them.

Normally we go big-on-big, because we don't want to put the back on a defensive lineman. The depth of the quarterback's drop dictates the type of pass-protection scheme we use. If it is a three-step drop, we may cut at the line of scrimmage.

This first drill you see is called a *slingshot* [Diagram 1]. You can do this on a sled and get the same result. This drill is done in a rack with two heavy-duty, elastic tire inner tubes chained at the top of the rack and then stretched and chained to the bottom. The player starts in a six-point stance, which is a kneeing position. We fit him into a perfect blocking position. The player puts his head through the opening of the two tubes. On the snap, the lineman uncoils and extends into the inner tubes catching one tube on each shoulder. He sinks his hips and brings his hands up in the punch. The elastic stretch allows him to experience the feeling of the hip thrust. The apparatus recoils and springs him back to his starting position.

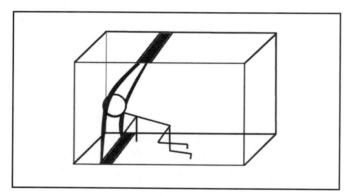

Diagram 1. Slingshot drill

The good thing about this apparatus is if you are not square when you hit the tubes, it will throw you off. It makes you hit it square and hold your balance. The continuation of the drill is to back them out of the fit position and let them hit the straps as if it were a sled. Back them off at a distance of two to three feet and let them attack.

The next drill is a *two-step drill*. The purpose of this drill is work on the short first step. I get the offensive linemen in a stance. I call, "One." I want the linemen to take a short first step, stay low, keep their balance, and freeze. I want them to freeze in their movement so they can see how big a step they took

and how high they have gotten. Next I call, "Two." They take the second step and stay low and freeze after that step.

After you do the freeze segment of the drill, you start to increase the interval by going fast in your count. It is a simple drill, but you pointing out the importance of the first and second steps in the blocking sequence is important. After you have gone several times increasing the step movements, let them go on their own without the commands.

The continuation of this drill is to puts dummies into the drill. You are still doing the one/two steps, but on the second step you are punching the dummy. In this drill we start out slow and speed up.

The next drill is called the *hit-position walk*. All we are doing is putting the linemen in a hitting position and making them walk. We want their legs bent and emphasize staying low. The purpose of this drill is to make the lineman keep their feet close to the ground. They are not stomping the ground; they are sliding their feet and keeping good contact with the ground.

The next drill is the same drill, except we add resistance to it. We have them pushing on another lineman to give them resistance. They have to maintain good foot movement, without getting their feet too far off the ground and maintaining a good base. They will find it is hard to keep their feet close to the ground while trying to push against something.

The next things you see are the *chute drills* we do. As you will see in the film, it is almost the two-step drill as far as foot movement goes. We are working on the hit position and taking short steps. We also use the boards in the chutes to keep their feet apart so they can maintain good balance.

We work with air first and then we put defenders in the drill. You can vary the resistance you use. It can go anywhere from passive resistance to live full speed. Those are the two basic tempos we use in this drill.

We do a *z drill* that works on the two basic steps in pass protection [Diagram 2]. They start out with a kick step to the left and a power step over to the right and repeat. After they work on the left side, they flip over to the other side and work on their right side.

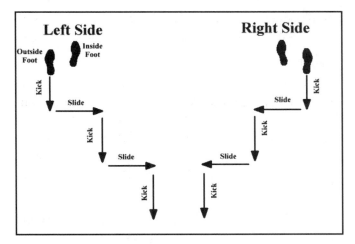

Diagram 2. Z drill

The next drill is the *mirror drill* [Diagram 3]. This is a two-man drill. There is one defender and one offensive lineman. The offensive lineman puts his hands behind his back, gets in a good pass-blocking set, and mirrors the defender. This is a non-contact drill. The offensive linemen is staying in front of the defender working on his foot movement, staying low, and keeping balanced.

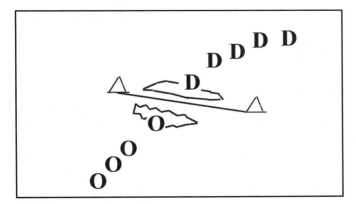

Diagram 3. Mirror drill

The companion drill is called *mirror dodge* [Diagram 4]. We line up two cones on a line five- to six-yards apart. The defender is on one side of the line and the offensive blocker is on the other. The defender moves up and down the line trying to fake the blocker and get across the line. The blocker is mirroring the movement of the defender. As the defender tries to cross the line, the offensive blocker uses a punch to prevent him from getting across the line. The blockers are trying to time the punch and keep their hands inside the defender's hands.

I talked about the *punch-and-press* technique in my lecture [Diagram 5]. This is the drill we use to work

on those skills. We have a five-yard square box with a defender and blocker at one end of it. The defender can use any part of the square he wants to rush the passer. The blocker has to counter the pass-rush techniques used by the defender. We work on everything from bull rush, swims, rips, and spins. The blocker uses the punch-and-press to keep the defender under control.

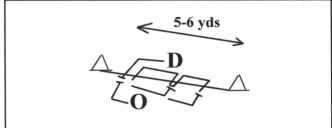

Diagram 4. Mirror-dodge drill

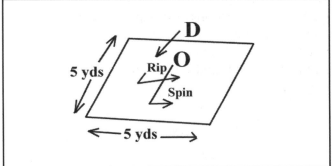

Diagram 5. Punch-and-press drill

The *hit-hit-hit drill* is a bull-in-the-ring type of drill [Diagram 6]. The offensive lineman is going to get three punches on targets coming at him from assorted angles. He has to stay alert and deliver a punch on each rusher. The coach stands behind the offensive blocker and points to a designated rusher who charges the offensive blocker. The offensive lineman punches and recoils back into his position waiting for the next rusher.

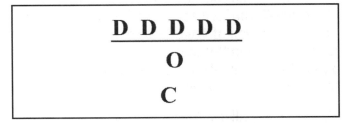

Diagram 6. Hit-hit-hit drill

I appreciate your attention. If we can do anything for you at the University of South Carolina, don't hesitate to call on us. Thank you.

GAME PLANNING AND RED ZONE OFFENSE

University of Oregon

Today I want to talk about game planning and our weekly preparation, along with the *red zone* offense. I know we all have been to a lot of clinics. I try to do what is best for me and I am sure you do what is best for you. Hopefully, I will be able to give you one idea that will help you in your program. If we can do that then our time will be well spent.

When we put together our game plan and our weekly practice plans, there are a couple of areas we must address. The first thing we talk about is being a *ball-security team*. We do not talk about fumbling the football, and we do not talk about throwing interceptions. We talk about ball security. We want our players to understand the responsibility of having the football in their hand. When they have the ball in their hands they represent the efforts of the other 10 players on the team.

We want them to know ball security is not limited to the individual carrying the football or catching the football. Ball security includes pass protection for us. It is securing the tract for the running game. Ball security is includes the pre snap by the quarterback in the passing game. We must take care of the football. I do not know a lot but I do know we cannot score if we do not have the football. We must take care of the football. In our practice plan we include ball-security drills each day.

We want to play physical football. On the film, you will see us running the power off-tackle play. It is a utility play good against fronts and any coverage. The play gives us an opportunity to establish our team as a hard- nose type team. By establishing that play as our personality play, it allows us to set the tempo for our offensive team and it sets the tempo for a great play-action game.

We want to eliminate mistakes and penalties. We want to be simple but have a multiple strategy. We want to give the defense as many different looks as we can while at the same time do the same basic things over and over. We want to give the defense a lot of different looks to prepare for and have to adjust to in a game.

We have a simple route in our offense that we call *gator* that is a smash corner. I think we have 39 variations on the play. We have different formations, different shifts, and motions, and the *over the bridge, through the woods, smash corner*. We want to find one thing we can hang our hat on. We feel it is a good play that will be good against multiple defenses and multiple pressures, plus the protection that is built into the play. We are going to find as many different ways as we can to give the defense different looks. When it is all said and done, the outside receiver is going to run the smash and the number two man inside runs a simple route.

We need to master *situational football*. When we break down the segments of the game we want to make sure our players know what to anticipate from the defense in all situations. We want to know what the defense anticipates from the press box in those situations. It is up to the players to make sure they are never surprised by what the defense throws at them in any given situation. It is my responsibility to make sure the players are never surprised by the play that I call in any situation. I have a great job description in my contract: "Don't break any NCAA rules and score points."

As we work on our game plan during the week, we must make sure everything we do will reflect on ball security, physical football, eliminating mistakes and penalties, simplicity and multiplicity, in all situations. When it is all said and done we must score points.

I want to talk about the following situations. I script openers. I script six runs and six pass plays. When I was at Fresno State we were a little more wide open. We threw the ball a little more because it fit our personnel. We would script eight passes and six runs for the games. We just adjusted the opening of the games because we wanted to throw the ball more.

I like to establish the sequence that the players know, and that I know. I want to give the defense as many different looks as possible with substitution groups and different formations, special plays, and looks on the field. We want an early, first quarter scouting report. We feel that is very important to the coaches as well as to the players.

In our game against Stanford this year we used six running plays and six passing plays in our first series. We try to work for balance in our offense. We go through a variety of personnel grouping. We give them a lot of different formations with motions and shifts. We tried to create explosiveness in the opening plays. We want to take a shot downfield.

We break down our running and passing game into different categories, such as first down, second down and medium, and second down and long. I work very closely with our offensive line coach. In the press box I work off the worksheet. I did not supply this information to the players. They knew these 12 plays were going to be run in the first quarter.

One misconception that people have about the opening plays is that we are not locked into these plays. It only gives me and it gives the players some guidelines. It works on first and second downs. When we get into third down we come off the script. Now we go to the third-down calls. We are not forced to running a dive play on third-and-long. Opening situations are for first and second downs.

We scored on 8 of the 13 opening drives this past year. I think we scored 6 touchdowns and two field goals. It was good for us and it helped us establish the tempo for the game.

Some teams have the first play to start a new series planned. We do not have our first-down play called in situations when we first go on the field. We break it down to second-and-seven. If we are in that situation, we have lost the first down. We want to win that first down. If we have second-and-seven, we have not gained four yards on the first-down play. A second-and-seven-plus to us is a second-and-long

situation. On our call sheet we have second-and-six. To me that is similar to a first-and-10 situation and I can call what I want to call. On second-and-one or two to go, there are two schools of thought. First, you can try to get the first down and move the chains. Second, you can take a shot to score the home run. Some people call this a wasted down. I do not like that term. I do not want to waste a down. My thought process was that I would much rather be in third-and-one than in second-and-10 to go. All of this can change with your personnel.

We talk about the *shot* mentality with the quarterback. There is nothing negative that can happen when you designate a play where you are going to take a *shot*. It is going to be a touchdown or it is going to be the next down. If it is a first down with 10 yards to go, it is either a touchdown or it is second-and-10 to go. If we design a play on Sunday night and the quarterback goes back to take a shot and the play is covered, he can throw the ball away. We can send out a two-man route on the shot. It is going to be a touchdown or it is going to be second down.

We break down the third-down situations into third-and-long, third-and-medium of five to seven yards, and third-and-short, which is one or two yards. On the goal line it starts on the plus three-yard line. I do not think there is anything unique in our approach. I just want to be sure our players are aware of what we are trying to prepare for.

We look at some contingency plans and some other items that need to be addressed. If we do not get to cover them on the practice field, we at least cover them in the meeting room, and especially with the quarterbacks. We want to know what the plan is if the defense turns the ball over. We want to get a first down after a sudden change. Then we want to take a shot coming right off the sideline. You need to have a plan and you need to make your quarterback aware of the plan.

We want to have a plan if there is four minutes left in the game and we are ahead by six points. We want the quarterback to know how we are going to *milk the clock*. We stress to the backs and receivers to stay inbounds. We do not want any fancy ball handling. We want to run straight at the opponents. We want to protect the edges and we want to throw the football on time.

Next we cover the *two-minute offense*. We must score in those two minutes before the half or at the end of the game. I am certain that more teams will lose a game in the *four-minute drill* than they will in the *two-minute drill*.

Our next situation is the *two-point play*. We go over all of those situations and let the quarterback know what we want to do here.

From here we talk about being *backed up*. To us being backed up is from the minus one-yard line to the minus nine-yard line. Each week we put the ball at the minus one-yard line and work on that situation. When we get into a backed-up mode, we have four areas of concern. First and foremost is *ball security*. We must take care of the football. Second, we want to get the ball *out to the minus five-yard line*. That will give 15 yards for our punt team to execute. Next, our concern is to *get a first down*. Now we feel we are rolling. Our fourth concern is to *get a touchdown*.

Every Thursday we place the ball on the minus one-yard line and I step into the offensive huddle. I repeat to them: *"Ball security, five-yard line, first down, touchdown."* As we get into the season the players will start chanting the four concerns back to me. That is a good thing because it means they are speaking the same language you are. They know what is expected of them and they know what is coming from me.

Our next point on sudden change includes *the last three plays and desperate plays*. We are trying to get a minimum of 25 yards per chunk. It may be at the end of the half or end of the game.

The last phase is our *overtime plan*. What do we want to do if we go into overtime is very important. We want to have a plan so it will not be just a guessing game. Those are the areas of the game that we want to address with the team and the quarterback.

How we address the situations in practice is very simple. On Tuesday we are going to run our base offense. We are going to run our core plays. It is a physical practice. It is a workday and it is the longest practice of the week. It is the most physical practice of the week. We look at live 9-on-7 and our inside zone drill. We install all our shifts and motions for the week. We start working on our play-action passing game. It is a hard physical practice.

On Wednesday we get into the *red zone offense*. Instead of working on our inside zone play live, we work on our passing game under pressure. We go against our defense and we are picking up the blitzes. We are checking our pass-protection rules against any look they want to show us.

When we split up and go against our scout team, we look at our opponent's specific blitzes. We work on our passing game under pressure. Again, the Wednesday practice is as tough as we can make it. We do not make plays up to give them. We show them what the opponents have show at this point in the season. It may not be what they do most of the time, but we have to be prepared for what they can do on defense. If they bring four men on the weakside and we do not have a player to block him, what are we going to do? We must know how to pick that fourth man up on the weakside and we have to be prepared to handle that situation. We must use our hot routes and sights routes. We must be sure the quarterback sees the fourth man to the weakside. We make the Tuesday and Wednesday practice as physically challenging as possible.

When we work on the red zone offense preparation, we get into the goal line and short-yardage situations. The goal line offense for us is from the three-yard line in to the goal line. Short yardage is third-and-one and third-and-two.

On Thursday we work on all of the third-down situations. We rehearse the opening plays. It is also a review where we go back and touch on certain situations that need to be tuned up.

In getting into the red zone offense, we try to get as much done as we can in one day. What is the number of goal line days you need to carry? It will depend on how many defensive fronts the opponents are showing. We like to carry three goal line running plays and three goal line pass plays. If the defense is multiple in their goal line approach, we may say that we are going to run a certain pass or run one way. This reduces our practice sets and we can get better at that play. If we practice six plays to each side that gives us 12 plays. We just say we are going to run two of these plays to the right and these two to the left side. That leaves us two plays that we can run to both sides. That allows us to be very specific in our preparation. Again, on Thursday we do come back and review the goal line plays.

One thing we do every day is our *pat-and-go drill*. Most teams run the drill but we coach the heck out of the drill. The reason I like this drill is because it shows up in every football game. If you throw the fade or go route, you will see the drill in every game. It is a simple drill where we throw fade routes to wide receivers and tight ends. Some teams use their running backs in the drill, but we do not. We want the receivers to get used to catching the ball over their outside shoulder.

Here is how we set the drill up [Diagram 1]. We put the wide receiver coach on one end, and we put the tight end on the other end of the drill. I work in the middle of the drill working the entire drill. We have a couple of coaching points in the drill and the film will point these out. It will show the good, the bad, and the ugly.

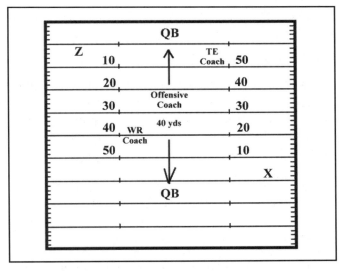

Diagram 1. Pat-and-go drill

Here are the *key points* we talk about in this drill. The wide receivers line up two yards inside the numbers. They run a press release versus air. It is not a full-speed drill. It is the first drill we use after loosening up. They wide receivers run a vertical push down the top edge of the numbers on the field. They run vertical down the field working to the top edge of the numbers. The key point is that we want them to fade only as the ball comes to them. If a receiver does not have to fade to make the catch over the

shoulders, that is great. We do not want them to fade unless they have to. We are trying to stay in the *box*. The box is the area from the bottom of the numbers to the sideline. Too many times we see the receivers in practice and in games get too close to the sideline. The quarterback wants to drop the ball over the outside shoulder of the receiver. The ball should be caught with the palms up and with *late hands*. We all have had receivers run for 10 yards with their hands outstretched in the air. We want *late hands* on the catch. We want the receiver to catch the ball above his eyes. We want the receivers to have their thumbs outside. If the receiver will arch his back, he will not turn back to look at the quarterback. He wants to stay arched and catch the ball over his outside shoulder. We work on this drill every day and it shows up in every game.

The next situation is the *red zone*. It is the area of the field from the plus 25-yard line to the plus 12-yard line. There are a couple of things to consider here when putting together your red zone plan. It is an area where the defense changes their personality. The defense has a different approach as far as their tendencies are concerned. Some defenses will blitz you all of the time. Again, we consider it a spot on the field where the defense changes.

Some teams need to consider the ability of their field goal kicker in their thought process. If you have a kicker that has an extremely long range, you can get into your red zone sooner. If you have a kicker that has a short range you may want to stay in your open-field offense longer.

Here is another point to consider. When you get to the 16-yard line, the field is twice as wide as it is long. Now the horizontal-stretch plays are going to become more of a factor as you get closer to the goal line.

In this past year Oregon lead the PAC 10 in red zone production. We were very effective when we got down to the red zone. The only concern is that we have to get down there more often.

Let me cover the specifics of the red zone. In our preparation we select our plays to run in the red zone. There are some plays we will run from the left hash mark that we will not run from our right hash mark. We have plays that we may say we are only going to run from the 15-yard line and in the middle of the field.

If we do not get that situation in a game, we do not run the play. It is a very specific and we may not run the play until the next game.

We have our *fourth-and-score* play ready. This is a play that we have to score on. You know the play and the players know it because they have practiced the play over and over. We want to make sure we have a plan and have all of the situations addressed.

We walk through our red zone calls on Friday. We cover the two-point plays. We keep a detailed sheet on all of the plays in the red zone. Basically it is a scouting report. We talk about being backed up to the goal line. Also, we talk about the overtime situations. To me, all of this ties into the red zone game plan.

We have a red zone grid that we break down the field in five-yard increments. We have plays that are only scripted from the left hash mark or the middle of the field. On play-action passes we are going to be very specific. We want to make sure we know what we are asking the quarterback to do in terms of play-action and the steps he must take. We want to keep the *hots* to his onside. We want to practice the plays from a certain position on the field and that is where we will call these plays in the game. We practice the plays on the grid on Wednesday. The players see this grid on Thursday and we walk through them on Friday. We will pick out 10 of the special plays and review them.

I have used this system for seven years and it has been good to me. It gives me a quick-hit list. We have all of the play-actions passes on it and it has the passes and the runs that we are going to use in the red zone. One thing I do is to script the entire play out. I want all of the plays down in front of me. You and I know in the heat of battle you may call a play and make a mistake on the call. You may call *right twin right – light* and the call should have been *right twin right – heavy*. You made a mistake calling the play. In the open field, the mistake will be covered up. But in the red zone everything you do is magnified. The closer you get to the goal line that magnification increases. As the play caller, I want to make sure the plays are coming out fast and efficient. We take the time on Wednesday and Thursday to review the plays and we write the play out.

If you throw on first-and-10 in the red zone, you must make sure you have a plan for what you will run on second-and-10. We like to use the *gap protection scheme* on the goal line. Things happen so fast on the goal line. If you are in a *man-to-man schemes*, there are some creases and seams available to the opponents. We want to box areas more so than man-to-man in our pass-protection scheme. You will see our power off-tackle play show up on the goal line in our red zone offense. Also, you will see the guard and tackle pulling on the play-action play. When we talk about the gap protection in the passing game, we are talking about the offensive line protecting the backside gaps as well as the onside gap in terms of speed option and sprint-out plays.

We talk about the *landmark throws*. We make sure we talk with the receivers, tight ends, and backs about the landmarks. If you want to complete the ball to the back of the end zone, you must practice the play. We use the pylon as a landmark. In the off-season you can put a trashcan out for the quarterback to throw at as the landmark. Have the quarterback start on the 10-yard line and take his drop and then throw the ball in the trashcan. We try to use every landmark we possibly can. At Oregon, the bottom of the letters is three-yards deep in the end zone. The letters themselves are four-yards tall. That leaves three yards at the top of the letters. When we talk about pushing into the end zone, we tell them to push three yards into the end zone at the bottom of the letters. It is a lot easier to see the bottom edge of the letters in the end zone than it is to figure out what three feet into the end zone is. We try to give the quarterback and receivers as many landmarks as possible.

We want to create lateral movement in terms of our *naked* and play-action game is concerned. When we are doing that we want to keep the *hot routes* to the quarterback's armside. This may not be as important in the open field, but when we get down to the red zone things happen fast. The closer you get to the goal line the faster they happen. We keep the hot routes to the openside of the quarterback so he can get ride of the ball if necessary.

We cover the double-move routes we use. Also, we go over our multiple-coverage beaters.

We do not throw curls and flat passes in the red zone very often. We do not want the receiver catching the ball with his back to the end zone. We are going to throw the slant routes, seam routes, and angle routes. We are going to throw the passes where the receiver has a better opportunity to advance the ball once he catches it. In the three-step drop, we run the slant routes. We may only run this play when we are in the middle of the field and at the 15-yard line.

We want to stretch the defense from low to high when we are in the red zone. I want to show the film and go over the points I have just covered.

(Film)

In the double-slant scheme, we want to *spread the defense*. It is a great multiple-cover route. We run the slant and the arrow on one side of the formation. On the other side we run the double [Diagram 2]. The quarterback comes up in his pre-snap read and looks for the safeties. If there are two safeties, we want to throw to the two-slant side. The progression is from the inside to the outside. If the defense is in cover 3 with only one safety in the middle of the field, we want to work on the slant-arrow route on the tight end side. A good cover 3 team will eat up a double-slant route. If the defense gives us a man-free look, the quarterback can pick the side of the formation he likes to throw the ball to.

If I were going to run this play in high school, the only time I would use the slant-out route would be when the ball is in, when the middle is closed, and I

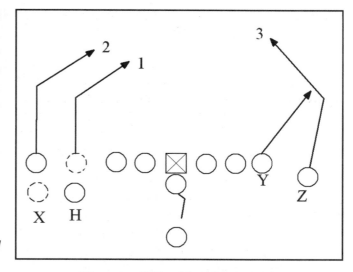

Diagram 2. Double-slant route

know it is going to be against a free-man defense. Otherwise I would keep throwing the double slant to the wideside of the field. In high school, the hash marks are wider and you can make that play. We want all three of our wide receivers to have their outside foot back and they run a three-step slant route. It goes outside, inside, outside, and then they break on the angle. If the receiver is getting pressure getting off on the route, he must time up his route.

I hope you got one idea out of this lecture. I really appreciate your time. I wish you the best of luck in the upcoming season. Thank you.

AFTER THE FOURTH QUARTER

Author, Storyteller, Educator

FROM THE EDITOR

John Mooy is a speaker, educator, author, sculptor, public radio presenter, and songwriter. He celebrates trial-and-error, out-of-your-comfort-zone strategies and believes each of us can dramatically and significantly impact our world. He has been speaking to groups and affecting change for over 21 years. He is widely known for his mesmerizing storytelling ability.

Without any legal training he served as a consultant to the United States Department of Justice in one of the biggest trials in American history. He worked directly with the lead prosecuting team in the trial of Terry Nichols in the Oklahoma City bombing case. John helped craft the testimony of hundreds of witnesses and the contents of thousands of documents into opening and closing arguments that were understandable to the jury.

As a teacher he was known for his creative teaching strategies, including his solicitation of celebrities with a request for a pair of shoes so his students could walk in the shoes of the rich and famous. He still has the golf shoes former President Gerald Ford sent his class.

Mooy Sauce, a book John wrote with a tongue-in-cheek style, demonstrated that effective communication using out-of-the-box thinking can have the desired effect.

In 1994, John gained national recognition for his song, "Fingertip Friends," about the Vietnam Wall, when it was performed live at the memorial in Washington, D.C., during the Memorial Day celebration that was covered by NBC and PBS.

The author of three books for children and other numerous articles, John also created a best-selling video, "Advocacy and the Art of Storytelling," for the National Institute for Trial Advocacy where he teaches attorney storytelling skills to enhance their courtroom presentations.

Thanks for that wonderful introduction. All week when I was preparing for this lecture, I thought of all of the things I was taught when I grew up. I thought I probably have more useful information on hand than 10 people. I was taught some things that will be with me forever. Let me share with you what those things are. I believe this will be the most uncomplicated approach to everything you will ever see. When you leave here today I hope this will work for you in any way it possible can.

It is easy to understand and it is easy to communicate and it is easy to implement. Here is what it is. See how this fits for you. This is the most uncomplicated paradigm to promote success you will most likely ever see. In a world filled with complications, this concept is built upon simplicity and awareness. Let me tell you where the concept came from, because that is important. It came quite innocently as the result of a question I was asked several years ago. As an educator, I was asked this question one day by a colleague while teaching in an alternative high school.

Here is the question: *"If I could go into every classroom in the United States grades K-12 and teach only once, what would I want everyone to know?"* My reply was very simple: "It does not matter if you are a football coach, a player, a businessman, an artist, or a car mechanic. *I would want everyone to know this:* **7 – 24 – 21 – 5**."

The first thing I would want you to know would be the number 7 — the first 7 seconds we meet another person, or another situation, and what we do during those 7 seconds. It is like going up to the line of scrimmage. During the first 7 seconds as the play initiates, I am either onsides or I am offsides. If I am walking into my classroom, it is greeting the teacher and looking him straight in the eyes. It could be the kid who created an impression on me. One day he roared into the parking lot and somehow was able to gesture with his hand held high above his head indicating that I was his number one teacher.

Think of the first impression. It is the first impression that is so important. It is the first impression in those **7** seconds. It is the first indication of how I carry out my assignment on the football field. Tremendous things happen when we create that first impression.

Many of you are teachers and you are teachers by being coaches as well. For 11 years I had a fellow teacher in a galaxy far, far away, and long ago, who every day would begin the morning by coming across the hall into my classroom and start out the day for herself and for me with a long face of depression. It was as if she was telling me we were doomed for another day at school. That attitude is so contagious. For those 11 years I refrained from looking at that teacher and telling her, "That is hard to believe because you are a real ball of fire." (Ha, Ha!)

I know in a football game you get a chance to repeat those **7** seconds every time you line up for a play. It is a matter of concentration for the entire game.

Then next number is **24**. There are **24** hours in a day. You need to ask yourself this question: What do you hope to get done today? The second question you need to ask is this: Do I have the tools to get the task done? Do I have the skills to achieve the goal? You are developing skills on the field each day. If I do not have those skills, can I develop them in a short period of time? If I cannot develop them in a short period of time then I need to alter that goal. I need to play for success. I need to plan to move forward. Every member of the team is counting upon the success of the role I play as a part of the team.

You can alter this second number. You could make the **24** the length of a game, a quarter, the length of a practice, or for 60 minutes. Break it down into a short-term goal.

"Okay team, I know we are playing a team that has superior ability. Let's see through this first quarter if we can hang close to that team?" Have them think about this every time they go up to the line of scrimmage - *(7 – 24)!*

The third number is **21**. The number **21** is the number of days generally recognized as the amount of time necessary to develop a habit. *Practice makes permanent.* There is an upside and there is a downside. The upside is that it develops good habits. The downside is that it develops poor habits. We become what we practice. It becomes part of us. It becomes permanent.

So you had better be aware of what it is your are emulating because those developed habits, good or bad, will become a part of you and a part of your team, and ultimately your teams successes and failures.

Think about this situation. In 1986, in a race across Alaska called the Iditarod, the sled came up to the starting line. The snow was blowing. As the sled came up to the starting line, everyone took note that the sled was being pulled by poodles. I get the same image. It is rather hysterical for me. It was not the little poodles with the little ribbons that smell really nice. They were the bigger poodles. That was not typically their job. They were not trained for that job. That year the poodle team came in 36th place of 52 teams that finished. Just to finish the race was a real key. The question you ask is this: How were these poodles trained? They were trained with huskies.

Coaches represent the huskies. You are the people that train the players. You are the people who others look up to and say, "I am going to do it like they do." You are upping the performance level. *Practice makes permanent.* The first impression is important. What is my goal for this quarter or for this football game? What are we going to practice, because it will become a part of us?

I grew up as a basketball player. I was always astounded when my coach would say to one of our players, "I noticed on your shots the ball always kicks off to the right of the rim. I want you to try this." He would show the player how he wanted him to shoot the ball. He would take one shot and reply, "That does not work." Practice takes place over a long period of time. It takes time to perfect a skill. We must practice it to the point where we can almost to the skill automatically. Practice makes permanent.

Vince Lombardi was asked, "How many plays does a team need?" His response was, "One, if you run it right."

I knew I had a different quality of kid come to see me when I was living in Des Moines, Iowa. He said,

"There is nothing to do." I asked him if he liked to play basketball. "Well, sort of. It is kind of hot today." I told him he could go down the street a half a block and shoot baskets. I told him to go down to the hoop and shoot 400 to 500 jump shots. He replied, "How do I get down there?" I told him to take the basketball and dribble the ball down there with his right hand. "Dribble down there and shoot the 500 jump shots and then dribble back with your left hand." He looked at me and he said, "You wouldn't give me a ride would you?"

I would like to set up something that is so contagious that people would say to me, "We do not have to quit now do we? Can we go longer?" I get the feeling from some coaches that there are some kids that do not want to be out there on the field.

Now we have a **7**, a **24**, and a **21**. Think of all the ways these numbers can interact with you and your coaching duties and in the classroom and beyond.

And now we arrive at the last number, which is **5**. It is a check list. The **5** represents the **5** characteristics that I believe successful teams possess a majority of, if not all of these characteristics. I started to ask myself what are the characteristics that all successful teams have in common. Here is what I came up with:

- Attitude: It is mine to choose.

- Ambition and energy.

- Ability to follow a direction.

- Ability to get along with others (team chemistry).

- Attendance: Being there. No great performance was ever turned in by someone who failed to show up.

There are a lot more elements. I included these **5** because I want to keep this very simple. I looked at the list and I asked myself this question. What kind of attitude do I have? I choose all of these points. What is my level of ambition and energy? Can I follow directions? I believe plays are all about following directions.

I enjoy the atmosphere of the football coaches here today. It is so much fun for me to be here today. I have always been a great spectator of football. It is all about stories. I am a storyteller. As Joe said in my introduction, I spent a year working on the Oklahoma City bombing trial as a storyteller. All we wanted to do was to make sure that people would understand when we told the story of what happened that day.

I could spend days with you and tell stories about you and your team. I would ask you some simple questions. "Who is the greatest player you ever had? Tell me about the greatest football game you ever saw? Tell me about a time when you thought the game was over and you were going to lose the game, but you came back and won the game." That is what you people deal with all of the time. You deal with stories. There will be more football stories in this place by the time you leave here than there will be in any other place in the state of Michigan. Stories are such motivating elements. My guess is that a lot of you showed your team the movie *Remember the Titans* soon after it came out. This is a story about coming together and working as one single unit. It is a story. Following directions is the third element.

I should say that to my students that do not show up half of the time. They cannot follow directions. I will say to them, "You have a real difficulty in answering questions. I have a question for you. Is there any chance you are going to become a heart surgeon? If you do, I would think you would be killing people left and right." Following directions is important.

I think of this when I get on an airplane. I know this because we have put it on film before. I want to know that the pilot is bored with everything except one thing: *flying that airplane*. I do not want to hear him on the intercom giving me instructions: "Good morning! Buckle up real tight and hold on. I had a dream last night and I have figured out how we can get this heavy load off the runway. Here we go!" I guess we would call this being really focused.

The fourth element is the ability to get along with others. This is team chemistry. "They were not the most talented team I ever had, but collectively these guys were great."

The fifth element is attendance. No one ever turned in a great performance when they were not present — ever in the history of any sport.

Think about what you can do with these four numbers: **7** – **24** – **21** - **5**. This covers about everything you ever do. Those are the elements through which you teach everything. "What were you thinking about when you did that?" You could look at these numbers and say it broke down at this point: when the punt came down and you thought you were going to run it back for a touchdown and the ball bounced off the top of the return man's helmet, that was a breakdown of the first **7** seconds. That was not a particularly good impression.

I have been in so many places to talk about these four numbers. This becomes my goal. I wrote a letter a year-and-a-half ago to Marty Mornhinweg. The Lions were mired in a tough time. This is what I wrote to Marty. "I know everyone is giving you suggestions on how to turn this dismal season around. I would like to come to visit with you and give this talk about the four numbers. It might be a starting point for you to get things moving in the right direction." Marty never wrote me back. We all know what has happened with the Lions recently.

I think the key word in everything is called *application.* I believe this understanding of the application can do great things for you. One of my goals is to have this happen. Let me give you an example. When the NFL sends performers out to the schools to do community service, and I hope some of you do that with some of your players, I hope the NFL guys will say something more than just *stay in school.* I have plenty of kids in my alternative classes where I work. They are there, but they are just not doing anything. I want to pass this message on to these people because I think it is a good message.

Let me tell you how it works. I am going to tell you two short stories. One of these stories you will all be familiar with. For the other story, none of you will be familiar with. Here is what I want you to look for in this story. I want you to look at the attitude. I want you to look at that first impression. I want you to look at energy and ambition and all elements in that number **5**. I have started to do everything through these eyes now. Everything! I am amazed at how in that first **7** seconds Tiger Woods addresses the golf ball. I think I have the potential as a golfer in a situation like that to tee off and kill numerous people. I just do not know how he can hit the ball straight every time.

I suspect it has something to do with the amount of time he has repeated practicing what he wants to be good at.

Next is my true story. I do not know the year. I do know the Buffalo Bills were playing the Dallas Cowboys. It was in that span when the Bills made it to the Super Bowl four straight years, but they never won a Super Bowl. They kept going back, as they did not give up on it. In the Bills/Cowboys game, the Bills were losing again by a substantial margin. They would have agreed with everyone that they were pretty much out of that game. They were at a point where people could have let a few things slide by. They could have let their attitudes slide, and they could have just gone through the motions. But late in that game the Buffalo Bills were driving the ball down the field. They were down near the Dallas goal line. Jim Kelly, the Bills quarterback, went back to pass and the ball was deflected out of his hand. It went into the hands of Cowboy linemen, Leon Lett, who had nothing but clear sailing to the end zone. Understand it is the thrill of a defensive lineman to catch a football and look up and see nothing between him and the goal line. Leon Lett took off and ran as fast as he could go. He went 90 yards down to the five-yard line. He thought about celebrating early. He made a mistake. It is now in the highlights of the Super Bowl games forever. Leon Lett held the ball out at the five-yard line to celebrate. But it made no difference to Don Beebe of the Bills. He chose not to follow the directions of just watching the play through to its completion. He set out to catch Leon Lett by running at top speed and chasing him the length of the field, finally knocking the ball from Lett's outstretched hand as he started an early end zone celebration.

Beebe saw the play through, regardless of the score, or the time left in the game, and in doing so created a memory we will never forget. It made no difference that the Bills were going to lose the game. It made all the difference in the world in the attitude he brought to the situation. I am sure a lot of you may remember this story.

Here is a story that you will not recall. I grew up in southwestern Michigan in a small town of Marcellus. My father delivered mail. My dad carried mail for 41 years. He opened and closed 219 mailboxes, six days a week, up and down 51 miles of gravel road.

He was really good at that because he had it down pretty well. He probably opened and closed those mailboxes a jillion times.

On his mail route was a man who's first name was George. George and his wife would come up from South Bend, Indiana, where he was a president of a bank. On occasions my dad would come home and tell me that, "George just gave me two tickets to the Notre Dame Football game. Would you like to go see the game?" My response was always something like this: "Are you kidding?" We got in the car and we drove to the Notre Dame Stadium. As a kid, I loved the atmosphere as we walked up to the stadium. We had two lovely seats way up high in the end zone. One Saturday I sat there with my dad and we watched the University of Pittsburgh, a good team at the time, play the University of Notre Dame, a poor team at the time. Pitt had an all-American end by the name of Mike Ditka playing for them. I do not remember what he did that day. They also had a kicker by the name of Fred Cox. He kicked the football the straightest I had ever seen a kicker do. You had to ask yourself how many times Cox could kick that ball through the uprights.

This story is not about Mike Ditka or Fred Cox. It is about a small Notre Dame running back by the name of Angelo Dabiero dropping back by himself to return a Pitt punt. He happened to be from a place called Donora, Pennsylvania. I looked it up in the record books. Donora, Pennsylvania, also gave us Tony Dorsett and Stan Musial.

Angelo Dabiero caught the ball near the sideline at about his 30-yard line and started up the field with the help of very little blocking. Quite simply, Dabiero refused to go down. He was hit, he twisted, he turned, and he moved left, he moved right, one yard at a time. I do not think the run covered more than 10 to 12 yards, during which time it seemed every Pitt player had either had his hands on Dabiero or had a clear shot at him. When he finally went down, the entire crowd rose up to their feet to salute Dabiero's effort with a standing ovation. Only two people here remember this story. I will remember it forever. Think of the first 7 seconds. Think of that first impression. The crowd stood to cheer his effort, and not a touchdown.

As I look back on this event, it exemplifies all of these four numbers. That is what we are all about. We are all about stories. You are trying to put together a better story than the last season's story. You will tell your kids all kinds of stories to move them forward. We are all about stories.

The question is raised concerning a player who does not look the coach in the eye when he talks to him. I would take this concept to the entire team. I would explain it to them as a group. I would tell the team to look me in the eye so I do not sound threatening to them, so we are all on the same page. We need to have them all doing the same thing. I do not think we need to tell him something like, "I notice you do not look at me when I talk to you; look at me." I would take a different approach to the situation.

I am a big believer in teaching in very subtle ways. I have a friend who was a very good coach. He used to do a lot of what I call *sideline teaching*. He would put his arm around the players and suggest that the athletes try it another way. I am a big believer in a lot of small successes lead to big things.

It is a thrill for me to be here. When I talk, someone is actually writing something down. That is a not what happens when I am teaching the alternative class. I will be around awhile. I would love to hear your stories. I would love to visit with you.

I think I can teach everything I need to get across to kids in those four numbers. I want you to take these four numbers and pass them on to your team. I want you to utilize them as a part of your teaching and coaching. Encourage your players to make these numbers a vehicle by which they can approach the next practice, the next game, and the rest of their lives. These numbers will not let you down. They all become a part of your story and a part of your teams' story.

Thank you for your attention.

DEVELOPING OFFENSIVE LINEMEN

Baylor University

I have been in this hotel for one hour and I already have myself in trouble. I got off the airplane about 11 p.m. last night. I got up early this morning and dressed so I could get to the clinic. I am like most college coaches today. If the schools did not give us coaching shirts, I would be naked. Baylor was not a Nike school before I got there, but we are in the process of becoming a Nike school. So I apologize to Ray Lamb for not having on a Nike coaching shirt. I have the Baylor green coaching shirt, but it is not a Nike shirt. Hopefully we will have that changed soon.

You might as well go ahead and get your chuckle out of your system. I have had over a dozen people between here and Waco asked me about *the play*. That play at the end of the LSU versus Kentucky game is now on the ESPN blooper plays. This year it was rated the number one play of the year in college football.

The thing that is funny to me about that play in the LSU game is this. You would have thought that Coach Saban made sure the same thing did not happen to his team. You would think they would have learned from what happened to us at Kentucky in that LSU game. But two weeks later LSU goes out and loses a game the same way. That just goes to show you that when you are dealing with young kids anything can happen.

I feel a little unprepared right how. I took the job at Baylor University on December 11, 2002. I have been running full speed ever since. I feel unprepared because I have not been able to find my overlays for my lecture and I have not been able to find tapes. I will wing it. If we get to a topic that you are interested in, stop me if you have any questions.

The first thing I want to do is to commend the high school coaches for the job you do. I have been a high school coach. I have been in the same seats you are in now. I commend you for the job you do with the young people. I do not say that just because the high school coaches are the lifeblood of any university, and not just Baylor, Georgia, or Kentucky. High school coaches are the lifeblood of all our programs. I just want you to know we appreciate the job coaches do with our young people in our country today. Our country is going to hell in a hand basket pretty quick. Just stop and think about it. This time next month we may be in a war. There are problems in Miami and most of the schools are locked down. Our kids have to go through so much today. It is unbelievable what kids have to go through today. Teenage suicides are higher than they have ever been. Teenage pregnancy is as high as it has ever been. Teenage alcoholism is as high as it has ever been. Teenage drug abuse is as high as it has ever been. I could go on and on. We have de-emphasized religion. I think our main problem is that the family structure has broken down. My point to you as high school coaches is this: *You are our last line of defense with the kids.* If it were not for the life skills you are teaching them, hard telling where some of these kids would be. It is bad enough as it is. I just want to say thanks for the job you do. I have been there and I know what it is like and I commend you for the job you do with the young people.

Over the last three years I have gotten a lot of letters, phone calls, and emails from people all over the country. Some of them have been from people that I know, some have been from people I have been acquainted with, and a lot of them were from people I did not even know. These people just wanted to congratulate me. They made comments such as, "Coach, it is so good to see an offensive line coach become a head coach for a change." I am not sure what your goal is, but I would assume most of you here today are offensive line coaches. If you goal is to become a head coach by coming up through the ranks, I can tell you it is not easy for a line coach to become the head coach. I will give you this advice: *"Keep on sawing wood. Be good people and keep battling."*

In my personal opinion, if more offensive line coaches were promoted to head coach, football would be in better shape. I know the football business would be a lot more stable than it is now. I mean this sincerely.

Everyone knows we make the jump from the University of Kentucky to Baylor University. We are going to carry our same system to Baylor. Some people tell me I am crazy to go to Baylor. They have won four conference games since they have been in the Big 12 Conference. They want to know why I would want to jump into that mess. Well, for one, it is a chance for me to go back home. Texas is my home state. I guess because of my background as an offensive lineman, I am just thickheaded. I like the challenge. I do not mind going head to head with the big boys. I like to head butt so we decided to go to Baylor and take on the challenge. Going to Baylor gives me a chance to get back home. It is only three hours to where my dad lives. I can see him more as he is getting older.

I was able to bring 10 families from Kentucky with me to Baylor. We took everyone that worked there. I was able to get all nine assistant coaches to come with me. We got the two G.A.'s to come with us. I think this is a testimony to those guys for following me to Waco. I can assure you if one or two of the coaches had come into my office and told me that they did not want to go to Baylor, we probably would not have taken the job at Baylor. That is the kind of staff we are. We do everything by committee. Our wives even get along. Our kids play together. We try to create a family-type atmosphere everywhere we have been.

Baylor is a unique school. It is the only private school in the Big 12 Conference. It is a small school with only about 11,000 students. Baylor is connected to the Baptist Church. It is a faith-based institution. They have chosen to maintain their ties to the church. In today's society there is a need for this. I think we can go out a find 20 to 25 kids that can thrive in that environment. I understand the loyalty to state schools. I understand how the game is played. But if you have anyone that may have Texas ties who would be interested in coming to Baylor, we would love to hear from you. Pick up the phone and call us. We will take care of your kids. We have a unique relationship with our players.

You talk about an emotional day, when I went back to Kentucky to tell the team I was leaving it was tough. The coaches were crying, the players were crying, and it was very emotional. But, we know how to take care of players. If someone wants to leave the state and come to Texas, just give us a call.

The thing I want to talk about today will not be related to schemes, but more about techniques and some thoughts about weightlifting that are beneficial to offensive linemen. What we talk about may not be for you. By the time you leave here you may think I am crazy. But if you can leave with just one little idea that will help you, then the time will be well spent. That is what these clinics are all about. It is sharing ideas and seeing old friends and talking football.

I want to give the young offensive line coaches some advice. The older coaches will know what I am talking about. In the old days when the coaching staff started dividing the players up, this is the way it was done. "Old Billy Bob is not much of an athlete. He can't do this and he can't do that. We will just make an offensive lineman out of him." Those days are gone. So when you get into those staff meetings and you start dividing up the players, the offensive line coaches need to get in there and battle for some of the athletes. At times the offensive line coaches get stuck with less talent than the other positions. That attitude is still prevalent. So it is up to you to get in there and fight for the players. It is going to be you who will get the criticism when you can't get a first down, or you can't knock teams off the ball. Defenses have just gotten too good not to have good players on the offensive line. We have to catch up athletically to our defensive linemen.

I enjoy going to clinics and other practices. I like to check out other coach's offensive line drills. That is what I go look for today. We all have our schemes. We all know what we want to run on offense. I am always looking for new ideas for drills. The safeguard is this: You go out and start looking at drills and you see a drill and you think it is just what you are looking for. The thing you must ask yourself is this: Will that drill help your players get the job done on Friday night? The drill must fit into your plan. If you do not watch out, you will end up with a lot of drills that do not help you teach the players what they need to do on Friday night.

It is important to stay on an *even keel*. This is true for all positions, and not just offensive linemen. I think players will survive in a predictable environment. I do not like to be around moody people. I do not know about you, but I just do not like them. If a coach is moody and not on an even keel, it will rub off on the players. Again, if you do not watch out, the players will become the same way. They will be higher than a kite one Friday and be on a low mood the next Friday. Do you know whose fault that is? It is your fault. That is because the players are up and down the roller coaster. We feel it is important to stay on an even keel.

Be very *positive* with the players. I think kids need that, especially nowadays. The thing of it is you must coach your butt off every day. You must coach as hard on the 20th day as you do on the first day. You must coach as hard the last game as you did on the first game. If you can be the same every day, the kids will appreciate that very much. Be the same guy every day. Another point that is important is to *leave your ego at the door*. An ego will take you down quicker than anything. It just becomes excess baggage you are toting around with you. It will rise up and get you.

To me, one word has become very prevalent in coaching circles. You hear it a lot at coaching clinics. That word is *philosophy*. Everyone has a *philosophy of this and a philosophy of that*. This is where I want to start as far as teaching offensive line play.

I will tell you a story that happened to me. I was interviewing for a high school coaching job in Paris, Texas. It was with the Paris High School Wildcats, home of Raymond Berry. It is the same Raymond Berry that I played for at New England in the NFL. I grew up near Paris, Texas. I always knew I wanted to be a coach. Coach Berry recruited me into the coaching ranks. He gave me a job at New England. That is where I started my coaching career. Later Raymond got cross with the owners and we all got fired. So I went back to Paris to see if I could get the head coaching job there. I was excited about the prospects of becoming a Texas High School Head Coach. I got an interview with the Paris School Board. This little lady was the school superintendent. I ended up in an all-day interview ordeal. I was just knocking the board dead. I was giving the right response to all of the questions and covering everything the superintendent wanted to know about. Everything was going great. I was thinking,

"This job is mine. I just have to last another 10 minutes with the board." I just knew she could not go much longer with the questions. She went over and sat down at the table across from me. She said, "Coach, I just have one more question for you. Tell me your *philosophy of life*." I thought for a minute and responded. "Lady, I am just happy my feet hit the floor every day." I could not see what my philosophy of life had to do with football. Needless to say, I did not get the job. I decided from that point on that I had better come up with ideas that I could say were my philosophy. I put several things down that I could refer to from time to time.

My philosophy for *offensive line play* could be used for any position on the field. I have used it for several years. It includes the things I believe in. This is what we talk about to our offensive line. These points are things I have learned through the years from my coaches and from others. I have revised it into my own words that make a little more sense to me. It is nothing new. Most of you may have the same ideas in your notebook. Hopefully this will reinforce your thinking.

You must have a hunger to succeed. If you want to be good at something, you must work at it. You must want to be good at what you are doing. One word we use a lot is *passion*. We have a passion for football. I have a passion for offensive linemen. That passion should drive you to be the very best you can be. You must do the same thing as your players. You must make up you mind what you want. Decide what you want and then go after it. You must give it everything you have. If you can convey that passion down to your players, they are going to have it. They are going to emulate the line coach. You are going to be their role model and you are going to spend more time with them than anyone. You must have that passion and hunger to succeed.

Be positive. Being positive is nothing but an attitude and how you see things. This is true not only in football but in everyday life. I am a *the- glass-is-half-full guy*. Some coaches work as if the glass is half empty. I do not like to be around those people that see things as half empty.

When you talk to your kids, tell them to be honest with themselves. If they do a good job, tell them they did a good job. Let them pat themselves on the back once in a while. If they make a mistake, let them know and make them accountable, but hug their neck and let them know you love them. I can assure you they will run through a wall for you. If they trust in you and know you care about them. Players do not care about how much the coach knows. To them it is *how much a coach cares*. Right! Fuss at them hard and be consistent. But you have to love them and pat them on the back. Tell them not to get too upset over mistakes. Everyone makes mistakes and they will make their share of them. It is a fact of life. Don't beat yourself up too bad on making mistakes. Take pride in your effort.

Coach with a blue-collar work ethic. I got credit for three extra years of coaching in my introduction. Thank you! I actually played 15 years in the NFL. The only reason I was able to stay in the NFL that long was because I had developed a work ethic early in my life. I thank God for my father. He instilled that characteristic in me. Ha, Ha! He used to kick my rear end regularly. But you know, I was glad I had that kind of work ethic when I went to the NFL in Philadelphia.

I was drafted in 1973. When I went to Philadelphia it was the first time I had been east of the Mississippi River. I was in culture shock when I got to Philadelphia. I think the people of Philadelphia were in culture shock after being around me for a day or two. I ended up living in a little Italian neighborhood in South Philly. I lived on Packer Avenue that was a small street that had row houses on it. It had one little house connected to another little house all the way down the street. It went for a block and a half. The houses were not big, but there were a lot of them in a row. It was right in the heart of Little Italy.

The Italian people are very resilient and they are very happy people. I had neighbors on each side of me. They would come out on the stoop each morning. The little guy would have a baloney sandwich in a brown bag. He would have the baloney sandwich and some fried onions or something like that for his lunch. The kids would come out and kiss their father by and he would go off to work. When he came home in the evening, the kids and his wife would rush out to the front to meet him. Everyone was just happy. Those men were just happy to have a job. He was happy he could provide food for his kids. The kids were healthy and his wife was not bothering him. He was a happy man. I thought this was a neat approach.

I would walk out to my stoop. I did not have to worry about lunch because I knew the Eagles would fix lunch. I could walk to the Vet Stadium. I would walk over there into the locker room. I would look around and I would see the total opposite of what I saw with my neighbors. This was back in 1973. The Eagles had just come off a 2-12 season. They were not worth a crap. When I walked into that locker room, I saw nothing but spoiled, rich, and overpaid football players. I should not use the term overpaid, but they did not appreciate anything. They had their hand out looking for someone to give them something. They did not understand how to work.

I thought about the situation and decided that my dad did not raise me that way. I stepped back from that situation and said, "This is not the type of person I want to be." I wanted to be like my little Italy neighbors. I have always been appreciative of what I have. I have a wonderful family. I think this is what really put the finishing touch on my work ethic. This is something you can control. How hard you want to work is up to you. This game is all about hard work.

You must be dedicated and committed to a purpose. All of the effort is not going to do any good if you do not have a purpose. Whatever you are doing give 100 percent to it. If you are in class, be a great student — be into it. If you are a football player it is the same deal. You must be into it 100 percent. If you are having knee surgery and you have a doctor standing over you and he is worrying about the stock market, you would be concerned. "Hey Dr., be 100 percent into fixing my leg." You must be dedicated and committed to a purpose.

You must have self-discipline. You cannot ask your kids to be disciplined if you do not have it. The kids feed off the coach. I have been very fortunate. I was in Philadelphia in 1980. We went to Super Bowl XV. During that year and a half, the Eagles were in Super Bowl XV. The Flyers won the Stanley Cup. The 76ers won the NBA. The Philadelphia Phillies won the World Series. It was a great time to be a professional athlete in Philadelphia. All four of those teams had discipline. It does not matter which sport it is, there is one common thread — *that is discipline*. If you do not have discipline, you are not going to win.

This is especially true today. We are a *reset society* today. The kids get on the *Play Station* and if things are not going like they want them to go, they just hit the reset button. They just start all over. With one little punch of the button, they have a clean slate. In today's world you must have discipline.

You must keep your emotional cool. We do not ask our players to do anything extra. We want them to do the same thing in a game that they do on the practice field. This is why we get on them about having great practices. We try to create as much game tempo as possible on the practice field.

We are only on the field one-and-a-half hours. We may go for one hour and 45 minutes at the most. But everything we do on the practice field is at high speed. We are moving from the time we step on the field. We do not walk from drill to drill. We try to get in as many reps as we can. Coach Goodner will have his defense set up and we will run two offensive teams at his defense, just one play after another. We go as fast as we can go. We want the kids to get a lot of reps. We do not coach a lot on the field. We go inside and coach off the tape. We try to show them as many looks as we can in practice.

You must be resilient. Everyone has problems. We win games and we lose games. We tell our kids we are not going to win them all, not necessarily, not all of the time. You are going to get beat, but you have to get over it. You cannot reverse the loss, but you can get yourself ready for the next game. As a coach you cannot spend too much time crying in your beer. If you do that, the next thing you know you will lose two games in a row. Then two games become three games. Hell, get over the loss and move on. You can't do anything about the loss after it happens. Do something about the next game.

You must have stoicism. You must know the difference in being hurt and being injured. A lot of the kids do not understand that thinking today. Most kids today have been pampered. After the first practice everyone is hurting. Everybody is going to hurt in football. You have to know the difference in being hurt and being injured.

Don't let early failure discourage you and never, ever, let early success satisfy you. Does that make sense?

Never assume the kids know or understand something you are teaching them. Take it for granted that you are starting from scratch. When you introduce a new play, or a new idea, or a new philosophy, do not assume the players know what you are talking about. Kids have a lot of distractions to deal with today. If you make an assumption that a player knows what you are talking about, you may find out he does not have a clue what you are talking about.

Try to put it all together on game day. You must play the game with great emotion. That is what this game is all about. I think kids today are afraid to show emotion. They are concerned their peers are going to make fun of them. Heck with that attitude. Emotion is what this game is all about. That is what the game was invented for.

You must keep focused. I got a chance to play for Coach Raymond Berry. He would draw a bull's-eye upon the wall and ask us what is that? "It is a bull's-eye." Then he would ask us what we had to do to win. We would say, "We must put the arrow inside the bull's-eye." He would reply, "No! You have to hit the center of the bull's-eye." That is what we are talking about when we discuss focus. Try to hit the center of the bull's-eye.

We believe in great effort. That is the one thing the kids can control. They can control their effort. If you demand it from them, they will give it to you. They are going to give you what you ask for. We demand a lot of effort from our kids.

The last point along this line is the fact *you must go out on the field game day and execute.* You must take care of the details.

This is about as close to a philosophy as I can come. I think it is important to set goals for your kids. Most kids like to have something to shoot for. You must make the goals tough, but make them so they can obtain their goals. It is obvious that you want short-term goals and long- term goals. You need to put those goals up on the wall and let the players go past it and see it day in and day out. You have to talk about the goals with the players over and over. An example of a short-term goal would be to average four yards per carry. A long-term goal would to be able to bench press 400 pounds by the time the player graduates. I think it is important to post those goals and go over them as much as possible at least once a week.

Next I want to talk about *strength training and conditioning.* Back when I was young, we did not lift a lot of weights. Coaches thought weight training would make you muscle bound. When I went to the Philadelphia Eagles as a rookie, I started on the offensive line. I weighed 217 pounds. Then about 1976, all of a sudden defensive teams started using the 50 defense or the 3-4 defensive schemes. Let me tell you, it is difficult to block Ernie Holmes at 217 pounds. That is when I started lifting weights and adding pounds to my body. Everyone realized there was something to the weight lifting. It has really boomed and started to take off today.

Today we *feed* our kids better than ever. We have more information about *nutrition and supplements*. There is no reason why there should not be great weight programs today.

Our whole deal is this: *We want to train the complete athlete*. I know sometimes strength coaches get carried away. Trust me, I love strength coaches. The thing we must keep in mind is the fact we are trying to train football players. This is where you as an offensive line coach must come in sometimes and let the strength coach know you are training the complete athlete or the football player. You must not lose sight of this.

We are going to *lift weights*. *Flexibility training* is also important. We have found out it is important to stretch. Most of you are doing conditioning during this time of the year. Off-season work is very important to offensive linemen.

We have talked about how important nutrition is to football players. There is no reason today that kids cannot learn to eat properly.

The *agility drills* that we do are specific drills to help us improve on the things we do on Saturday, which is to play the game of football. We lift free weights. I think this is important especially for offensive linemen.

Our philosophy of weight training came from a gentleman up in Columbus, Ohio named Louie Simmons. He is fantastic. He is training about 85 percent of the world-class power lifters and world record holders. He also understands how to train football players.

What he does is to use chains and the big, thick rubber bands with the athletes. If you get a chance

to hear Louie Simmons talk, it would be worth your time. I can tell you the amount of weights the players can lift is going up and up. In the two years we were at Kentucky, all of our players improved on this system. We are going to use the same set-up at Baylor.

Let me see if I can explain how the system works. When you bench press and push the weight up off your chest and you go through the full range of motion, the weight never actually changes from the time it leaves the chest until you get it to the top of the lift. What Louie has done is this. He has a big rubber band mounted into the floor that is attached to the ends of the bar. The athletes sit on boxes when they do these lifts. The boxes are easy to make. The rubber band attaches to the cleat on the box and to the end of the bar. The principle is that as you go upward through the full range of motion with that bar, the rubber band starts to kick in as you take the slack of it up and you get more resistance at the top end of the movement. You are adding weight as you go through the full range of motion. You can do the lifts with rubber bands on the end of the weights or you can do it with chains. When the bar is sitting on the chest, most of the chain is sitting on the floor. As you start the weight upward the chain moves up off the floor. The weight increases through the full range of motion.

The way they have explained this system to me is that the gain is coming at the top of the lift. As the band starts to stretch, or the chain comes off the floor, the weight becomes heavier. The extra strength is coming through the full range of motion.

I had my doubts in the beginning. I am old-fashioned and I had to see it myself. Men, it works. It is cheap to use this system. You can start out by wrapping the rubber bands around a couple of 45-pound weights to get the tension on the rubber bands.

On our *dynamic days* we are going to do the following lifts. We do the bench, squat, incline, power clean, and snatch. We lift heavy twice a week. We are on a split routine. We lift Monday and Tuesday, take Wednesday off, and work Thursday and Friday. Monday and Tuesday are heavy days; Thursday and Friday are light days. We still use the rubber bands on light days. We just take the plates off the rubber bands. We may use about 50 percent of the mats. Now we are working for speed through the whole range of motion. Course stabilization is a fancy way of saying we do a lot of crunches. We want to build strength in our stomach and midsection.

I want to talk about a few drills and pass protection. We throw the ball quite a bit. We threw it more when I was at Kentucky with Coach Hal Mumme. When I became the head coach, I decided to become more balanced and so we run the ball a little more now. A perfect world for me would be to throw the ball 60 percent of the time and run it 40 percent of the time. Last year, with the SEC Offensive Player of the Year at tailback, we gave him the football a little more often.

As the offensive line coach, you are always in a battle with the quarterback coach. The quarterback coach will tell the line coach, "You must get those sorry-ass linemen blocking. We do not have enough time to throw the ball. My quarterback can not get his reads with the defense on top of him." I know that feeling. I have been there.

The offensive line coach will respond, "Hell coach, the quarterback can't stand back there and take all day to throw the ball. He has over two minutes to throw the ball. He has to get the ball out of there. He is drifting all over the place. How do you expect us to protect him?"

I guess this battle has been going on forever and it will continue to go on forever. However, there are a few things you can do to reach a happy medium. It is good if the line coach is also the head coach, I will tell you that. I know who is going to win that battle.

One thing we did to help both areas at Kentucky was to junk our seven-step passing game. We do not throw the seven-step game anymore. We could not protect the seven-step game. Generally speaking, we have done a good job of protecting our quarterback over the years. We pride ourselves on this. We threw the ball a lot and our sacks ratio was as good as anyone else's in the SEC. We went back and charted our offense and found that most of our sacks were coming on the seven-step game. That is when we dropped the seven- step game. We run the *three-step and five-step game*. We throw the ball in .9 seconds on the three-step drop, and 2.2 seconds on the five-step drop. We do not want to hold the ball any longer than 2.2 seconds. If we do not get the ball

away in that time, we are going to find us a new quarterback or a new quarterback coach.

The thing that is important is for the quarterback to become conscious of getting rid of the ball on time. You can use a whistle or horn and have a ball boy blowing the whistle or horn. You can get a horn and set it for a certain time to go off. I did not think it would be effective with our quarterback. But after a few times they start hearing the horn sound and know they had held the ball too long. The horn made the quarterback aware of throwing the ball on rhythm.

On the three-step drop, the quarterback is going to drop 4.0- to 4.5-yards deep. On the five-step drop, he is going to drop to 7.0- or 7.5-yards deep. The offensive line must visualize what that distance is to protect the quarterback. To get this across to the linemen, we have the offensive line drop down on a knee at the distance the quarterback is going to setup at. We have them take a knee. Then we put the quarterback on a chalk line and have him take the snap and take his drop. We want them to see what the distance really is.

We have the quarterback drop three sets on each drop. This helps the offensive linemen to understand what the quarterback is doing on his drop. The linemen get a mental picture of the 4.5 yards, and that is the spot they have to protect. They can understand this point. We did the same thing with the three- and five-step drops. It is important to let the offensive linemen see the landmark you are asking them to protect. You need to make sure the offensive linemen know where the quarterback is setting up.

On any offensive pass play you run, the offensive linemen must know the depth of the quarterback and where he is setting up. Is he going to set up on the inside leg of the tackle on the shotgun snap? Is he going to set up behind the center on the straight dropback pass? The line needs to know this for each play. As coaches, sometimes we assume the players know this. That is not really the case. They must know where the quarterback is going to be and they have to be able to count on the quarterback being there. The quarterback must make sure the he knows where he must be on the set-up.

How do you ask five players to protect a spot when the spot changes on every snap? You cannot do it. It is all a simple matter of *geometry*. That angle makes a big difference to that offensive tackle. They must know where the quarterback is going to be on the drop. The quarterback must be disciplined to be at the spot designated for each play called. Make sure the quarterback is getting there.

It is okay for the quarterback to have that mental clock because he has to get that ball out on rhythm. The offensive linemen must know they cannot have a mental block. We are striving to block for as long as it takes. The quarterback has to throw the ball in the time period we allot for each play. The linemen block forever, and must not worry about the time factor it takes for the quarterback to get the ball away. They cannot have a mental clock on the time they have to continue to block on pass plays. You have to teach the kids to hang on forever, or as long as it takes for the ball to come out of the quarterback's hand.

The problem linemen face is that they block for a period of time and then they start looking backwards to see if the pass has been made. That is when they get themselves in trouble. We tell them, "The crowd will tell you when the ball is gone. If we have a big completion, the crowd noise will let you know the pass has gone."

When we go out looking for players who can pass protect, we look for *natural knee benders*. We look for players that have a lot of athletic ability. Again, we are trying to catch up with the defensive linemen.

You can drill a player until he is blue in the face, but if he is not a knee bender and the good Lord did not bless him with that trait, you cannot help him a lot. Now, I can go recruit that type of player as a college coach. I understand you inherit the high school players. It all goes back to getting those players that are good knee benders. They need flexibility at the ankles and knees and hips. Go watch them play basketball. See if they can handle the ball and see how they move around the court. If they can do that, they have a good chance of being a good pass protector. This is my personal opinion and that is the kind of kid I look for. I like players with good flexible hips and ankles.

In all of our drills, we base the fact that we want our offensive linemen to be *lateral movers*. We want

them to be able to move side to side. We want them to be able to slide their feet. In each drill we teach them not to turn away from the line of scrimmage. We do not want their hips and shoulders to open. We want everything square and in front of the lineman. They have to be like a baseball catcher. If a good catcher gets a pass ball, he does not stick his hand out at the ball. He slides his body over in front of the ball. He must have lateral movement to get over in front of the ball. It is the same for the offensive linemen.

When we decide what drills we want to use, we select drills that teach lateral movement. We go through the *running ropes* everyday. We go down through the ropes straight ahead first as a warm-up drill. We will hit every hole, with high-knee lifts [Diagram 1].

Diagram 1. Running ropes – warm-up drill

Then we hit every other hole [Diagram 2]. We want their hands about chin high. We want their arms flexed like a boxer. We want their hands six to eight inches from their chin so they can still punch. We go down and back, down and back as many times as we think they need that day. We ask them to lift their front foot, step over the hole, and bring their back foot over. This is not a speed drill. Slow them down and make them very deliberate and get out of the drill what you want. We want their hands chin high, six or eight inches from their chin, with their eyes up. The first week of running the drills they are going to look down at their feet. That is natural. The more they run the drills the better they will become and they will not have to look down at their feet.

After they get the drill down pretty well, I will start standing beside the ropes. As they come through the ropes, I will reach out and grab them by the shoulder pads. We are going to distract the lineman. We may slap him in the helmet, hit him in the crotch, or do anything to distract him. I want him to move his feet and keep his eyes on what I am doing. I want him to take his hands and knock my hands down, up, or knock them off his pads. There is no rule in the book that says the offensive linemen cannot use their hands. They can keep the defensive man's hands off them. This will take them a few weeks to get good at it, but this will teach them to pick up their feet.

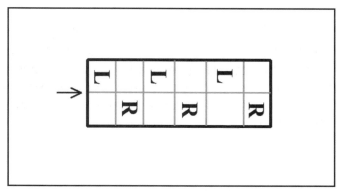

Diagram 2. Running ropes – every other hole drill

We run a *wave drill.* You have seen those big linebacker standup dummies. They have a cone shape to them and we lay them down long ways [Diagram 3]. We put a player in between two dummies. I get in front of him and I give him directions with my hand. I want him to go over the dummy on the right and then come back and go over the dummy on the left. It is a really simple drill. He is going to lead with his front foot and lift his back foot. It teaches him to get that front foot over the dummy and his back foot comes over. Then he goes back the other way. It is a good movement drill.

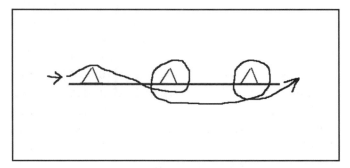

Diagram 3. Wave drill

The wave drill emphasizes *change of direction* and *lateral movement.* You can have some fun with this drill. You can catch the linemen off balance when

they are not concentrating. It is a good drill to teach lateral movement and to keep their shoulders square. They want to be perpendicular to the line of scrimmage.

The next drill we do is the *spin drill* [Diagram 4]. Here we stress the fundamentals of keeping the *shoulders square, proper balance,* and *body control.*

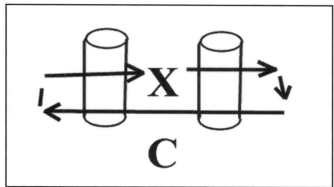

Diagram 4. Spin drill

We have a big bag that holds about 300 pounds of sand. We call it *Big Bertha* [Diagram 5]. We bang on that bag every day. It is hung on a swing set apparatus. We have the managers pull it up off the ground so it swings on the swing set. The players bang the bag, keeping their feet open, and their shoulders square. You can put the offensive lineman down in a two-point stance or you can back him off the ball. As soon as the bag swings forward he hits and lifts the bag. You can put him in the three-point stance and snap the ball and then have him take on the bag. We just keep working against that bag for four to five good pops. This teaches the players how to use their hands and how to punch.

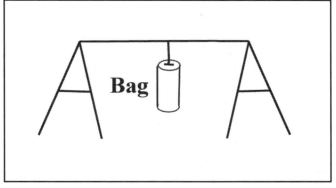

Diagram 5. Big Bertha bag drill

We use another drill we call the *softball toss* [Diagram 6]. This drill teaches *lateral movement.* The coach gets in front of the offensive lineman five- to six-yards apart. You take a softball and roll it on the ground to the lineman three to four yards to his right or left. The lineman must slide his feet to get over in front of the softball, field it, and toss it back to you. You go three or four times to each side. This forces him to move his feet. He must slide his feet and shuffle over to get the ball. After he picks the ball up he tosses it back to the coach. Then he shuffles back to the middle of the drill. The one thing you do *not* want him to do is to click his heels. He must keep his feet fairly wide. This is a good hand-eye coordination drill. It is a good conditioning drill as well.

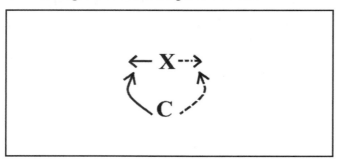

Diagram 6. Softball toss drill

I want to talk a minute about the *offensive lineman's stance.* I am not an etched-in-stone kind of coach. I give our kids a lot of room to experiment with their stance. You may have a 6'5" offensive tackle. You may have a 5'8" offensive guard. One year that happened to me when I was coaching in high school. The 6'5" player may be your best athlete. That small player inside may have stiff hips. The center may be okay but he has a certain problem. None of those positions are the same. That is the reason I cannot understand why a coach would want everyone to line up in the same stance. All payers are not made the same. God made everyone of us different. Some of us have more flexibility than others and some of us are a lot stiffer than others. We do not try to make five players look like a bunch of clones.

I am not a big coach on having the right hand down if you are in the right-hand stance on the right side. If you are left-handed, I think you can still play on the right side. You may get the best results with them using the right hand on the right side and the left hand on the left side of the line. But if a kid tells me he cannot get the hang of it by making him put the hand down that he is not comfortable with, then I will allow him to put that other hand down. If you don't

allow him to do it, he is going to fight you. It will take you forever to convince him he can do it. Let him be in a left-handed stance. I do not see a big deal about all of that. We let the kids get into a stance they can get into where they feel they can make all of the moves we ask them to do. They must be able to pull, drive block, pass set, and do other blocks. If the player is not comfortable he will start tipping the play off. You are trying to put the player in a stance his body will not allow him to get into. Let him find a stance, as long as it is fairly sound, and he can do the things you ask him to do.

I think *balance* is the key in a stance. You ask them to do a lot of things from that stance so they have to be balanced. I like my linemen to be a little wider with their feet. In conditioning drills, we always tell them to be shoulder-width apart. If you have a player who is 6'5", then shoulder-width apart is not wide enough for him. Let him get his feet a little wider. You want to lower his center of gravity by lowering his hips.

I do not teach traditional *toe-to-instep stagger.* I want a big player to spread his base out. We want his feet wide and we want him to get a little stagger. Give them a day or two to experiment with their stance.

I want them to come up with their arms relaxed and their arms on their knees. I want them to be in a position where they can reach out and touch the ground with their hand. They have very little weight on their hands at all. They must be able to flick the grass and stay in that stance. When they pick the hand up, they do not want to fall forward and they do not fall backwards on their heels. That is what we mean by being balanced. When you first start teaching the stance the players cannot sit in that position for a long time. The quads are not used to this. They can't sit there long because the quads are on fire. They are not used to using those muscles.

On the off hand, or the hand not on the ground, you can put it on the opposite knee or down on the ankle. I do not like the elbow on the knee with the hand up in the air. That is a personal preference. We do not want their shoulders tilted. So it is up to the coach where the off hand goes.

After you get him in a comfortable stance, then you can start working on him on the moves you want him to do. When you start teaching the moves, take it one step at a time. "We are going to take one step with the right foot." The next day we add another step to the drill. Then you build on the drill. Then you go one, then two steps. "One, two, right foot, left foot." You work on this until the players get comfortable coming out of the stance doing what you want them to do. The teaching must be very deliberate. Drill the heck out of them.

The key to *pass protection* is how fast the players can come out of the stance and get them to where they want to be to blocking their defender. It is a matter of how fast the offensive line can go from spot A to spot B. You must get the blocker to the point you want him to be at to block the defender.

On a three-step drop, our players are going to take a six-inch drop at the most. That is as deep as we want them when we are throwing the three-step drop pass. The blocker must be really firm. It is almost a matter of replacing their feet, now that we have them understanding how deep they have to be to block the defender.

Most defensive teams offset the defensive linemen. To help the other offensive linemen is to teach them how to *set up on an angle.* Most offensive linemen will jump and turn when they are trying to block the 3 technique. That is old school. If you open the hips and shoulders, you give that defender a two-way run at the quarterback. I want my linemen to set and drop straight back off the line of scrimmage. It does not matter how fast the defender is, you do not have to drift more than six inches outside to take care of the speed rusher. If you will take that six-inch step and back up, the defender must cross the line to get to the quarterback. I want the tackle to sit in there as square as he can be. As soon as the defender makes a move toward the quarterback, now he starts to open. He is just reading the defensive end. When he turns to come to the quarterback, that is when the tackle starts to open. He should be fronted up and it should put him right down the middle of the defensive end. The big mistake I see is the offensive linemen opening up too soon. We want to take the defender deep before we open. The key is to get some depth and get them back off the ball, but not at a big angle. We want them to stay square. When the defender comes to the quarterback the blocker must open, drop his hips, and work his body down low. This is where all of the drills we teach come into play.

When the defender comes to the blocker, we want to be heavy with the inside hand. When we first start teaching these techniques, we make the offensive lineman bury his outside hand. We make him use one hand on the drill. If you only had one hand as an offensive lineman, which hand would you want to use? The *inside hand* unless you are the center. We make them stick the outside hand in their shorts when we start teaching the drill. He must stick his inside hand under the defender's breastplate and grab him. To the official it looks like he has a closed fist. When the defensive lineman gets up the day after a game, his chest should be black and blue from the number of times the blocker pinched him in that area. If you bring the hand outside you are going to get called for holding. The key is to get those handles on the breast. That is what they made those breastplates for as far as I am concerned. If I can get him by those breastplates, I can steer him around. He is not going anywhere. If he wants to go outside, we can stretch him with the outside foot and push him with the inside arm all the way to the sideline. We can let his momentum carry him outside the quarterback.

If he wants to come back inside, I must square back up. I am going to take my outside arm and take him down inside and push him over the pile of players inside. We have help down inside. We do not want to try to redirect the defender. Take him the way he wants to go. The same is true for the inside blockers as well.

Against *zone stunts*, you want to have the five offensive linemen set up at the same depth. Against *man stunts*, you have room to adjust with individual moves. But against the *zone blitz*, you must draw the line two- to three-yards deep all across the line so they can pick up the stunts at the same plane.

I have a lot more I could talk about, but I am out of time. You are welcome to come to Baylor to see us. I enjoyed visiting with you. Thank you.

COACHING HERITAGE AND OVERTIME STRATEGIES

University of Arkansas

Men, it is good to be home. It does not seem that long ago that I was the head coach at Murray State University. I had four great years at Murray State. I will never forget the day before I was hired at Murray State. I was an assistant coach at the University of Arkansas at the time. I was in one of those situations where I did not know if I was going to stay at Arkansas or go to another college to coach. I went in to see Coach Frank Broyles. He is a great man. I was the last student-athlete that he signed at Arkansas. He is still our athletic director at Arkansas.

Coach Broyles asked me this question: "What do you want to do in life?" I told him I wanted to be a head coach in college. Coach Broyles has a southern draw when he talks. He is an unbelievable speaker. He replied, "That is what you should dooooo!" I did not have the courage to tell Coach Broyles there were not many colleges that wanted me to be their head coach. I had been an assistant in college for 16 years.

A week later a friend of mine was at Murray State. He was the basketball coach, Scott Edgar. He told me one of the applicants for the football head coaching job had dropped out of the running and he told me he thought he could help me get the job. The A.D., Mike Strickland, called and asked me if I would be interested in coming over for a visit. I said, "I would love to visit with you at Murray State."

I went in to see the head coach at the time, Danny Ford. I told Danny I was going to visit Murray State about the head coaching job. Danny told me I would not get the job, but it would be good experience for me to go for the interview. That is a good example of the confidence others can give us in times of transition.

I went to Murray State and it was an unbelievable experience. I was blessed to get the head coaching job at Murray State University. At times, people have a tendency to pour cold water over you in a situation such as this. I had friends come up to me and say,

"Congratulations, you are a head coach now. But tell me, why would you take that job?" Murray had led the nation in number of losses for the last several years. That started getting to me after a few others said similar things. I started getting nervous. I could not hire a staff for a couple of months. We did not have enough helmets and shoes. I did not realize we were going to be in the fund-raising business.

To make this long story short, it comes down to this: *It is what you make of the situation*. This is the reason I have an awesome respect for the high school coaches. My dad was a high school coach for 37 years at the Arkansas School for the Deaf. I grew up as a coach's son. The best days of my life were at the Arkansas School of the Deaf. That is where I learned about *family*. This is where I first understood the word *team*. I was the one who always got called off the court. I was the one who was talked to during the time-outs. I was the coach's son. I loved to sit on the old school bus and ride to the away games. I had a job to do on the bus. My dad would give me a box after the game. In the box would be baloney sandwiches. After the game my job was to hand out the baloney sandwiches. I would go down the aisle of the bus and pass out the food. I was only six years old when I started doing this. I was fired up after the game because I knew my job was to hand out the sandwiches. Here is what was great about this job. At the bottom of the box there was always a baloney sandwich leftover — always one left. I would say, "Dad, all of the sandwiches are passed out. There is one left." My dad would ask, "All of them have been passed out?" He would tell me that last sandwich was for me. That baloney was about one-half inch thick. There was nothing like it. I did my job and I was rewarded with the baloney sandwich. There is nothing like being a coach's son.

Also at the Arkansas School for the Deaf, I learned about family. Some of the deaf people felt like it was *us against the rest of the world*. The deaf people knew no color. If you could talk with the deaf people you were on their team. Again, it was an *us-against-the-world* attitude. On the playground there was a dirt basketball court that is not what most of you are familiar with. You can't just say, "Hey Johnny, throw me the ball." You must use your eyes and you must use your mind. If you could communicate with them, you were a member of their family.

I went to Murray State University as the head coach. I will never forget that first team meeting. I was all ready for the meeting. I had my Bear Bryant and my Frank Broyles speech down pat and I was ready for the players. I had so much fire and ginger in me because I had been waiting for this day for a like time. I was nervous, just like I get before a kickoff of a game. I could not wait for that first team meeting. The meeting was scheduled to start at 7:00 p.m. It became 7:00 p.m., and all of three bodies were sitting in the chairs. I looked at the A.D. and asked him, "Mr. Stickland, did you get the word out to the players?" His reply was this: "Oh yes, they know it is a 7:00 p.m. meeting. You must realize they are usually late for meetings." I thought about it and replied that this was going to stop. I am the new coach and they should be here on time. About 7:15 p.m., another 15 bodies wandered into the meeting room. As time went on, more and more players showed up. The thing that got to me was their attitude as they came into the meeting room. To them I was *just another head coach*.

By 7:37 p.m., all 69 of the so-called football players were present for the meeting. They had won only two games the year before. They did not win but one or two games each year for about four years before I came to Murray. I could tell football was not real important to them. I could not take it any longer so I went after them.

"How many of you here tonight knew we had a 7:00 p.m. meeting?" I still did not get much out of them. I asked the question again if they knew about the time of the meeting. Again, there was no response. "I tell you what I am going to do. I am going to set my watch back to 6:45 p.m. We are going to walk out of this room. We are going to empty this room. We are going to walk back into this room as a family and on time. You are going to put your butts in the back of the chairs and you are going to look me in the eye. We are going to do that because it is the right thing to do."

I was a nervous, 35-year-old coach who was on new ground, new territory. Now guys, I love earrings on women, and I have accepted them on men to a degree, but I had some players in that meeting that had earrings that hung down from their ear lobe down to their shoulder. They were dangerous on them. I told them they could not play ball with those things on. They just did not look like football players.

One player in the back of the room said, "Is this some kind of *nut* here?" I felt he was making fun of my name. That was my first confrontation. I went back to that guy and told him that everyone was leaving the old team. "You either get in or you get out. We are going out at 6:45 pm and we are going to come back in this room as a team. What are you going to do?" He replied, "I will go along with you."

Now, what is this story all about? This is where you come into the picture. In that first job that I was so nervous about and so uptight about, there were some good things that developed out of the time I put in there. I wanted to be a head coach so bad and I wanted to be successful so bad I gave it everything I had. In the four years I was at Murray, of the 69 players in that first meeting, 33 of them have gone on to become coaches. This is the reason you are a *difference maker*. As a coach, you do not know whom you are going to affect.

In that first meeting, I kept thinking, "Boy, I am glad Coach Frank Broyles or Coach Lou Holtz are not here. They would really laugh at me now." For me, this is where it all started. It is what you make out of the situation you are involved in that matters. It is your *attitude* that counts. It is what you make out of the job that really counts.

Within two years we were champs of the Ohio Valley Conference at Murray. In my first year they were discussing the possibility of getting rid of the game of football. They talked about Kentucky being a basketball state and not interested in football. But we changed that in a short period of time.

I asked the A.D. about the student involvement at the football games. We had a beautiful stadium at Murray. It seats 16,000. In the years 1990 to 1992, the students numbered about 200 at each home game. We had 9,000 students at Murray and only 200 of them were going to the games. I asked the A.D. how much it cost for the students to attend the games. He said, "The student can come to the games free." That is all I wanted to hear. I told the A.D. I was going to get 6,000 students to come to the games. He told me that Murray was referred to as a *suitcase college*. You know, when it gets to be Thursday and the students start packing those suitcases and start heading home for the weekend. They told me a lot of that stemmed from the fact that Murray was in a dry county.

I found out that a fraternity was having a party and about 2,500 students would be there. I asked if I could make an announcement about the football game at Racer Stadium that Saturday night. I told the person in charge that I would be at the party early to make my spill and leave. "I will be there about 7:00 p.m." The guy looked at me and said, "No, no, coach. You do not want to come at 7:00 p.m. or even 8:00 p.m. You want to come at 12 midnight. That is when they will all be there and that is when they will be feeling good. If you will come at 12 midnight, we will let you go up to second floor of the frat house, crawl out the window on the roof, and we will give you a bullhorn and everyone can hear you." I said, "Great!"

The night of the party I got ready to go. My wife Diana asked me where I was going. "Honey, you are not going to believe this. I am going to a fraternity party. I am going to recruit me some fans for our game." I told her what I was going to do. "You are going to a fraternity party at 11:30 p.m.? You are going out on the roof with a bullhorn in your hand?" I told her that was indeed what I was going to do.

I went to the party and they introduced me. I went out on the roof with the bullhorn. Let me tell you, the students were oiled up. They were having a good time. I simply asked them to come to the game. "I need your help. I want you to sit on the side of the field where the opponents come out on the field. I want you to make it a bad night for them. Make it tough on them. You will get a free ticket to the game. Can I count on you being there?" They assured me they would be at the game.

The record for the number of students at the games had been 300 students. We had 3,600

students at that first game. We broke a record for the attendance and the students liked what they saw. We did not win, but we started becoming a team that night. That is when our program started to show a little hope. Our players started believing. When that happens, that is when you start achieving goals.

Today there are not as many *touch-football games* as there use to be. I think this is where we as coaches come into play. My son is 14 years old. He is almost 15 years old now. If I do not start the pick-up touch game, it does not get started. I understand this situation. Kids today like to play video games. They would rather put in a DVD or watch something on TV. I will yell at my son to come with me and throw the ball in the yard. It is important that we keep the games going. "Hey son, get a football and let's get a game going." Those games come during some of the best days of a young player's life. These activities are difference makers.

I have been very fortunate. As I said before, my father was a high school coach. Most of you here tonight are difference makers and you do not even know it. How many of you here tonight have been in coaching five years or less? Guy, I am here for you. We need difference makers in coaches. My dad was a difference maker. Deaf players still come to our door to tell my dad that he did a great deal for them. I could tell you story after story of the deaf players that have come back to thank my dad for making a difference in their life.

I had the privilege to play for Coach Frank Broyles, Lou Holtz, and Eddie Sutton. Eddie Sutton's assistant coaches were Pat Foster and Gene Keady. I got to play for Lou Holtz. He is a great coach. He was really tough in the 1970's. He was really tough on quarterbacks. I thought he was a lot tougher on me than others. I had the opportunity to play for Jimmy Johnson at Oklahoma State. I thank Jimmy Johnson today for what he did for me. I had a dream when I was nine years old that I was going to be in the NFL, NBA, or both. Things were going according to my plans when I was a senior in high school. I had over 250 offers from colleges. I had offers from Bear Bryant, Ron Meyers, Dick Vermeil at UCLA, Frank Broyles of Arkansas, and Jim Stanley at Oklahoma State. I went with my home state of Arkansas. But after Coach Frank Broyles retired at Arkansas, I transferred to Oklahoma State with Jimmy Johnson. He had been at Arkansas as an assistant and had helped recruit me to come to Arkansas. I played two years for Jimmy Johnson. I thought I was going to play in the NFL. I spent a total of two hours in an NFL Camp. I was cut in a heartbeat. Boom! I was back in Stillwater, Oklahoma. I was getting out of the car when I returned from the NFL tryout. Jimmy Johnson came up to me and asked me what I was going to do now that I had been cut. "Coach, I am going to continue to work because I know I belong in the NFL. I am going to be in the NFL, NBA, or both." He replied, "That is great. But until that time comes you are still six hours short of your degree. Why don't you come to work for me?"

I was the freshman coach and lived in the Hank Iba Dorm. When Jimmy told me I was going to live in the dorm, I walked away. My thoughts were this: "Who does this guy think he is talking to me like that with his can of hair spray, telling me what I am going to do? I am going to live in the dorm and make about one dollar and sixty-five cents per hour?" Little did I know in 1980 if I had turned down that job, Jimmy could have had hundreds of applications for that job in no time at all. Jimmy Johnson did me a favor and gave me a job.

When we were in the meeting room at Oklahoma State, I was in awe. On the staff were Dave Wannstedt, Pat Jones, and several other important coaches. As a grad assistant, I sat in the back of the room. I was the *gopher*; I was the G.A.

In 1981, we were in the meeting room and Jimmy Johnson said, "We have not had one freshman quit the team this year during two-a-days. We have not had one freshman get a DUI. We have not had one freshman pull a fire alarm or kick a window out. The credit for this goes to Huston Nutt."

I was in the back of the room. I nudged Pat Jones and asked him what did Jimmy had said. Pat said, "He is talking about you silly. Listen! He said you did a good job, Houston." I was on cloud nine after that.

I could not wait to tell my future wife this story. I said, "Diana, you are not going to believe it. Jimmy Johnson bragged on me in front of all of the coaches. Now, here comes the cold water again. This is why you must fight cold water, even with your best buddies. She replied, "Houston, are you talking about that dollar-and sixty-five cents an hour job you

have?" She was a geologist. She went straight from the classroom to a job making $35,000 a year in Oklahoma when the oil was hitting just right. "Houston, are you still living over in the dorm with those boys?" She already had a checking account. She was buying appliances for her house and I was living with boys in a dorm. This was the way she looked at it. I was getting excited about a coach that had told me I had made a difference in the life of the freshmen players.

She asked me if that was what I wanted to do. I answered her with this: "*This is what I want to do. I want to be a coach.*" She asked me if I would only make one dollar and sixty-five cents an hour. I explained that I did not expect the pay to be that low all of the time. "You have to pay your dues. You have just ruined my day because Jimmy Johnson said something good about me today."

Men, there is nothing like the coaching profession. You are a difference maker in young people's lives that need you more today than ever before. When I go to see young athletes and coaches, there is a bond between them that I cannot explain. We sign close to 25 players per year. For the last 9 or 10 years, 18 of those 25 players have come from a one-parent home. Who is going to be their father image? You are, coach. You do not know what is sticking with the players you are working with. As a coach you affect people's lives.

Do you think we knew that 33 of those players at Murray State would go on to become coaches? They became teachers and affected people's lives. We never know how we affect the young people today. Coaching is an awesome profession and we must keep it going. It seems every day there is someone trying to tear the profession down. It is all about *attitude*. I believe you must have a great attitude. I believe we must have *character*. We must have *integrity*. Kids are looking at the coach. You are their *role model*. You are their *leader*.

After Jimmy Johnson gave me a chance at Oklahoma State, I went back to Arkansas and was a G.A. for Lou Holtz. That was about my fourth year as a G.A. I equate that to a high school coach who wants to be close to the kids. But I wanted to be a college coach and I stayed on that level. I told Diana I was going to give it one last year or I was going to go back to my high school alma mater, Little Rock Central High School.

Lou Holtz taught me some important lessons. He was very exact. He was a perfectionist. If you do not get anything from this lecture tonight, be sure to get this point. It is the best example I can give you about coaching.

Lou Holtz gave me the task of coaching the fullbacks at Arkansas. That is a tremendous responsibility for a G.A. Here is where I always got a knot in my stomach. I will assure you, the G.A. that works for him today has a knot in his stomach. This is because Lou Holtz expects perfection. I had the fullbacks and I was a grad assistant. Lou smokes a pipe. I can smell that smoke right now. He would puff on that pipe in those meetings. "Coach Nutt, are you going to get those fullbacks to take that six-inch step today?" I would assure him I would get the fullbacks to take that six-inch step.

When we went to the field that day, I knew I had to get one thing right. I had to get a fullback in a perfect stance and I had to get him to take a six-inch step. I had to do this because Lou Holtz asked me to do that. "Will you get it done?" Things were going just right until period seven. I had a fullback take a false step. Now, picture this on the practice field. "Houston, I thought you said you could get the job done today with the fullbacks? You have had your chance, now move out of the way." I was embarrassed because I did not get the job done.

After supper the coaches would come back and go over all the film of practice. Here is the lesson I am going to give you that helped me forever. This is why I love Lou Holtz today. I love him because of this. One night we were watching the film of practice and Lou Holtz asked me if I had gone over a certain play with the fullbacks. For some reason, I guess I was frustrated, but my response was this. "Coach Holtz, I went over that play 100 times with the fullbacks." Coach Holtz turned off the projector and started puffing on that pipe. I could hear him sucking on that pipe. I knew I was in deep trouble. Here it is. He said, "What did you say?" I said, "Coach, I went over the play 100 times with them." He responded with this. "Then I question your teaching ability if you went over the play 100 times with them. Let me ask you something, Mr. Nutt. What is so significant about the

number 100? Why not 1,000 times? Why not 2,000 or until the job is done?"

Men, I assure you that was the right answer here. If you do not get anything else out of this talk, take this point home with you. Young coaches, he taught me that night that it did not matter if I went over the play 500 times in my mind; *you must go over the play until the kid gets it right*. You must go over the play until they get the play right and you have to tell them why they are or are not getting the play. You may have to do something extra to get the job done. It may not be a nine-to-five day for you. This is what you love about teaching and coaching. You are going to make a difference if you believe in the kid and you go over and over the play until they get it right. That is coaching. That is it! That is what Lou Holtz taught me and that is why he is one of the best teachers in the world. He is a great teacher, disciplinarian, motivator, and all of those things. The same is true with Jimmy Johnson and Eddie Sutton. All of the great coaches have that ability to teach. They knew how to get the job done.

My mother was an English teacher at the Arkansas School for the Deaf. Each day after school I would go to my mom's room. One day I got to the room and my mother was going over a simple sentence with a seventh-grade student. She went over the sentence several times but the student was not getting the point. I asked my mother if she could hurry with the student so I could visit with her and then go to the gym to play. It seemed like a 45-minute time span was like two days. I wanted to know when I could go play. She told me I could go play when she finished. She had *perseverance*. She had a *never-give-up attitude*. That is the type of teacher we must be. That is what it is all about.

I wish I had a dime for every time I heard someone say that they wished they were 6'2". Or they will say, "If I just weighed 200 pounds, and if I could just run 4.6." When I hear those remarks I want to hit them over the head. "Young man, we recruited you for a reason and we believe in you. You have everything you need." I tell them to take the 4.8 and try to get to 4.75 first. That is what we do. We take what they have and we try to build and improve on what they have.

Every day we ask them these three questions. First is the question of trust. *Can we trust you to do what is right?* Can we trust you to be on time? Can we trust you to do what is right when no one is looking? The second question is *are you committed?* Commitment means you are willing to do what it takes for the good of the team. The third question is *do you really care?* Do you care about your coaches? I know the coaching staff cares about the players. Do you care about us? If we can say yes, he can be trusted; yes, he is committed; and yes, he cares, then we feel we have something.

I am so excited about coaching. I cannot say enough about the job you are doing with our young people. That is why I am here on Valentine's night. I feel I owe so much to Murray State University. They were willing to take a chance on an assistant coach. I had a chance to meet a lot of the high school coaches that are here tonight. They helped me at Murray. We won two championships when others said there was no way we could win. I think it is important to win regardless of the level you are on. Don't let people pour cold water on you, your profession, or where you are located. If you can make one kid better, then you can make another one better. Then it becomes contagious. Then you can start to build that trust and that family spirit. You do not know where it will take you in your career.

If they had told me back in 1991 that we were going to win two championships at Murray and we were going to win the first playoff game in the school history, I would have said, "No way."

When I went to Arkansas, the players did not believe we could win. We cannot keep all of our athletes under one roof. Because our president wants our athletes to live in the dorms with the other students, we have a hard time checking on our athletes. We can only house our redshirt freshmen and sophomores in one place. The others can stay in the dorms with the other students. Do you know how long it takes to do a bed check at night in this situation? It takes a good two hours. Why? Three players live in one apartment, two live in this duplex, and three more live down the road a mile from the others. It is hard to build family in this atmosphere.

In that first year at Arkansas I kept the door to my office open all of the time. Not one player came in to see me. At Murray State the players lived in my office all the time. They wanted to talk. At Arkansas the kids just went about their way. They were not used to talking with the head coach. They did not want to get involved in my life. So I decided to get involved in their life.

So one night at 10:45 p.m., I started out to visit them. I knocked on a door of the players. It was great. I knocked on the door of a real good athlete. Knock — Knock! "Who is it?" "It is Coach Nutt!" This is what I heard. "Right! Yea! Get out of here." They had not had a coach check on them in four seasons. Knock — Knock! Finally they came to the door and said, "Coach Nutt, what is up?" I would proceed to tell them that we had study hall tonight and that you two did not make it the study hall. The tutor said you two were like all the other jocks who did not care and that was the reason we were getting beat at Arkansas. Now, we had 28 of the 30 players at study hall. But you do not hear about the guys doing things right. You hear about the ones that are not doing things right. I told those two players they had to find that tutor, apologize to him, and make the time up. I think it is important that they know they must be held accountable. We had a little reminder to help them to remember to be on time, and to do what is right. I wanted them to know that someone was listening to them. There comment was, "No one is looking at me, because I am second team." I let them know that it did not matter if they were a backup, someone was watching them. I think it is important to ask the players what kind of shadow they are.

I have rambled enough about football 101. I was asked to talk about overtime games. I do not know if Earl Browning, the Clinic Director, remembers this or not, but I begged him to let me speak on this clinic for three years when I was at Murray State. I would call Earl and ask him to let me speak at the Louisville Clinic. He would tell me to wait until the next year. I asked him year after year. In my fourth year we had won the OVC and he said, "Houston, I want you to speak at the Louisville Clinic." Finally, after all of those years, I finally got to speak at the Louisville Coach of the Year Clinic.

This year Earl asked me to talk about *overtimes.* Earl said, "Houston, you are an expert on overtime games." I told him I did not know about that. He pointed out that we had been in four overtime games at Murray State, and one at Boise State. We went seven overtimes two years ago against Mississippi. Last year we went six overtimes against Tennessee. He said, "You must know something about overtime games."

I do not have a lot to say about those games, but I do have some ideas that you may be interested in. After that first year we started bringing more *two-point plays* to the game with us. We ran out of two-point plays in that first overtime session with Ole Miss. You do not think about the two-point plays beyond one or two plays. You must think more about the two-point plays. What do you think you want to do on the two-point plays? You must know how to approach the overtime games.

I love the 25-yard line deal. Rules in the college game are a little different than in high school. I think the overtime rules are an exciting way to decide a football game. David Cutcliff and I had this discussion after our seven overtime games. David did not like it because it took the kicking game out of play. Our overtime rule is not like the NFL rule. In that game in Oxford our offense had over 110 plays in that game. I did worry about the condition of our players. I like the rules we play under now because it makes the game exciting.

In the first two overtimes you can score and kick an extra point. In the third overtime period you must go for a two-point play. I want to share some thoughts we had during our overtime games. I am going to show the film of the overtimes and comment on them as far as the points I think are important to consider in an overtime game.

The first consideration is this: What have you done well in the game up to this point of the game? We consider the run and the pass. One thing that helped us is that we started doing more passing in the red zone. Each day we tried to make that a part of our practice plan.

Here we have a fourth-and-one situation. We are going against Eli Manning, the Ole Miss quarterback. I am scared about our kicker on a field goal because we had already missed one field goal attempt. It was fourth-and-one. I did not think a field goal would win the game at this point. You have to discuss those types of things. We had a couple of coaches looking at me trying to tell me to kick the field goal: *"Kick it!"* We did not kick the field goal. We had been consistent in getting a hat on a hat, so we went with our *zone weak play*. We had a good back that could run and we scored.

The thing about overtime is to decide if you want to go on offense or on defense first. In most situations you want to put the opponent's offense on the field first. But, when are going against such a good quarterback as Eli Manning, who is so accurate, you know you will have to score seven points to win the game. Those are the things you must talk through before the game.

The next situation is when we get a fumble after we were on defense first. Then we went conservative. That was my fault. All we had to do was to kick a field goal and we would win. We were conservative lining up the field goal and we missed it.

Then we went to the third overtime. We noticed the backside end was stretching very hard on every stretch play. We told our quarterback, Matt Jones, to fake the stretch and keep the ball. We did not want him to throw the ball, we wanted him to fake the stretch and then keep the ball. Matt Jones runs a 4.6, so he had speed to get the ball in the end zone.

Now we had another two-point play. We never considered calling five, six, or seven two-point plays. Basically we just ran out of two-point plays to run. Sometimes we make it more complicated than what it really should be. You must take your best plays and play.

The first two-point play we tried was a *reverse play*. We always have some type of reverse in the game plan. We had never before had a reverse play for two points fail. Low and behold in Oxford, Mississippi, it failed.

Our quarterback is Matt Jones. He is really a neat person. He can throw the fade, and he can throw play-action passes, but he is not a real tough passer throwing the ball outside. But here is what he does best. He is the best backyard player I have ever seen in my life. He is a real sandlot player. He can make it happen. He does what we call *overcome coach* a lot of the time. That is what he did in our overtime.

The thing we found out in the overtime game was the fact we had more errors by the players then than during the rest of the game. We had mental errors during the overtime. That is something you can talk about in planning your overtime. You may want to go back to the basic plays. That is what I think you should do in the overtime games. We are going to keep it simple so we do not have a busted play. The errors kill your momentum in the overtime. Even if you are tired, you should be able to make the fundamental plays.

Next we went to the *mid-line play* in the overtime. It is a play that Coach David Lee brought to us. It is an interesting play because it starts in the I formation. It is a true *read play*. We are reading the 3 technique. If the 3 technique closed down inside, we want to keep the ball. The tailback is coming to block the linebacker. Now the free safety must make a play.

When we got into the overtimes, we tried to run plays that our quarterback did his best on. We made so many mistakes in the Ole Miss game it was a miracle that we won the game, but our quarterback still found a way to make some big plays for us. We felt it was important for our players to be on *automatic pilot* in the overtime period.

When we got to the sixth overtime, our offensive line coaches were telling me to "run the ball, their defense is tired." They were barely getting down on one knee on defense. We decided to run straight at them. Our offensive line was able to move the pile.

During the overtimes we only ran three or four different plays. We ran the plays we felt the players could run in their sleep. When you are running the 110th play, it is difficult to keep from making mistakes.

In the Tennessee game this past year, we had the second longest overtime game in the world. We played at Tennessee in front of 108,000 people. That is a lot of people in that big house of theirs. We tried to add a few different formations but we ran basically the same plays. We stressed the basics in the overtime. We did not want any foolish penalties, no mistakes, and we wanted to execute the fundamentals. We believe you must always coach them during the overtime. We did not want to beat ourselves. We had just gone 11 weeks of winning the turnover margin against our opponents. We really tried to emphasis that point to our team. We had 36 take-a-ways at the end of the year. Our backs did not fumble until the bowl game.

We stressed the plays we felt the offense could execute the best during the overtime game against Tennessee. We still made too many mistakes. We are going to put the ball in hands of the players we feel will make the plays for us.

In the Tennessee game we got a turnover, very similar to the turnover we got in the Ole Miss game. We got the ball. All we had to do was to score and we would win the game. We can kick a field goal and win the game. I got too conservative again. We should have lined up in the middle of the field, run it up inside three times, and then kick the field goal go home. We missed the dang field goal and had to go to the next overtime.

We really stress that we do not want any foolish penalties during overtime. It does not do you any good to hit someone in the back 20 yards down the field.

If you have young players on offense, it is important to give them just a few plays in the overtime. You know what your players can do, especially after they have played 15 to 20 more plays than what they are use to doing. You want the players on automatic pilot. It seems there are always one or two players that do not get the idea and make mental errors. This is especially true when the players are tired.

We are going to stay with the best plays that got us to the end of the game. If you do not have designated two-point plays, then run the plays that have been good for you during the game. Keep it simple, and run the plays the team can execute best. Sometimes we do not follow our instincts and we do not do what our players do best. It all goes back to the basics and the fundamentals. You must run plays the team believes in. These are plays that we run over and over.

Arkansas does not have a lot of all-American players. There are two million people in Arkansas. We do not have that many SEC high school players in the state. That means we must go outside the state to recruit players. The bottom line is that we must do what the players do best.

In overtime I would suggest this: *Don't be too complicated.* Do what your team does best. I appreciate your attention. I feel like this is home. Louisville, Kentucky, has been real good to me. I appreciate all the coaches I came in contact with when I was coaching at Murray State. They helped me win two championships. It is good to see so many of our former players who are here as high school coaches today. I appreciate your attention.

QUARTERBACK DRILLS AND TECHNIQUES

Penn State University

My dad is a tough act to follow. Today is the first time I have ever gotten the last word at my house. As far as my mother's concerned, she thinks I am a good coach. At least she thinks someone in the family can coach. If any of you have an opening on your staff let me know. I may not have a job at Penn State after that last comment. I really do appreciate the Pittsburgh Clinic giving me the opportunity to speak with you. I am going to keep it very basic. I want to cover some of the things we do to develop our quarterbacks. I will cover the entire package. I will cover the mental and physical aspects of the game and the things we do to get them ready to play.

It is neat for me to speak to the coaches of southwestern Pennsylvania. Coach Joe Paterno mentioned Bob Phillips earlier. Bob was the quarterback coach at Penn State when I was in the ninth grade. I went to the football camp at Penn State when I was in the ninth grade. Art Bernardi was my individual group coach. Twenty years later I am coaching on the Penn State staff and Art Bernardi is working at our camp. I am sure it freaked him out to see me coaching at Penn State. But it has been neat coaching at Penn State. It is just a nice place to coach. I have really been impacted by a lot of coaches over my career. I feel I owe something back to the game of football.

I want to start out by giving you a scenario of what we ask our quarterbacks to do at Penn State. Playing quarterback at Penn State obviously has great rewards. However, there is a lot of responsibility that comes with the position. On game day we dress in our practice facility. Our dressing room is about one-half mile from the stadium. We get our pants, shoes, and t-shirt on and put the jersey on over the shoulder pads and helmet. Then we take the bus ride to the stadium. It is a neat experience going to the game on that bus. When you are a player, you do not really appreciate it. We take the bus up to the stadium and the people tailgating honk their horns.

It is a tradition at Penn State to have the head coach in the front seat on the right. The front left seat is for the starting quarterback. It is an unspoken tradition, but it is symbolic of how we feel about the quarterback at Penn State. The quarterback is our *coach on the field*. When we get to the stadium, the first person off the bus is not the head coach. It is the starting quarterback. When he gets off the bus there are 2,000 people cheering for him. When he walks into the stadium there are 110,000 people cheering him. When we played Nebraska there were close to 111,000 in the stadium. The first player the fans are going to cheer or bitch about is the quarterback.

When we evaluate the quarterbacks, we find there are things that we want them to have in their passing package. There are a lot of great passes out there. Some players can throw the ball through the wall. They can throw the ball 70 yards. They can do all kinds of things with the football.

The first thing we look for in a quarterback is *mental and physical toughness*. We talk about toughness and that is number one. The second thing we look for in the quarterback is his *footwork*. The third thing is his *vision*. If the quarterback has those three things, you have some talent.

As a coach, we feel we can develop two-and-a-half of those three things. By the time they get to our level, they either have the physical toughness or they do not have it. When our freshman quarterbacks come in that first year, we do not put a red scrimmage vest on them to keep them from getting hit by the defense. Now, after they have had a year under their belt and have played in games, we do put the red shirt on them. We do not feel we need to beat them up after they have had that experience of being hit in a game. Our defense knows if they see a quarterback under the center with a white jersey on, it is tee-off time. The defense waits for that day. That is one way we try to build toughness.

A lot of the mental toughness comes with *classroom work*. Joe talked about teaching your players. The most underestimated phase of coaching is in the meeting room. I am talking about our classroom setting. We have to do a great job as coaches in the classroom.

We used to give the players a scouting report. The players look at the report when you hand it to them and they comment on the fact they have played against some of the players on the other team. They will tell you they know all about the opponents. Then they lay the scouting report down and it never leaves the room. So what I have done in the last three years is to make them write down everything we have on the scouting report. I have a lot of board space in my meeting room. On those boards is the game plan laid out. We go over the personnel, our goal line package, and all of the other facets of the game. We plan it on the board for them.

On Monday we talk about the *personnel of the opponents*. We talk about the personnel groups. We may pick out one cornerback and decide we can beat him easier than we can beat the other cornerback. Sometimes we are right and sometimes we are wrong. We make our quarterbacks write all of this info down. We make them write down our goal line package. "These are our passes we are going to use on the goal line." We have them write down the two-point plays for the week. We have them write down all the new plays we are going to use each week.

Next we go into *situations* with them. We have them write down the different down-and-distance situations we can face in the game. We give them our game plan for *going in* when we get down on the goal line. They are writing all of this information down. We go over all of the first-down plays. Then we cover the second-and-long and second-and-medium plays. I talk with them in terms of the thought process that goes into the game plan.

We sit down and go over what we want to do in the passing game each week. I discuss the passes we pick for the week and go over the situations where we will use each pass. As the week goes on, they get a feel for the game plan. By Monday night we have the game plan for the passing game all set. We go into Tuesday with all of the game plan for the passing game. If we cover it in the meetings we have them write it down, we look at the films, and then we go out and practice the plays selected.

Certain aspects of the game we practice every day. On Wednesday we work on the going-in offense and the red zone offense. We look at the defense we expect to see in those situations. The only thing I write into their game plan is at the bottom of their sheets. I will write down the defenses our opponents have used in their last five games in the goal line situations. I cover the number of times they blitzed, and their top coverage in each situation. I quiz the quarterbacks on this information. When we are watching the tapes of the opponents, I will give them the situation and ask the quarterbacks what they expect in each situation. They must be able to respond immediately. This is the way we build the game plan.

Next we go over our *coming-out offense*. We go over the running plays. We cover plays coming out from our end zone. We cover the deep passes coming out. We go over the formations that give us the best chance to be successful. Again, these are things they write down and they learn as they go through the week. You would be surprised at the number of times the quarterbacks tell me they knew I was going to call a certain play. They may tell the person on the headset to tell me in the press box they knew that was the play to call. They know we have practiced these situations all week. At least I know they are paying attention.

As Joe mentioned, we want to spend time with our players. We do not spend time with them just to get to know them, but we want them to learn how their minds work. Don't be afraid to explain things to them. "This is why we are running this play."

We talk about coverages. I make the quarterbacks draw up the coverages. I do not give them a scouting report. I make them draw up the fronts. They have to know how everything works. When our quarterbacks walk on the field they have almost as much information as the coaches have. They can react accordingly. That is how we build the mental-toughness level. They have learned it in the classroom, they have watched it on the video, and now they go to the practice field and put the game plan in action.

We run our two-minute drill at the end of practice. We want them to practice the two-minute drill when they are tired just like they would be in the fourth quarter. Again, that is another way of building mental toughness. We are in a fortunate situation in that we can recruit the players we want to play with.

The thing I would tell you as you look at quarterbacks for your team is that you always get one player that looks like he has all of the potential in the world. On the other hand, you may get the player who gets in the game and never complains and gets the job done but is not flashy. Do not underestimate that player.

I want to put on a tape of the drills we use for our quarterbacks. These drills are *footwork drills*, *visual drills*, and at the end we will show you some *combination drills*.

(Film)

The first drill is the *board drill* [Diagram 1]. We use this drill to start most of our practices. It is a footwork drill. We are teaching them to move their feet in a tight space. The quarterback takes his pass drop and then sets up using the shuffle. They do not take the big steps. We want them to the point where they are almost hopping. We want their eyes downfield.

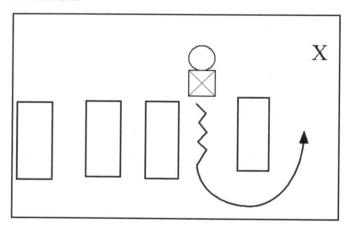

Diagram 1. Board drill

I stand down the field and look to see if they are looking downfield. If they are not looking downfield, I will hold up my hand with a certain number of fingers up. I make them call out the number of fingers I have up to make sure they are not looking down at the board.

After we hold up the numbers to make sure they are looking downfield, we make sure they have both

hands on the ball. We try to strip the ball from the quarterback as he takes his drop.

Next we go to the *six-yard square drill* [Diagram 2]. It is just a five-step drop square. We want to spend as much time as we can in our individual drills working on our drop run. I spend a lot of time working with them on their running techniques because they spend a lot of time in that run in the six yards. As they run around the cones, their eyes are straight ahead. The players are not down looking at the cones. They eyes should be downfield. When we are in spring practice or preseason practice, we will move the cones out to 15-yards apart. Now it becomes a 60-yard drop for them.

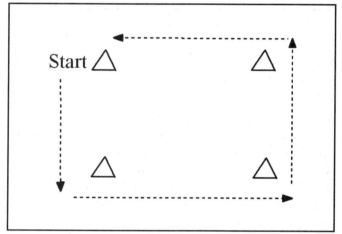

Diagram 2. Six-yard square drill

We stress getting back and away from the center as fast as we can. The ball is moving from side to side as the quarterback drops.

Next we go into some vision drills. This is a *peripheral vision drill*. To set up the drill, we tell the quarterbacks to go back and set up where they would normally drop on a pass play [Diagram 3. We tell them to set up on their drop. We place two receivers in the drill on the outside of the quarterback. They start moving outside almost to the point where the quarterback cannot see them. We want the quarterback to see the entire field or area between the two receivers. He must be able to see both receivers without staring at them. I am going to be in the middle of the field and the quarterback has to look at me. He can still see everything that is going on in this area. I will tell one of the receivers to raise his hand when the quarterback gets to his fifth step on the drop. The quarterback must find the receiver who raises his hand. Then he turns his head, locks on, and makes the throw.

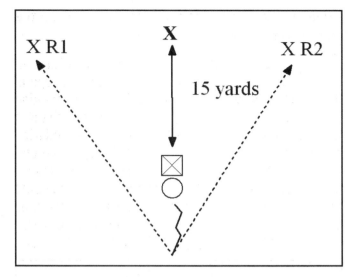

Diagram 3. Peripheral vision drill

I do not know how many of you saw the movie *Top Gun.* In the fight scenes where they were flying those jets, once the pilot got the target in range he locked on the target and shot the missile. It is no different than this drill. He is not staring at either receiver. We want him to be looking straight down the field so he can spot the open receiver. In the game, the defenders who are going to tell you who the open man is will be in the middle of the field.

The next drill is the *anticipation drill* [Diagram 4]. The hardest thing to do is to get the quarterback to throw the ball before the receiver is open. The difference in a good quarterback and a great quarterback is the ability to throw before the receiver is open. When we first started using this drill when I was coaching at James Madison, we used dummies on the drill. Now we use live defenders on the drill. As the quarterback drops back he is looking straight down the field. We put the receiver down the field at 10 yards. We do not want the receivers running 15 to 16 yards on the plays every time. The receivers do not start to run until the quarterback hits on his fifth step. Once the quarterback hits his last step on the drop, the receiver takes off on his route. The linebackers drop to their spots. The outside linebacker takes the curl and the inside linebacker takes the hook area. The receiver comes into the window between the two cones. We want the quarterback to know where that window is going to develop. The ball should be gone before the receiver gets around the cone.

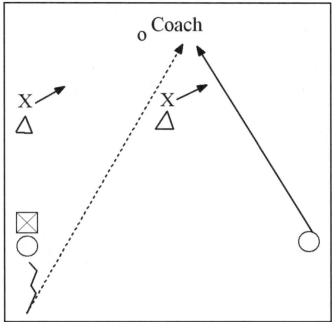

Diagram 4. Anticipation drill

This drill teaches the quarterback to anticipate the receiver's move to the open area. The other thing we want to teach the quarterback is to hit the receiver in the front part of the window. The reason for that is because the near linebacker is opening his shoulders to the outside. It is very difficult for him to turn his shoulders back to the inside. We also want to stay away from the farside linebacker. He has the best chance to tip the ball based on his shoulders tilted toward the receiver and can flow to the area. Our receiver has a chance to make the catch and get upfield and make a big play. Now we want to get the ball to him early in that window so he is away from the linebacker and he can turn and get upfield.

Using films is a great way to show the quarterback how to throw the ball before the receiver is open. He can see where the receiver is when he lets the ball go. The receiver has not made his break when the quarterback releases the ball. When the ball is released, the receiver is not open. But based on where he is going to be when the ball arrives he will be open. The quarterback must anticipate the receiver being open. The quarterback keeps his eyes downfield until he sees the receiver nearing the window. Then he turns his head and throws the ball.

If we have a young quarterback who has a hard time getting this concept down, I will get on the backside of the window and tell him to throw the ball to me. I stand at 16 yards and tell the quarterback to hit on his fifth step and then throw the ball to me. This gives the quarterback a mental image of the receiver already being in the window. Again, we want to throw the ball where the receiver is going to be and not where he is at the time of the release. We do not want the receiver to leave on his route until the quarterback hits on his last step.

Next we go into read drills. Again, these are vision drills. Now we run a *2-on-1 drill* [Diagram 5.] We have one receiver run the curl and the other receiver run the flat. You can run the smash combination. You can run the curl with the outside man and have the inside receiver run the flag behind the curl. However you set up our 2-on-1 passing situations in the game is how you should set this drill up.

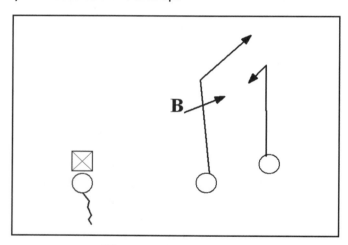

Diagram 5. 2-on-1 drill

The big mistake we all make is to go out and run the 7-on-7 drill. Coaches do not break it down into the basic components. In spring practice we work on these drills in our individual drill periods. When the quarterback drops back he is not staring at the receivers. When he hits on that last step he turns his head and shoulders in one motion. He locks on the receiver and throws the ball to the flat.

Next we go to our 3-on-2 drill [Diagram 6]. Now we have a receiver running the inside route, another receiver running the curl, and the third man running the flat route. You can set it up the way you run the 3-on-2 situations in a game.

Now the quarterback must see five things happen. Again, we are building up on the drill where

he can get into the 7-on-7 situations. The more you can break it down for the quarterback, the easier it will be for him when you get to the 7-on-7 drill.

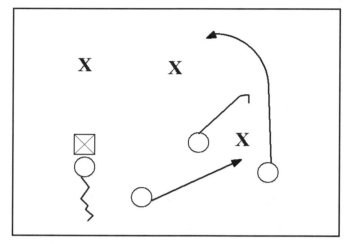

Diagram 6. 3-on-2 drill

The next drill is what we call our *board-scramble drill* [Diagram 7]. We go back to the boards. We have two receivers downfield. We are teaching the quarterback to scramble. He scrambles to his left or his right. You set the drill up the way you want him to scramble. We work on the drill both ways. The quarterback goes back to set up and scrambles to his left. We have a defender that shadows the quarterback. The defensive man can come up any of the lanes he chooses. As the quarterback scrambles we still want his eyes downfield reading the receivers. As he starts to move he must be able to feel the rush defender. If the defender gets in front of him, we want him to come underneath the defender. He may have to step up in the pocket as he would when he is flushed out of the pocket. It is not just a reset-and-throw situation.

The big mistake quarterbacks make when they get flushed out of the pocket is they tuck the ball and run. They do not look downfield for the receiver. As quarterbacks gain experience, they gain the confidence and start looking downfield. That is where the big plays come from. We want our quarterback to find the receiver at 16-yards downfield and then have the receiver turn it into a 60-yard play. Those are back breakers for the defense.

In the drill, we point to one of the two receivers downfield and tell them to scramble with the quarterback. I can wave them off on the drill. I do not want the quarterback to think he has to throw the ball every time he scrambles. The quarterback must read and make a decision and go with it.

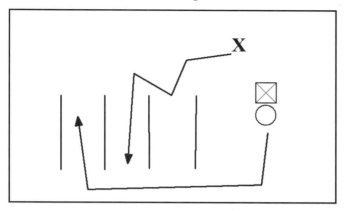

Diagram 7. Board-scramble drill

A key coaching point is for the quarterback to keep his eyes down the middle off the field as he scrambles. Now this drill becomes a peripheral vision drill as he moves. As he scrambles out of the pocket he must be able to read the receivers on the run.

Now we take the drill one step further. Instead of getting flushed up in the pocket, we get flushed outside the pocket [Diagram #8]. Now we are outside on the run. We use live defenders on the drill. You can use live defenders on the board drill as well. The quarterback comes outside looking downfield at the two receivers. If the defender comes up to force the quarterback, he dumps the ball to one of the receivers. If the receivers do not come to the ball, the quarterback has to run the ball if he is gets pressure from the outside.

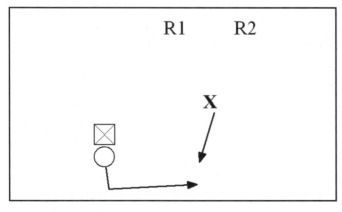

Diagram 8

Here is one coaching point for this drill. We do not want the quarterback looking all the way back to the other side once he has been flushed outside. If he sees someone open deep he can throw the ball deep. Even if the ball is picked off it is just like a punt. That does not bother us. We do not want the quarterback to throw anything underneath on the backside.

Our next drill is our *pass-reset drill* [Diagram 9]. Here we work against the defensive end coming upfield. In this drill we are not getting flushed. It is a situation where the defensive end has gotten a big jump on the offensive tackle. The tackle is still on the defensive end and he is going to run the end beyond the quarterback. It could be the end makes a move inside and the tackle runs him by the quarterback. The quarterback is only taking two shuffle steps in the drill. As he takes the two shuffle steps, he keeps his eyes downfield. He can see what is happening in front of him and he can react to them. We tell the defensive ends what we want on the drill and I tell the receivers what I want on the drill.

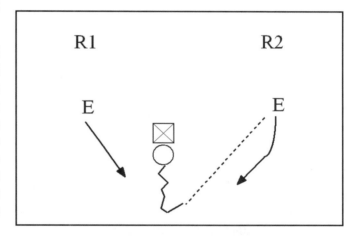

Diagram 9. Pass-reset drill

The quarterback takes two quick shuffle steps and throws the ball. We do not what him running out of the pocket. We want him to reset his feet. That is why we call it the reset drill. The quarterback can see what is happening downfield.

The next drill is our *play-action read drill* [Diagram 10]. It is hard to create a read drill when the quarterback is on the move. It is a play-action pass as we fake to a back. We read the free safety. We have a post receiver and a flat receiver. After the quarterback makes the fake he must get his head around on the play. It is a hard fake and the quarterback is going to stick the ball in the mesh area and pull his hand out. After he gets his head around he must find his keys in a hurry. He must find the safety very fast. If the safety bites, we will let the quarterback pull up and throw the ball deep. If the safety stays deep, we want the quarterback to come off to the linebacker. He must be able to read these defenders on the run. As he gets his head around he can read the defense.

One thing to help the quarterback on the fake is this. We have the other quarterbacks stand where the defensive end will be and have him tell the quarterback if he can see the ball. If the defense can see the ball, they know it is not a handoff. As the quarterback comes out of his fake, he must get his shoulders turned and he must find his target and get himself headed in the direction he is going to throw the ball.

Any time you can break down the drills so they can see what is happening, it makes it easier to teach. Once the quarterbacks learn the basics they can go to our 7-on-7 drill.

One last point I want to cover. I am a big fan of Dave Letterman. I am sure you have seen the *Top Ten List* that Dave does on his show. I decided to come up with 10 things I have learned about coaching quarterbacks. Here are the 10 things I think you should know about coaching quarterbacks.

Ten Things You Should Know about Coaching Quarterbacks

- You never want to second-guess them or make them look bad in front of their teammates. It is okay to get in their face, but you cannot second-guess them. If you do, it becomes very difficult for them to be the leader in the huddle. It is vital for them to have leadership in the huddle.

- Even in bad situations, find things the quarterback does correctly. For example, the quarterback may be making the correct reads but is missing the throw. If he is making good throws but reading the wrong man, tell him he is making good throws but try to find the open man.

- Encourage the quarterback to take chances and to force throws in practice. We let them force the throws in practice. This lets them test their ability to get the ball into tight spaces. If he does not try it in practice, he will never know if he can do it in a game. It does not

matter if he throws 10 interceptions in practice. Now, by the time of the game, he should have a good idea of what he can get away with as far as forcing the ball into tight areas.

- In terms of dealing with the press, take the blame for a bad game as much as you can. You can say things such as, "We did not help him out very much. We could have called a better game for him." This will help alleviate the blame and it will help build his confidence for the future.

- If the quarterback senses a lack of confidence in him, he will play the way he feels. You may not feel good about the quarterback, but you must get it out of your mind. You must show confidence in the quarterback or he will know it.

- Make the quarterbacks write down their five favorite passes. Don't be afraid to use those plays. If you get in key situations and the quarterback is struggling, you can pull out one of those five plays and call it. The guy has all the confidence in the world in those plays.

- You can never do enough footwork and vision drills. We have talked about those situations.

- Always stress speed in setting up on the pass. The longer he holds the ball the more the pass rush will come.

- It is hard to teach the quarterback to throw the ball before the receiver is open. Again, we covered that point.

- The quarterback must think like his coach. If you are calling the passes and the plays, he must think like you. You must spend time in meetings and outside of meetings talking about situations so he can get a feel of how you call the game.

What we do in our meetings and what we do on the field all tie in with these 10 points. Let me give you my email address. I have a drill packet and I will send you the drills. Just send me a note at jvp4@psu.edu. Make sure you include your mailing address. Thank you for your time and attention. I appreciate coming to visit with you.

REFLECTIONS ON FOOTBALL OVER THE YEARS

Penn State University

Wow! I did not expect such a warm welcome. Didn't you guys see the Capitol One Bowl Game? That was some greeting. I did not expect a standing ovation. I get a big kick out of coming back to the Pittsburgh Clinic. Some of you hear stories about all of the old guys. Well, that is what we have here. We have Earl Ceh and all of the old guys up here. The old gang is back in town. We can't shoot straight, but we are back in town.

When I started coaching as an assistant coach, I started out recruiting in western Pennsylvania. I did not even have an automobile. I hitchhiked down to Altoona, Pennsylvania, and then took a train. I had a great friend by the name of Red Moore pick me up at the railroad station in Pittsburgh up in Beaver Valley, and drove me around to all of the schools. At night I could see the smoke coming out of the chimney from the houses and you could see the smoke from the steel mills. It was a real exciting time for me and I have never forgotten that time period. I have a lot of ties to this area.

I got a kick out of talking with Ralph Friedgen earlier today. Ralph's father and I were on a clinic together one time about 100 years ago in New York. I had not tied the name of Ralph's dad to him until we talked about it on a Nike trip two weeks ago in Hawaii. About 25 Nike coaches were together in Hawaii. The Nike people pick up the tab for the coaches and their wives. We get together and visit about our problems and we tell a lot of lies to each other. I accused Ralph of cheating, I accused Bobby Bowden of cheating, and Bobby accused me of cheating. You know how those things go when you get together. It is just like most of you do when you come to this clinic. It is no different, except we were in Hawaii! (Ha Ha!) Okay, there is a little difference. Nike picks up the check for everything on that trip.

I knew Ralph Friedgen 40 years ago. If you notice, I have a tan having spent a week in Hawaii. Now, Ralph and Bobby do not have a tan. I do not play golf. They spent all day looking for their golf balls in Hawaii. They took 140 shots per round. They are not going to get much tan looking for golf balls.

Pete Dimperio asked me to come to the clinic and I agreed. Of course I knew Pete's father for a long, long time. He would take me down in the basement of Westinghouse High School. Now, I am going to bore some of you, but what the hell! I would go to Westinghouse High School when Pete's father was the coach. He was a great coach and he had some great teams. We would go down to the locker room in the basement and he would let me see all of his players. He really had some studs on his team. We had a lot of fun.

When Pete called me to be in the clinic, I asked him what other speakers were going to be in the clinic. He told me that Ralph Friedgen and Bobby Bowden were going to be in the program. I told Pete that Bobby Bowden had to be in the program after me. I told him I have to keep him behind me in more ways that one (number of wins in college football). If Pete had put me on after Bobby, I would still have come.

It is good to be here. There are a lot of things I would like to talk with you about. Earl Ceh suggested a couple of topics: *"how to identify leaders,"* or *"how to develop leadership on a team."* That is a very difficult thing to do and I am not going to be able give you much here. I have had kids who have become leaders on our team and I had no idea they would be leaders when they came into our program. I am not talking just about athletics. I am talking about the *character* of the team. I think all of us at some point in time try to figure out what the team is all about. What is going to make this time go? Who will be the players you can count on when you are down and out?

Today I can get up here now and feel a lot better about our program. The last time I was here we were not doing so well. We have some losing seasons. You have a better appreciation of where you are and what it takes to get straightened out when you are down. Last year we came back and won all of games except one game and that game was disputable. This year we had a good football team. We had a good team, but not a great team because we could not win the close games. With a break here or there we could have been a little better than we were. We were not a great team but we are getting back to where we were in the past.

The question about *developing leaders* is a very good question for me to answer. The only thing about that is the fact that I really do not know the answer. I only know there is a chemistry that you get with your team.

You may look at your team and have some thoughts about them. "Boy, if I was on Normandy Beach and we just landed for the invasion of Europe, and I was next to this guy, and the Germans were shooting the devil out of us, I would want that guy to say, 'Let's get the hell up and get out of here.'" He would lead us out of the hole we were in. You get to that point with two or three of your kids. You would not care where you went with them, you would go. You would be willing to put them in a room with anyone in a fistfight. They would have a shot of coming out of that room alive. It is very difficult for me to tell you how to identify those type players.

As you get older and the longer you have been coaching, you can develop a feeling for identifying those players. You can get a feel for what you want for your program. Our program is different from others. For me to get up here and tell you this is how you develop leaders would not be fair. I have seen other great players and I have talked to other coaches about their players and they have told me what great leaders they were. But, I am not sure they would have fit into our program. You must constantly look at the situation and you must evaluate the situation for your program.

I think you must look at the kids who are willing to make a commitment for you to have a good football team. You need that so you can have a chance to compete in the league you play in.

I am not in the high schools that much now, unfortunately. But you look for kids who can handle themselves and kids who the other students look up to. Leadership is not something that you just take and apply to football. It is something a kid has that everybody in the school likes. He must be strong, fair, and understanding. He must reach out to other people. I think you have to observe the kids and find those who can be leaders. You do not need a lot of leaders. You only need a handful. If you get three or four players to be leaders, it is great. We have 130 players and if I get three or four leaders I am elated.

When I talk about leaders I am not talking about a player who is always yelling, "Go on – let's go." We get a lot of leaders that like to yell, but they are not really leaders. When the ball is snapped, they get knocked on their rear end. So I am not talking about those yelling guys and I do not count them as leaders.

A leader must help you get the things you want done. They must believe in your philosophy. If you can get three or four of those guys and cultivate them and make them understand that we cannot have a good football team without their leadership, then you've done a good job.

When I first started coaching, I picked out a few guys who I thought would be good leaders. I would ask them if they were taking care of the other players. I had one player tell me not to worry about it. If we had a player who was drinking, he would take care of it. He would get that player in the locker room and put him up against the wall and let him have it. "Tom, if you go out drinking on Wednesday night I am going to kick the crap out of you." That would scare the crap out of that player.

I have had a few other leaders who would keep the kids straight. They would wake the kids up in the morning. They would see that the players went to class. Once you get potential leaders, you have to develop them.

I do not want to belabor the topic of leadership, but I do want to talk to you about a couple of things. I have been very happy with out staff over the years. I think that has a lot to do with creating leadership. I am more fortunate in that respect in that I can recruit players and coaches. By doing that we can make sure our coaches are all on the same page. I have been fortunate in that I grew up with a great coaching staff. When I got to be the head coach at Penn State, the only coach I hired was Bob Phillips who coached right down the road from here. Our staff was close and we all got along. We would go out together on Thursday night and have dinner. Now I have had to replace a couple of coaches. We have had the same staff the last two years. I made a commitment to coach a few more years simply because we have some great assistant coaches. I will miss a few of the older guys who were on the staff. Jay Paterno is working with our quarterbacks. Jay's mother thinks he is a good coach.

I want to spend the rest of my time talking about what it takes to be *successful*. I feel better talking to you now than I would have before we have those two off years. I had to start thinking about what had happened and what I had to do to straighten the program out.

The first thing I realized was the fact that *coaches must be salesman.* I have talked about some of these things before. About 300 of you have heard me talk too many times, so hang in there with me. You have to be a salesman to the point when you lose games, the people and the players do not blame the coaches. They cannot blame the offense or the defense. We have been fortunate that no one was pointing the finger when we want not winning a lot of games. Fortunately, the players were willing to go back to work.

Regardless of the level you are coaching on, *you must be organized.* You must be a teacher and you must be a salesman. You must sell, sell, and sell. You must sell your program all of the time. You must be organized. If you are not organized, you are wasting people's time. If you are not organized, you are misjudging the people you are working with. Those things are important.

The best teams that have won the championships are the teams that have made the fewest mistakes. They have done the best teaching job. They are coached by individuals who know the most important thing is not the X's and O's, but who those X's and O's are. I think Jim Tressel of Ohio State has done a great job. I think Walt Harris of Pittsburgh has done a tremendous job with the material he has to work with.

I have no doubt about the X's and O's situation. I can get up and draw plays on the chalkboard. It depends who the players are in those positions. You must keep this point in perspective. You must analyze your personnel.

I would like to cover several errors related to coaching. Those errors include the errors of teaching methods, tactics, strategy, judgment, off-field relationships, and the errors of developing morale. I think all of these things I am going to talk about you have heard over and over again. It may not hurt to review them again at this time of the year.

I think one the biggest problem with coaching is the mistake of not using time effectively. It may not be the biggest problem, but we do not use time effectively. We must recognize the time factor. I think you must play. Planning is making valuable use of time. If we spend too much time on one drill or aspect of the game, you create boredom. Most of my time is now spent on watching the other coaches to see how much time they are spending on different areas of the game. I like to critique their coaching. At times they spend too much time on one thing. They do not realize they have six or seven more practices to get that aspect taught to the players.

If the players get bored, the learning goes down the tubes. Football players have short attention spans. They are very active kids. I may ask my assistants how much time they need for a meeting for their players. If they tell me one hour and 15 minutes, I tell them that is too long. If the meeting goes beyond 45 minutes it is too long. The players will be asleep. If you turn the lights on after a long film session, you will find half of them asleep. We have put more players to sleep than most teams. I stress this point again: *hold to you time schedule.* If you have something to get across to the players, organize it and stick to the time element.

The next point I criticize coaches on is for not explaining what they want do on the field. They go on the field and ask players to do things that are not really going to help them. I ask them if what they are doing is going to make that player a better football player. If they do not know if the activity is going to help them or not, then they need to quit doing that activity. Working for 8 to 10 minutes on a drill is enough.

I think you must *explain* to the players why they are doing the drills. Explain what you are trying to accomplish in the drill. Explain why and then you can show how.

At times in the teaching profession we are impatient. You can't teach the kids to do certain things until he can do the basic things. The kid has to be able to come out of a stance before you can teach him to block. If he does not understand how to come out of a stance, you cannot teach much else. There is a *proper teaching progression*. You cannot teach a kid to do something until he does the basics.

In 1955 I went to visit Oklahoma coached by Bud Wilkinson. I spent a lot of time with Bud. I was just an assistant coach at that time. He was very gracious to me and he talked to me at length. I asked him about some drills they were using. I asked him why they had spent as much as 30 minutes on one drill. He explained it to me like this, "The defensive backs cannot perform the next skill until they learn the technique we were teaching today. It is a teaching progression and we need to make sure they have the first phase down before we go to the second level." Bud talked to me at length about this situation. It is important to remember not to go too fast in the teaching process.

Back in those days, the colleges had six weeks of spring practice. Now we only get 15 days. It is quite different. We are under the gun to do things differently.

Now, I have talked about two things here that make conflict. I have talked about time being a factor. You cannot spend too much time on one thing or the kids get bored. The question is how do we relate to this spending so much time on the stance, or working with the defensive backs? This is the difference in a good teacher and an average coach. These points do not come together where you can separate them. I cannot tell you how much time to spend on a drill. You must have a gut feeling for that.

I think we have too much verbal instruction on the field. Really, how much can a kid learn from verbal instruction on the field? Chances are he has his helmet on and he has been on the field for 40 minutes, and he is sweating like a pig. He has a headache and he is asking himself this question: "What the hell am I doing out here?" He is not going to listen to your verbal instructions very much. How much can he learn?

So we do the *how* and we do the *why* on the blackboard. You do it with tapes and with walk-throughs. You teach assignments before you go on the field and then you *correct on the field*.

The first Liberty Bowl game we ever played in was in 1959. Bear Bryant brought his first Alabama team up to play us. We beat them 7-0 in Philadelphia in the Liberty Bowl. I was not the head coach then. Rip Engle was our head coach. He introduced a *chair drill* at practice the week of the bowl game. He took his entire football team inside because the weather was so bad. He sat the team in chairs in the positions they played on offense. The players would point to the defenders they were to block on certain plays. He got all kinds of publicity out of this. But the important part was that he recognized the importance of getting the players on the field and he understood the theory in teaching them the play assignments. He did not want a lot of demonstrations by the assistant coaches.

My high school coach was a great punter when he was in college. He coached George Sternweiser who later played with the Yankees. George would come over and kick with our punters in practice. George would punt 30 times, my coach would punt 35 times, and our regular punter would get to punt three times. We would all stand there and watch them. I can't stress enough the importance of not doing too many demonstrations and not being on the field too long.

It is better to have your team *rested* than tired. How long do you practice? I haven't the slightest idea. I do not know your school schedule. I go back to that meeting I had with Bud Wilkinson in 1959. He has had a great impact on my coaching philosophy. He said if one coach on his staff mentioned the fact they were practicing too long, he would start cutting back on the practice sessions. As the season goes along you have to cut back some. You have so many games in which you can play your best games in. You must get your team geared up for the big games. Be careful how much time you spend in practice.

Next I want to discuss errors in strategies and tactics. You do not win many games because of tactics. You still have to block better than the other team and you have to out-tackle them. You have to out-hustle them.

I was talking to Rick Neuheisel of the University of Washington when we were on the Nike trip. They had a hard time in the first part of the season and were not doing very well in their conference. They were struggling. He was able to save the season by ending with wins over Oregon, Oregon State, and Washington State. He lost the bowl game, but they had a decent year.

I asked him how he handled the situation and turned things around. I am always trying to find out new things, so I wanted to know what he did to turn the program around. This is what he told me.

He said, "I sat them down and told them we needed to win the Northwestern Pacific Championship. We still had to play Oregon, Oregon State, and Washington State. I gave the players the *three F's.*" I asked him what he meant by he *three F's*. He said, "I sat them down and talked about *field position*. I asked everyone on team, regardless of the position they played, to contribute to field position for the next games."

I asked him what the second *F* was. He said, "The next thing we are going to do is *fight*! We must fight as hard as we can." I asked him for the third *F*. He said, "We are going to *f&@%* them*." I went along with him and asked him what he meant by that remark. He said, "The f'em was for the media. We were not going to let them get too us regardless of what they say in the media." His three F's were: field position, fight, and f'em.

It is not a matter of tactics and outsmarting anyone. It is a matter of *executing the fundamentals*. I was with Andy Reed at the Maxwell Dinner the other night and we were talking. I have always had a belief that you do not win with tactics. You win games because you *intimidate teams*.

Red Sanders was one of the greatest coaches who ever coached in football. He had the biggest impact on Bear Bryant and Bud Wilkinson than anyone. He was a coach at Vanderbilt and UCLA. He was the coach who changed the whole practice routine.

When I was in high school, here is what you did at practice. We walked around bent over picking up rocks and throwing them over the fence. When my high school coach had enough confidence that we have enough rocks out of the field, we would scrimmage. That was practice. Then Red Sanders came along and changed the format. He introduced agility drills and breakdown groups. Red Sanders told coaches you had to intimidate the opponents and make the say, *"Ouch!"*

I will never forget what Vince Dooley said to me. When we played him in the national championship, we took the ball to start the game and went straight down the field and scored. This is what he said to me. "Joe, first drives never impress me."

I was talking with Andy Reed and we were talking about the game with the Eagles and Steelers. The Eagles took the ball and went down and scored the first time they had the ball. I said to myself that drive was too easy. You have to make teams say *ouch* sometimes in a game.

You must have a philosophy on what you are going to do. You must decide what you want to do on offense and defense and stick with it. Don't let the fans change your philosophy. I am sure you get the same kind of crap I get from the stands, and the media.

Be *realistic* with your players. Do not ask them to do something they can't do. This is not easy. Some of the young coaches may not have been around as many good players as older coaches have. We have been fortunate at Penn State in that we have had a great staff and we have had a lot of great football players. We have had a lot of ordinary players at Penn State as well. Because of character and desire we have been able to win our share of games. You have to evaluate your teams and you must be realistic about it. Don't ask them to do things they cannot do. When the chips are down, go back to the basic fundamentals.

I have been influenced by a lot of people in my coaching career. Billy Cannon played running back for LSU when Coach Paul Dietzel won the national championship. Dietzel would not play Cannon much in the first and second quarters because he always wanted him fresh in the fourth quarter. They were playing against Mississippi and it was late in the fourth quarter. Mississippi was leading LSU late in the game. They punted the ball to Billy Cannon and he ran it back for a touchdown. He had fresh legs and was able to outrun the Ole' Miss kicking team. It is important to know your players and to keep them rested.

In discussing the off-field relationship, we have a very unfortunate situation today. We have too many coaches who are not in the high schools with the players. People do not understand what the situation is at Penn State. I have spent a lot of faculty at Penn State. I spend a lot of time with the student body at Penn State. They are non-athletic people. I think that environment helps you create the things you want on a football team. We sell more student tickets to football games than any school in the country. We sell 30,000 tickets to students. We have to cut the ticket sales off at that number. We are constantly on our kids to get involved as students. I do not want our players to think they are big shots and I do not want to be a big shot. I want everyone on our faculty to understand what their problems are I want to make Penn State a better place. I am not just talking about athletics. It does not matter what area we are working with at Penn State, I just want to be able to help. I think you must understand this. Think of the gains that come from working with the other people in your school. Respect for the student body has a great carryover.

The last part of this discussion is how you *handle* the media. That includes television and the radio. Does anyone have any advice for me in this area? How do you handle officials? Does anyone have any advice for me on this? (Ha, ha!)

No matter how you handle these situations, it comes down to what these people think of you. We get some pip-squeak who never had a jockstrap on in his life and he thinks he can say what he wants to say and it is gospel. You have to spend time with them and you have to give them something to write about. My problem is that even after 53 years of coaching, I still have problems dealing with some of the reporters. I cannot get use to a 27-year-old reporter telling me I did not do something right. I have to tell them something like this: "Well, maybe you have a point." You cannot get away from them. You have to understand them. The problem is the questions they

are asking me today have been asked 30 years ago. There just are not that many questions you can ask about a game.

I like to tell a story about this subject. Years ago we played Texas and they were a good football team. We were supposed to be a very good team. It was our opening game of the season. We lost that opening game to Texas. We ended up having a good team, but Texas had a better team that year. After the Texas game was over I went into the press room and I was trying to put some things in my head as far as how I was going to handle the press. We started the press conference and they started asking questions. "Why didn't you do this? Why didn't you do that? What happened here?" Everything they brought up was all negative. Finally I said, "You guys need to knock it off. I honestly believe we played about as well as we could play. If we played Texas five times, Texas would beat us four of those five times. I think Texas has a better football team than we do." That did not satisfy them. They started asking more questions. I said, "Let's knock it off. Let's leave. Texas was a better football team today than we are. Now, let me go home and be with my wife." Oh God! I got letters from all kind of people. They wanted me to go see a doctor on sensitivity. I went home and told my wife what I said and she knocked the hell out of me. You just have to be careful what you say and who you say it to. It was not always that way, but it is today.

The last part of the discussion is about *morale*. We make a lot of mistakes in dealing with morale. Football begins with morale. If you do not have good team morale, you can forget about it. You may win a game or two with the kids against a natural rivalry, but if you want to be a consistent winner, it all starts with morale. Our game is played with the mind and heart first, and second with the body.

When you talk about morale and you say you are going to practice a certain amount of time, you must stick with it. If you have rules, make sure you enforce them. Do not have rules you cannot enforce.

George Welsh use to be an assistant at Penn State. He used to say the difference between the Marine Corp and the Navy was this: "The Marine Corp only had rules they could enforce. The Navy had all kinds of rules, but they could not enforce them." If you put in a rule, make sure you have the guts to enforce it. Drinking is the biggest problem we have in college. That and cutting classes.

You must have *discipline*. I do not care what you decide about the rules. I tell my kids no earrings. I do not think if a kid sticks an earring on that he is not a good kid. But you have to challenge the players today. The players must have discipline. I think discipline creates pride. Pride creates morale.

Most of you have heard me tell the story when my brother who went into the Marine Corp. My dad wanted him to join the army. My dad was smoking, "I do not want a Marine in my house. I did not bring you up to be a Marine. You had better not come back home brainwashed about the Marine Corp."

My brother went away and was gone for 17 weeks. He came home from the Marine Corp on a leave. He had his Marine uniform on when we went to mass. He wore the uniform all day, even when he came home. My dad was still upset about the Marines. He asked my brother, "What do you think about those phony Marines?" In my house, if my father said black, you said white. If he said red, you said green. My dad kept giving my brother a hard time over the Marines. Finally my brother got up and went over to my dad and screamed at him. "Dad, knock it off! The Marine platoon is the greatest fighting unit ever put on the face of this earth!" My dad rocked back in his chair and said, "They got you! They got you!" Dad hated the Marines and he had one right in front of him in his house. That is a great example of pride and discipline. This is the way we all want our football teams to be like. It is difficult to get that on a team.

When you have been in coaching as long as I have, you have so many obligations. You have so many people associated with your program. I had to go to a funeral today. I do not spend as much time with my players as I used to. I think you must have a real interest in those young people. They can't just be football players. They must be more than football players. They are looking for you to lead them because you are something special in their lives. You can *guide* them and help them over some tough spots

in their life. You must understand this fact. If you want a group of kids to band together and go to war with you, you must understand that point. You must be concerned about the player's studies, where he is going to college, and what he wants to do with his life. You must find out if he has a problem at home. You must reach out and make sure you understand the kids today.

The last point is to *coach your own way*. I could get up here and talk until the words came out of my ears. Tommy Protho said one time, "Your high school coach was not as tough as you think he was." Now, you think about this. Some of my staff played for me early in my career. They tell me I was tougher when they were playing. I may have yelled at them a few more times, but I am not really different. The point is this: *you be you!*

It is time for me to turn this over to Jay Paterno and let him talk about our quarterbacks. My goodness, my Rolex watch is missing. Has anyone seen my Rolex? I will tell one more true story.

Years ago I made a speech in a small town in northern Pennsylvania. Penn State asked me to go up there and talk at their high school banquet and I did. The A.D. sent me a check for $1,000. I sent the money back. I told him that high school coaches help us so we have to help the high schools. He told me that was the amount of money they gave Woody Hayes the year before. I was probably making more money than Woody was making. So I sent the money back. In a few days he sent me a box. I opened the box and I saw this Rolex watch. Being a boy from Brooklyn, all I needed was a Bulova watch. I opened the box and I kept looking at it. I decided to put it in a Federal Express box and send it back. That was in 1968. I said what the hell, and kept the watch. That is how long I have had this watch. It still does not keep time.

I am really proud of my staff at Penn State. They all have done a great job over the years. Most of you know our other coaches. I am going to ask Jay Paterno to visit with you tonight. Thanks for paying attention.

THE 4-2 DEFENSIVE PACKAGE

Texas Christian University

I am excited about getting the opportunity to speak at this Nike clinic. I spent several years in this area and I always liked the way the kids played football here. I know the players that come out of the high schools here are hard-nosed kids.

To get a chance to move across the nation and just talk football is a dream come true for me. If I had my choice I would be in a tee shirt and sweats because I am a defensive coach.

My topic today is the *4-2-5 defense*. We are in a small profession. I don't keep any secrets. The way I do clinics is to tell you what I know. I'm going to talk fast and try to get through as much as I can. However, if there are any questions you would like to ask or have me explain something again, hold up your hand and I'll be glad to do it. I like to conduct these clinics like we were a bunch of coaches sitting around a table talking football.

I was very fortunate to be a head coach at a Division-1 level. This is my 22nd year in coaching. I coached with Dennis Franchione, who is the head coach at Texas A & M, for eight years at TCU. When we were at TCU, he had a system set up that allowed me to be a head coach.

I'm not going to talk too much about philosophy. I am going to spend most of my time talking about our defense. I think the way you run your program is how you win football games.

At TCU we do not put our coordinators on the road recruiting. If I am recruiting a kid, I want to make sure when he gets to TCU we have something to offer him. We have been to five bowl games in a row. In the last four years we have graduated over 80 percent of our players. Three years ago we were 10-1 and number one in the nation in defense. There were 24 out of 28 players on that team who graduated on time. Last year we graduated 13 out of 14 players. This year we graduated 21 of our 22 players on time. The one who didn't graduate is our linebacker who left early for the pros.

We are trying to do the whole scope of things. We have to take a Division-II, high school mentality when it comes to our weight program. If you want it done you have to do it yourself. We don't leave it up to the strength coach to get our player strong. He is in charge, but all the coaches work in the program.

Last night in our weight program we had our *night of champions*. I want to share some of those results with you. We had two guys bench over 600 pounds, one guy squatted 860 pounds, and another had a 465-pound power clean. We had 62 players power clean over 300 last year and 17 players power cleaned over 400. In the last three years we've had 17 guys drafted or who've gone as free agents into the NFL.

We draw up new set goals every six weeks. One of their goals is to increase their maximum lifts by 10 pounds every six weeks. Those goals run for three years. We have a *night of champions* and invite TV stations and newspaper reporters to watch our lifters. We take our top 16 lifters and they work their maximum lifts. It is not just the first-team people who take part. We had a walk-on wide receiver who participated in the ceremonies last night. We are going to move him to fullback. We want to be known as the school that develops football players.

There a lot of Division-1 schools in Texas. The recruiting in Texas is extremely competitive. We don't get the high profile recruits who go to Texas or Texas A & M. We can't recruit against the University of Texas. They are going to select and we are going to recruit and evaluate. We are going to be able to recruit against Texas A & M in some cases. We have an advantage on out of state recruiters, because the instate kids know if they come to TCU we are going to give them a chance to play.

Last night our freshman quarterback benched 440. You don't have to be that strong to be a quarterback. The key is that the weight room only gives you a chance to win. It doesn't mean you are going to have a good football team. What it does mean is that the players have accountability and work ethics. Our punters, kickers, quarterbacks, and our managers are all going to lift in the weight program. Everyone has to have the same work ethics if you want to win.

When you start treating somebody differently, you are going to have a problem. If you start making someone special as far as work ethics, you are going to have a problem.

At the end of the year we *reevaluate our team*. We ended up the year number one in the conference. After watching our cut-ups, I don't think we are worth a crap. What you see on film is what you coach. You think you are pretty good, but after you watch the cut-ups, you know it is a never-ending battle to succeed. When you get too high on yourself, you better back up, because there is someone out there that is going to prove you wrong.

At the end of every season we sit down and go through our game films and evaluate ever defense and coverage. We are going to find out what we did well and what we did poorly. When we find out what we are doing wrong, we want to make corrections and adjustments so we don't have to go through the same thing next year.

In the state of Texas, we don't always get all the guys that we want. But we recruit guys who will play hard for us and kids who can develop. We try to develop our program like Colorado State has done. They have taken guys who are hard runners, mixed them with some good players, and tried to make everybody else better. They make sure they have 11 guys who will go on the field and play their butts off.

Our coordinators start in January with developing a plan for the upcoming season. The coaches are going to run the indoor program. Our whole program in January and February is about maturing, chemistry, accountability, and getting kids to grow up.

With 85 scholarships, you are going to have to play with some redshirt freshmen. Now is the time when we get those kids to start growing up and accepting accountability for what goes on inside our program.

We *set goals every six weeks* and then set out to achieve those goals. It is not just about weightlifting. We set academic goals and goals to help a player in his social life. Our job is to make sure they can be successful in life. It is not about playing football. We have to win football games to keep our job, but if you recruit kids who want to be successful, you have a chance to win.

Our coaches work with their players until the summer break. That is when the strength coach takes over. We can't work with them after that until practice starts in September. But between January and April we are going to work on all the things you have to do to win football games.

Last year we were picked to finish fifth in the conference. One of the things that happens in our conference is the fact that we don't recruit against anyone else in our conference. No one really knows each other and all the sport writers pick the ways teams will finish in the conference.

The one thing we recruit on defense is *speed*. When you are building your program, you have to have consistency. At TCU, our off-season program is the lifeline. Five straight bowl games and three conference championships is tied to that lifeline. The players who do not buy into our program and are not getting stronger will not be around long. If it takes them until they are juniors or seniors to get ready to play, they are not going to be too happy in our program. They have to improve in a hurry if they expect to play in our program.

When I get to the film, you will see number 49 at defensive tackle for us. He was a linebacker when he came out of high school. He now is 6'1" and 282 pounds and plays a 3 technique. He probably should play defensive end, but we had no one else to go inside. He runs 4.6 for the 40-yard dash. He benched 560 pounds, squatted 700, and power cleaned 475. But he didn't do that when he came to TCU.

Last year we had six safeties bench over 400. If you have to take on 290-pound guards, you better find some way to stay healthy. When you play an eight-man front, your safeties are going to be in some positions where they have to take on those big people.

We believe in the *K.I.S.S. system*. We say *multiplicity is simplicity*. One of the things we want to do in our system is to limit the game planning. What we did in the first seven games we want to eliminate because this is the eighth game.

We want to make sure we have a blitz package. We want to play zone man, a front with a zone package, and bracket coverage. We teach all those things in the first six days of two-a-day workouts. You can take the packages you want from those things and you don't have to be as extensive if you don't want to be.

We divide our packages into *attack groups*. The four down linemen and two linebackers are one segment of our defense. We align the front six and they go one direction. The coverage behind them is what we call a *double-quarterback system*. We play with three safeties on the field. We have a strong, weak, and free safety. The free and weak safeties are going to control both halves of the field. They are the quarterbacks and they make all the calls.

Our fronts and coverages have nothing to do with each other. The front is going to be called by the use of a wristband. We break down our first six or seven opponents and put the defenses on the player's wristbands. We don't have to teach anything new to our kids during the season. The teams may change, but the fronts remain the same. We teach every week but we don't have to re-teach our fronts.

Three years ago we were number one in the nation and we blitzed seven percent of the time. We played our zone and robber package with our slanting front and we were really good. This year we blitzed 38 percent of the time. But we had an inside linebacker who was only 208 pounds. He was not 240 pounds like the linebacker we had three years ago. We had to do something to make him successful.

He had 28 tackles for losses and 12 sacks. He was a great blitzer. We didn't have to change our package in the off-season; we started emphasizing something that was already in the package.

In our coverage scheme, we are going to divide the formation at the center every snap. We play with five defensive backs in the secondary. The front is going to have two ways to make a formation call and two ways to call the field and boundary. We are going

to call *tight* and *split* as a formation call [Diagram 1]. If the tight end is left, we call *Liz* and the defensive tackle aligns in a 3 technique to the tight end side. We do not flip-flop our defensive ends. If the defensive ends have a tight end, they align head-up on the tight end. If there is no tight end, they play a loose 5 technique. The noseguard aligns on the center in a backside shade.

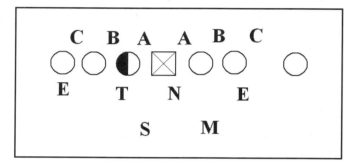

Diagram 1. Front alignment

We flip-flop the noseguard and tackle. The noseguard is generally big enough to be a two-gap player. We usually can find only one guy who can run like we want our tackle to run. That is why we flip-flop those two guys. If we want the tackle to align to the split end side, we call *rip*. That means the tight end is left and the split end is right.

If we don't want to adjust the 3 technique to the formation, we call *field* or *boundary*. If we are on the left hash mark and we want the 3 technique into the wideside we make a *field* call, which will align the 3 technique right. The noseguard knows he is to align on the backside shade of the center away from the call.

If we call the letter *G* in our front call, the noseguard is going to line up on the guard away from the call [Diagram 2]. If we call *tight G, split G, field G, or boundary G,* the noseguard goes away from the call and aligns head-up the backside guard.

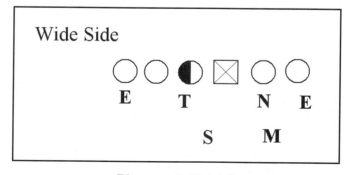

Diagram 2. Field G

One of our defensive ends was a wide receiver in high school. He is now 6'5" and 270 pounds and runs a 4.59 40-yard dash. The key to this defense is speed. Everyone that plays on the defense can run.

We feel if we are going to be a top defensive team year after year, we have to average between a 4.62 and 4.66 in our top 22 defensive players. That figure includes defensive linemen as well as defensive backs and linebackers. When we establish our 40 times, we time our players running in pads. Our noseguard weighs 275 pounds and runs a 4.9.

The coverage part of the defense is separate from the front. The linebacker will get the front lined up. We have two people signaling the signals from the sidelines. One coach is signaling the front call and the other coach is signaling the coverage.

For the diagram, I am going to use a one-back set. I'll put a twin wideout set to one side and a tight end with a split receiver to the other. We call that formation *spread.* What determines the strength of the passing formation are the twin receivers. With the twin set left, the free safety calls *read* left. The free safety is going to talk to the left corner, strong safety, and the readside linebacker. The weak safety aligns on the other side and talks to the right corner and right linebacker.

Starting in spring practice, the first Monday we teach *cover 2.* On Tuesday we teach our *blue* coverage, which is quarter coverage. We are still in shorts, so we can't bang anybody around. On Wednesday we teach *squats-and-halves* coverage. After that we are done teaching our zone coverages.

When I was growing up we played a 50 front. If you wanted to get the safety down you had to rotate the cover. We double-called the coverage. One of the coverages was for single-width formations and the other coverage was for double-width formations.

We don't worry about formations any more. When you divide the formation down the middle, to each side there are only three formations the offense can give the secondary [Diagram 3]. The offense can give you a pro set, which is a tight end and wideout; a twin set, which is two wideouts; or some kind of trips set that the defense will have to defend. That is all they can give you.

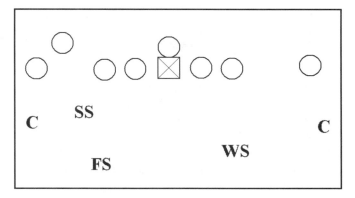

Diagram 3. Secondary alignment

In three days we teach our kids to line up in all three coverages against those formations. We don't practice on Monday, but on Tuesday when we start talking about our game play, we never talk about lining up. All we talk about what the opponent is going to be doing and how we are going to adjust to it.

Unless the offense lines up in a three-back wishbone or a no-back set, there are only three ways the offense can be aligned and be sound. Unless we want the coverage to overplay something to one side, we don't worry about formations.

In our front we use a *Liz* or *rip* call to set the front [Diagram 4]. If we follow that term with a *T-word*, we are going to slant toward the call. If we call *rip tank* or *Liz toro*, all four down linemen are slanting to the call.

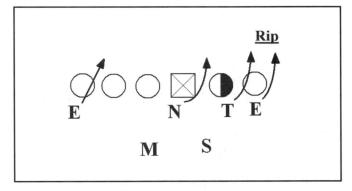

Diagram 4. Rip tank

If we call the front and use *A-word* after the call, we are going to slant away from the call. If we call *Liz army*, we are going away from the call [Diagram 5]. It doesn't matter where we set the eagle side of the defense, we are going to slant away or toward the call.

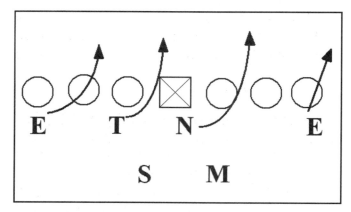

Diagram 5. Liz army

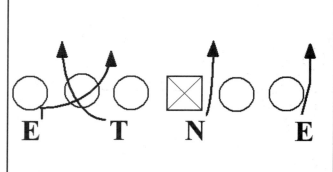

Diagram 6. Tex stunt

You need to remember the way we call the slant, because as we start to add the blitz package to the front, it will sound like an English class. We have 157 different calls with this system. The key is the limited amount of teaching you have to use with each position. The defensive tackles have to remember *six words*. That is all they have to remember no matter what blitz we are running. All they need to know is *army, toro, Tex, ex, Tex-ex,* and *twist.* We build sentences that tell the defense exactly what to do.

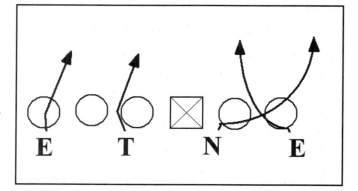

Diagram 7. Ex stunt

The *Tex* call is a tackle and end stunt with the tackle going first on the stunt [Diagram 6]. The *ex* call is a tackle and end stunt with the end going first on the stunt [Diagram 7]. The *Tex-ex* is a double stunt with one side running a *Tex* stunt and the other side running an *ex* stunt [Diagram 8]. And the *twist* is a stunt run between the noseguard and tackle [Diagram 9].

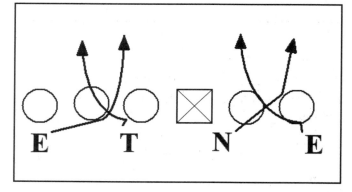

Diagram 8. Tex-ex stunt

The next thing we do is put the calls together in combinations. For instance, if I want a run defensive call and bring the safeties off the edge, I'll call *smoke.* Since it is a run-type of defense, the front call will likely be army or tank. I would call *tight G army double smoke* [Diagram 10]. That call puts the 3 technique toward the tight end and the noseguard over the backside guard. The four down linemen are slanting away from the tight end, and we get a double blitz by two safeties off the edges.

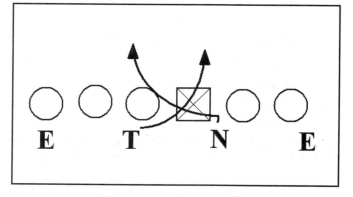

Diagram 9. Twist stunt

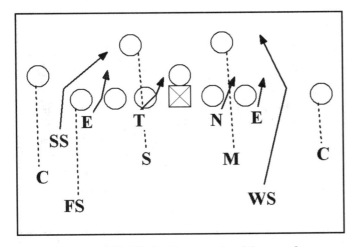

Diagram 10. Tight G army double smoke

That takes care of the running play. If the offense comes out in what we call *10 personnel*, the formations looks like a passing set. Ten personnel to us is one back, no tight ends, and four wide receivers. I might bring a nickel back into the game for one of our linebacker, since I am going to bring a double smoke blitz. To stop the draw inside and confuse the offensive line's protection scheme, I run a different line movement. I call *field G Tex-ex double smoke* [Diagram 11].

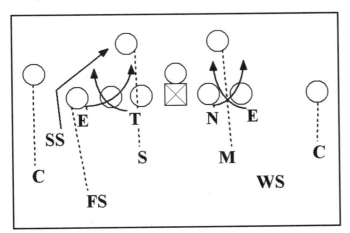

Diagram 11. Field G Tex-ex double smoke

The 3 technique aligns to the wideside of the field. The noseguard is aligned on the boundary side guard in a head-up position. The fieldside runs the *Tex* stunt between the tackle and end and the boundary side runs the *ex* stunt between the noseguard and defensive end. We are still blitzing two safeties off the edge. Did the call present any communication problem for the defense? All we did was to create a different sentence and run the same stunts.

Many years ago when I was a young coach, I was a salesman. We were trying to tell people what we were doing defensively was good. We were trying to sell our players on the idea that we could take things away from the offenses.

When an offense has to game plan for TCU, they must handle the twist game, slide game, and the double-blitzing scheme. The offense has to go to slide protection in their passing game. We don't play teams that try to man protect against us. If they try to man protect, they are going to be in a lot of trouble. The offense cannot grasp all those schemes. It is easy for us because we taught all those things in the first three days of spring practice.

After six practices we have put in everything that we are going to use. On the seventh day we go back to the beginning and re-teach the schemes again. That also includes our offensive line.

When we call these fronts we don't put any coverage into the call. We are going to call a slant or twist for the defensive front four. If we call *blitz*, we are going to tell the linebackers where to run through. They will run through the A, B, or C gaps or come off the edge.

The secondary doesn't care what is going on with the front and linebackers. All they know is there is going to be a *blitz* and both linebackers are going to rush. That tells them they have to cover everybody if there is a pass.

If there is a double smoke being run, the free safety knows the strong and weak safeties are blitzing off the edge. He has to talk to the two linebackers to get them into coverage.

One of our best packages is our *dog package*. That is bringing four defenders off one side and we are not going to let anyone come free to the post. You may not believe this statistic when I read it to you. This year we ran 158 snaps in the dog package. Teams ran the ball 85 times out of the 158 for 73 yards. That worked out to be 0.89 yards per carry. They threw the ball the other 73 times for 275 yards for 3.77 yards per completion. The biggest surprise of all was there were only three touchdowns. Two touchdowns came from inside the five-yard line when we ran the dog stunt. We had one passing touchdown against the dog.

The way to beat robber coverage is to blow the top off the safety. The safety is reading the number two receiver's route. If the route goes outside, he can play robber on the outside receiver. If the number two receiver goes deep, the safety has to take him and the outside receiver beats the corner on a dig route to the inside behind the safety.

I still call the defenses at TCU. The reason I do this is because of what I have seen in a lot of head coaches. I figure I am going to get only one chance to be a head coach and I was going to make the most of it.

Every year it seems like I am doing a little bit less. But I am very involved with the special teams and defense. On the offensive side of the ball, I hired four coaches. One had been a head coach on the college level and the other three had been coordinators. I leave them alone and let them run the offense. Just because I have the word *head* in front of my name doesn't make me smarter.

I have been coaching for 22 years and have watched head coaches stop coaching something that they were good at. The only reason they stopped coaching was because they became the head coach. I'm knocking head coaches, but I felt like in my position, I didn't want to take away something that I was good at.

We play the defensive end on the tight end in a top category. We play it against 11 or 12 personnel. That type of personnel has only one back in the backfield. We play the defensive end on the tight end man-to-man. We do that against zone teams and against one-back sets because the offense doesn't have an extra blocker in the backfield.

That is the defense we run most of the time. We play *0 cover*, which is man-to-man coverage with no free safety, with the blitz scheme.

We also run some *zone-blitz schemes*. If I am going to bring a secondary player and a linebacker on the blitz, I call that *white dog*. If I don't want to play man coverage in the secondary, I call *spree* and roll the coverage into a three-deep coverage. The only guys who are doing anything different are the five secondary people.

I played at Kansas State and we played three-deep coverage a lot. The thing that drove me crazy was that every week we changed our three deep. It got to the point we didn't know how we were playing three deep. If we are going to change something in cover 3, we add a word. The cover becomes 3 *change* or 3 *free*, or 3 something like that.

I went to Texas Tech one year to see their defensive scheme. The defensive coordinator was John Goodner. They were playing the 4-2 scheme. They used something in their package that was called *slide backs*. What they were doing was sliding a safety into the box when they played against a two-back team. They played a man-free coverage scheme. We play a little three-deep scheme with our package, but not very much.

Our free safety has to be the second leading tackler on our team. We depend on him to make tackles fewer than three yards away all the time. Usually our free safety is going to average between 85 and 105 tackles a year. The strong and weak safeties will follow him in number of tackles made. The number one tackler will be our eagleside linebacker.

We are going to wrong arm all blocks in this front and bounce the football to the outside. The problem with the 4-2 defense was the alignment of the eagleside linebacker. To the eagleside, the tackle was the B gap player and the defensive end was the C gap player. The eagle linebacker is the A gap player. When teams ran the off-tackle power play we ended up short-handed with defender on that side.

We needed a way to borrow from the 4-3 principles and make it fit the 4-2 concepts. We came up with the work *slide* [Diagram 12]. When the offense comes to the line in a pro set with two backs, one tight end, and two wide receivers, the secondary call is *2 blue*. That is robber cover to the strongside.

If the off fullback sets to the tight end side, the offense has overloaded to that side. The weak safety moves up and makes a *slide* call to the linebackers. Before the ball is snapped, the Sam linebacker slides from a 10 alignment in the A gap to a 50 alignment over the offensive tackle. The Mike linebacker moves from a 30 alignment in the backside B gap to head-up on the center and becomes the A gap player.

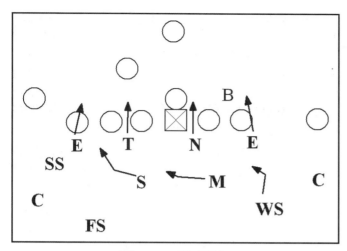

Diagram 12. Slide

The weak safety aligns in his half position, and before the ball is snapped, he moves up. He comes up into a position outside his defensive end and four-yards deep. He is cover in the backside B gap. He doesn't fill the B gap unless the ball shows there. To get that adjustment made, the weak safety talks to the two linebackers and the corner on his side. The defensive linemen are not affected. The robber cover to the strongside is not affected at all. The adjustment is made with limited communication.

If you can't get your team to play fast, you are in trouble. They can't play fast if they are thinking all the time about where to line up.

In the secondary we have *three zone coverages.* We split the difference in those three coverages and it gives us nine coverages. We play *cover 2,* which is our robber coverage; *blue,* which is quarter-quarter coverage; and our *5 coverage* that is squats-and-halves coverage. We can also play cover 25. That means we are playing cover 2 to the free safety side and cover 5 to the weak safety side. The first digit in the number is the free safety side and the second digit is the weakside.

The last four schools I coached at had very limited success before I got there. I was at Utah State and they had not been to a bowl game in 30 years. We went to two bowl games. I went to the Naval Academy and we went to two bowl games there and they hadn't been to a bowl game in 16 years. I went to New Mexico State and they hadn't been to a bowl game in 36 years. We won a bowl game there. Then I came to TCU and they had not been to a bowl game in four years and now we have been to five straight bowl games.

I am not saying we invented the wheel and have some revolutionary plan. All I am saying is find ways to get players into positions where they can be successful. We feel we can play this defense with players that we have developed from average players. If the players have chosen to come, we have to deal with them and develop them into being the best they can be. If they can slant, twist, and stunt, they can play in our front. If we can play zone coverage, we certainly won't kill ourselves.

I'm going to use Colorado State as an example of using their tight ends. They set their tight ends and make the defense declare the front. After the front is set, they shift the tight end to the other side and run the ball that way.

This year when we played them, they had a tight end who could play as a fullback. That meant we had to play against a 21 personnel scheme, which are two backs and one tight end. They made us play against a 12 personnel scheme, which are one back and two tight ends without changing their personnel on the field.

They came out in a two tight end formation with one back in the backfield. We called *tight G Liz* [Diagram 13]. We made the Liz call because the fieldside was to the defense's left. The number-one play run from a one-back team is the *zone play.* Because your linebackers don't need to fast-flow the linebacker against the zone play, we moved our linebacker up to two-and-a-half yards and played gaps. They got up in their gaps and played football. We were overmatched in size so we cut the distance down and plugged the gaps. The free and weak safeties became really active on this type of defensive adjustment.

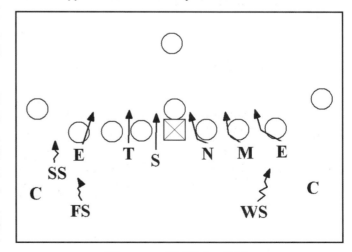

Diagram 13. Tight G Liz

If they come out in a two-back set, we move our linebacker back to four- and-a-half yards. We play fast-flow from that depth.

If the offense comes out in two tight ends set, they can adjust the set and put one of the tight ends in motion. This allows the offense to get into an overloaded set. Our weak safety makes a *scoot* call to the linebackers [Diagram 14]. That puts us in a 4-3 look against an overshifted offensive set. The weak safety is forcing the counter coming back and is the pitch player on the option. He makes a solo call to the corner on that side that puts the corner in lock-up man cover on the wide receiver. The weak safety is vertical on that play.

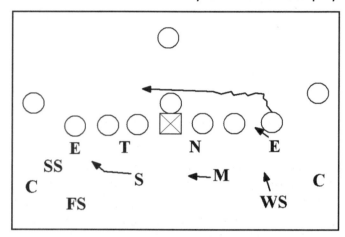

Diagram 14. Scoot

I was a front coach for many years before I became a secondary coach. There is nothing worse than a secondary coach who is always worried about getting beat deep. We have to get up to stop the run. Our goal all year was to hold people on first down. We wanted to put them in a second-and- long situation. This year we did that 71 percent of the time.

We lead the nation is rushing defense, but more importantly, we were second in pass efficiency. This is the first year in my 22 years of coaching that we held people under 40-percent completions. The offense had an average of 38-percent completion against our defense. Usually a team that ranks high in rushing defense can't stop the pass. Or a team that ranks high in the passing game defense cannot stop the run. Nobody throws against them because they don't have to. People who play us want to keep us balanced. They don't want us to overshift our front.

I'm going to show you some film on the things I've been talking about. In this defense the safeties have

to be a big part of your run game.

(Film)

We call our *dogs* just like we call our defensive front. We have *T dogs*, *S dogs*, *W dogs*, *F dogs*, and *B dogs*. The initial in each dog call means *tight*, *split*, *wide*, *field*, and *boundary*. If we want to run a field dog stunt we call *field G army* [Diagram 15]. That is one of our regular fronts. It is a four-man slant into the boundary of the field. The linebacker looks at his wristband and sees that he is supposed to run through the fieldside B gap.

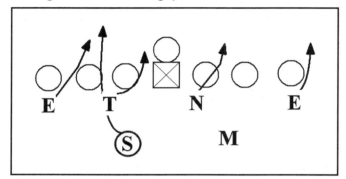

Diagram 15. Field G army

We spend most of the time on defense working against 50-gallon trashcans. We do middle drill against an offense, but 40 minutes a day we spend working against those trashcans. The reason we do that is *alignment and assignment*. We do all the inside runs in middle drill. Anything outside is done against trashcans. I got tired of losing my best defensive linemen against a scout team. After the scout team got tired, we didn't get anything out of the scrimmage, because the defense dominated the scout team in every phase of the game.

This teaches the defense to run to the football. If it is a dropback pass, the defensive line takes three steps up the field or runs the stunt that is scripted and stops. As soon as the ball is thrown, they turn and run their butts off to get to the ball. There is no scout team in the way and you can see if anyone is loafing.

Most people are scared of the blitz because they are afraid they are not going to get everyone covered. We have *three categories of blitzes*. We run *bullets*, *smokes*, and *dogs*. If the offense comes out in a no-backs set and the blitz is bullets, the free safety reads the passing strength of the set. He knows since the set is empty it is going to be 5-on-5.

If the offense comes out in a wishbone, the defensive call is a *wide dog*, which is a safety and linebacker coming from the edge. The first place the safety is going to start the count is the side the dog is being run to. The safety has to know where the blitzes are coming from so he gets the right count on the receivers.

The safeties shuffle and read eyes. They need to know what type of pass is being thrown [Diagram 16]. If it is play-action, he reads until he knows it is a pass. His eyes immediately go to the number two receiver. If that receiver is running vertical, the strong safety shuffles inside of him and plays him.

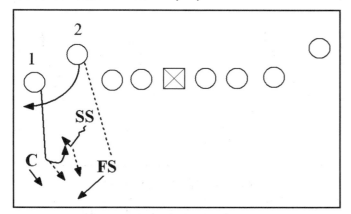

Diagram 16. Robber coverage

If the number two receiver runs an out route, the strong safety's eyes go from number two to the number one receiver. He is playing curl to post on the number one receiver. He is keying the hips of the receiver. If the hips sink, that means the receiver is breaking his pattern off and is going to stop. If that happens the safety jumps on the pattern. However, if the hips don't sink, the safety knows there is a post route coming. He doesn't go to the receiver; he picks a junction point to intercept the post route and takes it.

Our corner is going to tell the safety exactly what the number one receiver is doing. If the receiver stops and runs any route under five yards, the corner calls *timing*. That tells the strong safety to look out for the smash, quick slant, or the hitch route.

If the number one receiver runs an in or out route inside of 12 yards, the corner will call *in* or *out*. The strong safety has the responsibility to get underneath those routes. The corner is not responsible.

The free safety is also keying the number two receiver. If the receiver takes an out route, the free

safety makes a *wheel* call to the corner [Diagram 17]. That call tells the corner he has an outside route working in his area. The corner can continue to play the number one receiver, but his eyes should go to number two. The *wheel* call also tells the corner that the free safety will take the post of the number one receiver.

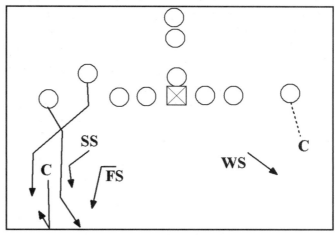

Diagram 17. Wheel coverage

The corner squeezes the number one receiver to the free safety and comes off for the wheel route of the number two receiver. Our experience tells us not to play the wheel route with the strong safety when there is a two-back set. As soon as the offense sees the strong safety take the wheel, they will run the fullback out of the backfield into the flat.

To the weakside, the corner does not have an underneath safety. The backside corner and weak safety are probably going to be in some kind of squat-and-half coverage.

If the offense is running man routes, we want to be in a zone. If the offense is running zone route, we want to play man coverage. Every year we are trying to find ways to get one more man at the point of attack than the offense has blockers.

The reason we can get away with doing some of the things we do is because we are playing five defensive backs. There are a lot of guys in the state of Colorado who can play this style of defense, because I've watched them at Colorado and Colorado State. I want speed on the field. I would rather have 4.5 safeties on the field than 4.8 linebackers.

If the offense can't outrun your defense, they may get some big plays, but there is a chance they won't score. That is our philosophy. Thank you. I appreciate your time.

THREE- AND FIVE-STEP DROP PASSING GAME

University of Louisville

First, I want to go over our base philosophy very quickly and then I will get into some football. Offensively, the first thing we are going to do as a staff is to get our kids to *play hard*, *play with emotion*, and we are going to *be a fast-tempo offense*.

The first thing we are going to do with our offense is to break the huddle and try to put the pressure on the defense. We are going to play a fast pace and we are going to get in and out of the huddle. The offense must stay after the defense play after play. The defense will try to intimidate the offense if you will let them. The thing we want to do is to put pressure on the defense and we are not going to let them intimidate us.

The way we are going to do that is by *running the football*. In order to win, we must be able to rush the ball in the fourth quarter. When the defense has 11 players flying to the football and gang tackling and getting after the offense, we want all of our offensive players running to the football. As receivers, we are going to run the football and force the defense to take the defensive backs out of the game. We do not want any stupid penalties, and we want our linemen knocking the defense off the line of scrimmage. We want the linebackers and defensive backs who are flying to the football to have their heads on a swivel. We want them to know they are going to get hit by our offensive players. So a big key for us is that we must be able to run the football, and we must be able to run it in the fourth quarter.

There are different ways we can do that. In 1998, when we had Chris Redman as our quarterback, we had four receivers who caught 50 passes or more. Our best play was the *draw play*. Chris threw for over 400 yards per game. When teams defended the pass, we ran the draw. Our back ran for over 1,200 yards that year.

Last year when Coach Bobby Petrino was the offensive coordinator at Auburn, their four best players were their two running backs and two tight ends. They would up and run straight at the defense.

What are we going to do this fall? I am not sure. We will have to find that out in the spring. It will be whatever fits our talent. If we can throw the ball and spread the defense out, we will do that. If we have good running back we will move the ball on the ground. We must be able to run the ball to win.

The second thing we must do on offense is to be able to *defeat the blitz*. In this day and age you are going to see all kinds of blitzes. Each week we must have a plan to take on the blitz. We must defeat the blitz. How do we do that? There are a couple of different ways to defeat the blitz. We must come up with the keys when the defense is going to bring the blitz. Against the zone blitz, we feel the best way to defeat that defense is to run away from it. We must be able to see the different types of blitzes and check the protection, and use maximum protection against them. We must be able to go after the defense and make big plays when they blitz.

Sometimes you do not know the blitz is coming because the defense disguises the blitz so well, you must do very well with your sights and do a good job that way.

The *three ways we are going to beat the blitz* is by running away from it, beating its max protection, and beating it by hitting the home run, or by sighting the blitz and getting the first down.

The third thing we must do is to *use play-action passes off the run*. If we can accomplish the first goal, which is to establish the run, then the third part of the play-action becomes easy. We are going to have a play-action package out of our personnel package and our formations. If we can have a good play-action package, we feel we have a chance to win the game.

The fourth thing we must do is to *throw the short pass but make it into a long run*. This is something we feel is important to any passing game. Most of the time this comes down to the personnel and the receivers you have. We are going to get the ball out of our quarterback's hand quickly and then hope the receivers can make something positive happen. We may throw a six- yard hitch route, but we want the receiver to take the ball to the house. We want the big play off the short pass.

The fifth point is to *utilize different personnel groups and formations*. We will use a lot of different personnel groups. We want to give the defensive coordinator fits. We want to be able to bring in a lot of different personnel groupings, but out of those different personnel groupings we want to be able to run the same formations. We may have two backs, two tight ends, one wide receiver in the game, but still run from an empty set. We do not want the defense to be able to say if we have certain personnel in the game we are going to run from a certain formation. We want to be able to run all of the formations out of the same personnel groupings. We do not want to give anything away.

The last thing we want to do in our basic philosophy is to *execute*. It is more important than all of the rest of these points. This is what it all comes down to. My father was a football coach and we grew up around football. This is something he preached to us every day when we played for him and when we coached for him. He taught us to rep the plays until they became habits. You have to rep it, rep it, and rep it until it becomes a habit. Here is what he would rip off to us when he talked about execution: "*Execution is created by constant repetition, which establishes sound habit formation that creates a conditioned reflex to any give situation.*"

What this means is that you must rep it, rep it, and rep it. We want the players to be able to run the plays in their sleep. We are going to rep the moves over and over, and we are going to coach on the run, and we are going to work hard, and we are going to have execution.

For us, it is never the coordinators offense; it is the staff's offense. Nothing bugs me more than to be around a coach who calls everything his offense or his defense. You hear them talking about "my guys, my players, my plays, and my staff." The best thing we did in 1998 at Louisville was to *game plan as a staff*. It is everyone's offense. Everyone takes part in the offense. We do not want those coaches who have a lot to say on Saturday after the game but never say crap on Sunday and Monday in the meetings. We are all going to have input in the game plan on Sunday and Monday.

I want to go over how we do our *game planning*. For example, doubles is our simple one-back set. We will look at the defense to see how they play against the double set. We will look at two games if possible to see what the defense is doing and how they adjust to the sets. We watch the tape as a staff. Each coach is going to be given a chance to throw out ideas and we are going to talk about it.

When the tape is over, we are going to the board and setting up our game plan. This is one of the best things we did as a staff before. We will list the four run plays we will use out of doubles against the defense [Diagram 1].

We are going to game plan by what is best from the different formations. We want to run the best play from each formation. Our *quick game* is our *three-step drop game*. We will list the plays we are going to run from each formation for that part of the game. Then we go to our *dropback game*. That is our *five-step* and *seven-step* game.

What I am saying here is simple. The more coaches you can have help you game plan, the better you are going to be. Five minds are better than one mind in this case. We are going to stay and work on it until we get the job done as to what we want to do from each formation.

Once we have all of the formations done, we go to executing the situations of the game. The first thing we work on is the third-down situations. We work on the short, medium, long, and extra-long situations. We all understand how important third-down situations are. We list the situations we must work on and go over each area [Diagram 2].

PERSONNEL FORMATIONS

1. RUNS

    1.

    2.

    3.

    4.

2. DRAW/SCREEN/DELAY

    1.

    2.

    3.

    4.

3. QUICK GAME

    1.

    2.

    3.

    4.

    5.

4. DROPBACK (70's/80's)

    1.

    2.

    3.

    4.

    5.

5. PLAY-ACTION/NAKED (BOOT)

    1.

    2.

    3.

Diagram 1. Game planning

EXECUTE SITUATIONS OF THE GAME

1. Third downs
(short - medium - long - extra-long)

2. Critical zone (+30 to +4}

3. Short yardage (third-and-one)

4. Goal line (two-point play)

5. Fourth-down plays (fourth-and-one, fourth-and-five, fourth-and-nine, fourth-and-ten+)

6. Last play of the game (+4, +8, +14, +25)

7. Two minutes

8. Four minutes

9. Coming out

Diagram 2. Executing game situations

The first situation we game plan is *third down and short*. We all understand how important third downs are. We start with third-and-short yardage. Everyone breaks it down different ways. We call third-and-short one to three yards. Some teams will call short one to two yards. Whatever we consider, third-and-short is on the cut ups. We all watch the third-and-short plays. We come up with two runs, one pass, and possibly one play-action pass in the game plan. One week we may have two passes and one run to mix it up.

Next we work on *third down and medium*. One big thing that has helped us here is to *self-scout* our defense and offense. By doing a self-scouting report, we know what the defense is watching from us. We compare what we are doing against third-and-short and compare it with what our opponents are doing in those situations. This also tells us what we are doing well. We watch third-and-short, medium, long, and extra-long.

I am going to touch briefly on the other areas we cover in executing the situations of the game plan. We look at the *critical zone*. We look at those situations from the plus 30-yard line to the plus four-yard line. Nothing is greater than game planning a plan and then to going out and execute the play successful just as you planned it.

We run the plays in the game plan against the defenses we expect to see in the game. On Thursdays during the season, we work on game situations and cover all of the different areas of the game plan.

Next we work on the *short-yardage plays* that are third-and-one-to-go situations. Then we work against the *goal line package*. We always have one or two two-point plays that we work on. Then we go to the *fourth-down situations*. We work on all of the fourth-down situations from short to long.

We always have a *last-play-of-the-game situation*. We select plays that we could run on the last play of the game that would give us a chance to win. We work those plays from the different positions on the field. We do not just call a play off the top of our heads. We know what we are going to run in those situations to win the game. We work on these situations so we have a chance to win the game if at all possible.

We always have a *two-minute package* in our game plan each week. It will differ from week to week. We go over it and go over it so we understand it. The *four-minute part of the game plan* is to kill the clock. We want to be able to control the ball and so we have plays set up that will enable us to kill the clock. *Coming out* is much the same way except these are situations where we must have the yardage to keep the football. We may have three plays that we select that will help get us out of the hole. We may have a run from the minus one-yard line. We will have a home run play from that same distance. Also, we will have a play that we feel will get us upfield to keep from punting the ball deep in our end of the field. We work on the situations from the different yard lines coming out.

As a staff, we believe this is a great way to game plan. It takes a lot of time but it has been successful for us. You may not have all of the machines to make the tapes but you can still get the job done. If you can make the cut ups, it will help you understand the defense more and it will help you in game planning.

Next I want to look at our *quick-passing game*, which is our three-step drop by the quarterback. I want to talk about the techniques of the quarterback and receivers. I will go over the details of how we teach the patterns. These are very simple and basic routes, but if you will execute them properly, they are very good routes.

The first route we cover is the *X/Z hitch pass* [Diagram 3]. The inside receivers must know the route they are running by the play call. We run the same basic pattern on each side of the ball. We run a five-step hitch route and a seam inside-shoulder flat-defender route. We teach step routes. When we get into our receiver stance, our outside foot is always going to be back. One reason we believe in step routes is because it disciplines you receivers. The NFL may not believe in the step routes. If you have receivers who are disciplined, you will be a better football team.

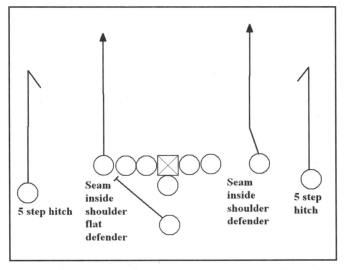

Diagram 3. X/Z hitch pass

When we run a simple hitch route we are going to coach them up. We are not just going to tell them to run a hitch route at six yards and let it go. We are going to have all of the little coaching points and be very detailed for every position we coach.

When we are coaching the hitch route to the receiver, the first thing we want them to do is to break the huddle and then look man on, first man inside, to the free safety. Their outside foot is back. We want our receivers to do three things when they line up to come off the ball. If you can get them to do these three things, you will have a lot of success. We want their eyes up, their hands up, and we want them to get a great get-off on the route. The eyes of the receiver must be up as he comes off the ball. The first thing a young receiver does when he is not running a deep route is to look at the ground. The receiver is not going very deep if he is looking at the ground. The receiver must have his eyes up and he must give a great burst to create separation. He must sell the route in the first three steps on the release.

When we run a five-yard hitch route, we call for three big and two little steps on the play. The receiver is going to come off the ball and go one, two, three big steps, and then one, two small steps. Bam! The ball should be on his outside shoulder.

The first thing the young receivers do is to come out of the hitch with their hands down. We do not want that to happen. It should be a simple catch to make, but it is tough if he has his hands down. We want the receiver to keep his hands up on the route. We want his hands up with his fingers to the thumbs.

We use a term to help the receiver on the hitch: *know where you left him*. As we come off the ball, we want to look at the defender. If the eyes of the receiver are up and he makes his hitch move, and the defender is left inside, the receiver is going to dip inside and then go outside. If he left the defender outside, he is going to dip outside and run inside. That is how you get yards after the catch. Again, we stress short throws and long runs.

Our quarterback on the X/Z hitch route takes a three-step drop. We want him to throw off his plant foot. We talk to the quarterback about throwing off rhythm and throwing off his plant. The quarterback is coming back one, two, three steps and throwing off the plant of his third step. He is thinking of throwing the ball as he hits that third step. He wants to throw the ball out to the receiver in the flat in the seam.

The big coaching points for the receiver on the hitch route are to make sure the receiver snaps his head around on the hitch, make sure he stays on that seam, and make sure he catches the ball in the seam area. Young receivers will look for the ball from the quarterback and drift inside. When that happens the linebacker will pick the pass off and everyone blames

the quarterback for the interception. It is the receiver's fault when that happens.

The next route we are going to run a lot of is our *X/Z out, Y double hook route* [Diagram 4]. Now our outside receivers are running a five-yard speed cut out. Again, their outside foot is back. We come off low and hard as fast as we can. Their eyes are up and we are looking through the defensive man. We are working the heck out of our arms. We pump those arms hard. We want the eyes looking to the hands when the ball arrives.

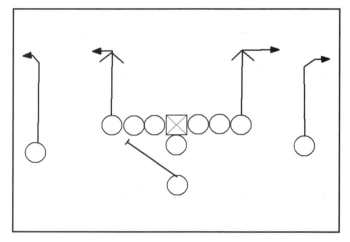

Diagram 4. X/Z out – Y double hook route

We want their outside foot back, with great get-off, and as we get to a depth of five yards, we plant the foot at a 45-degree angle and roll out of the pattern and catch the ball at six yards. We want to catch the ball and go down the sideline and score.

The key is great pad level, great get-off, and a nice low stance. We are going to play in a low stance. We want our shoulders lower than the defenders shoulders.

The tight ends come off the ball at six yards and they are going to hook inside, hook outside, or break outside depending on what the defense is giving them. You can take these two routes and go play in a passing tournament. You can move the ball up and down the field with this play.

If the defense pressures the outside receiver, he converts the route to a fade route. If the defense is playing off the receiver, the quarterback takes a three-step drop and is thinking of throwing the out route all the way to the best receiver. If the flat defender covers the flat route, he throws the ball to the tight end.

If the defense goes to a two-high defense, it means they have four secondary defenders. Predominately they will have three linebackers. One linebacker will be tucked inside more than the others. The quarterback reads the linebackers and looks for the tight ends. The only throw the quarterback may struggle with may be the six-yard out route to the field. You may want to tweak that part of the play a little more or you may want to rep it more and more.

The next route is the *X/Z slant, Y arrow* [Diagram 5]. Here we run two slants to the two-receiver side and a slant and arrow to the tight end side. Again, we are teaching the step route. It is a three-step slant route. His outside foot is back. The corner is head-up on the receiver. We want the receiver to get great get-off. If the defender has inside leverage, we may have to squirm up. If we do not square up it does not become step route any more. If he is head-up to the outside leverage, then we will have great get-off, and run the one, two, three steps and stick that foot in the ground on the plant. If you want to help the receivers with their routes, teach them to stick that plant foot on their routes. Teach them to stick the route and then burst out of the plant. If you can get them to do that they will get better.

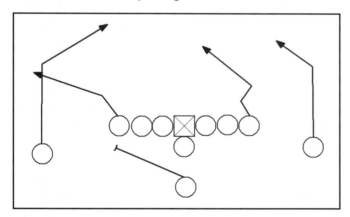

Diagram 5. X/Z slant – Y arrow

We use to teach the receiver to run a 45-degree angle out of the break. Now our aiming point is the outside shoulder of the near safety.

If we have a two-receiver side, the inside receiver is the hot man. If both receivers are covered tight we tell the inside receiver to win *quick* and for the outside

receiver to win *late* on the route. The quarterback should see the inside man first and the outside receiver second.

On the slant route, the pass may be thrown off the plant or the quarterback may have to sit on the ball to give the receiver time to get to the open window. In the three-step game, the quarterback must know if he is throwing off his plant step or if he is going to sit on the throw later. He must read the defender and get the ball to the open receiver.

This next route is one of my favorite routes. It is something I think we teach really well. In 1998, the University of Louisville was number one in offense. We averaged 560 yards per game. We converted 39 third downs on this play. We did it from a lot of different formations. The play is our *inside option route* [Diagram 6].

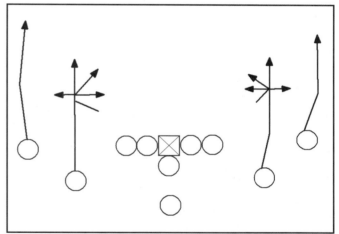

Diagram 6. Inside option route

The two inside receivers have the option routes at six-yards deep. Some teams will run the five-step drop and run the routes at 10 yards. Not a lot of teams run the option routes at six-yards off the three-step drop.

This is how we teach the play. We always check the defender on the receiver, to the first man inside, to the free safety. If I am the inside receiver, as I come to the line of scrimmage I must look for a man-on look by the defense.

We want to come off the ball full speed. We use speed release straight ahead, arch release outside, or stem release inside.

Against cover 0 (man coverage), we must push to six yards, step on the defenders toes, and run by him or snap off to a skinny post. If the defender is playing man we are thinking home run or a touchdown. If we do not break the defensive back's cushion, we are going to break out at six yards, sit down, or break inside at six yards. If we are worried about the first defender inside, we are going to break it off and run the six-yard out route.

We use three different releases on this play. We run a speed release, which is straight ahead. We use an arc release that comes outside, and stem release that goes inside.

Against the *one-high look*, we want the receiver to have great get-off and then push to six yards, then break in, break out, or sit down. Against *zone under* we want to sit down. Against *man under* we run away.

In our three-step drop game, we will package what we do in a game. The first time we call the hitch route we may call *Z hitch, W option*. We may run a hitch on one side and an option on the other side of the formation. If the corner plays the hitch receiver soft, we throw the hitch. If the corner plays the hitch receiver tight, we read the option route to the other side of the formation. You must do this a lot of the time now because the defense disguises their alignment so much.

Now I want to show some tape of our three-step drop game. I will review the four routes I have covered.

(Film)

I want to get to the five- and seven-step drop game. The first route is the *Z/X curl*. To the field we have a curl and a seam route. To the boundary we have a curl and an arrow route. We step route our curl routes. If you come to see us practice, you will see us teaching the step routes all of the time. We can go step routes or we can run point to point. Point to point is yardage.

The first curl route we teach is called *5-4 curl*. We break the steps down where we take five steps on the first step and then push up four more yards on the second stem [Diagram 7]. Again, their outside foot is back. We must have great get off to threaten the corner. On the fifth step we want to plant with the outside foot and accelerate to the second stem. On

the second stem the receiver must get his eyes inside on the flat defender to beat the underneath coverage. On the last two steps of the four steps we want the receiver to take a look inside. If the defense is playing zone under, we have to beat the underneath man on the coverage. He must come back to the football.

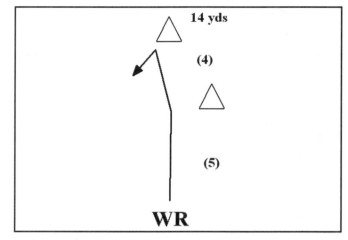

Diagram 7. 5-4 curl

We run all of our routes off these steps. If you think the defense can read these steps they are going to beat you anyway. We run all the different routes from these steps.

Next we run the *4-5 curl*. Now we break on four yards on the first stem and five yards on the second stem [Diagram 8]. Against a jam corner we run an inside release to avoid getting jammed. We push to the second stem straight upfield. On the second stem we want the receiver to get his eyes inside on the flat defender to beat the underneath coverage. We must find the hole and beat the underneath coverage.

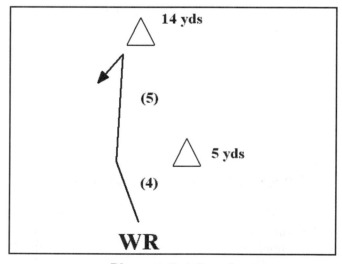

Diagram 8. 4-5 curl

Here is the way the play looks with all of the receivers included [Diagram 9]. The quarterback takes his five-step drop and throws on rhythm. On his first three steps his eyes are on the *hold* linebacker. On the last two steps he keys the flat defender. Against two-high coverage he reads the X end to the running back. Against a one-high coverage he reads Z to Y receivers.

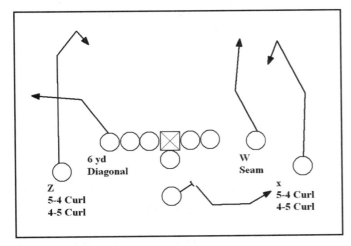

Diagram 9

Quickly I want to show you the individual routes on the *X/Z out, W read/Y drag* [Diagram 10]. We run the X/Z out at 12 yards. It is a six-step speed cut out. Again, the receiver must have great get-off. The receiver plants on his sixth plant step inside foot and rolls out of the break. His aiming point is at 12 yards. Against a press defender he runs a 12-yard trace route. We want him to catch the ball and sprint down the sideline.

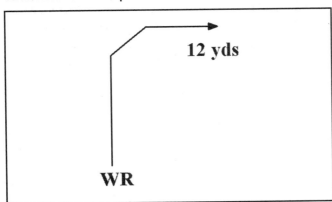

Diagram 10. X/Z out – W read/Y drag

On the *Z/X out, W read* route we use a speed release or arch release. The receiver must push to the second level behind the linebackers [Diagram 11]. He threatens the safety and then snaps the route off. He

must read the middle linebackers drop, and catch the ball in the first window or go to the second window. Against man coverage he must run away from the coverage. We want him to catch the ball and get upfield.

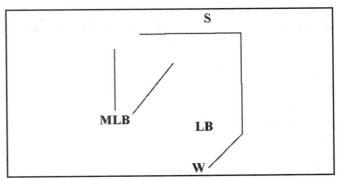

Diagram 11. Z/X out – W read

Here is an example of the play with all receivers involved [Diagram 12]. For the quarterback on a one-high coverage, it is a five-step timing throw. We want him to throw off the plant. He must key the defender and read the Z back to the running back or read the X receiver to the Y receiver.

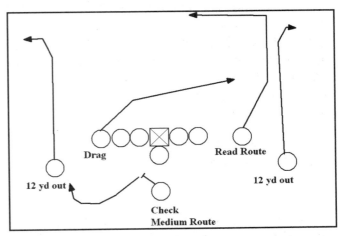

Diagram 12

Against the two-high look, it is a five-step rhythm throw. On the first three steps he reads the middle linebacker. On his last two steps he must key the weakside linebacker and read the W receiver to the Y receiver.

You are always welcome to come to our practices. There is no one in the world that I have more respect for than high school coaches. My dad and my brothers, and my high school coaches are the most important people in my life. I think you guys are awesome. Anytime we can help you let us know. Thank you.

WIDE RECEIVER TECHNIQUES AND DRILLS

University of Kentucky

As most of you know, when I accepted the opportunity to speak at this clinic I was coaching at the University of South Carolina. Now that I have moved on to the University of Kentucky, I want to apologize for the films I will show. I have not had time to put any new films together for this lecture. The film you will see will be some films from South Carolina and some from Notre Dame, where I once coached.

I want to give you a general outline of what I give my players. First, we talk about football in general. We talk about *stance*, *catching the football*, *elements of blocking*, and *point-of-attack blocking drills*. Then I will show you some tapes of our drills. If I have time, I will talk about our triple-pass plays that are flood routes to us. I am talking about flood routes strong and flood routes weak.

A lot of the coaches I have visited with in the last few days have asked me how it was working for Coach Lou Holtz. I can assure you he is a great motivator. I had a great time working for Coach Holtz. I want to give you a couple of points I got from Coach Holtz that I feel are worth passing on to you that helped me as a football coach.

People who do not read good books and other materials are no better off than those people who cannot read. This means a lot to me. I relate this to an athlete. If a player is a great athlete but is not willing to work, he is no better off than the average athlete, and not as good as the average athlete who works his tail off.

Championship teams start when the quarterback is *mistake free*. I want our quarterback coach, Paul Hudson, to hear this. That is when you have championship teams.

The third point I want to pass on relates to *motivation*. Motivation is spending personal time with the players. You must see them improve. When they improve they become disciplined. When they are disciplined it means they want to be disciplined like you as a coach. You must give them discipline.

The next thing Coach Holtz taught me was to *coach for the love for the game*. You must coach because you love the competition and the challenge of the game. If you are in the game for any other reason you are in the game for the wrong reason.

The fifth thing I took from Coach Holtz is something I will always take with me. He said you can *strengthen a team* with these three things. First, is by *addition*. If you are a high school coach, you can strengthen the team by adding new members to the team when the next class moves up. You can also strengthen your team by *deletion*. If a player is a bad apple you must delete him from the team. The last point is *player development*. This is by developing the team to be good players. That is how you strengthen your team. Those are just a few of the things I took from Coach Holtz. As I said, I get a lot of questions about working with Coach Holtz. It was a great experience for me working with Coach Holtz and his staff.

When I start talking with our receivers, I ask them three questions. And again, I got this from Coach Holtz. First, I want to know if I can trust the receiver. Can I trust you? Then I want to know who cares. Do you care about your teammates? Who cares about the staff? Then the third question is who is committed? Those are the three qualities we talk about. *We talk about trust, care, and being committed.*

We want to know if we can trust them, if we can trust them to be in the right place at the right time, and if we can trust them to be in class on time. Can we trust them to get off the blocks and be in the proper football position? Does he care about his teammates and the other players on the football team? Is he committed to the things we ask him to do? Those are the things we talk to them about all of the time.

Next I want to talk about *the position coach*. These are points I believe in. I think it is important for a position coach to demonstrate. They are a must as far as I am concerned. The position coach must be fair, firm, and he must be consistent. He must be firm and lay the law down. He must be fair in administering the rules. He must be consistent in his coaching techniques.

The position coach must teach and lead and he must communicate. He must coach the heck out of fundamentals. He must coach fundamentals from the ground up. We start with footwork and work up. The same is true with discipline. You have to coach the heck out of the offensive and defensive philosophy. The team must understand what the philosophy is to become a team.

You must coach *togetherness*. It cannot be offense versus the defense. It cannot be the offense against the special teams. You must get the team to believe in themselves. You must convince the team that the coaches believe in them. The team must believe in your coaching staff. You must coach the plan. The players must understand the plan. They must understand field position. They need to know why we are punting on fourth down. They must know about turnovers. They must understand hitting. You must out hit your opponents. Those are some general points that we talk about.

Next I want to talk about what I call *wide receiver alerts. First, the receiver must know the situation.* He must know the down-and-distance. He must know field position. He must know the difference in coming out or when we are backed up coming out, from the red zone, or when we are on the goal line. We want to make sure they know down-and-distance and field position.

The second alert is the assignment. They must know the base play. They must know the audible that goes with the base play. We want our receivers to know why we use the audible.

Next they receiver must know alignment. He must know if he is going right or left. He must know the split rules. Is he going to be in a tight split or a normal split? He must understand motion as a wide receiver.

The fourth alert relates to adjustments. On pass plays he must know the route conversion. We may have an out route called. If the defense plays cover 2 with a squat corner and a safety over the top, he must understand the route conversion. He will convert the route to the fade route. A comeback route may be converted to a corner route against a cover 2 look. The receiver must be able to adjust to the run. He must know the different type of blocks.

The next alert is the P.S.L. or pre-snap look. The first aspect is to know the elements of man coverage. Second they must know the elements of zone coverage.

From the stance, the receiver must be able to see two defenders. He must be able to see the corner and the safety. He does not need to know what the defense does on the backside. Those two defenders will tell him what the defense is playing.

The next alert is that the receivers must be able to R.O.M. -- read on the move. They must be able to read and adjust on the move. They must be able to change directions both on the run and on the pass.

The last alert is on big plays. Again, we stress this on run and pass. Big plays happen because the wide receivers did something to make it happen. It may be that a player makes a catch and then makes a big run. It may be on a great catch of a pass. And it could be a block on a pass caught by another receiver. The same is true on the running game. In the past, a big run for us was a 15-yard run. If a big run happens it is usually because we have done something as a wide receiver. We must have the big plays in the running game and our receivers must be downfield blocking.

Next is my *wide receiver game goal sheet* [Diagram 1]. I will go over these goals with the wide receivers.

Our first goal is to *win*. We list all of our opponents across the top of the sheet. Our goal is to win. It does not matter if the score is 3-0 or 55-44. We do not care, we just want to win.

Our second goal is 15 knockdowns per game. A knockdown to me is when the defender gets both hands on the ground or he goes down to one knee.

Games > Goals v	1	2	3	4	5	6	7	8	9	10	T
Win											
15 KD's											
150 Yds. Rec.											
2 TD's											
Avg. 5 YAC											
5 Big Plays											
Perfect Assignment											
Perfect Ball Security											
No LOS Penalty											
No Efforts											

Diagram 1. Wide receiver game goal sheet

Next we want to gain 150 yards receiving in each game. This is total yards for the entire group of receivers. We do count the tight ends and running backs in the total.

We want to have two touchdowns per game for our wide receivers. We want to average five yards per *Y.A.C*, which stands for *yards after catch*. We want to average five yards after we catch the ball.

We want five big plays per game. A big play for our group is a 20-yard pass, a reverse for 16 yards, or a jet sweep for 16 yards. If we can make five big plays, we will win the game. We want all of our players to perform perfectly on assignments. We do not want to miss any assignments. It is hard to win with missed assignments. We want to have perfect ball security. We do not want any dropped balls and we do not want any turnovers from our group. We do not want any line of scrimmage penalties. I say no line of scrimmage penalties because we must be able to line up. We are going to go hard until the whistle blows. We may get a late hit and get the 15-yard penalty. However, we do not want to get the five-yard penalty. We cannot have a misalignment by our receivers. We cannot have any illegal motion or illegal procedure penalties. We do not want to receive a *no* on effort on our goal sheet.

I received a definition of effort from a friend of my. It came from the Tampa Bay Buccaneers. Their definition of effort is this: *don't get passed up.* If they pass, you go after them. If you are lying on the ground, get up and go after them. Don't stay on the ground too long. They do not want to see a change of speed by the receivers. They want to see nothing but speed.

Next I go over our *grade sheet* [Diagram 2]. This is what we look for on the film.

OPPONENT'S NAME: _____	U.L.	Murray State	Bama	IU
Plays				
Plus				
Minus				
GRADE				
Catches				
Yards				
YAC				
Drops				
TD's				
Runs				
Yards				
TD's				
Big Plays				
MAD Plays				
Effort				
MA's				
KD's				
C. Error				
Penalty				

Diagram 2. Grade sheet

First we have the number of plays a player is involved in. We give plus and minus on the grades at the point of attack. We go through all of the categories on the sheet. M.A.D. stands for *make a difference plays*. We talk about their plays that made a difference in the game. It may be a reception for eight yards, a block, or it may be a fumble recovery.

We do not want the M.A.'s or *missed assignments* in the game. We do not want any *critical errors* and we do not want any penalties, especially the five-yard types.

Next I want to talk about the *receiver's stance*. We are in a *two-point* stance. We want his inside foot up. We are in a two-point stance with his knees up over his toes. We want the majority of his weight on his front foot. The back of his heel is pointed to the sky. His back is flat, his arms are relaxed, and his head and eyes are pointed inside. The majority of his weight must be on his front foot.

There are two definitions for a *false step*. One is when he does not have enough weight on his front foot. The first thing a young receiver does is to pick his foot up and set it inside and then take off. The second definition is when he does not have his back foot back far enough. If that happens he will drop step when he starts. The two mistakes are not having enough weight on his front foot and not having his back foot up underneath him. He should roll off his front foot and push off his back foot.

If we get press coverage, we will square the stance up so we can move side to side. If we have soft coverage, we want the weight forward.

Let me move to *catching the football*. The first things we talk about here are the eyes. If you ask the young receivers how they catch the football, they would tell you with their hands. We tell them we catch the football with the *eyes, feet, and then the hands*.

You need your eyes to find the football. You use your eyes to locate the ball. You use your feet to get into the best possible position to catch the ball. If the ball is thrown outside my framework, I must use my feet to get over to the football. The last point is to catch the ball with your hands.

I like to tell the receivers to have their thumbs together, creating a triangle with their fingers. We want to extend the arms but we do not lock the elbows out. If you have a little bend in your elbows, you have a better chance to catch the ball. We use the arms as shock absorbers. We look the ball all the way into the tuck.

If the ball is below my waist, I must extend my arms. Now I want my thumbs apart. My feet are spread wide. If the ball hits my arms, I use them as shock absorbers. I want to look the ball in all the way to the tuck.

Next I want to talk about the *elements of blocking*. I want to cover blocking on the perimeter. We may use this block on the option, bubble screen, or on a sweep play. I will tell you the techniques and drills we use.

We cover four points on the blocking aspects: *stay square, good football position, outside leverage*, and *effort*. The number one point is to stay square to the line of scrimmage. Any time we are blocking the perimeter, we must stay square to the line of scrimmage. We want to stay square in good fundamental football position. We want to keep outside leverage and put the inside knee in his crotch. I want to keep outside leverage. If he moves, I move. If the target moves, I move. We want to shuffle with the defender. We do not want to click our heels.

The defender is two-yards away from us when we square up on him. If he settles, we settle. We break down and we are ready to attack. Now we are just like an offensive lineman. We want to stay on the same level with the defender. We mirror the defender and keep outside leverage. We shuffle with the man. We do not want to click our heels.

The last aspect of blocking is *effort*. Blocking is nothing more than effort. If they will not give you effort, you can't win.

Everything we do in football starts from the ground up. The thing I want to do with receivers is to get to their feet. You can coach so the receivers get quick feet.

The following are the drills we use to teach our blocking. We call them *P.O.A. blocking drills*, which means *point of attack*.

- *Foot-fire drill* –- We use two cones five-yards apart. We have them shuffle through the cones several times. We have them hip-hop from one cone to the other. We add a cone and have them touch the cone as they go by the cones. They go as fast as they can. Some people call this the tapioca drill.

- *Mirror drill* –- Start with a defender against the blocker. We want the inside knee inside the defender's crotch. We go back and forth. Our offensive linemen do the same drill. However, they actually put their hands behind their backs on the drill. They defender slides down the line and we keep our leverage on him.

- *Fit-and-finish drill* — We have the cones five-yards apart. We have the receiver with his knee inside the defender's crotch. We are going to block him outside. We fit up under the defender and get under his pads. The defender slides side to side and the blocker stays with him keeping his butt square to the line of scrimmage. The *finish* aspect of the drill comes when the blocker feels the defender coming off the block. When the blocker feels the defender coming off, he wants to finish him off by lowering his hips into him.

- *Two-point extension drill* — We have one man on offense and one man on defense. The man on offense will place his chin on the chest of the defender. He has his hands down between his legs. He tries to come up between the defender's chin to his helmet. We want him to put the two screws in his helmet through the defensive man's chin. We can see this drill on the tape later.

- *Tripod drill* — It is basically a tackling drill. Now we want the offensive man in a breakdown position. We stand behind the defensive man and point in a direction we want the blocker to go. He will lead step and roll his hips into the defensive man. He must throw his hips into the defender and get his butt underneath his feet. It is like a tackling drill except we do not lock up with our hands.

- *Punch-and-shuffle drill* — We started using this with our bubble-screen play. For example, we have a middle receiver in a three-receiver set. We have outside leverage on the middleman. He has to battle to keep outside leverage. The number three receiver runs the bubble and the number one receiver blocks the man over him. We want to punch and shuffle to keep leverage on the middle defender. We do not turn our hips on the play. We keep our butts square with the line of scrimmage. We want the runner to cut off our block. We punch and shuffle, running to the sideline.

- *Punch-and-shuffle cut drill* — When you are blocking the perimeter, there are times you get mismatches. If our receiver is overwhelmed by a big, strong safety, we use this drill. We will punch, shuffle, shuffle, and then cut block on the man.

- *Run-off drill* — We run the defender off the line of scrimmage. If the defense in playing man-to-man, we will run him off the line of scrimmage. There is no need to block him. We will run another drill with the wide receiver going inside to block on the safety instead of running the outside defender off. We will take the second man inside instead of the outside man. We just tell the receiver to *take two*.

Now I want to show you a tape on these drills. Again, these are old tapes and not from the University of Kentucky. I will be around if you have any questions. Feel free to come to visit with us. Thank you.

BUILDING THE DEFENSIVE GAME PLAN

Marshall University

It is certainly an honor to be with you today. I am very happy to see this many coaches here. The last time I spoke at a clinic there was one, two, or three coaches present. I asked the person who ran the clinic if he had told the coaches I was going to lecture. He replied, "No, but I am going to find out who did tell them." (Ha, ha!)

I want to talk to you about the things we do at Marshall University. Before I get into the defensive game plan, there are some things I should tell you. First, let me give you a little of my background. I was a high school coach for 14 years. I graduated from Marshall University in 1965. I had a dream of one day coming back as head coach at Marshall. I had tried the professional game and Coach Landry tried to make a tailback out of me. It did not last very long. That is when I got into high school coaching.

In 1979 I had an opportunity to go back to Marshall as an assistant coach under Coach Sonny Randle. I actually took a $10,000 pay cut to go back to Marshall as an assistant. That is how bad I wanted to go back to Marshall. I stayed four years at Marshall as an assistant.

I then went to Wake Forest as an assistant coach. While I was at Wake Forest, the Marshall head coaching job opened up. I applied for the job but they gave the job to Jim Donnan. Jim came to Marshall and really did a great job. He started Marshall on the road to winning a lot of games. The A.D. at Marshall told me that I was a good football coach, but they were going to go with Jim because of his experience. He told me I needed to get more experience at schools that had a winning program.

At Wake Forest we played in so many homecoming games that we started taking our own homecoming floats. So at that point I decided that I needed to move to other schools if I wanted to be a head coach in college. I did not want to leave Wake Forest but I felt I had to. I had worked for Al Groh who

is at Virginia. I was his defensive coordinator. Also, I was the defensive coordinator for Bill Dooley at Wake Forest. Wake Forest is a great school. The only bad times at Wake Forest are the three hours on Saturday during the game.

I left Wake Forest and went to the University of Mississippi. We won at Ole Miss. We went to the Gator Bowl. Next, I went to Tulane as the defensive coordinator for two years. Then Coach Steve Spurrier called me to come to the University of Florida as his defensive coordinator. I was with Steve for two years. While I was at Florida, we only lost one regular season game. From there I got the head coaching job at Marshall in 1996.

It took me 31 years to realize my dream to become the head coach at Marshall. Along the way I met some great head coaches at the schools where I coached. I learned something from all of them. Then I had to put my package together at Marshall of what I wanted to do.

What we try to do at Marshall University is to do the things that will help us win and build tradition. We want *consistency* in our program. We have been fortunate in that we have been able to do that. We have a really good situation. The big thing is the fact that we have good players. That is the first important thing about our program. *Good players make good coaches.* We have been fortunate to win 80 football games in the seven years I have been at Marshall. This is the most wins by any Division-I team in the last seven years. The key to this is that we have had good players.

One thing we have been able to do is to assemble a good staff. We put our plan together in 1996. We have lost some good assistant coaches who have gone on to better paying jobs. The coordinator at Florida was with us. The coordinators at Minnesota, SMU, and North Carolina State worked for us. What I have tried to do is to keep someone on the staff who can move up to replace any coordinator that we lose. When we lose a coordinator we promote within the staff every time. By doing this we keep the consistency in the program. We keep the same terminology the same in our program. When someone new does come in, it helps us in that we can tweak our program and add to or take away something without making a complete change.

If you have heard me talk before or if you have seen us play, you know that we use the phrase *we play for championships*. That is our motto. This all started in 1996 when we were still in Division I-AA. We were 15-0 and won the National Championship. In the next year we moved up to Division-I football. Marshall University had not had a winning season in Division-I football since 1964. That was the team that I played on. Marshall had winning seasons since then but they were in Division I-AA.

There was a lot of apprehension about the success of Marshall in Division I. That first year we went 10-3 and lost to Ole Miss in the Motor City Bowl. We lost that game 34-31. After the game in a press conference, a reporter asked me if I was extremely pleased with the performance of the players against a Southeastern Conference team. My response to him was this: "I am proud of the effort of the players, but at Marshall University we are used to playing for championships. That has been our standard and our goal." Since that time we have played in 21 games that meant the divisional, bowl game, or conference championship, and we have won 19 of those games. We lost to Ole Miss that year and two years ago we lost to Toledo in the MAC Championship game.

What we are trying to do is to set a standard among our players, fans, and coaches that we expect to play for championships. This morning I talked to our team in our workout. I talked to them about being a champion and what is expected of them.

We lost a lot of good players last year. We lost a great player in Bryon Leftwich. I think he will be the first player taken in the NFL draft. If he isn't taken first, he should be first. At Marshall University we have had three Heisman Trophy legitimate candidates in the last six years. That is something special. You will hear me discussing in my talk about *exploiting your strengths and managing you weakness*. In our recruiting we talk to the prospects about playing for

championships. If you have a team that does not have any jewelry, you have a problem in college football. The players want those championship rings. In seven years at Marshall we now have seven rings. That is what they want and that is what they expect. Today I asked our senior class if they were going to be the class that does not get a championship ring. In the MAC, if you do not get to the championship game there is a good chance you will not get invited to a bowl game. I think you have to build that attitude.

I was fortunate enough to be around some teams that have won a lot of games. At Florida we were 11-1 the first year and 12-0 the second year. The next year we were at Marshall and went 15-0. The next year we were 10-3, 12-1, 13-0, 9-4, 11-2, and 11-2 last year. That is a lot of wins.

I want to leave you with something that I think is important. You must *set the standards and expectations* for your program. We do not believe in rebuilding. I do not talk about rebuilding at Marshall. I do not talk to our fans about rebuilding. I talk about winning championships. I talked to a big alumni group the other day and the first question I got was this: "Coach, how are we going to do next year?" My reply was this: "We are going to be hard pressed *not* to be better than we were last year." I really believe this. We have good players. If I give them an excuse not to play up to their potential, I am building in an excuse for the players. That is the last thing I tell our players before they leave the locker room. "We want to play as close to perfect as possible." We realize that no one is perfect. I think we set the standard very high for our program.

There have been two tests for us in this span of time I have talked about as far as playing for championships. In the 2000 season, we lost Chad Pennington and several other good players through graduation. We lost to Michigan State and we lost to North Carolina by two points that year. We are 49-1 over the last seven years at home. The only team to beat us at home was Western Michigan in a televised game on a Thursday night. We came back that year and beat Western Michigan at home in the playoff game.

To start the season we were 2-4. We had just lost to Toledo 41-0. We lost a close game to Western Michigan, we lost to Michigan State, and then we won two games, and lost to North Carolina. After that Toledo loss, we were humiliated. We did not do very many things very well.

We all know when things do not go well people start pointing the finger and blaming others. The question was what we were going to do to turn this season around. This is what I did and hopefully it will give you an idea that will help you in a similar situation. It worked very well for us.

On Monday we had a team meeting. I did not tell anyone on the staff what I was going to do. I figured it out; it was not getting better. I went to Lowe's and bought 44 flashlights. Also, I bought a big bag of rubber bands.

At the meeting I had the first-team offense stand in one corner. I gave each of them a flashlight. I had the first team defense go to the other corner of the room and I gave them each a flashlight. I took the special teams starters and gave all of them a flashlight.

Next I had all of the room lights turned off. Then I told the offensive team to turn their flashlights on. All 11 of those lights were turned on. Then I told the right guard to turn his light off. "Men, we only have ten players on offense doing it right. The right guard just missed blocking the linebacker. We got our quarterback sacked for a five-yard loss." I told the guard to turn his light back on. Then I told the halfback to turn his light off. "Men, the halfback just ran the ball down the field for a 20-yard gain but he fumbled the ball and the defense recovered the fumble. Again, we have ten guys doing it right and one guy doing it wrong."

Next I had the offense turn their lights off. I asked the defense to turn their flashlights on. I did the same thing with the defense. I had the linebacker turn his flashlight off. "We have ten players doing it right and one player hurting us. We just called a blitz and he hit the wrong gap and they hit the dive play for 80 yards and a touchdown."

Those are the type of things that happen when things are not going well. We have nine players doing things right and two players not getting the job done. We were so close to being perfect but we have one or two players who let us down.

Then we did the same thing with the special teams. It was the same situation. Finally I had all of

the players with the flashlights turn them on. As a team we could light up the room. This illustrated to them that they had to *play as a team and work together*. We had to somehow become a team.

I gave each one of them a rubber band. They wore that rubber band every day and every practice until the end of the bowl game. One rubber band by itself is not very strong. But if you put a bunch of rubber bands together, it is strong as hell. Our saying was this: *We were going to band together and get better*. We can be a strong force. We were going to have faith and we were going to believe each other.

We turned it around and beat a team in the championship game that had beaten us by 28 points in the regular season. At the end of the year we were playing as good as any team that has ever played at Marshall University. We did it with the same players who had gone 2-4 in the first six games. We won all of the games from that point on and we won the MAC Championship and went on to a bowl game.

The other situation I want to tell you about is when we were playing East Carolina in the Mobile Bowl two years ago. We were down 38-8 at the halftime. It was not very pretty to say the least.

I like to tell this story about that game. Our offensive coordinator and offensive line coach, Mark McHale, was walking off the field with me at the half. Mark got me by the arm and said, "Bob, whatever you say, make sure it is positive. When you go in to talk to the team be positive." We were on national TV and we had played terrible. I told Mark I would do the best I could to be positive. We got them in the locker room and got all of the little things out of the way and then I got them together to talk with them as a team.

I looked them in the eyes and this is what I said to them: "Men, Coach McHale has asked me to be positive in my talk with you. Men, let me assure you I am going to be positive. *I am positive your ass is going to walk home if you do not start playing better*."

We started playing better when we told them the things we stood for in our program. We reminded them of our championship season.

We talked to them about having *faith* in each other and in the coaches. It is the same thing with the good Lord. We all have faith when He is in this room.

We have to have faith in our football team especially when things do not go well for our football team. So let me assure that adversity strikes every program.

You have to *believe in your teammates* and you have to *believe in the system*. You have to *believe in your coaches*. The coaches must *believe in the players*. Everyone must pull together. I do not think this just happens. You have to talk about it and you have to work on it and you must make the players believe in it. Any time you work with young people, what you give them is what they are going to give yourself. The first play you put in on offense is usually your best play. I want our players to be ecstatic over the way we play. I want them to be excited to kick the crap out of the opponents. I want them to be upset when we win but they do not think they played well. I want teams to know when they play the *Herd* we are going to play hard for 60 minutes.

Let me cover our *defensive philosophy* related to our game plan. We start with the basic principle of playing Marshall football. Everything we do, as an individual, will be focused on becoming a close-knit team. We will stress and believe in the team concept, not the *I* concept of football. No single member of this squad is more important than the team. Put he ball down and play wherever and whenever the ball is spotted. This will be the attitude of our defense:

A defensive player's value to his team can be measured by his distance from the ball at the end of the play.

When we start talking about the game plan we are going to keep it simple. We want the players to be able to go out and play. I want to go over a few things that we do in putting in a game plan. We put first things first in our practice. We stretch and then we kick, and then we go to what we call *first things first*. These things are the fundamentals of football. These are the fundamentals that we try to get across to our players in practice and in a game. These are very simple principles and fundamentals of football. It is a simple way to communicate with the players.

The first thing we talk about is the *stance*. If you have to move to move, you have a poor stance. If you have to move to go in the direction you want to go, then you are in a poor stance. If I am a wide receiver

and I have to drop step to get off the ball, what am I doing? I am moving to move. I want to be in a stance where I can go on the snap of the ball. You have to adjust your stance so you can move without taking that false step.

We do not want to have a drastic level change of in our back. If you have to make a big change in your position, you are going to be off guard. You cannot play the game of football with a straight back. You want to play the game with your wrist below the knees. We are talking about the bent knee position. If we do that we can usually play the game from that position.

To tie all of this in together we talk about two kinds of stances. One is a *speed stance*. We are trying to run fast either forwards or backwards. If you are trying to run fast you want to keep your feet inside your armpit. That is the speed stance.

If I want to hit the opponent, I want to use a *power stance*. Those are simple points that we cover with our players. We want their wrist below their knees with their head up and their butt down. We explode from the hips and make the hit. We go from speed stance to power stance and from power stance to speed stance. This gives us a uniform method of communicating with our players about the stance. Some of you may have a different way of expressing the same thing we are doing.

I am just a simple guy from East Beckley. It is a small town in West Virginia. I know two big words. Those two big words are refrigerator and mayonnaise. I am pretty good with those two big words.

Communication with the players and staff is very important. It doesn't make any difference how much football you know, or what I know, but how much the players know. They have to be able to regurgitate it back in the action of the game. A confused football player is a slow football player. He is slow to react and he looks like a coward at times. He looks like he does not know what to do or where to go. You have to make it simple so they will know what to do and know what is going on.

When you evaluate your game film you will find that missed alignments and missed assignments will get you beat more times than talent will. If you are making those kinds of mistakes you are not doing a very good job of teaching them in practice. If we are teaching them too much, we may have to cut down on the amount of things we are asking them to do in a game. We want our players to execute.

We have graduated over 80 percent of the players since I have been at Marshall. We have won an average of 11 games per year in the last seven years. We try to keep a system that does not change. We try to keep the system something they can learn. We give the system to the players in time segments. The big problem we have on defense today is the way teams are changing on offense, but we still try to call the perfect defense. It is hard to make the perfect call on defense. We think it is better to make a call and line up in it and go at it as best as we can.

I do know this much. I keep in mind a sign I saw in a yard. It read, *Slow Children Playing*, and had nothing to do with the traffic. So we are going to try to keep the things we are going to do very simple. We are going to do the things we are capable of doing.

The last point related to the stance is to *point your toes in the direction you want to go*. It is very simple. Point your toes where you want to go. These are simple little things that we try to communicate to our players.

Talk to the players so they can understand what you want and have fun with them and you will be a lot better off as a coach.

Let's get into the *game plan*. Some of these following things I'm going to go through quickly. You must have a *positive way of communicating with your players* instead of saying don't fumble the ball or wrap it up. We say wrap the ball up. Coach the player's positively, not negatively. What they hear last is what they remember. Always find a way to talk positively to them.

The next thing is so fundamental but true. We call it simply *alignment, assignment, and good stance*. You have to align right, do your assignment, and get in a proper stance. When your team gets beat, how many times did you line up wrong, didn't know what to do, or didn't get the call in time. Those are three things a player should be able to do every time. If you can't get your players to that point, you need to stop and start over. You should be able to get them lined up, teach them what they have to do, and get them in a good stance. If you do this you will win more than you lose.

How many of you saw the film *Remember the Titans*? The third team the Titans played was a team that I coached. I was the head coach at Rosen that played T. C. Williams High School. That story was a little distorted with some of the things they were saying. When I first went to Groveton High School they had lost 31 straight games. They only had 17 people in the program and had scored only six points the previous year. We got a little better as time went on. They had three high schools in Alexandria, Virginia, at the time and they combined the three with T. C. Williams High School. Coach Boone and I are still real good friends. He did a great job at T. C. Williams.

We were not very good when I went to Groveton High School. But I told the players we did not have to look bad when we lined up. I told them we should be able to get into our stance right, and we should be able to line up right. We had nice uniforms. We could warm-up and look good doing it. That is part of the game.

In the movie where the T. C. William's team did all of the chanting before the game was interesting. I will never forget that experience. Sometimes I give the same chant to our team. "Ah T.C. – You are the one for me. Ah – Ah T.C." They would come out on the field and give all of those chants and try to intimidate the other team. I told the guys I was glad we had yellow game pants on when we played them. Believe me they were something special. But we ended up playing them pretty close.

You should *point your toes in the direction you want to go –- you can't play straight legged*. We've already talked about that.

You should always do walk-through. I am a firm believer in this. We do a lot of walk-through. The reason I do them is because it is a good teaching technique. If a player can't walk through a play right, how do you expect him to do it at full speed? Go at a speed where the players can do it right. It may be walk-through, or half speed, three-quarters speed, or full speed. Basically, that is the way our practice is organized. We do a lot of walk-through.

I think this next point is really important. *Pick out the teams you have to beat and do a study on them*. Whoever you have to beat to keep your job, or to win the championship, do a study on them and learn everything you can about that program. There are a lot of ways to get this done. You can get a lot of information just by talking to other coaches in the league.

My first year at Florida, we went to the University of Tennessee and shut them out 31-0. To learn about Tennessee, I went around the country trying to learn about the Tennessee offense. I visited Penn State and everyone else that played Tennessee the year before. I understood Tennessee's offense. When Tennessee had a tight end or fullback in the game, the offense was the same. It did not matter where the fullback was lined up. If they have three wideouts and a tight end in the game, the offense was the same. The tight end is just a fullback, and the plays were the same. The formations were different but the plays were the same. When they had one back in the offense, they were running the draw. We shut them out. That was when Peyton Manning was a freshman.

Have a system for developing a game plan with the players. Give drafts to them early and a folder to keep all the scouting and game plan material in. We start on Monday doing our game planning. We get the TV copy of the game of anybody we play. On TV they give close-ups of the quarterback. You can hear snap counts, checks, and signals. If you get enough tape you can figure out a whole lot. Find out everything you can about your opponent. However, it doesn't make any difference how much you know. It is how much they know and can execute. When you do it, find a good system that works for you.

One thing that we do is this. We make out *improvement sheets* after every practice. Each coach makes a list of any player who is going to play in the next game and what he needs to improve on in the next practice. We do this from what went on in practice and from practice films. We list what they did wrong and what they need to improve on. We give those lists to each player. What it tells the coach is how well he is communicating his techniques. If they are making the same mistakes on Thursday that they made the day before, there is something wrong with the teaching methods — it's too complicated, they don't understand, or they can't do it. If that happens, we take out whatever the technique or play was.

If they are making the same mistakes in fundamentals, the coach needs to spend more time on fundamentals and less time on scheme. If you want to be a consist winner you have to do those things.

I see Coach George Perles out there. He has coached more good defenses than most coaches, including me.

Here are some *principles of good defense.* You have to keep leverage on the ball, gap control, have an alley player, and take care of the cutback. It doesn't matter what scheme you run or stunts you use if you have the principles of good defense. If you teach something that doesn't have one of these principles in it, you better tell your players. If you run a stunt that leaves you with no cutback player, you have to tell your defense so they can make the adjustments to play that type of play. Someone has to get off a block to cover that. If you don't tell them, they will lose faith and think you do not know what you are doing. If it goes against the principles, tell them so they know you understand.

Keep it simple so they can line up and play. A confused football player is a slow player. He has to know what to do. Do lots of walk-through with them.

Know and understand your opposition. Do they count people? Do they count five in box, six in the box, or seven in the box? Is it a run or pass? What do they do? Do they favor the three-man side, or the four-man side?

Know and understand the blitz control and pass protection. Do they ID the Mike linebacker or four-man side? Do they ID the hot defense by pointing? You should know how the offense is going to protect according to the look you give them. If you know their offense, you can dictate where they will run the ball by your defensive alignment. If you face a throwing team, attack their protection. You must cover the receivers and attack the protection.

If you play a three-deep coverage against a good passing team it is tough. If you play a three-deep against Marshall, our quarterback will beat you every time. He will light the defense up in that coverage. You cannot stop anything in the passing game in three deep. Understand on normal downs such as on first-and-ten, second-and-medium, and third-and-short, you must stop the run and make them throw the ball.

On long yardage downs, let them run the ball and stop the pass.

Somewhere in between you must disguise the defense. If you line up and let them see the defense you are playing you are in trouble. That is the whole theory of the offenses a lot of teams are using today. Teams line up and get the play from the sideline because they want to see how the defense lines up. You must disguise your defense and you have to move your people around.

I see Coach Ron Zook in the back. "How are you doing Ron?" Ron is a great football coach and a good friend of mine.

Take the great player out of the game. Do not let them wreck the game! Make them go somewhere else to make plays. When we play teams that have a great running back, we put enough people in the box so they can't run the ball. We make them throw the ball. When I was at Wake Forest we had to play against Bruce Smith at VPI. We did not have one play that we planned to run in that game where we didn't double-team Bruce Smith. He was a great player but we just double-teamed him. He was that good, but we took him out of the game.

We had Randy Moss play for us as a wide receiver. Any time he was 1-on-1 we threw him the ball. We did that 100 percent of the time. He was better than any man the defense could put on him. If you play someone that good you better take his butt out of the game. Some teams put three defenders on him. But you need to take the great player out of the game and do not let him wreck you.

If the quarterback runs the option play well, you better put two defenders on that quarterback. Make him pitch the ball. Do not let the great player wreck you on defense.

Move and stem the front and secondary. With 12 to 15 seconds to go on the 25-second clock, we distort the quarterback's reads because they do not have time to check off. Distort the receivers' coverage reads and linemen's count and gap control. Which gets you beat most, mental error or physical ability? It is the mental error that gets you beat. Create confusion on the offense.

You have to have a plan to handle personnel groupings. How are you going to play four wideouts?

Stop the run to win. You have to stop the run, and you have to be able to run the ball to win big games. Three out of the last four years we have been one of the leading teams in the nation in touchdown passes. But to throw the ball you have to be effective running it, too. Make the offense throw the ball. Understand the count, gap control, leverage, cutback run, and the alley player.

Have your players understand the hidden yardage in football. Those are the yards created in the kicking game, penalties, and turnovers.

Stop what your opponent does best. If they are a running team, make them throw. Make them play you left-handed.

I think my time is about up. We never close practice. You are welcome to come down to visit us at Huntington any time. Thank you for allowing me to visit with you.

THE NO-HUDDLE OFFENSE

West Virginia University

It is a pleasure being here tonight to speak to you. Last year was a good year for West Virginia. I thought we played hard all year long and I hope that sets the stage for next year.

I don't know if you have been to our campus before, but we think we have one of the best situations in America. I am a native of West Virginia and it is nice to be home coaching at WVU. If you were to see our facility you would certainly be impressed.

One reason I think we were able to turn this program around from going 3-8 in our first year to 9-2 this year was what I call a *hard edge*. Our kids understood our schemes better on both sides of the ball after being in the program for one year, but the hard edge was why we won. We referred to the hard edge as competing hard on every play of every game.

Everyone is going to have deficiencies and strengths on their football team. What we did was play to our strengths and hide our weaknesses. We got our player to play the hard edge all the time. To have a good season you have to win a few close games. We won one in Cincinnati when a last second field goal hit the goal post. We won a game with Virginia Tech on the next to the last play of the game. Our kids played every play as hard as they could and did not worry about the scoreboard.

I used to be known as a passing coach. Now I'm known as a running guy. We changed our method of attack this year. We played to the strength of our team. We were like a high school team our first year at West Virginia. We had to play with the personnel we had. Colleges can recruit to fill the needs of their system. We haven't been ability to do that as of yet. We are only in our second year. I probably did a poor job the first year I was here of playing to our strengths. I learned my lesson last year in that regard.

We had an experienced offensive line, good running backs, and an athletic quarterback. But we were only average at wide receiver and we didn't have a big playmaker. Our strengths were the players involved in our running game. We didn't want to abandon our philosophy, which was to spread people out and run the *no-huddle offense*. I think the no-huddle is the greatest advantage you can use to control the tempo of a game. The only thing we did differently was to emphasize the running game over the pass. We had enough multiplicity in our offense that it allowed us to attack with our running game and not abandon our base philosophy.

We didn't change our offense, we only changed our focus to what we were doing. You have to keep what you are doing simple. Not necessarily so your players can understand it, but so your coaches can. Rick Trickett, my offensive line coach, told his players that he was going to give them everything he could base on an 11 ACT score, because that was exactly what he scored on it the sixth time he took it. He coaches his players in a simple manner and they learn with no mental mistakes. We try to confuse the other team, not our own players. A confused player plays slower than a player who knows exactly what he is doing. We did the same thing on defense. Our defense was new this year. We went to an odd front with three down linemen, three linebackers, three safeties, and two corners. We kept it very simple all year because the coaches were still learning the defense.

I'm not the smartest guy in the world, but *I know what I don't know*. That was the best piece of advice I got early in my career. We get coaches at our level who think they know everything. I can promise you, I'm a lot smarter now than I was a year ago, but I better be smarter next year than I was this year. What I don't know I can try to learn. You should know what your players don't know. That is part of teaching and coaching. No matter whether you are coaching offense or defense, your staff had better be on the same page.

We have a game plan sheet like every other team in the United States, but we don't use it very much. The thing we look at between series, halftime, and during TV time-outs is what I call the *answer sheet*. It has on it what we are going to if the defense plays a certain defense. If a team is playing a bear defense, the answer sheet tells us what our adjustment is going to be. We have a series of plays that are the answers to the types of defenses people are running against us.

We establish the answer sheet at the end of spring practice or at the end of two-a-day practices. You sit down with your coaches and establish what you are going to do against different looks you are going to see. The answer sheet does not change during the season. You have to have more than one answer for each situation. We do the same thing on defense. If a team is hurting us with the off-tackle power play, the answer sheet tells us what to do to correct the situation.

Our base offense is based out of a *spread shotgun set* and is always no-huddle. It is not always pass or fast-tempo types of plays and we are not always in a shotgun, although that is our base. In offensive and defensive schemes, you have something that is your base and you branch off of that.

I'm going to talk about two running plays. We have about six runs, but our best plays are our *zone and trap plays*. I don't want to talk philosophy too much, but I do want to explain the basis behind our offense. This will be real quick and then I'll get to the nuts and bolts of the offense.

Our offensive philosophy starts with *spreading the field both horizontally and vertically*. I think the best thing you can do as an offensive coach is to make people defend the offense in space. The hardest thing a defender has to do is make open field tackles. We are going to make the defense tackle us in the open field. Every play we have in our running game is designed to get to the safety. We want the safety to make the tackle. When we crack back on the safety, we make the corner make the tackle. We do that because most corners don't want to tackle anybody. That is why we spread the defense horizontally.

We spread the defense vertically by running receivers downfield. I am not going into receiver techniques, but if the receivers don't block, they don't

get to play. Our receivers have a very simple rule in the running game. If it is man coverage, run the defender off. We keep running him as long as the defender runs with the receiver. If the defense is zone coverage, the receiver stalk blocks the defensive back.

The way we distinguish between zone and man coverage comes from the way the defensive back covers the receiver. In the first three steps our wide receivers are attacking the outside shoulder of the defender. If the defender's eyes are on the receiver, we treat that as man coverage and run him off. If the defender's eyes are on the quarterback, we treat that as zone coverage. It may not be zone coverage but we still stalk block the defender.

If the defender closes on the receiver immediately, we cut block him. We are allowed to cut on our level. If the corner rolls up on the receiver, he chops him down.

If the defender is running with the receiver in man coverage and looks back to the quarterback, the receiver stops running and stalk blocks the defender. We tell our receivers that someone is going to be responsible for him. It is his job to block the defender covering him and not let him make the tackle.

We always play to numbers, angles, and grass. Numbers mean we count the number of defenders on each side of the ball and run at the fewest number of defenders. There are exceptions to every rule.

The angles refer to the blocking angle we get with our offensive line. I would rather run at a 1 technique than a 3 technique. It is easier for a guard to block down on a 1 technique than it is to reach block the 3 technique. If the numbers are the same, we run at the 1 technique.

The reason we like the zone play is the fact that the 1 technique doesn't stay a 1 technique after the ball is snapped. Generally the 1 technique is slanting somewhere else. The zone play allows us to zone block moving linemen.

We run the ball to the grass. That means if your numbers and angles are the same, we run to the wideside of the field. If the defense is head-up on their techniques and evenly defended on both sides of the ball, we run to the wideside of the field. That gives us more room to run the ball.

The most important thing is the numbers. We want to run and throw to the numbers of the defense. If the defense is in a cover 0, you should be throwing the football 100 percent of the time. If there is one safety deep, you have numbers to run the ball.

The last thing I can't emphasize enough. At our level, I think it is the most under-utilized thing in football. Your offense has to control the tempo of the game. We do that with our *no-huddle and indy* schemes. You don't have to be a no-huddle offense to do it. To help our defense in practice, we have huddled, broke the huddle, sprinted to the line quickly, and snapped the ball. We haven't done that in a game but we have the capability to do it.

The two advantages you have on offense relate to the fact *you know where you are going and you know when the ball is going to be snapped*. We change the tempo by snapping the ball in five seconds, 10 seconds, or 15 seconds. No-huddle is the best way for us to control that part of the tempo because conditioning is always a factor.

When you go fast in the no-huddle or you have the ability to go fast, you make the defense tire physically and stress them mentally. Of course it is harder on your offensive linemen physically and mentally as well.

I knew we were going to be a better team this year. The no-huddle gives your linemen less time to think about what their assignments are offensively. When you don't run this kind of offense, the linemen have time to talk at the line of scrimmage about assignments. In this offense there is little time at the line to talk about assignments. This year we knew the offense better and were more comfortable in what our assignments were.

In a five-minute period, with a traditional offense, you get about seven plays run. *In our offense, we run 13 plays in five minutes*. When you do that, you have to coach on the run. We tell our players we are going to yell at them and chew some butt, but it is going to be quick.

I do not like to repeat plays. That works for a lot of people to run the play over. We don't do it unless the play is a total cluster. Normally we do our corrections on the run and go to the next play. If you want to run this offense, you have to practice that way. If you are a no-huddle team and you never go fast, you may as well be a huddle team.

If you are a no-huddle team and you just line up and never go fast, you have made it easier on the defense, not harder. At least if you break the huddle the defense has to identify where your players are. If you are a no-huddle team, sometimes you go fast and at times you go slower. The defense doesn't know what to expect. They call the defense and get aligned quickly, because you might snap the ball.

The no-huddle is no more pressure on the quarterback then any traditional offense. Everyone thinks the quarterback is making all the calls and audible in a no-huddle offense. He's not making any of them. Like I have said before, I'm not letting an 18-year-old kid who watches cartoons on Saturday morning make those calls. I make the calls. I want my quarterback to execute the play and make good decisions.

I don't want the pressure put on the quarterback. He doesn't know as much as the coaches and has not watched enough film to make the right audible. If you play a no-huddle offense, you could change the play three times if you chose to do so. Don't put the pressure on the quarterback to make the correct audible.

We don't ask the quarterback about the audible, we ask him about his execution or his decision-making. If you've seen us play, after the quarterback has called the play, he looks to the sideline. We tell him to stay in the play, to Xerox the play, or give him the audible of the play we want run. When I say *Xerox the play*, we mean to run the same play to the other side.

What you would like to have is your quarterback on the same wavelength as the coach. The first year the quarterback will look to the sideline and stare at the coach. They really want to make sure they have the call. The second year they don't stare. They look at the coach quickly and then look at the defense. The third year the quarterback looks to the sideline and waves the coach off. The fourth year they flip the coach off.

If you have a really smart quarterback, you can get some things done quicker. Make sure you remember this point. Whatever offense or defense you run, it has to be simple enough for you dumbest starter to understand. If you have 11 dumb starters, you better run one formation and one play. Whatever you do, be able to execute it well and know why it didn't work.

The worst thing that can happen to a coach happened to me a bunch of times this year. When something is going wrong and you're not moving the ball, what is the first thing you do? You say, "What in the heck is happening out there?" When you ask your kids what is happening on the field and their answer is, "I don't know," you are in a world of trouble and going to hell in a hand-basket.

The offensive linemen have a better view of the play than you do. The beauty of this offense is the offensive line will be able to tell you what is happening on the field. That way we can come up with the answers to correct our mistakes.

The easiest thing you can do to add multiplicity in your offense is to *add formations*. You can add a formation just for window dressing, but some one on the other side of the ball has to deal with how to defend it.

If the offense adds a player in a formation close to the quarterback, the defense is going to do the same thing. That makes the defense harder to block. If you add a player in the spread, it is no big deal for anyone, particularly your offensive linemen. The players you have to worry about are the five guys in the offensive line. As long as you don't confuse them, you are okay with formation additions.

This first formation is called *rip* [Diagram 1]. The wide receivers are X and Z. The X is the split end and the Z is the flanker. The slot receivers are H and Y. The quarterback is the Q back and the tailback is the F back. We used to be in the four wide receiver look about 70% of the time.

In our base set, rip and Liz, we used the landmarks on the field to align our receivers. The college hash marks are at 20 yards and the high school marks are 17 yards. If you want to align as we do your numbers will be different. We align our receivers on the hash marks. When we say plus five and minus one, we are describing the receivers' relationship to the hash marks. They are five-yards outside the hash mark and one-yard inside of them. The best advice I can give you is to make sure there are six yards between the wideouts.

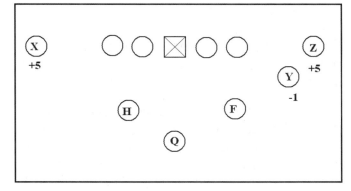

Diagram 1. Rip formation

We have four wide receivers. The receivers who catch most of the balls are our X and Y receivers. The X receiver catches a lot of ball because he is our boundary receiver. The Y is the strongside slot back and is matched up against linebackers and nickel backs. The biggest problem high school coaches have with the four wide receiver package is they don't have four wide receivers who can catch the ball. We can recruit and sometimes we don't have four receivers either.

My suggestion is to play your wife's relative or a booster's boy at the Z receiver, especially on a running play. It doesn't matter how fast he is. He can run off a defensive back or stalk block him. In fact, the slower receivers make better stalk blockers.

If you want to throw the ball to the Z receiver's position, move him to the X receiver side and put the X receiver at the Z position. This is good advice if you have a situation like this. If you have a booster's son or a wife's relative, you can tell the daddy or your wife that the kid is going to get on the field 30 to 40 snaps a game.

If you break the huddle with more than 11 players, it is a penalty. However, if you are a no-huddle team, you could have your whole squad on the field. If you go no-huddle you can run your whole team onto the field and run them right back off.

Any time we find defensive coaches who substituted defensive personnel to match the offensive personnel, we run a special play. We send a *personnel group* onto the field. They continue to run until they see the corresponding defensive personnel come off the sideline. When they see them coming onto the field they stop, wave to them, and run off the field. We have a heck of a time. I forgot which team it was, but the coach was really complaining to the referee.

If they change that rule I am really going to be upset. I would love to coach in the NFL just for one game. All the NFL coaches are really into personnel substitutions. I think it would be fun.

Over the years I have gradually gone to the rip or Liz set 50 percent of the time. I have added the two tight ends and two wide receivers set, and *three wide receivers and two-backs set* [Diagram 2]. I had two really good tailbacks this year in Avon Cobourne and Quincy Wilson and an athletic quarterback in Rasheed Marshall.

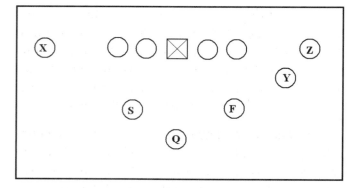

Diagram 2. Three wide receivers and two-backs set

We wanted to play to our strengths and get our best players on the field. We went to a three wide receivers, two running backs set, with the quarterback in the shotgun for a large percentage of the year. That gave us three players who could really pack the mail.

We aligned the Z at plus five and the Y at minus one. The X aligned at plus five to the weak side of the set. The backs were aligned toe-to-toe at the width of the offensive tackles and the depth of the quarterback. They were slightly in front of the quarterback's alignment. The quarterback was in the shotgun. Being in the shotgun gives us an advantage.

Our offensive line splits are about two feet. If we are getting a lot of movement in the defensive line, we will cut the splits down. Some teams go wider, but we like to keep them the same. As they become more experienced they can adjust their splits to take advantage of the defense. For instance, if we are going to trap a defender, we may split him wider.

We also run *two tight ends with two wide receivers*, with the quarterback in the shotgun or under center. That set presents a problem for the

defense because they end up with a nickel back down on a tight end, and it gives the defense one more gap to cover.

Those are our three basic sets, but we have more. From the two tight end set, we bring the X over and align him with the Z receiver wide. Another one we like is to take the H receiver and align him at the tight end position to the Y and Z side. That gives us a triple set right and a one-receiver alignment left. In all these formations we run the same plays and no one is affected.

I'm going to show you why we run the *shotgun*. I'll draw it up in the three-receiver look. On most of our running plays we never block the backside defensive end [Diagram 3]. If you go under the center you can't see the defensive end until it is too late. To run the zone play from under the center, the quarterback has to turn his back to the defensive end and open up at five o'clock. From the shotgun you can see if the defensive end is chasing the play down the line or hanging back for the bootleg. The quarterback has time and distance to read the end.

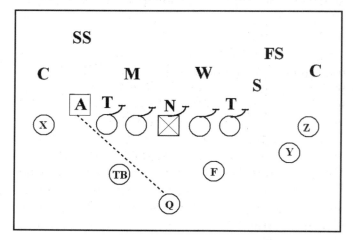

Diagram 3. Shotgun formation read

In the shotgun, either the quarterback or the tailback is responsible for the *mesh*. Most times it is the tailback's responsibility for the mesh area. On the trap, the mesh is the quarterback's responsibility. The quarterback gives the indicator to the center to snap the ball. We change the indicator weekly. The center snaps the ball and the quarterback reads the backside end.

The back goes to the quarterback. He takes a open step, crosses over, and on the third step he is in front of the quarterback. The back is responsible for the mesh. If the end is chasing and crashing down the line of scrimmage, the quarterback keeps the ball. He doesn't have to ride the back; he simply keeps the ball and runs out the backside. If the end comes upfield or the quarterback has a doubt about the end, he gives the ball to the tailback.

The *shotgun snap* is not as difficult as you think. The center we had last year had never done it until we arrived. The center I had a Clemson had never done it. The center at Salem College had never done it before we got there, and in fact, I don't think he even had played football before we got there.

That reminds me of a story. When I took the job at Salem College, I was the youngest head football coach in America at 24 years of age. At 25 years of age, I was the youngest fired head football coach in America. In 1988 I had just finished my first year as a head coach. I had 21 of 22 starters coming back. I was putting in new offense and everyone was fired up about the next season.

At Salem College, if you could spell Salem they would let you enroll. If you couldn't, they would give you the S, A, and L, and hoped you could come up with the E and M. We had a lot of people coming and were loaded for bear. The previous season I started 14 true freshmen. I was really moving up. I decided to buy my first house for $33,000. I bought my first car for $7,000 and proposed to my present wife.

I was supposed to get married in two weeks. I went to the office on June 17, 1989, and received a phone call from the Associated Press. They wanted to get my reaction to the fact that a Japanese University had bought Salem College and was dropping football. Five minutes later I got call from a West Virginia State coach inquiring about my players since we were dropping football.

About that time the athletic director walked into my office and told me there was going to be a meeting at 1:00 p.m., which was going to be detrimental to my program and that was all he could tell me. I went to the meeting and found out that no contracts would be renewed and I had one week to clean out my office. At 25 years old, I was fired for the first time.

The quarterback in the shotgun can block the backside defensive end by reading him. That is why we like to run the shotgun with our quarterback. If we run the zone play from under the center, we get a tight end into the formation on the backside to keep the defensive end from running the play down from the backside.

Even though we had a very athletic quarterback, the best runners are going to be your tailbacks. We wanted to hand the ball to the tailback. The quarterback doesn't have to be really fast. He has to be fast enough to outrun the defensive end as he redirects his charge.

Your blocking scheme depends on the *ability* of your offensive linemen. Remember, you should always play to your strengths and never your weaknesses. If your linemen are athletic you can do more man schemes. If your linemen were short, fat, dumpy players, I would use all zone schemes.

I had one player play for me who was two inches from being a complete circle. He was 61 inches tall and 59 inches around. We tried to get him to be a complete circle. We bought him a bunch of cheeseburgers and fries.

If you have a lot of those kinds of linemen, you will be all right in the zone play. However, I don't think you can run the trap or the dart play. Your linemen have to pull on those plays and they will never get there. If you have athletic linemen, you will do well on the trap and dart play.

The whole key to running the football is the *number of players left in the box*. When I first put this offense in 12 years ago, the hash marks were at 17 yards. I liked trips open better than the double set.

If you notice in the NFL, since their hash marks are almost in the middle of the field, they don't use many unbalanced formations. They don't use three receivers to one side and one receiver to the other because everything is run from the middle of the field.

The reason we liked the *trips open set* was the fact we had more room to displace the linebackers. We wanted to get the linebackers out of the box. The first man we look for is the free safety. If the free safety is on the hash mark, we expect to see another player on the hash and there will be five players in the box.

If the safety is in the middle of the field and deep, which is 10 yards or more, the coverage is cover 1 or cover 3. If that is the case there are six defenders in the box. I don't know what kind of front it is but I do know there is going to be six in the box.

We have six blockers to handle six defenders. We actually have seven blockers because we are counting the quarterback's block on the defensive end. If the defense plays two deep, we have seven blockers on five defenders in the box. If the defense has two safeties deep and you cannot run the ball, you are going to be in for a long night.

One thing I learned this year was to be patient in your offensive sets. There is a misunderstanding a lot of people have about no-huddle teams. They think they are only quick strike and big-play teams. I would rather have a 12-play drive that goes 80 yards, than a two-play drive that goes 80 yards. The long drive gives you defense a chance to rest, but a more important thing is it demoralizes the other team. When the offense holds the ball and controls the game, it demoralizes the other guy. On a 12-play drive the defense has to play 12 plays at full speed and still get scored on.

When I had hair, back in my younger days, a three-yard gain wasn't a big enough gain. I wanted to throw the ball. My thinking today is a lot different. Three yards on first down and four yards on second down means I've got third-and-three and I think we can make that. The offense becomes a lower-risk game.

We were second in the country this year in turnover ratio. We had 13 turnovers in 13 games. We had five games in which we didn't have one turnover.

To run the *zone play*, the offensive line needs to give a little ground to gain a little ground [Diagram 4]. We don't give as much ground as traditional zone teams because penetration is going to kill you. We take a quick give step, turn and put the hat on the outside of the breastplate of the defender and try to move the defender. We would like to knock the defender down the field, but a lot of time it is not going to happen. If the offensive lineman is good enough to get in front of the defender and get run over slowly, that is good enough for us.

That theory is the same with *pass blocking*. In the pros you might see an offensive lineman lock up a defensive man, but at the college level it is few and far between. We coach our players to get in front of the defensive lineman, get a good hold on him, and get run over slowly. The coaching point is to make sure he comes over the top so the lineman can pull him down as he falls backward.

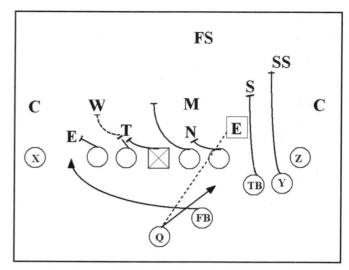

Diagram 4. Zone play

If the noseguard stays in a 1 technique, the offensive guard calls *help*. He is going to stay on the noseguard until the center can come to take him over. When the center takes the noseguard over, the guard climbs up for the Will linebacker. The coaching point for the guard is not to get in a hurry to get to the linebacker. He stays on the 1 technique as long as he can. The faster the guard gets to the linebacker, the faster the linebacker steps up.

As long as the linebacker stays deep the guard can stay on the 1 technique. The backside guard zone steps to the inside and climbs to the next level to cut off the Mike linebacker. The backside tackle zone steps and tries to reach the 3 technique. If there is movement in the 3 technique, the tackle won't be able to reach him. In that case, the tackle pushes him down past the hole and the back runs on the backside cutback lane. That is a hard thing for a back to do initially but it is not as hard as you think.

The way the back runs this play is the whole key to the play. He is toe-to-toe with the tackle in his width. He open steps, cross steps, and on the third step he is parallel with the quarterback. The biggest mistake a tailback can make in the zone play from the shotgun is to immediately start downhill after he receives the ball. When the back starts downhill, the Will linebacker starts downhill. When that happens the guard can't block him.

The aiming point for the back is the outside hip of the offensive tackle. After he receives the ball he goes two more steps parallel before he starts to press his aiming point. I don't care how wide open the play looks; he has to take those two additional steps.

We don't run the outside and inside zone plays. We run *a* zone play. There are three paths once the tailback presses his aiming point. We call the paths *bounce, bang,* or *bend.* The *bounce* path is wide to the outside. The *bang* is off tackle, and the *bend* is running the cut back lane. When the tailbacks get smart they understand the fronts they are running against.

If it is an even front, the tailback is going to *bounce* or *bang* on his path. He can't bend it back to an even front, because the backside 3 technique is playing a cutback lane.

If the front is an odd front, with a 0 technique and two 4 techniques, we tell the back he has a *bang* or a *bend.* Every few teams sit in their fronts. On the snap of the ball they are moving. That is the way Miami plays their defense. Even though they align in an even front, we treat it like an odd front because of their movement.

It is easier for the back to bend the play back when the quarterback is under center. He can do it from the shotgun but it takes a lot of reps for him to be good at it. He has to learn to be patient and learn how to turn his hips and cut off his back foot.

If the defense leaves your X receiver 1-on-1, you should be throwing to him on a slant, hitch, or fade route, or running a speed option that way. The X receiver is our best receiver and the defense will very seldom leave him without some underneath help. That underneath help has to be the Will linebacker or the free safety over the top. If the defense moves the Will linebacker out, that leaves five in the box. The zone play becomes even better with those odds.

The defense will put the Sam linebacker in what we call the *gray area.* The gray area is the linebacker moving back and forth between the coverage on the receiver and the box. If we see this happening we run a quick screen or sprint out pass toward him.

Miami made an adjustment on our zone play [Diagram 5]. They started out with two safeties on the hash marks. It looked like a two-deep coverage. As the ball was being snapped, they brought the free safety down into the box. That let the Will linebacker step out on the bounce. The three wide receiver set

takes care of this adjustment. The other tailback comes out of the backfield and blocks on the Will linebacker. It gives you a lead blocker on the Will linebacker.

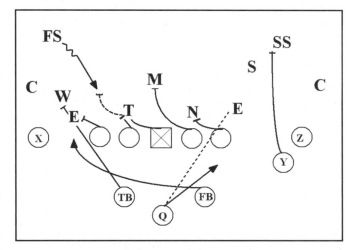

Diagram 5. Mac formation

You can run the ball either way and you still have the threat of a passing game. The first complimentary play off the zone play is the *naked bootleg.*

The first compliment as a running play is the *trap* [Diagram 6]. Teams that defended the spread running game began to realize if they put the down lineman away from the back in a 3 technique, it made it hard to run the zone play. The trap play is easy to run into that alignment.

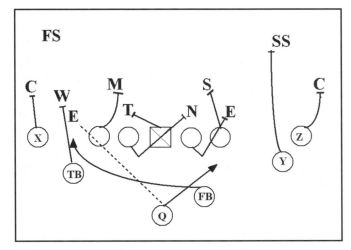

Diagram 6. Trap play

The backside tackle makes a quick flash step toward the defensive end and climbs the inside breastplate of the Mike linebacker. The center blocks back for the pulling guard. The frontside guard influences with a pass set and blocks the defensive end. The frontside tackle comes down on the Sam linebacker. The backside guard pulls and traps the A gap. We tell him to trap the A gap because the influence block sometimes brings the trap man upfield and we simply turn up in the hole with the pulling guard.

The problem we had with this trap when we first started to run the play was the mesh. We couldn't get the play to hit quick enough. We tried to direct snap the ball to the tailback. The way we solved our problem was to make the quarterback responsible for the mesh. On the snap of the ball the quarterback stepped up and stuck the ball into the back's belly. That let the back take a path directly to the hole.

The linebackers couldn't tell the difference between the traps and zone because the first step was the same. The back took an open step and his second step was directly to the hole. The quarterback stepped up and handed him the ball. On his third step he was parallel with the hole. The quarterback is still reading the defensive end chasing from the backside.

The defense is constantly trying to counter what the offense is doing to it. They crashed the end down the line, which told the quarterback to pull the ball and run the naked. What the defense was doing was crashing the end and stepping the Mike linebacker outside to make the play on the quarterback.

The offense had to have an answer for that play by the defense. Our answer was to make a *lock call* to the offensive tackle [Diagram 7]. A lock call for the offensive tackle told him to lock on the defensive end and block out on him. This basically means the defense has two men outside and opened a big lane inside of them. The offensive tackle was not going to zone step on the zone play and he was not going to block the linebacker on the trap play.

When the defense knows you are reading the defensive end, they are going to do something to mess up your reads. Another thing you can do to counter that adjustment is run the option to that side. We did it our first year but we did not do it this past season. The slot back drops off the ball and becomes the pitchman on the option.

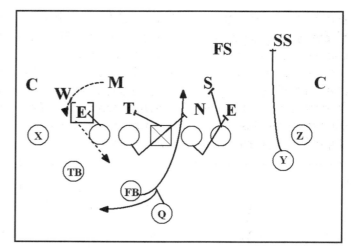

Diagram 7. Lock call

We have run sight-adjustment patterns on running plays. We signal the sight adjustment into the game. The quarterback does not change the play because the receiver has seen the sight-adjust signal. He simply throws the ball to the receiver. The ball is thrown behind the line of scrimmage so it doesn't matter if we have linemen downfield.

We throw the sight adjusts when the defense is trying to get the safeties down in run support. The corners are actually playing halves and the safeties are coming down for run support or playing a robber technique underneath. We read that as the wide receivers uncovered because the corners are aligned nine-yards deep on the inside shoulders of the X and Z receivers playing soft.

Our wide receivers look to the sideline like the quarterback. When the quarterback gets the signal, he doesn't have to relay it to the receiver. They saw the signal when it was given. The shotgun allows you to do that.

That is something that is easy to build into this scheme. You don't need a lot of plays; you need the answers to what the defense is doing to you.

The hardest defense to run against is the *bear defense*. It is tough to run the zone play and you can't run the trap because center and guards are covered with a defensive lineman. The thing that kills the bear front is the speed option.

If you have a good running quarterback, this play is a good adjustment to the lock play. We call the trap and add the letter *P* to the play. It is called *trap P* [Diagram 8]. Everything is run like the trap play in the offensive line. The only exception is the lock call to the tackle, which blocks back on the defensive end. The quarterback, instead of handing the ball to the tailback, fakes it and runs right into the vacated area of the Mike linebacker. On this play the quarterback puts the ball in the tailback's pocket and rides him slightly.

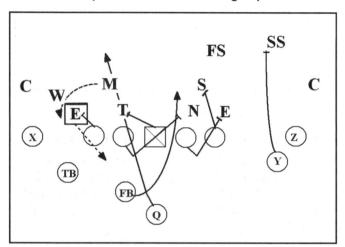

Diagram 8. Trap P

You could also fake the ball to the tailback going one way and run a quarterback zone play going the other way. These are simple adjustments to the base plays. They are not new plays. The reason we don't run the quarterback on all these plays is we want to keep him healthy. When you run the quarterback at the college level, he is going to take some shots.

Off your best runs you should have play-action passing to go with those schemes. We are going to run a *naked* or a *bootleg*. The only difference is the bootleg has the security of a pulling guard to protect the quarterback. It doesn't sell the run because of the guard pulling, but it gives the quarterback more time to get the ball deeper. We gap protect and pull the offside guard.

When we run the naked play, that is exactly what it means. He is alone with no blocking scheme for him. We tell our offense lineman on a naked to block the play that has been called but don't go downfield. They can't chase linebackers. They like that because they get to stay right there with the rest of the fat boys and block the crap out of someone.

We have all kinds of combination patterns, but we primarily run a curl and flat, with the backside

receiver coming into the deep middle [Diagram 9]. We have done all kinds of things from that base pattern. We have run the tailback out of the backfield down the sideline and throw back to him. A popular pattern we run is a go route by the Z and a hook out by the Y receiver.

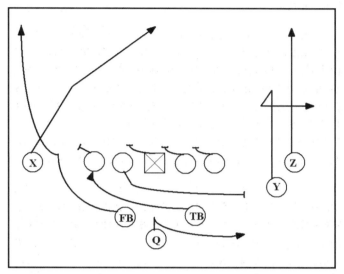

Diagram 9. Play-action pass

The defense is reading the hat level of the linemen. If we are running the naked play, all the linemen have to work hard to keep their helmet and shoulder level down. Our players like the naked because they don't have to chase the skinny guys down the field. If we run a trip set we want somebody deep, someone in the immediate level, and someone in the flat. If we give the signal for zone naked or trap naked, the patterns are the same. The offensive line blocks either the zone or the trap.

If you haven't been to West Virginia, we welcome you to come up to visit us. We have a real nice facility. People in West Virginia get excited about football. I think our attendance for home games ranked first in the Big East this year. We brought 50,000 people to our bowl game. We played awful but we had a great following.

I have a nice situation at West Virginia and I am very fortunate to be there. My greatest accomplishment after my first year was going 3-8 and getting my contract extended. This year we had some success. I have a great staff and this year we signed a long-term deal. I'm going to be there a long time. Thank you.

COACHING TODAY'S ATHLETE

Louisiana State University

I certainly appreciate the warm welcome. You guys are a dedicated group because I am going to talk a lot today about inspiring people, the psychology of coaching, and coaching today's athlete.

At LSU, we just had the number one recruiting class in the country. It is important to do a good job of recruiting. It makes you a better coach when you have good players.

We had an interesting season last year. We had the angels of football visit us when we played Kentucky up here last year. We scored a 75-yard touchdown on the last play of the game on a Hail-Mary pass. The pass bounced off about five Kentucky kids before one of our receivers caught it at the 27-yard line and ran it in. That play was proclaimed the *Bluegrass Miracle*. In the last game of the season, we were visited by the football demons at Arkansas. They got the ball with 31 seconds to go on their own 19-yard line. They completed two passes over our heads while we were in a prevent defense and beat us. That loss prevented us from going back to the SEC championship game for the second straight year.

We had a season of tremendous highs and devastating lows. You have to relate all the good and bad things that happen to you to some individual play or player. Sometimes players hide within the team. They don't do what they are supposed to do. I see it in the fourth quarter or in our off-season program all the time. What it boils down to and what I address with the players is, "You don't get what you want, you get what you deserve." You are going to get out of the program to what you put in it.

The Bluegrass Miracle was nothing but luck, but it was an individual player making an extra-effort play. The kid did a good job of staying with the play. He ran his butt off, the ball got tipped, he made a play on the ball, and he scored. You never know when it is going to happen.

We got the ball thrown over our head at Arkansas in a prevent zone defense. An individual player made a grave mental error of not playing the three-deep zone properly. An individual player in each of those circumstances had something to do with the outcome of the game. That is what I'm going to talk about.

In high school coaching, you have fewer coaches in the building. They don't have as much time to work with their players as they used to. At the college level, the NCAA has cut the number of coaches we have and installed the 20-hour week for our players. But the expectation of what you are supposed to accomplish continues to rise. Fifteen years ago no one ever got fired for having a winning season. John Cooper at Ohio State and Jim Donnan at Georgia got fired after an eight-game winning season. High School coaches have been fired because their teams don't get into the playoffs. The expectations keep going up, but you have fewer tools to work with.

The challenge is greater for coaches, plus the kids are different. Are kids different today or does it just seems that way to me? I have a 16-year-old boy and a 12-year-old girl at home. They are different because they are not allowed to suffer through anything. We coach a competitive game. In that game there is adversity and failure. In that game you have to play the next play and try to *overcome* that adversity and failure to receive self-gratification. That is really important.

None of the kids are allowed to suffer. As soon as something gets hard for them, someone fixes it for them. They grow up not knowing the difference between *cause and effect*. When I grew up we played checkers. If you made a bad move, you got jumped and you lost that checker for the game. My children grew up playing Nintendo. I can't tell when they lose because, all they do is push the restart button and see if they can go further the next time. They have no reaction to the game. They don't understand cause and effect.

We are supposed to take these kids, with fewer coaches and less people that have relationships with them, and teach them how to be a dominant team. We are supposed to make football players out of these guys. Coaching is really teaching. The biggest asset in teaching is the ability to inspire learning. Teachers have to have the ability to inspire the kind of commitment and attitude it takes to be successful.

Jaromir Jagr is a hockey player who plays for the Washington Capitals in the National Hockey League. He wears 68 as his jersey number. He played on the Czechoslovakian Olympic hockey team. I don't know what Olympic year it was, but his team ended up in the finals playing the Russians for the gold medal. In 1968 the Russians invaded Czechoslovakia. His grandfather and many other Czechs were killed in that encounter. That is why he wears the number 68. It is a constant reminder of that fateful year. His coach came into the locker room to get the team before the gold medal game. He asked Jaromir if he was ready to play, to which Jaromir replied, "I've been ready to play this game all my life!" He said his commitment as a hockey player was to beat the Russians for all the people they killed including his grandfather in 1968.

I told our players that story. I go back to them on occasion and ask them what their 68 is? What is the reason they are committed to this game? Why do they want to play? A lot of them don't have any idea.

I heard something from a Martin Luther King speech that I had never heard before. He told a story about going to get his shoes shined. He went to the same place and had the same guy shine his shoes all the time. He said he went there because this guy was the best there was at what he did. He was the absolute best shoeshine guy in the world. He said he had to wait his turn, but he didn't mind waiting. The point was, *whatever you do be the best you can be.* This shoeshine guy shined shoes like Michelangelo painted and Shakespeare wrote literature. If you can be the best with what you have, you master life.

If you can't be a highway, be a trail. If you can't be the sun, be a star. That is a very old speech, but it is very inspiring. Kids today don't want to do anything that doesn't give them self-gratification immediately. If the task is difficult, they want to do something else. They grow up with so many choices of things to do, it is hard to decide.

Discipline is getting people to do what they are supposed to do, when they're supposed to do it, and the way it is supposed to be done. Discipline is not punishment. Discipline is changing someone's behavior to get him to do what you want him to do. The prison guard mentality has never worked in our prison systems. In the old days a lot of coaches coached that way. If you don't do what I say, we are going to punish you. That doesn't work any more in today's society. It is a lot easier to coach that way, but you can't get the job done that way.

Whatever you take away from the players in terms of discipline had better mean something to them. We have a simple rule at LSU. *If the player doesn't do what he is supposed to do, he doesn't play in the game.* I figure they all want to play in the game. It is the same with school work. We have gone from last in the SEC to second behind Vanderbilt in graduation rate. We have one rule in academics. We have a nine-point system in academics. There are nine things they have to do in a semester to stay current in their academics. Included in those nine things are going to study table, going to class, and other requirements. If they don't do those nine things, they don't play.

I have suspended seven players for academics in 10 years of being a head coach. We are 7-0 in the games where I had that player suspended. I also told my player that story. I told them we were undefeated when I suspend someone for academic reason. Outside of the quarterback, how much does one guy affect the game of the football? It is our responsibility as coaches to get them to do the *right thing*, not enable them to do the wrong thing.

Some times as coaches we don't have a good answer for that last question. I had to suspend our free safety this year. We were 6-1 at the time. One of our star players broke his arm one week, and our quarterback broke his foot the next week. The next week we beat South Carolina and I had to suspend my free safety for disciplinary reasons. We lost three out of four leaders on our football team in three weeks. We were 6-1 and ranked fifth in the country at the time. We finished the season at 8-5. I had a choice. I was either going to enable this guy to do the wrong thing or suspend him. If I had allowed him to stay on the team, I would have told the rest of the players that good players don't have to abide by the rules of this organization.

I showed the suspended player there was a consequence for not doing what you are supposed to do. He didn't play; however, I called the athletic director and chancellor and told them I was going to do the right thing. I told them when I suspended this kid I wanted them to support my decision. They agreed to do it because it was the right thing to do. I also told them we probably would lose a game or two because of it. The suspended player's replacement was the one who made the mistake in the Arkansas game. He is also the guy who made the mistake when Kentucky went ahead of us inside the last minute of that game.

I would do the same thing again. The bad thing about it is the suspended player is no different then he was before. But for the rest of the guys on our team it made a difference. Everything you do as a coach affects everyone else. Everything your players do affects everyone else and they have to understand that.

As teachers and coaches, we have to get guys to understand the reasons behind doing things a particular way. That is the best way to coach. Everybody has to have a vision of what they think they can accomplish. You don't have to be able to see it to do it. Ray Charles sings "America the Beautiful" better than anyone I know. Everything he is singing about he has never seen. He has never seen the sky or the mountains but he has a *vision*. It is important that people understand what they want to do and how they want to do it. I think you have to have a road map and direction in your program so guys can see that.

We have *principles and values* in our program. Players have to know what is important within a program. Our principles start with helping the individual become successful as a person. We want the player to be more successful for having been in our program than he would have been if he were not here. We want to continue to develop the commitment and character of the players.

We want our players to get an *education*. We have an academic support program that will help the players get that education. The players need to know that their welfare and best interest is at heart with the coach, his staff, and the people who are trying to help them.

We want every player who comes to LSU to have the opportunity to win a championship before they leave. Since I have been coaching here, all our guys have had a chance to do that. There are no individual goals included in this section.

All the resources available at LSU are here to help the player launch their careers when they leave. The people at LSU are committed to helping the athlete to get on with his life. That is what we stand for. Everyone in our organization knows they are here to support the player to do that. Everyone means *everyone*, from the athletic training staff to the janitor in the gym, and we are all here to help these guys.

What is success? *Success comes from consistency in performance*. People who have consistent performance do it a certain way. The first thing on our list is, "What is your 68?" Knowing what you want to accomplish is almost as important as accomplishing it. It doesn't matter how bad I want them to do it. The only thing that matters is how committed they are to accomplishing their vision. The coach has to help the player see the vision.

Everyone has a commitment. It was like Harrison Ford in the movie, *The Fugitive*, when he was being chased by Tommy Lee Jones down the drainage pipe. When he got to the end of the pipe, he turned and told Tommy Lee Jones, he didn't kill his wife. Tommy Lee Jones told him he didn't care. He was a marshal and was committed to catching him. He didn't care whether he was guilty or innocent. Having a commitment is the only way you can get people to work and invest their time to be successful.

After the 9-11 tragedy, I had a psychologist from Louisiana who worked at the Kennedy Space Center for NASA, come in to talk to our players about stress management. Our players were watching the news and asking questions I could not believe. They didn't know what the selective service draft was. They were asking if they could be drafted out of school in case of war. They didn't understand the system and were getting upset in terms of what could happen.

No one goes to the army anymore and gains that natural discipline. And very few people have ever worked on a farm. The old adage, *you reap what you sow,* is probably the most significant true statement that we could ever have. Maybe everyone should have to work on a farm for a year. On a farm you till the soil and plant the crops or you sit on the porch. When it comes time to harvest, you actually reap what you sow, and you get out of it what you put into it. Sometimes it's not what you put into it for yourself but what you do for others.

How can you overcome adversity and beat the system if there is no suffering? If you are going to be *persistent* you have to fail at something. You have to have a negative experience. You have to be able to bounce back from a negative experience and make it into a positive experience. You can't get frustrated. If we show our frustration to a player when he doesn't do something right, he learns to show his frustration. Don't let your ego get in the way of coaching. If you think a player's poor play is a reflection on your coaching and you chew his butt out for it, you are wrong as a coach. I tell my coaches that all the time. We need to teach him for the next play.

The player won't know how to compete on the next play if they are frustrated or you are frustrated with them. That is the key to success. There has never been a perfect football game that any of us have every played. There is not a player or coach in this room who has ever played a perfect game. There is no one in this room who didn't have to overcome adversity or get beat on a play. How you respond to the negative play is the most important thing.

I will not allow my players to put their hands on their knees or show in their face they are tired going into the fourth quarter. If they do, they are going to get their butt whipped. If they do that, they are showing the other team they can be beat.

One of the greatest true stories I can tell you about someone not showing his frustration in a game was about a middle-weight championship fight involving Bernard Hopkins and a guy from East Lansing. No one ever heard of this guy. I knew him personally because he trained in a friend of mine's gym in East Lansing. He was undefeated when he got his shot to fight Hopkins. I think Bernard Hopkins is a competitor. Everything I have talked about today is what Bernard Hopkins stood for. This fight took place at the height of Hopkins's boxing career. The fight was at Caesar's Palace in Las Vegas. After the first three rounds my man had won all three of them. He came out in the fourth round and almost got killed. Hopkins knocked him down three times and finally knocked him out. It was brutal. He went to the hospital and was really hurt. I saw the guy two months later and asked him what happened in the third round. I figure he would tell me that Hopkins hit him with a good shot and he couldn't defend himself. He told me at the end of the third round he hit Hopkins with his best shot. It never phased Hopkins. He told me he knew he couldn't beat him after that punch. I don't know if Hopkins was hurt or not, but he showed nothing in the way of frustration or how he felt. He broke his confidence and killed the other fighter psychologically to the point he didn't think he could win the fight.

People have to go through the process to *improve.* The bad thing about today's athletes is they don't think there is a process to go through. They think they are good from the start so there is no process to go through. Coaches are all about the process. I signed the number one running back in the country this year. He thinks he is going to come to LSU and gain 1,400 yards next year. He hasn't even taken a handoff. When the noseguard lights him up the first time that will probably be the first time he has ever seen stars.

Our quarterback broke his foot and I had to put Marcus Randall, our freshman quarterback, into the game. I took him aside and told him he only had to play average today. I just wanted him to help the other guys on the team play okay. I know this kid. I know he wants to play good, make every play, and be the star, and that is how you want him to be. But I know he is full of anxiety. When a player hasn't played and has no experience, it is awfully easy to get frustrated when things don't work out right. Their expectations are so high that ,they set themselves up for failure and frustrations. Failure, frustration, and anxiety do not help you perform.

Who creates the expectations? Most times it is the media that cause the expectations. All these so-called recruiting gurus probably don't know a football player from a load of coal. He has the expectations of being the best guy and has no idea the process he has to go through to be a better player. I asked Marcus Randall a simple question to make him realize there was a process he needed to go through. I asked him if he thought he would be a better player when he got to be a senior than he was right now. He said he would. That meant he did believe that by gaining experience, knowledge, getting coached every day, making mistakes, and going through the process for the next three years, he would be a better player.

I told him if he made a mistake in the game, it was nothing but a learning experience. It is not something to get frustrated about. I gave the best speech of my life, he went out and played a great game against South Carolina, and we won the game. I thought he was ready so I didn't do much the next week as to his mental development. We went to Auburn the next week for an 11:00 game.

The press had laid out the season in the newspaper. We were going to beat Auburn, Alabama, and Arkansas, win the SEC Championship and go to the Fiesta Bowl to play for the National Championship. Some fat guy who has never played a down has put all this expectation on this freshman quarterback to go out and win the game. I should of known how that would affect this kid. I didn't and he thought he had to go win the game. He threw four interceptions in the first half for 200 yards in return yardage. We were behind 17-0 at halftime. For every 100 yards of field position you give up in a game, it usually equates to about six points. I did a poor job of helping my quarterback be a consistent performer.

The best example I can give you about persistence was a commercial Michael Jordan did for Nike about three years ago. He pulled up in a limo and was going into the back door of the gym. The announcer was giving a lot of statistics about Michael Jordan. He said he had missed 26 game-winning shots and he had missed 2,963 shots as a NBA player, and he had lost 293 games in the NBA. Michael opened the door, looked at the camera, and said,"Because I fail is why I succeed."

I think everyone should play the game of baseball because if you make two outs every three times you bat, you get into the hall of fame. What sport do we have where you can fail two out of three times and get into the hall of fame?

It is hard to overcome adversity because we live in a day and age where no one is allowed to suffer. Let me tell you a story about Woody Hayes. I was at Ohio State coaching for Earle Bruce. We had a tremendous team in 1980 and should have won the national championship, but we lost to Michigan the last game of the season in Columbus. Things took a big change in 1981. We were rebuilding and hadn't had a very successful season going into the Michigan game. We were 8-2, which was a disappointment for the Ohio State fans. We were a 17-point underdog. Michigan was leading the Big Ten was scoring at 35 points a game. The fact was, however, if we could win the game we could tie Michigan for the Big Ten championship.

The last week of practice was cold and snowy and we practiced like we didn't want to play the game. Usually the week of the Michigan game we always had to be careful in practice because we don't want to get any body hurt. During that week guys went crazy, they were so hyped up. That was not the case that year. We were getting some heavy criticism from everyone and the kids just didn't think we had a chance to win. I even felt that way too. I don't think anyone thought we could win the game.

We had a tradition at the last practice, where all the seniors would make their last tackle. They each hit the bag for their last tackle and we had a speaker come in to address the team.

Earle Bruce was the coach then, and Woody Hayes hadn't had anything to do with the team or the school since the incident in the bowl game against Clemson. We got him to go on a trip with us and come and address the team. His speech centered on this statement: "*There can be no great victories in life unless there is tremendous adversity.*" He talked about all the adversity surrounding the Michigan. He talked about the point spread, the weather, and all the other bad things that were affecting their attitude about the game.

He turned all the adversity into opportunity. He equated it all to the war in the Pacific during World War II. He said the war in the Pacific was the greatest victory ever for the United States because to win that war we had to go through tremendous adversity. He went on to talk about Pearl Harbor and the role it played. By the time he was finished, the whole team had come from doom and gloom to looking at this game as an opportunity to do something great. I felt the same way.

We had an opportunity to go to Michigan and do something special. We went to Michigan and played our butts off. They didn't score a touchdown. We won the game 14-9. Still to this day, after all the games I've play or coached in, that is the number one game I remember. I was just the secondary coach, but that is the greatest game I can remember.

The game that ranks second in that category was the SEC Championship Game last year. We played Tennessee, who was number two in the country. Everyone had them going to Pasadena to play Miami for the National Championship. Everyone knows we won the game, but we had the best running back in the SEC who went down with an ACL in the first quarter. Our quarterback got his ribs cracked in the second quarter.

In the second quarter I was choking because we lost those two guys. We had fourth-and-six-inches on our own 23-yard line. I went for it; we got stuffed, and didn't make it. We had a 7-0 lead but Tennessee had scored two times in a row on long passes. I thought we had to change the momentum of the game so we went for it. We went out on defense, knocked them back and they settled for a 49-yard field goal. The score at halftime was 17-7.

We went in at halftime and I apologized to our team for the mistake I made in going for the first down. We went out in the second half and won the game 31-20. The senior told me after the game, when we went for the first down on fourth down, that it was the first time they thought that I thought we could win the game. That is why we played like we played the rest of the game. You never know. But that was the second best game I've ever been involved in where we had to overcome extreme adversity.

How do you create these things? It is not easy. I think the one thing we need to do differently in motivating players and helping them be successful is not to talk about results. Our goal next year is to be a dominant football team that is a nationally recognized program. It doesn't have anything to do with winning the SEC championship, going to bowls, or how many game we are going to win. All the expectations will be made up by that little fat guy, who never played a down and writes for some newspaper. I like all those guys, but they are the ones who create the expectations.

If you don't get result-oriented with the kids, you can focus on the things in the process that are important to them being successful. That is the only way they are going to compete the way you want them to. It is hard to create a relentless competitor. To get a player to play every down, play hard, with toughness and responsibility, and do a good job is the most difficult part of coaching. There are three intangibles that take no athletic ability that aids a player in being responsible for his own self-determination. Those three intangibles take the most time in coaching in my opinion. Those intangibles are *effort*, *toughness*, and *assignment*.

When I talk about toughness, I'm talking about *mental and physical toughness*. The player's ability to make the play when the game is on the line is mental toughness. The assignment part of those intangibles is to know what your job is. Every time we don't have a successful play, it goes back to a mental error, missed assignment, or lack of technique trying to carry out that assignment.

When you talk about results, you create problems for yourself. If you can focus on intangible things, your players will compete better for you. They will overcome adversity better for you. I really do believe that. Everybody wants to win a national championship. But why would you put that as one of your goals? What happens when you lose the first game? Are you going to change the goal board? The personality of your team should be what you try to get them to define, not the results.

We live in a front-running society. Confidence goes up and down like the weather. I grew up in West Virginia. The only team I saw play college football was West Virginia. There were only a few games on TV. The exposure these kids get now is incredible. It is amazing about the perceptions these kids get as a result of who wins and who loses. Their perceptions are all result-oriented. Everything is about front running and dogging the other guy.

How do you make players believe in themselves? I ask my players what they think everyone in the room thinks of them. Forget about yourself; it's about how you affected anybody in this room. I know players today are self-absorbed. That doesn't mean they are selfish. If you are self-absorbed all you think about is how it affects you. If you are selfish you want it for yourself. When you are self-absorbed, you have a hard time thinking about how what you do effects someone else.

They have to take ownership for something big. I ask our players how big their frying pan is. That comes from a story about a fisherman in West Virginia catching catfish. He was throwing all the big fish back and keeping only the small ones. He was asked him why he was throwing the big fish back. He said he had only a nine-inch frying pan at home. His whole deal as a fisherman was based on how he could cook them. That's what I ask our team. How much capacity do you have for success? How much do you believe in yourself? What do you expect to accomplish? The answer is not in wins and losses and championships. I think it is how you play the game. That point seems to have lost its importance in today's game.

There is no substitute for knowledge. Knowledge and experience is what help you make an excellent play as a player and as a coach. My wife is really mad at me. I have not been home one weekend since the beginning of August . I told her as long as I was coaching I was going to be the best I possibly could be in this profession.

My dad owned a service station in West Virginia. I had to pump gas when I worked there. The later I came home at night, the earlier the station opened. There were seven coal-mining towns in the county where I lived. His station was at a crossroads. When the shifts changed in the mine was the time you had all your business and pumped all the gas. If I got home after midnight instead of opening at six the next morning, we opened at five. I worked there from the time I was 11 years old until I had gotten married and was a junior in college. When I was a sophomore in college, I wanted to get a job at a construction company. I could make $11 an hour. That was a lot of money in 1971. My father asked me what I wanted that I didn't have. I said nothing. He said, "Get over there and pump gas for $2 an hour." That's what I did and

there was no conversation about it. That is the only job I ever had until I got married.

The most difficult thing there is to do is get your team to *play together*. You have to have a good product. In the coaching business, our product is the principles and values of our organization. Since we are in the people business, the people have to think that you are for them. You have to know the competition. The category also includes you. We always know the opponent, but we don't know ourselves as well as we need to.

I told our players to always play to their strengths. If you are a fastball pitcher, use your best pitch. Don't lose a game because you tried to get someone out on a change-up. *The key is to work on your weakness, but play to your strengths*. Never make your strengths weak by trying to do something else.

When I was 15 years old, I was a sophomore in high school. I was the starting quarterback for my high school team. We played a team called Masontown Valley. They were leading us 18-0 at halftime. I was the quarterback and called all the plays. Earl Canter was our coach. He never called a play.

We came back in the second half and we got the football with two minutes to go when we were behind 18-12. We got down to their 25-yard line with 25 seconds to go in the game. It was fourth-and-12 and Earl called time out. I was relieved because I thought he was going to call the last play and take it out of my hands.

If we won the game we were going to go to the playoffs. If we lost, we were out. They were third in the state and we were fifth. I went to the sidelines to find out what we were going to run. He told me he wasn't going to call a play. He told me I had to call the play. I asked him what he wanted to do. He told me we had the fastest guy in the state playing left halfback, who ended up an all-American at West Virginia, and an all-state wide receiver. He didn't care what play I ran, but he wanted the ball in one of those guys' hands at the end of the play. I went back in the game and called a play-action pass where I faked the ball to the left halfback and threw the ball to the split end. We scored a touchdown and won the game.

After the game, Coach Canter told me that at a critical time in the game *don't think of plays, think of players*. I remembered that.

You should never let the other team determine what you are. General George Custer overestimated and General George McClellan underestimated their opponents. You cannot let the other team destroy what you are. You will not win or lose or have success based on what the other team is. You will have success based on *what your team is*. Team work is a funny thing. You can have a 427 Corvettes with oversized cams that will run 160 miles an hour, but if you don't have the lug nuts for one tire, you are not going anywhere.

Every player has his own strengths and weaknesses. There is not one perfect player on anybody's team. I went through six drafts in the NFL. I saw a guy get drafted in the first round and sign an 18 million dollar signing bonus. We had a list of problems with that guy that was a mile long. But that list was shorter than the next guy's. There are no perfect players and every player has a role in which he can contribute. You have to bring those guys together so that the lug nuts do their job, the 425 engine does its job, and the tires to their job. When all this happens you have a well-oiled machine. If this is to happen, your players cannot be selfish and self-absorbed. The best way to keep players from having those traits is to give them *ownership* and make sure they understand the *big picture*.

On the field, you can't develop leadership if the coaching is doing all the leading. The players have to play and the coaches have to coach. The coaches can't continually tell the players what to do. Bill Belichick would make the coaches go to the sidelines all the time when we had team drills. He would say to *let the players play*. I have senior meetings all the time. When we have them, I give the players ownership in those meetings. We have a peer group from every class that serves in a Peer Intervention Program. This program centers on behavioral issues. They deal with drugs, alcohol, agents, how to treat the other sex, spiritual issues, or any other behavior issues both positive and negative that you might have heard about. It actually is a tool to develop leadership within every group. I need groups that I can meet with to find out what is going on and be a sounding board for the team.

There are no decisions made on this team that I do not control. I can frame out any situation for them and get them to do what I want done. But they think it is their team and they are making the decisions. If you give them that type of ownership, they will lead and effect the other guy.

To be a good player on your team, you have to affect someone else on the team. You have to cause them to play better by the way you play. You affect other players with the *character and attitude*. To be a great player, you have to affect your entire unit. If you are a great player, every player on that unit plays better when you are on the field. The number one thing on any team that will keep your players from being selfish is *respect for the other players*. Having respect leads to trust and from that they begin to believe in each other. That is the way it works and that is the way it has to be.

If the players think there is a division between the coaches and players, you will have trouble within the team. Leadership has to be and can be developed on your team.

I tell our players that someday the NFL will want to sit down and talk about them. I ask them, "Would the organization draft you by the way you act, play, and represent yourself?" I have had a lot of good players who were high draft choices in the NFL. Some of those players were high-maintenance players. Not one of them ever thought the people in the program would have their best interest in mind. They all felt like they had a voice, but they understood even if they didn't like the discipline, they did it any way. I tell them all the guys that own those NFL franchises and the coaches of those teams think just like I do. They have the same kinds of rules in their organization that we have here.

Before I go let me say one other thing. I think we all have a professional responsibility. We are in this business to help each other. I know LSU is a good distance from here, but I want you to know that our staff is committed to promoting professionalism. What you guys do with high school football player in developing them makes our jobs a lot easier and better. That is why we have success. We appreciate that and I appreciate your time today. If we can do anything for you at LSU, give us a holler. Thank you.

LINEBACKER TECHNIQUES AND DRILLS

University of Notre Dame

Let me say it is indeed a pleasure to be invited to the Coach of the Year Clinic by Nike and Earl Browning. I got a chance to know Earl when I was Oklahoma State. They were a Nike school and I spoke for him in a little different of a place than Louisville. I spoke at the Hawaii Clinic. The weather is just a little different over there.

Hopefully I can share some of the things that I believe in as it relates to *linebacker play*. I am proud to be a part of the Notre Dame staff. We have a great head coach. Tyrone Willingham not only has impeccable credentials, but also is a great person to work with. It was his vision that enabled Notre Dame to get back on track.

Growing up in Ohio, I always wanted the opportunity to coach at Notre Dame. When Coach Tyrone Willingham called to offer me the job, it was a no-brainer. If you know anything about Notre Dame, from the Golden Dome to Touchdown Jesus, it is a special place to coach.

I believe a linebacker has to be coached just like a quarterback. There are some *special characteristics* that go with a linebacker. The first thing we do as coaches is go right to the drill and technique work. I have learned over the years that before you can teach techniques and drill, you have to ingrain *leadership* at that position. All positions are important, but the linebacker is critical on defense. Everything that goes on within the defense goes through that individual. Everything the coordinator sends into the game comes out of the linebacker's mouth.

Everything he says affects the entire defense. When I first got to Notre Dame, I sat down with my linebackers and asked them why they wanted to play linebacker. There are qualities that the linebacker coach and coordinator expect the linebackers to have to play that position. We expect the linebacker to be the *heart of the defense*. Playing linebacker is a privilege and with any privilege comes responsibility.

He has to understand the privilege he has been given and be ready to fulfill its responsibilities.

Leadership is the first and most important quality you look for in a linebacker. Leadership is influence. John Maxwell said, "People catch our attitudes just like they catch our colds; by getting close to us. One of the most gripping thoughts to enter my mind centered on your influence as a leader. It is important that you possess a great attitude, not only for your own success, but also for the benefit of others." The linebacker has to have the right *attitude*. I spend a lot of time with our kids giving them things so they understand the importance of leadership in the position of linebacker.

Clarence B. Randall was quoted as saying, "The leader must know, must know he knows, and must be capable to make it abundantly clear to those about him that he knows." The linebacker has to *increase his knowledge of the game*. He has to study film. He has to call the right defense. The players in the huddle have to believe that the linebacker knows what he is saying. In the huddle, the linebacker has to be in charge at all times.

Leroy Eims stated, "A leader is one who sees more than others see; who sees farther than others see, and who sees before others do." The linebacker has to recognize blocking schemes, formations, and be aware of what is going on around him. He has to anticipate things and give that knowledge to the group.

As coaches, we have to let the young men trying to play linebacker know what we expect from them. Your signal caller in the huddle must be your defensive leader. Never let this be questioned. He has to look into the eyes of every man in the defensive huddle and make sure they are looking at him. He has to have *discipline* in the huddle. He has to be sure that every man has heard and understood the call correctly. He breaks the huddle sharply. He always looks up and never makes a bad call in his own mind.

I had two linebackers this year who called the signals. One of them was clearly established as the leader in the eyes of his teammates. He got hurt and the other linebacker had to make the calls. He was not seen by his teammates as being the natural leader. Consequently, when he got in the huddle to make the call, it appeared as no one was listening to him. It was because of his presence in the huddle. He had not learned to have control and huddle discipline. He had to develop the attitude and charisma to get in the huddle, call the defense, and break the huddle without offending the player next to him.

The linebacker has to *execute the defense the best*. You cannot be a linebacker and not be the best. We expect the linebacker to know the defense position by position. He has to know what everyone on the defensive front is supposed to do in a particular defense. If one of your teammates lines up incorrectly, the linebacker should recognize this immediately and move him into position. If the defense is breaking down through an error of a teammate, he should be able to explain the error. In order to do this, he will have to study football.

In football we always talk about *effective communication*. Here is a saying that I've picked up that illustrates that idea. I pass this along to my coaches and players. It is called the *miracle of dialog:* "Every man is a potential adversary, even the ones he loves. Only through dialog are we saved from this hate toward one another. There is only one qualification for this dialog. It must be mutually perceived by the parties and pursued relentlessly." I know I'm talking about the position of linebacker, but I'm also talking about what happens between a coach and another coach or a husband to his wife.

When a linebacker is in the heat of the game and has to adjust the position of one of his defensive lineman or another linebacker, he has to use a *command* that reflects his leadership. If he gets emotional and curses at one of his teammates or coaches, oftentimes that person will get offended by it. If the linebacker says the right thing, players will follow direction and coaches will listen to you. I have seen players at the wrong time of a ball game stop communicating with one another. The wrong time is

when the offense is driving on the defense. That is the time when communication has to be the clearest.

When you look at your films and find players out of position, the general excuse for the misalignment is, "I didn't hear the linebacker make the call." The reason he didn't hear the call was the way the linebacker said it. I happen to believe the way players talk to one another on the field is important. I believe when you are coaching a position, you need to take time to cover these communications. I do it in the spring when I have more time.

The linebackers should always *know and be aware of the down-and- distance*. The down-and-distance will predict every defense we call. The linebackers need to know what to expect on each down-and-distance situation according to the position.

He needs to be aware of the *field position*. This is equally or even more important than down-and-distance. You should know what the opponent will do when he is backed up to his own goal line. We have to know when he is likely to gamble on offense. We want to know at what position on the field they will go into their regular offense. When is the offense likely to use trick plays and when will they gamble on fourth down?

The linebacker has to know *how much time is left in each quarter*. Many games have been lost because a team misjudged the time left to play in each half and what an opponent can do during this time. In games where two teams are equal, the time employed intelligently by a team often determines the winner. The linebacker should know the number of time-outs his opponents has left, as well as how many time-outs he has left. Proper use of time-outs will win games for you.

Linebackers are not born with that kind of knowledge. The coach has to give him the tools and teach him to think. If you have a smart player playing for you and you want him to reflect your coaching, you better give him the tools to do his job. You have to give him those leadership qualities that you want. You are the coach and you have the knowledge and wisdom to pass on to these players. If you give them the wisdom and guidance, it is easier when the situation arises to talk about those things.

The linebacker needs to know the *tendencies and formations that the opponent is going to use*. We need to know if the offense runs away from the formation or runs to the formation. In addition to knowing the formation, he has to know the favorite play run from each formation. If we know his favorite play, we can force him to run something else to try to win the game. The linebacker has to make sure he adjusts the defense correctly to the formation. Formation tendencies and checks to those tendencies are the responsibility of the linebackers.

I have not had the opportunity to coach pro football, but I've been to several camps to observe. The one thing that impresses me about a pro defense is the amount of communication that is going on among the defensive players. When we get back on campus that is the one thing we wish our players would adopt. The reason they do it is because the coaches practice it, coach it, and give it to them. When the defense is communicating, we are really good. When we don't get that communication, we are not nearly as good. We are just not consistent at talking as a team.

The alignment of the linebacker is based off his *gap responsibility*. We have to spend time talking and practicing different techniques and alignments. The linebacker will be aligned in a one shade, a 2I, a 20, 30, 40, 50, and a 70 technique. They have to know where to align and which gaps go with those alignments.

The way I teach is called the *whole-part-whole system*. I teach the whole concept of the defense and then go back and break the defense down into its parts and the techniques that go with each part. When I do drills, I believe it is important for the players to know why you are doing particular drills. I do drills that are direct carryovers to the linebacker's responsibility as it relates to the defense.

These drills are used to teach and learn the basic fundamental skills of linebacker play. When we begin to do our drills, the basic drills are divided into several areas. We teach in a *progression of drills* that relate to the specific techniques of linebacker play. We teach movement drill. There are warm-up drills that we do before practice. Bag drills are used daily to improve foot movement and agility. We tackle daily in some type of tackling drill. We teach sideline tackling, circle tackling, and other forms. We teach proper position starting with a fit position, to a hit position, and finally to an approach and complete tackle. We systematically teach block-protection drills, which covers the rip and cut block. Finally we teach key drills, which feature stance, alignment, and key.

I'm going to show these drills on film and I'll go back and forth with their description and use them as I go through them. We don't use all the drills every day. Depending on the time of year and the opponent we are playing, the drills will be selected and adjusted.

There are certain things you must keep in mind and practice to improve yourself as a linebacker and a football player. Repetition is important to improve your skills, but you must avoid boredom in the drills. When you are doing drills, you have to pay attention to the little details. If players want to improve their skills they must work hard on the little things.

Your players have to *help each other improve*. They need to encourage each other in drills when things are done well and help each other to correct mistakes when they are made. If the players practice drills at full speed, they will learn to play at full speed. Each drill starts with an offensive movement and ends on the whistle. The player has to go all out from movement to the whistle.

Time is precious and time can't be wasted getting into position to run the drill. If a player doesn't know why we are doing the drill, how to do the drill, or how to correct of a mistake, he should ask. We want the linebackers to be competitive in a game-like situation so it helps them to become better. The harder the player goes in a drill, the better he makes himself and his teammates. It is always good for the player to know the tempo of the drill. He has to understand the difference between a teaching drill, thud drill, tag-offense drill, and scrimmage.

We have a *fundamental teaching progression* that we use in teaching stance, start, and keys. We are in a two-point, balanced stance. Having a balanced stance is the best position to start laterally without rising up, dipping down, or false stepping.

In our starts, we want to be able to start forward without giving away our stunts. In the lateral start we have to move the away foot first. We want to be able to lean in the direction of the key and start laterally by sliding or crossing over without false stepping.

There are a number of things we key. The linebacker keys the near backs inside shoulder. The linebacker keys the heads of the offensive lineman they are over. They have to key men in man-to-man coverage. If we are running a stunt, the linebacker knows where he is going regardless of the flow. He keys the ball to get a good takeoff and keys the linemen on the run. In the pre-snap read, the linebacker keys lineman or backs for tips by their eyes, stance, or alignment.

We use a number of different techniques in *shedding blocks*. We use position techniques first. On an aggressive high block, the linebacker uses his position technique getting his shoulder pads under the pads of the blocker. On the low block, the linebacker uses his hands to keep the blockers off his feet. Against a pass blocker the linebacker wants to use his hands and not get involved with the body. If the linebacker gets blocked he has to use a rocker step, give ground, and go. When he is facing a trap block, the linebacker uses lateral body reaction, stays square, and if caught he uses the rocker step and gets off the block.

When we teach *tackling*, we are looking at the man and want to run over him. At the moment of contact, the linebacker explodes, accelerates his feet, squeezes as tight as possible, and takes him back. When he gets into the squeeze part of tackle he wants to wrap up his arms and grab cloth.

We start our practice with what I call *movement drills* [Diagram 1]. They are general agility drills that are worked over dummies or bags. We don't do the same drills every day. We change them up to prevent boredom from setting in. This gets our blood flowing but we are practicing linebacker skills. We do a lateral run to start with. It is important for the linebacker to explode for five yards after he crosses the last bag. They start in a good football position with their shoulders down. They shuffle over the dummies, keeping their shoulders down and in a good football position. I watch their foot work as they go through the bags. I want the linebackers to move their feet. I don't want both feet down in the same hole. As one foot hits the ground the other foot should be up. I don't want both feet on the ground at any time. When

one foot leaves the ground the other should be on the ground, and when one foot comes down the other foot should be off the ground. When we change direction later on in the drill, the linebacker will have a short step in between the bags. We work on not crossing over with their feet. We want them sliding and not crossing their feet. We want their eyes up feeling the bags and their hips as square as possible. In this drill we do the lateral run, buzz feet, lateral run, change direction, and forward-backward change direction.

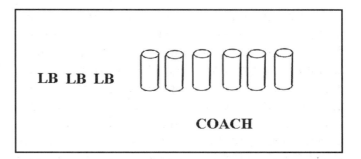

Diagram 1. Movement drills

If you want to add something to the drill, use your managers to flip balls to them as they go down the bags. They catch the ball and flip it back to the manager. You can use two or three managers to do this. At the end of the dummies you can roll out a ball and have them scoop it up and score or recover it. You can have them angle tackle at the end of this drill. These drills relate to things that are going to happen in a game.

We use a drill called *shuffle-run-shuffle* that teaches the linebacker the techniques in pursuing a ballcarrier. We set up four cones. The first two cones are five yards apart with ten yards between the next two cones. They are five yards apart, just like the first two cones. The linebacker shuffles between the first two cones. He turns and sprints between the next two cones. As he reaches the second set of cones he has to square his hips and shoulders and go into a shuffle. This drill teaches the shuffle down the line of scrimmage, the sprint to the ball inside out, and the squaring up at the end to make the tackle.

We use a *downhill agility drill*, which teaches the rip and an angle tackle [Diagram 2]. We have a group of ballcarriers and linebackers in this drill. The coaches stand at the break dummy. The linebacker's dummies are aligned at an angle coming downhill to the ballcarrier. As the ballcarrier moves, the linebacker steps over the dummies. He is coming downhill to the break dummy where he buzzes his feet. The dummies he steps over are simulated blocks. We have blocker with arm shields to make the linebacker rip as he is coming downhill. We are ripping through those blocks. Once the linebacker gets to the break dummy, the back makes a cut off the dummy. The linebacker executes an angle tackle on the ballcarrier.

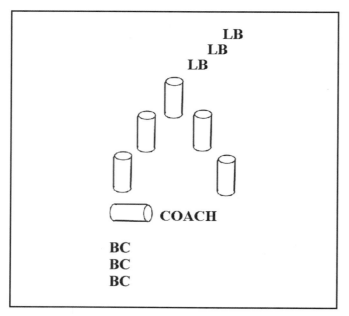

Diagram 2. Downhill agility drill – rip angle tackle

The next drill is almost the same drill, but instead of the rip technique on the blocks we are playing a cut block [Diagram 3]. We don't do this drill every day except when we play teams like the Air Force Academy. When you play teams that are going to cut your linebacker, you better do these types of drills every day. That is the only way you can teach your players to stay on their feet. The object of a load-option football team is to knock everyone down. The drill is almost the same except for the dummy where the coach is positioned. That dummy makes the ballcarrier go one direction. At the end an angle tackle is executed.

When you teach *angle tackling*, everyone seems to have their own version of what and how they teach it [Diagram 4]. When I teach tackling I start backward. I start with a fit position of a perfect tackle. We get the hips sunk and the arms wrapped grabbing cloth. After we put them in the fit position,

we back them off one step. We teach the lead step into the tackle. The lead step keeps the tackler from crossing his feet. We lead step right and lead step left and make a tackle going both ways. If the tackler gets into a crossover step, the ballcarrier has a distinct advantage. He can cut back on the tackler and run through him. If we are going to tackle with the right shoulder, the tackler takes a step with his right foot and leads with his left foot. On the left-shoulder tackle, he steps with his left foot and leads with his right foot. If the back cuts back, the tackler simply steps with his other leg and does not have to cross over. Great tacklers never have their feet together. You have to have them apart with a wide base.

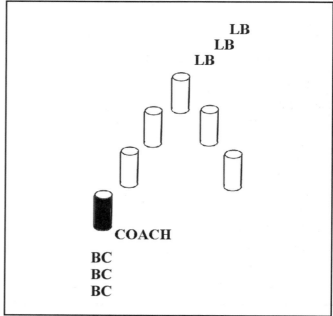

Diagram 3. Downhill agility drill – cut angle tackle

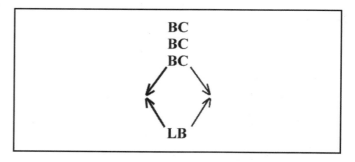

Diagram 4. Angle tackle

The drill that teaches base is what we call the *hunter tackling drill* [Diagram 5]. Space five tube dummies three yards apart with a ballcarrier in each slot. In the first part of this drill, the linebacker shuffles down the line of dummies moving into each slot and making a form tackle on the ballcarrier. This allows him to make four form tackles. He shuffles into the first slot, makes the form tackle, recoils, and shuffles to the next slot and repeats the tackle. Each tackle is delivered with a shoulder tackle, wrap up, and extension lift. He repeats the drill four times.

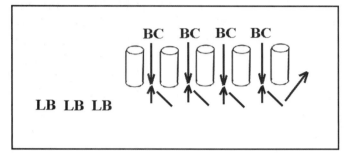

Diagram 5. Hunter tackling drill – A

The second part of this drill is to align the ballcarriers in a line opposite the linebackers to the side of the dummies [Diagram 6]. On movement of the ballcarrier the linebacker begins to shuffle down the dummy. He keeps an inside-out angle on the ballcarrier. The ballcarrier can turn into any lane of dummies he chooses. The linebacker attacks the ballcarrier when he turns into a lane and makes a good angle tackle. This is a full-speed drill. If you want to add something to the drill, you can let the back one fake into the alleys. If he fakes into one alley he must run through the next one.

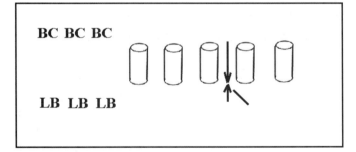

Diagram 6. Hunter tackling drill – B

The first block protection drill we use is called the *cut drill* with an angle tackle [Diagram 7]. We line up four dummies with a line of linebackers. The blockers push the dummies at the feet of the linebacker as he shuffles down the line of dummies. The linebacker uses his hands to punch down on the dummies to keep them out of his feet. At the end of the dummy line he comes off and makes an angle tackle.

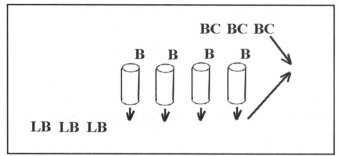

Diagram 7. Cut drill

When we teach block protection, we teach what we refer to as hat and hands. This called the *rip drill* [Diagram 8]. We line up the offensive linemen in one line and the linebackers in the other line. We start out in a head-up position and work out to a shoulder position. The offensive lineman is using a scoop block. What we teach is *hat* in the V of the blocker's neck and *hand* underneath on the breastplate. We press off, lock out, and rip through with the inside arm. We use the rip to knock the offensive blocker's hands off the linebacker. He has to get off the block in a hurry and squeeze back into his gap responsibility. When we use this technique, I tell my linebacker to get off as quickly as he can, because that blocker is usually 320 pounds. Leverage is very important in this drill. We give the linebacker the option to come underneath the block if the lineman gives too much space upfield. However, that is a dangerous move if the lineman is quick.

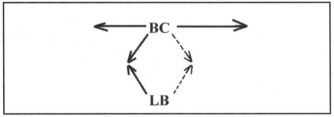

Diagram 8. Rip drill

As the linebacker comes downhill on the scoop block, there is a point when he reaches the edge of the shoulder of the offensive guard, he has to rip through with his inside arm and not get pushed any wider. He has to squeeze back inside to keep the running lane at a minimum. Sometimes you have a linebacker who is a great athlete. We tell him to rip if he needs to, but if he doesn't, he goes to the ballcarrier. Coaching is great but you have to understand that sometimes ability takes over. Never take the athleticism away from the good athlete. If he can make the plays, let him make them. Of course, the opposite side of the coin is where his athleticism gets him in trouble. That is where the coach comes in and shows him how to play that area.

In the *down line shed drill*, the linebacker is playing off three blockers working downfield [Diagram 9]. We set up four dummies at an angle going downfield. We put three blockers and a ballcarrier in the slots of the dummies. He uses his shed techniques as he moves down the line and executes an angle tackle at the end.

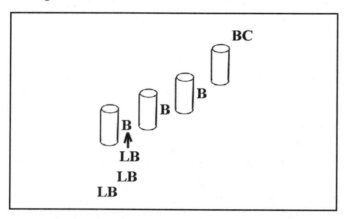

Diagram 9. Down line shed drill

We use a *fit shed drill* to teach the proper fit on the offensive lineman [Diagram 10]. This is a simple drill. The linebacker fits into the block of the lineman, sheds him, and makes the tackle. We go right then left on this drill.

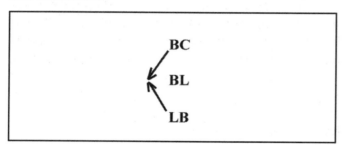

Diagram 10. Fit shed drill

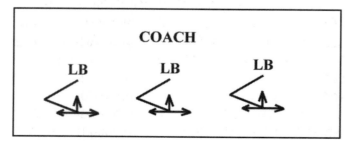

Diagram 11. Wave drill at 45 degrees

I'm running out of time so I'll talk about these next two drills together. This is a pass-drop drill where we drop at 45-degree angles on the direction of the coach [Diagram 11]. The coach gives them two movements and makes the linebacker break up, left, or right.

In the second drill is called a *90-degree wave drill* [Diagram 12]. The linebacker tilts and runs straight back as if he is covering a tight end going vertical. At some point the coach levels the linebacker's retreat and makes him break left or right.

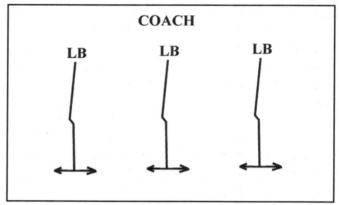

Diagram 12. Wave drill at 90 degrees

I'll briefly cover this next drill [Diagram 13]. I know you've seen it before so I won't talk too much about it. It is a simple drill that teaches linebackers their proper fit on flow. We line up an offensive line with one back five yards behind the center. All we do is give flow with the back; the linebackers react to the flow and make their fits to the line of scrimmage on the offensive blockers.

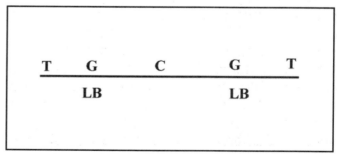

Diagram 13. Read drill

Gentlemen, I appreciate you inviting me down here. I hope I gave you something you can use. If you get an opportunity to come to Notre Dame, make sure your drop in. I know I was going fast at the end, but if you want a copy of this tape I will make you a copy. Thank you very much.

FOCUS ON THE MOMENT

Ohio State University

I was able to catch the last minutes of the lecture by Coach Nick Saban of LSU. One of the neat things about our profession is that we share ideas with one another. We at the university level feel as if our task is to serve, not only our team and our university and to try to win games, but also to serve other people in the profession and to serve the high school programs. We want to serve the young people that want to play the game of football. I am no different than all of the other college speakers that have been on this program. You are certainly welcome to visit with us at Ohio State any time. Our doors are open and you are welcome to visit with us.

My job as the head coach is this. First, is to stay out of the assistant's way. The second thing I must do is to devise the overall approach to their football experience at Ohio State.

I must try to design the program where we fit into the big picture at the university, within the state, and within the profession, and then try to serve from that standpoint. Every one of us has a role that we serve for the big picture and my approach is aligned toward the overall program. That is what I want to do today with you. I want to cover the overall approach to the program. If I get a chance at the end of the lecture, I want to talk about our major approach on how we train our quarterback. I do not want to get into the details, but I do want to get into the things that I feel make a difference. I have had six different quarterbacks take us to the National Championship. They all did different things, but they all did some of the things I think are what the team needs and I will try to share those with you at the end.

The clinic people started asking me for a topic back in October. Some of you know how Earl Browning is. He's the Clinic Director of the Louisville Clinic. He called and told me he needed my topic for this lecture. I told him, "Earl, we are playing Purdue this week and they are tough." The next week he would call again. I would ignore him. We were playing Penn State and I did not have time to think about a topic. Well let me tell you, Earl Browning is relentless. He called during the Michigan week. I told him, "Look, we are focusing on what is going on now. I do not have a topic." Then it dawned on me. It may be one of the reasons we had a little success at Ohio State because it was something that we start talking to our people about from day one. This is not revolutionary and it is not something you have never heard before. But when you sit and think about your overall approach, whether you are the head coach, a position coach, a parent, a spouse, or whoever you happen to be, if we could just learn to focus on what is going on in that moment, we would be much better at what we are doing. We do not want to have our heads, minds, and thoughts elsewhere. If we can do that, we have a chance to be successful. It does not matter if we are working with a walk-on player who will never play, or who may not even be good enough to play on our scout team, and we are in conversation with him, we need to focus on that moment. It may be our daughter trying to show us her English paper. It may be that we are visiting someone in the hospital who loves Ohio State or loves your school. They may say, "If I could just meet Coach Jim Tressel." If we can focus on whatever is going on in that moment, we have a chance for success.

Each year at Ohio State University and I am sure it is like it is at your school; everyone wants to know: "Are you going to win the championship? Are you going to beat your rival?" They ask you: "Are you going to be the National Champs or State Champs," or whatever it is at your level. That is what people want to talk about. The media is trained *not* to focus on the moment. They are trained to get things discussed on what may go on in the future, even though it may not have anything to do with the preparation aspect of what you are trying to do at the moment.

Our task is to help our young people, for the good of the team, to focus on what is going on. This includes all meetings, at all times in practice, especially the last 15 minutes when they are exhausted and their minds can drift. Our task is to have them *focus on the moment*.

This task really gets hard when you are winning and your record is 7-0. And it is really tough when you are having a losing season. It is like Coach Jack Harbaugh of Western Kentucky University who won the Division I-AA National Championship. When his team started the season they had won two games and had lost three games early in the year. It was difficult to get the players to focus. What were some of the players thinking about? "Oh man, I wonder if we can have a winning season. I wonder if our team is very good. I wonder if coach is going to replace me." It is obvious what Coach Jack Harbaugh did. He got the team to forget the 2-3 record and focus on winning the rest of the games starting with the next day's practice and the next game.

They are the same things we talked about when we were 7-0. Forget about the record. Forget about the BCS Ratings. The media wanted to know if we were mad that Ohio State was not in the top three in the BCS Ratings. Who cares! I told our players if we did not win the next game we would not be in the top 20 in the BCS Ratings.

All of you have computer points with the state high school playoffs. Everyone wants to talk about where you are in the state ratings. Our job is to *focus on what is going on this moment*. That is our job. If we can teach our young people anything, we need to teach them to focus on the *task at hand*.

Once Miami had defeated Syracuse and Virginia Tech to go undefeated, and both of us were selected to go to the Fiesta Bowl, everyone wanted to know how we felt about being the underdog. They would make comments like "there is no way OSU can beat Miami." They wanted our players thinking about the game. They all wanted us to talk about what was going to happen on January 3.

Our players needed to think about what Miami did on offense and defense. We needed to study Miami. We needed to get ready for final exams. We needed to continue with our training. One thing I was proudest of this year was what I did with our line. We probably did not have the greatest line play in the world this year. We were a little inexperienced, a little overweight, and we had some injuries. From the day of the Michigan game in November to the day of the Fiesta Bowl on January 3, our offensive line lost an average of 12 to 15 pounds each. The only way to lose weight is to focus on today. You cannot think about being down to a weight of 308 pounds the day of the Fiesta Bowl, and you now weigh 320 pounds. You must focus on this moment. I felt we understood focusing on the moment with our offensive line when they made the commitment to focus on each fork full of food they were eating. They were focused on each extra stair climber, or treadmill, or whatever. They were able to focus on what needed to get done at that moment.

If we can teach our players to focus like the offensive line did, when they go to biology class, even if they hate biology, they can make it. They may not understand what biology is going to do for them in the future, but they are there. They need to be there. They had better be in those classes. Second, when they get there they need to focus on what is going on in class. I know some of them want to go on to the NFL. I know they do not give a biology test in the NFL. The players that make it in the NFL are the players that can focus every second on whatever they have to do. At the present time our players are asked to take biology. That is the deal. Focus on the moment at hand. If we have a chance to do that, we have a chance to progress. The minute we start thinking out of the moment at hand, we are dead.

When we came off the field on January 3, actually it was January 4 by the time the game was over, the press wanted to know if we were going to repeat as champions. I am sure the same thing happened when Jack Harbaugh of Western Kentucky walked off the field after they won the Division I-AA National Championship. I told the press that next championship game is 365 days from now. I told them I wanted our guys to focus on the moment. I told them, "No, we are not going to think about next year. We are going to celebrate tonight and focus on what is going on now." That is very, very important.

One thing we talk about is the task we have as teachers and coaches. It is an important task. Every moment we have the privilege of coaching we must make sure everything we do is focused on what it should be.

This is what hangs up in the Ohio State locker room. We feel this is important. Again, you can get tied up with X's and O's in coaching. On the same token, you can be gone because of a lack of wins. We understand that situation. This is what we have hanging in our locker room:

> *Concern for man and his fate must always form the chief interest of all technical endeavors —never forget this in the midst of your diagrams and equations.*

> *— Albert Einstein*

In our case the students and players are the people we affect. A lot of you are involved in the X's and O's and a lot of you think this is really going to make a difference, and it does. The X's and O's are important. They are part of the formula, but all technical endeavors, concern for man and his fate, must always form the chief interest. No one messes around with diagrams and equations more than we do.

The first time I saw this quotation was five years ago. My son was visiting Ohio State with the honors program. I was not the coach at Ohio State at the time. While my son and I were visiting Ohio State and the Honors Program, an engineering professor started his recruiting pitch with this thought. I was sitting out in the audience just as you are today. As I listened to the professor I realized this was true for football coaches, as well as many others who teach. No one messes around with diagrams and equations any more than we do. We want to make sure we follow the rules every second. In every decision we make, and every time we talk with one of our young people, every time we decide this is how we are going to do something, we must concern ourselves with the well-being of our young people. Sometimes that is very hard. When things are not going exactly as we like, sometimes we let our emotions take over and we say things that are not in the best interest of our young people, and we question how we are bringing them up as adults. There will be a day when no one will remember who the 2002 Division I-AA National Champions were, or the 2002 Division I Champions were. There will be a day when we will be a *trivia question.*

With this in mind, we had to decide when we came to Ohio State University two years ago what our mission was going to be. We knew what the people at Ohio State wanted us to do. They wanted us to fill the stadium, graduate every player, keep the players out of trouble, go to every alumni meeting in the country, and win every game. That is what they want us to do and we know that. But what is our mission? So we wrote a mission statement. It is written on a large banner in our team meeting room. It is about 10-feet tall and 5-feet wide. When our players come into that room they have to look at that sign. We make sure they read it every day.

Before you can focus on the moment you must decide where you are going. You may say, "let's go to the mall." First you must decide what the mall is. Then you can decide the direction you should go to get to the mall. Then you can focus on every turn and every stoplight. So the question was this: What was our mission and where did we want to go? We wrote the following mission statement so there was no miscommunication or misconception as to what and how we wanted to accomplish the mission:

OHIO STATE FOOTBALL
FAMILY MISSION STATEMENT

UNDERSTAND THE TEAM CAN ONLY PROGRESS WITH LOVE AND RESPECT!

I. We must show class and humility on and off the field.

II. We must always compete with the idea that we deserve to be Big Ten and NCAA Champions.

III. We must respect the proud tradition of the past. We will be the class of college football.

Notice we start with the team. One of the problems we have at Ohio State is the conception that the players are only stopping by for a short period of time before they go to the NFL. That is a problem we have at our level. I had that problem when I was coaching at Youngstown State. One year after our banquet I had a mother come up to me and ask me if I thought her son was going to get drafted. Now, he was a backup defensive back and smaller than I am. I looked at her and said, "I do not think we are going to war anytime soon. I do not think he is going to be drafted." Now, I may not be able to say that today. She looked at me and said, "I mean the NFL Coach Tressel." He was a backup player and she expected him to be drafted in the NFL. I am sure you have the same type of problems at your level. The players must understand it is the *team*. The team is the reason we are here.

We wanted to make sure from the get go that the players understood that it was not going to be about X's and O's with us. That aspect of the game was not going to make any difference. I have been very lucky. I have been coaching 28 years in college and I have been in the National Championship finals eight times. It is not the X's and O's that win championships. It is the intangibles, those spiritual things that make a difference. The players must have respect for one and another. Again, the X's and O's are important. I promise you, *love and respect* are more important than the defense we play.

We commit ourselves to reaching our full potential, whatever that is. We happen to think we can attract good enough players, and if we can reach our potential, hopefully some good things are going to happen. But, we are still going to commit ourselves to reaching our potential. We know every action we take must be made with the team in mind. If I am out in a social situation and I am focused on the moment, I better have the team in mind. Do we bat 100 percent with this? No! If we batted 100 percent they would not need us. If all of our players did the things we wanted them to do they would not need coaches? Let me tell you something. Coaches, moms, and dads are needed more now than ever before in this world. So we have to teach that all of our action must be made with the team in mind. An unwavering loyalty to the team must be built into the system. That is our mission. We want to build unwavering loyalty to the team, especially during the tough times.

I promise you when Western Kentucky University was 2-3, if they did not have unwavering loyalty, they would not have gone on to win the National Championship. It would not have made a difference what offense they played or what defense they played. If they did not have unwavering loyalty with that group of people, it would not have happened.

Fun will prevail for all. One of the things we are accused of in football is that the players do not have

any fun. It is true to a degree at the high school level, very true at the college level, and certainly true at the professional level. We all have players come in to see us and tell us, "Coach, I am going to quit the team because football is not fun anymore." In most cases that player has a problem — he either is not playing enough, he does not like the team, he does not like conditioning, or something similar to this. Do you know what? We cannot write off the fact that this is just his problem. I do not know why you would go to a football camp for five days and get down in a football stance each day. That is not fun. We must create ways for our game and the situations to be fun. We must create the situation so it is fun. It cannot be stoic work. If you work like crazy you can still make it fun. That is part of our mission statement. *Fun will prevail for all!*

There will be an absence of special privileges. Another thing we get accused of in sports is letting the star players get by with certain tings that the other team members do not get to do. The players must know our policy is that there must be an absence of special privileges. Now, this does not mean it is going to be a flat out democracy.

I learned when I was playing college football that football is not a democracy. I was one of the captains of the team at Baldwin-Wallace College. My buddy Sums, who was also a co-captain, went into to see the head coach, who happened to be my dad. We went to see the head coach because one of the players had been late for practice; this player always had something wrong when it came time for conditioning. It was a combination of things with this one particular player. He was a little lazy on some of the drills and as captains we wanted to address these problems with the head coach. I told Sums to talk to my dad. I was going to be there with him for moral support. We walked in to the office and Sums told dad that we were representing the team as co-captains. Sums explained that we did not think one particular player was doing all of the things the rest of us were doing. He explained the problem was a concern for the rest of the team. My dad looked at us and asked if there was anything else. We said, "No!" Dad went on to tell us that this particular player had problems that were none of our business. We thanked him and left the office.

Later I asked my dad why he had not supported us and why he had not told us what was going on with this one particular player. He said, "You guys had no idea of what was going on in that particular player's life. I appreciated the two of you coming to me with the situation because I needed to know what some of the feelings were." He went on to tell me that sometimes the players are not going to know what is going on in every situation. "I was not going to say that some player's father was just put into prison, or that some player's aunt that raised him just passed away. There are some things where you are not going to get to know the entire story. I am glad both of you felt you could come and see me and express your concern."

While there is an absence of special privileges, we must do our best to make sure everyone feels they are being treated the same. We all know as coaches that some players need a little more care and concern than some of the other players. This is just parenting, teaching, and coaching. We must work like crazy that we do not error and give special privileges that need not be given. We must do this so we can follow our mission.

Part of our mission is this: *We know we are going to get what our works deserve.* From day one in our mission we must understand this. *We are going to get what we earn.* It has nothing to do with the officials. It has nothing to do with the weather. It has nothing to do with the way the ball bounces. *We are going to get what we earn.* We know that no one is going to walk into our dressing room and hand us a game. No one including a referee is going to come into our dressing room and take away a game.

I have heard some comments about the interference call in our overtime game with Miami. I understand this. People like to talk about things after the game. They want to focus on that play but the game is over. Our players could have moaned and groaned with two-and-a-half minutes to go in the game when we clearly caught the ball inbounds that was not called in our favor. If we get that call the game would not have gone into overtime. Our players and coaches could have cried and moaned then. We did not do that. We had to punt the football and they ran the punt back into our end of the field. Our players did not think they were going to lose now that Miami had the ball in our territory. Instead, our players bulled their necks and played defense. Miami did a great job and kicked a long field goal to tie the game and send it into overtime.

Miami got the ball in the first overtime and scored. Our guys could have folded their tent and quit. We had fourth down with 13 to go. Our players could have *not* focused on the moment, but we converted. We ended up scoring a touchdown. Yes, we got an interference call. I do not know if that was a right or wrong call. I have been watching the films and there are a lot of right and wrong calls in a game like that. That is the human aspect of the game with the officials. They were trying very hard to do their best. It is the same with our coaches. They were trying to call the right play.

We go into the second overtime and we scored. Then Miami got the ball down deep and had first-and-goal on the two-yard line. That is when our guys were able to *focus on the moment.* We kept Miami out of the end zone. I really and truly believe that we earned and deserved the National Championship. *We will get what our works deserve.*

We are committed to growing mentally, physically, and spiritually. When we recruit young players we do not sugarcoat it. It is not a deal where we tell them to come to Ohio State and win the Heisman Trophy and then go to the NFL. That is not our approach. Do you know what? We may lose some players because of this approach, but that is our approach. That is one of the things we would like for a player to do who comes to Ohio State. We want them to come and be a Big Ten Champion, win the Heisman Trophy, and go to the NFL. All of this is fine. However, that is not all you are going to do at Ohio State. There are going to be moments when we can teach players so they can grow mentally, physically, and spiritually. When that happens we are going to focus on those aspects of our program. The whole deal at Ohio State is not going to just be Big Ten, National Champs, and the NFL. That is not the whole picture. The players must know that when they come to Ohio State.

We want them to recognize that they are students first and athletes second. We have 30-plus players in the NFL. We will probably have six or seven more drafted this year. That is not a high percentage of the players that have gone to Ohio State. The rest of the players who leave Ohio State must go out and serve society. It is our job to prepare those players for the future just as it is to prepare those players that go to the NFL. Just because we are called football coaches does not mean that is all we coach. We coach the whole picture. We understand they are students first and athletes second.

We will personify class and humility on and off the field. I just talked to the Ohio State Alumni Club of Louisville, Kentucky. I told them there were two things I noticed about Ohio State when I took the job two years ago. First, they wanted to win. Second, they wanted to *win with class on and off the field.* That is their school. They want to feel good about the players wearing the jerseys of their alma mater. They want the players to win on and off the field. That aspect needs to be a part of our mission. We need to focus on this point.

We seek to get better every day. We work on it every day. We do it to develop consistency. *Consistency! Consistency!* We want consistency in how we practice, and how we go to the study table, and how we work in the weight room. We grade every lift in the weight room and we grade every practice. We give a letter grade for every practice and every lift. That is the way it is. We want the team to know that every moment is important. It is very important that we develop consistency through the relentless execution of fundamentals each and every moment.

We will always compete with the best to become the best. We will play with passion and deserve to be the Big Ten Champion. That is our mission. It is not something we accomplish all of the time, but that is our mission. That is what we are seeking to accomplish. We want to deserve the Big Ten Championship and the NCAA National Champion. That is our mission. We realize this can only be accomplished by extraordinary focus. We want to take it one step at a time. We say extraordinary focus one moment at a time.

Understand at Ohio State there are 25 to 30 sports writers at everything you do. Those writers want to pull the coaches and players away from whatever their task is and get their minds thinking elsewhere. So we tell our coaches and players that it takes extraordinary focus to accomplish our goals. We must have that if we want to be champions.

The next part of our mission is that *we will respect the proud tradition of the past of Ohio State.* We will provide further greatness and tradition for the future. That is a goal that we have. It is a part of our mission. It is a privilege to play at Ohio State. It is a privilege to play at the University of Louisville, and it is a privilege to play at LSU. It is a privilege to play at your high school. It is a privilege to play for whomever you represent. We will do so at all times knowing it is our responsibility to serve as a positive role model. I do not care what Charles Barkley said. It is our responsibility to serve as a positive role model for the youth of the great State of Ohio. This is especially true in our case because we are on the news every day for those kids. We have a responsibility to serve as a role model for all of the young and old alike that we are able to touch in these United States. We all know it is a small world. We have people in the Armed Forces in Afghanistan that tell us they watch every game. We are exposed. Now we have a chance to be a role model across the world. I am not saying that we are there at this time, but a part of our mission is that *we will be the class of college football.* That is what we would like to be. To do this I think you need time, tradition, and gratitude for where we are today. This is crucial for us to teach.

I shared this next thought with our Alumni Club of Louisville earlier today. We took a book this past season and went through it as a team. You have never seen the book. It is not a best seller. It is a book written by Don Steinberg called *Expanding Your Horizons: Collegiate Football's Greatest Team.* Don played at Ohio State and wrote the book about the 1942 National Champs at Ohio State. That was our first National Championship. This is what he wrote about: first, this is what Ohio State football is all about; and second, here is what became of the team members of the 1942 Ohio State Buckeyes in later life. This is our legacy. Yes, we won the National Championship in 1942. Very few of you knew that but obviously that is not such a great accomplishment. But what these team members did later in life is very significant. There were 43 players on that team. After the Championship season 34 of them left school and enlisted in the Armed Services. They went to serve their country. Three of those 43 men lost their life in the war. I shared the story of Charles A. Csuri with our Alumni this morning. Chuck Csuri was an All-American in 1942. He was an underclassman. He was voted captain of the 1943 team. He enlisted and went to the war. He was a stud as he was voted All-American. He was a good leader as he was voted captain of the 1943 team. The same qualities he displayed at Ohio State were displayed in the service. He was in Europe battling like crazy for our freedom. Some of us here today were living at that time and some us here were not living at that time.

Chuck happened to be a part of a battle that was very pivotal in which the direction of the war was going. It just so happened he was among the battalion that got surrounded by the enemy. The commander told his men that they had lost communication with the Allied Forces. The Allied Forces were not aware of where the enemy was now. They did not know that Chuck and his men were surrounded. They did not know they were losing the ground they held. The commander said, "We need someone to get through the enemy line and regain communication with the Allied Forces and tell them where the enemy is located." Charles Csuri raised his hand and said, "I will go."

He broke through the enemy line. On the way through the enemy line he had his helmet and belt pack shot off, but he made it to the Allied Forces. They were able to regain communications. He let our armed forces know, "This was not a good play we had called. We need a new play. This is not the right defense to be in. We need to change what we are doing."

You all know the end results of that game. We turned the war around in Europe and won World War II. That accomplishment was much greater than winning the 1942 National Championship at Ohio State.

There were many others like him from that group. This season Charles Csuri came in and spoke to our team. Today he is 82-years old. He looked very frail and showed his age. Our players all knew about Charles. We read the whole book together. He was not that impressive to look at, compared to our players today. But our players had read about him and they knew what he had done when he was in the war in Europe. Our guys, coaches included, had not done anything like Charles had done.

Charles talked about one thing with our players. "No matter what you are doing, if it's football or staying in school, you need to focus on your role." He happened to love school. He came back to Ohio State and got his degree. He did not play any more football but he loved football. He spent 40 years on the Ohio

State Faculty. He invented all of the video imagining that you see in the movies today. He and his students are the ones that designed the video imagining for *Jurassic Park* and *Shrek* and all of those kinds of movies. He is world famous in that arena as well. He said, "Whatever it is you are working on, you better focus on what your role is. You need to focus on what you need to get done."

Now, our guys knew what he had accomplished. He had been an All-American. They had not been All-Americans. Well, one or two of our players were returning All-Americans. He had been a National Champion, and none of our players had been a National Champion. He was a college graduate, and none of them were college graduates. He had a successful career and the players knew he was world famous in his element. None of our players were world famous in their element. They knew he had the courage to give up everything he loved to go fight for our freedom. Our players' eyes were riveted on him. I knew we had a chance to have a good football team after that meeting.

That meeting was prior to our first game of the year. I knew what we had shared with them was special, as far as the tradition at Ohio State and the responsibility we all have to further the tradition of our great school and our great country. I knew all of this, but you never know if the players understand all of this. I could tell the players were beginning to understand what we were trying to get across to them as they listened to Charles Csuri. I am not sure they understood everything totally. I never fought in a war and I am not sure if I understand totally what people gave up so I could be free; the freedom that I take for granted every day. But I could begin to see that our players were beginning to understand a lot more about what we were trying to get across to them.

We went out and played our opening game against Texas Tech. Our team was as focused for an opening game as any team I had every seen. From that day on I knew we had a chance to be okay. I also knew we still had a lot of good teams to play. I knew we needed to stay healthy and we needed to do the right X's and O's. We needed to continue to stay focused on the moment.

I think it is important for all of us at the college level, and all of you at the high school level, to help our young people to understand how fortunate we are as a nation, and the tradition our country has. It is becoming a little more real to all of us right now.

Our team is going to the White House to be recognized on Monday, February 24. A few of our players are kind of scared. They watch CNN News. They see the tanks outside the White House. They see the reality of what is going on. I think it is our responsibility as coaches and teaches, especially after 9-11, to help the players understand our tradition. You can remember how it was with your players after 9-11. They were scared. It is our responsibility to talk about things beyond football. When it is time to focus on blocking we must forget Iraq. We are going to block. When it is 4:00 p.m. we are going to block. When it is 10:00 a.m. we are going to be in biology class. When it is 10:30 a.m. we are going to be in the weight room. When it is 11:00 p.m. at night we need to get in our rooms. We don't need to be out.

One sign we had hanging at Youngstown State coming down our ramp was this: *WHAT ARE YOU GOING TO DO NOW?* It was real simple. What are you going to do now? It was appropriate for everything. If we were coming in at halftime and we were down by 12 points we saw that sign. *What are we going to do now?* Coming down the ramp we may be up by 12 points. *What are we going to do now?* It was the same thing coming in at the end of practice. *What are we going to do now?* We had the same sign as you entered our weight room. They saw the same sign leaving our weight room. Focus on the moment. At Ohio State we ask that same question. We were 14-0. *What are we going to do now?* All they want to do now is to have celebrations. *What are you going to focus on now?* This is important.

We need to know what our mission is. Our mission will not change. We are not going to put up a new sign. The mission is the same. The only way we can be sure we have a chance at our mission is to focus on the moment.

We have a Latin phrase that we like to talk about. It is really appropriate now. *Macte Virtute!* It is an imperative statement. It is like when I say, "Hey, close the door." That is an imperative statement. We do not have to discuss the statement, just close the door. It is imperative. This is the Latin imperative phrase that means *Increase Excellence!* Increase your

excellence! This is for whatever level you are at. We were 7-5 the first year at Ohio State. We needed to increase our excellence. We had 46 players get a 3.0 average or better this fall quarter. We want to increase our excellence. We had 27 players that were All-Academic Big Ten. The next closest in our conference was 17 All-Academic Big Ten players. We still want to increase our excellence in everything we do. *Macte Virtute!* That is imperative. It is not something we want to consider. It is imperative.

The question raised is in what ways do we want to increase our excellence? On the other side of our team meeting room, opposite our 10-foot mission statement, hangs our *Block-O of Life* sign (Diagram 1). It is nothing original. At Youngstown State it was called our *Wheel of Life*. It is no different here as it is anywhere else. In the Block-O of Life are six areas where we need to increase our excellence. We designed this idea 17 years ago when I was at Youngstown State. We asked the question in what areas can we help our young people? If our role was to have a concern for our team, in what ways could we help them? We came up with six areas. We call them our Block-O of Life. It is on a 10-foot sign in our team meeting room.

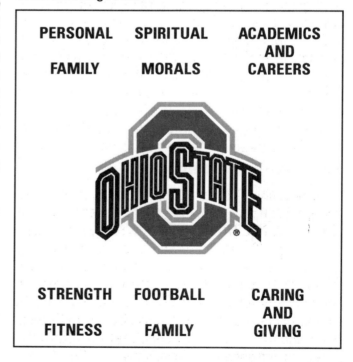

| PERSONAL | SPIRITUAL | ACADEMICS AND |
| FAMILY | MORALS | CAREERS |

| STRENGTH | FOOTBALL | CARING AND |
| FITNESS | FAMILY | GIVING |

Diagram 1. Block-O of Life

At the top of the sign are the *spiritual* and *moral* areas. If you do not do things right, and your morals and ethics are not right, nothing you accomplish is going to be fulfilling anyway. When you are around any group of champions you can ask people what made them champions and they will tell you it was something you could not touch. It was something special. The media likes to say chemistry because they are afraid to say spirit. They are afraid to say there was something spiritual or something untouchable about the team. It is something they could not explain. Just like you cannot explain a mothers love for her child. How do you explain that? You cannot explain it. You cannot touch it.

We want to teach our guys to grow spiritually and morally, and whatever path they enjoy personally or family-wise. If we can teach our team to grow spiritually, making sure that morally and ethically we know the difference between right and wrong, it does not matter how many games we win. If we can do that they will have a chance to go out in our society and do the right thing and be the right kind of people. That has to be at the top of our chart to increase our excellence.

Obviously in college, personal family takes on a different tone. That is because the athletes are away from home. Mom is not there to wake you up every day. Dad is not around as much. It is a different situation. But, it does not make it any less important. Probably from this time on they are not going to have the daily contact with their family that they use to have. The players must come up with a way to increase their excellence in a way to keep that family bond intact and let the family appreciation be known as best they can. It is something we have to increase our excellence in and it takes on a different chapter in their lives.

Obviously we stress *academics* and their future *careers*. I do not care where you play; everyone is not going to the NFL. If you do go to the NFL you are going to be about 26-years old when you are done playing pro ball. The way health care is today you will have to work until you are 60 anyway. So we must get each player ready for this endeavor. It is mandatory to increase our excellence academically. We want them to be able to focus in on a career that they can fall in love with and become compassionate about. That is why we are here today because we love what we are doing. I feel sad for some of my friends. They are more excited about Ohio State Football than they are about their accounting firm. Some of them will tell

me they are upset because they are going to miss the Ohio State game this week because they have to work. We want to find something our guys are passionate about.

On the bottom of our chart is *strength* and *fitness*. This is huge. It is very critical. Our players want to know how to get into the NFL. Great! "Here are the players that play your position in the NFL. Those players jump this high, they run this fast, and they weigh this much." There is nothing wrong with that goal. At the same time we tell them the teams that win in our league run this fast, jump this high, and they are a certain size, and they play hard for four quarters. Strength and fitness are crucial.

If we are considering man and his fate in our teaching, there is no greater help you can give young people than to help them develop good health habits. There are some heath issues that genetics take care of. If that happens you are in trouble, or you are in good shape, one or the other. There are a lot of health aspects that we are responsible for. There are certain things that are controllable. If we can help our players learn the health lessons we will be giving them a financial boost they do not even know about. The cost of staying healthy is extraordinary. If we make sure we increase our excellence in that area of health we are taking care of them again.

For the football family, that part is easy. All we ask them to do when they are thinking about increasing their excellence in football is to start with the *team* issues first. I do not care if they want to be All-Big Ten. That is great. They can put that down as a goal. If they want to be All-American, that is great. Put it down. If they want to go to the NFL, that is great. Put it down. But first, I want to hear what they want for their teammates.

After they write down all the things they want for their teammates and the things they want for themselves, then we talk about how they are going to do those things. Anyone can write goals. Anyone can talk about how to increase their excellence. The issue is how are we going to do that? They must be willing to learn what it takes to be a champion and to be excellent.

The last point in our Block-O of Life is in the area or *caring* and *giving*. I have no idea why I was born into the family I was. I got to watch my dad coach every day. Our house was next to the stadium. They did not pay my dad much, but they gave him a house. So I lived next door to the stadium. I got to watch my dad work every day. Then I had great high school coaches. Then I got to play college football for my dad and his coaches. Then I got to work for Jim Dennison and then Tom Reed, and then Dick MacPherson, and then Earle Bruce. Then I got to be a head coach at Youngstown State. I do not know how I got blessed to be a head coach. Now I get to be the head coach at Ohio State. Are you kidding me? I do not know why I am blessed from that standpoint. But I do know this: I am blessed and the responsibility for being blessed is to care about and give of yourself and give of your blessings to others. That is your responsibility. Just because I am blessed doesn't mean my responsibility is to just sit back and count the money. That is not my responsibility. My responsibility is to take my blessings and help other people.

We must make sure our players understand this fact. When you walk into our locker room you will see some good-looking players. They are big, strong, fast, and they are good academically. They have been blessed. They have had lots of good high school classes. They have had lots of good support at home. They have been blessed. They had better not get out of Ohio State without the understanding that with those blessings goes a responsibility of giving to others. At Ohio State we have a community outreach program and it is crucial. I have a staff member whose job is community outreach and development. He does not coach, but his job is important to us. It is important that we increase our excellence in terms of the fact that we are very, very blessed. It is time for us to share. That is our responsibility.

In each of those Block-O of Life areas we have our players set goals each year. This is true in all six of those areas. We have them set up a plan to accomplish these goals. Then we have them set up what we call their *dream*. What do they dream about? This may be down the road but we have them set the plan. It works nice and the coaches do the same thing. I just spent two hours with each of my assistant coaches talking about their new goal sheet.

The interesting thing about setting those goals after you win the National Championship is this: The only goals that really change much are the football goals. Those other areas are ongoing. It does not matter if we are 7-5 or National Champions. As our coaching staff goes over our goals, some of them may say, "Do you know what? I am not sure I did as good as I said I was going to do in the family area."

Today we have everyone patting us on the back telling us how great we are now that we have won the National Championship. But when we look at those goals and see what we said we wanted to improve our excellence, a year later they have some second thoughts concerning the fact that they did not increase their excellence as much as they could have. I think this is healthy and it makes us get better as individuals and as a team.

Goals must be specific and must be measurable. Our players set goals to get better grades and to study hard. What does better grades and study hard mean? They need to be specific. This is what they must say: "I want to get my grades up to a 2.82 average. I know I have to be at study hall from 7:30 a.m. to 8:45 a.m. That is a rule we have, but I am going to study that first hour of the day, after study hall." You can measure that goal. You either do it or you don't do it. It is the same thing with coaches. When we write our goals on how we are going to increase our excellence, we must be specific and we must write goals that are measurable.

Next, we must face our goals. February and March are the times we face our goals. We ask our players to keep their goal sheets in a strategic place so they can bump into them every once in a while. We do not want them to put them in a drawer and forget them.

We talked about our mission. The mission in some ways can be a little abstract, so you have to focus down into the statement. We have three basic goals at Ohio State.

First, we want to *graduate all of our players* — all of them. I do not get concerned about the NCAA graduation report. Let me give you an example why I am not too concerned about the NCAA report. Eddie George went to the NFL for seven years. He has worked his way back to Ohio State and he has graduated. This will work for me. That does not work for the NCAA. He does not count because he did not graduate in the first six years of college life. I do not care, he did some other things. He is doing alright. I don't care how long it takes, I want to graduate all of our players with a meaningful degree. I want them to get a useable degree that will prepare them to be responsible citizens. We must constantly talk about this and make that a goal as a staff.

The second goal we have is to *win*. Hey guys, at Ohio State you have to win. How much is enough? No set number is enough. You have to win more than you could ever dream of winning. You cannot win enough at Ohio State. That being said, you better define success so that it is obtainable. You just can't win enough to please everyone. Our Alumni that were here today are happy today. If we walked in here with a 0-12 record, most of the Alumni would not have been here. And those that did show up would have something nasty on their minds. So we must decide what success is at Ohio State. Here is our definition of success. We could go to the dictionary where it says, "The accumulation of material possessions, prestige, rank, or power." We could use that definition. Or, we could use what we have chosen to use for success.

"Success is the inter-satisfaction of peace of mind, knowing I did the best I could possibly do for the group." I think the last three words are the most important: *for the group*. You can add these words as well: "For the team; for the school; for the community, for the country." I did the very best I could possibly do. Do you know what? There are going to be years when we are not 14-0, I will promise you that. This does not mean we were not successful if we do not win all of our games.

I feel we get good enough players that we should win on the scoreboard, too. I think we *should* be able to win on the scoreboard. However, I am not going to measure my self-worth solely on the won-lost record. Guess what? We did not have a perfect season last year. Yes, we were 14-0, but we did not have a perfect season. So I am not going to measure myself the other way either. I am not going to say we won 14 games so everything must have been wonderful. Every player was affected positively. But we did not meet all of our goals. Success must be defined.

Our third basic goal is to *create a positive impact* on our institution of Ohio State, in our community, our great state of Ohio, the United States, and the entire world. That is our goal. We want people to say we were champions and that we were first-class champions. That is a goal we have. We want our players to know in some ways we have a broad abstract mission, but we have some specificity to it, and we have some goals that we need to own up to as individuals and as a team as we go through life.

How can we get all of this done? Sometimes we can't get it all done. The only way we can accomplish our goals is to focus on every moment. When I worked for Coach Earle Bruce at Ohio State, he used to talk to us about dealing with players. He would ask us how we could see a player walking down the hall with his head down and a coach would ask the player what was up and the player would say, "Not much coach," and that coach could not figure out that something was wrong with the player. Coach Bruce would ask, "How could you walk by him and not know he has a problem?" A coach does not always know what is going on in a player's life. You need to focus every second on the moment. That gives us a chance to perhaps complete our mission. That gives us a chance to have a much higher concern for the fate of man than the diagrams and equations that we enjoy doing so much. That is crucial for us.

Let me shift gears on you. I am not going to do the X's and O's. I apologize, but my assistant coaches do not let me get the chalk much. We think there are three things that can make a difference for us at the quarterback position. It does not matter if we have an option-type quarterback, straight dropback quarterback, or a rollout guy, a tall guy, a short guy, or a fast guy.

Three things must come true for our quarterback to make the contributions to the team needs to be successful. It is the same three basic points we have always stressed. First, he must make *great decisions*. What I love about this aspect is that it has nothing to do with recruiting. The quarterback does not have to be tall, big, tremendously skilled, or whatever to be a good decision maker. If this is the most important thing the quarterback can contribute to the team, then how can I as his coach help him? How can I help him?

First, I can help him gain a total understanding of our offense and opposing defenses. This does not take talent. It takes a lot of work.

Second, we can put the quarterback into situational learning experiences. We can put him into situations that are going to be as game-like as possible before he is in a real game. Again, that does not take talent. It just takes a little creativity on our part.

Third, we can give him repetition under fire. I got highly criticized when I got to Ohio State. The charge was that I was letting the defense hit the quarterbacks. I had a lot of people trying to tell me what we needed to do with our quarterbacks over this situation. "You do not understand this is a different level of football." To be honest with the quarterbacks, I thought I was helping them to be a better player in the games. Guess what? Michigan is going to hit the quarterback. Purdue is going to hit the quarterback. Penn State is going to hit the quarterback. I think you need to put them under fire.

One of my quarterbacks at Youngstown State taught me this several years ago. I pulled him out from under the center and brought him over to put a special color scrimmage vest on him so the defense would not hit him. He said, "Coach, don't put one of those special vests on me. When you put that thing on me it changes my footwork, it changes the way the defense comes at me. Put me under fire in a game situation." Now, don't *kill* the quarterbacks. Don't go back to your school and tell the moms of the quarterbacks that the Ohio State Coach said, "We are sorry, but we will have to kill your son." The point is to get the quarterback under fire in practice. Don't let them just play touch football and then on Friday night get mad at him when it is tackle football and he does not make good decisions.

We can help the quarterback with films and mental gymnastics. We watch film and video, do walk-throughs and talk-throughs. Again, that does not take talent. He does not have to be a talented quarterback and you do not have to be a talented coach to do those things. He will become a better decision maker as a result.

The other way to really help the quarterback is through experience. At some point in time you must throw the quarterback into a game. He has to learn in real-game situations.

What made me feel good about our quarterback this year was this. Last spring after the signing date, people wanted to know which of the two quarterbacks we had recruited were going to start for us. We recruited two of the top quarterbacks in the country and everyone wanted to know which one would start as a freshman. The people all wanted to tell us we did not have a quarterback that was good enough to play other than the two freshmen. I just enjoyed the heck out of the fact that we had a fourth-year junior, who did not play before, that stepped into the slot and was what the team needed. Now, all of a sudden he is 14-0. Now Craig Krenzel is the most popular guy in Columbus. He gained experience as the year progressed.

The second thing our quarterback must do for us is to *make big plays*. Well, that does take some recruiting. You can recruit within your school. Don't let all of the big-play guys just be basketball players or baseball players. Don't let the guys that have that knack of making things happen get away from you. You have to recruit them, just like we do. But you must recruit them within your school.

I think the quarterback that is confident has a chance to make big plays. How does he get confident? By doing all of the previous things that we just covered. He must have knowledge of the offense and defense. He must have experience to make the big plays.

The third thing our quarterback must be able to do is to *eliminate the turnovers*. In the last 30 Super Bowls, the team that won the turnover margin has won the game 28 of the 30 games. I can show you stats where teams that win games also win the turnover margin.

How can we make our quarterback a player who is going to do a good job in eliminating turnovers? First and foremost he must believe that this is his most important role. Some quarterbacks remember the big pass play they hit in a crucial situation. They remember the long pass they forced into the receiver. The good quarterbacks remember the mistakes they made. They must be able to say, "I know why that mistake happened and I am not going to make that same mistake again." He must believe the most important task he has for our team is to eliminate the turnover.

Second, we constantly talk to our quarterbacks about delivering the ball to the receiver who is in front of the defender — the ball must be delivered at the numbers or lower. *Numbers or lower –- numbers or lower.* In 7-on-7 drills, practiced against air, or any drill, if the ball is not delivered at the numbers or lower, the quarterback gets a minus on his grade sheet. I do not care if we catch the pass or not. There will come a day when the ball is above the receiver's numbers and the receiver reaches up to get it, and then the ball careens off his hands and the defense makes the interception. The quarterback says, "He should have caught it." Yes, he should have had it, but it was above the numbers. If the mistake happens where the ball is at the numbers or lower, then where is the ball going? It goes down to the ground. We do not have a problem with that type of pass. *Numbers or lower –- numbers or lower.* They get sick of hearing this comment.

The next thing we want to stress with the quarterback is not to force the ball into the receiver. I would rather punt than force the ball and have it intercepted. Our goal on offense is to have every offensive series end in a kick of some type. The extra point is ideal. The field goal is okay. But a punt is better than an interception. I do not want a series on offense ever to end up any other way except by a kick. It is okay for us to punt. We can play defense. It is not okay to turn the ball over. We do not accept the quarterback commenting that, "I thought I could get the ball in there." *No!* That type of thinking will not work. "Let's not get it in there; let's punt." Don't force the pass.

We feel pressure on the quarterback in practice is important. If you do not put pressure on the quarterback in practice and you put him in a game and he turns the ball over, it is the coach's fault. Don't make him a redshirt in practice and have everyone keep five feet away from him. It is not going to be that way in a game. I do not mean that you go kill him. We have a good defense and they will get to our quarterback. They are smart enough to know that they can come running full speed at our quarterback as long a they do not knock the snot bubbles out of him. It does not help us if they slow down three yards from the quarterback. That does not help us. They need to get into his face.

The last point is the *experience factor.* You have to put the quarterback into the game to get game experience. There is no substitute for game experience.

There is one last thing I want to cover in the decision-making process. I feel this is crucial for the team and the quarterback. We must practice hard on situational aspects of the game. We have *coming-out* scrimmages all of the time. We tell our punt team this: "If you can drop the ball inside the opponent's 10-yard line, and our defense can stop them from getting a first down, we are going to get the ball back across the 50-yard line after the punt. We are going to score about 70 percent of the time when that happens." So coming out defense is huge, and we scrimmage that situation a lot.

For the offense it is the same deal. If our offense gets the ball back on our four-yard line and we do not get a first down, we will have to punt. If we have to punt in that situation, the opponents will get the ball across our 50-yard line and they have a very good chance to score even though our defense is very good. We tell our offense, "We cannot get stopped *coming out.*"

Here is a stat that I could not believe happened to us this year. We scored 31 percent of the time when we got the ball at our own 10-yard line or less coming out. *Wow!* That may never happen again at Ohio State. I think part of this was because we stressed the importance of *coming out* and we scrimmaged the heck out of it. This is important to our team.

The other part of the stats that I saw yesterday was the fact that there was only 15 times in 14 games where the opponents got to start their drive on our side of the 50-yard line. That meant they had less than half the field to go for a touchdown 15 times in 14 games. That helps your defense. Keep in mind we got to start on the opponent's side of the 50-yard line 39 times. That really helps your offense. That helps your team. So we practice those situations that we know are going to come up in games.

Short-yardage plays are big. We have a different way that we practice short-yardage situations. Let me explain what I mean by this. Let's say the ball is on the minus 42-yard line. We will scrimmage our number one offense against our number one defense full speed, smack them up, on third-and-two from the 42-yard line. We start the series with the third-and-two situation. *Bang!* If you make the first down the offense gets to go to third-and-two at the minus 48-yard line. *Boom!* If the offense makes it, they get to go to third-and-one-and-a-half at the plus 41-and-a-half-yard line. *Boom!* If you make it, you get to go to third-and-one at the plus 31-yard line. *Bang!* If you make it, you get to move up to third-and-one at the plus 21-yard line. *Boom!* If you make it, you get to move up to the 11-yard line. *Boom!* If you make it, you get to move up to the one-yard line. Now we tell them it is fourth-and-one for the touchdown. We tell them it is the last play in the world.

What is funny is the fact our season ended on a fourth-and-two-to-go situation for the National Championship. It was the last weekend of college football, and it was the last day of college football, and it was the last play of college football. Our season ended with the last play in the world right there on the two-yard line. It may have been on the one and-a-half-yard line.

Now, in all of those situations, if the offense does not make it, the second unit comes in and now it is number two's against number 2's in all of those situations. We start back at the minus 42-yard line. If they make the first down, they keep going. If they get stopped, they go off the field and the third teams come on the field until they are stopped. When they are stopped the first teams come back on the field. They will start where they were last stopped. If they did not make the first down at the 21-yard line on the last attempt, they will start at the 21-yard line the next series. I think it is important to have full contact with tremendous competition.

If the defense wins the down, they are off the field. If the offense wins or gets the first down, they get to stay on the field and continue to drive the ball down the field. That is what we call *situation learning* and we need to practice that way.

The next area we discuss is the *red zone*. If I had to say what the greatest improvement Ohio State made from 2001 to 2002, I would say it was the red zone. Why? There were a lot of reasons, but we just emphasized it a lot. We did not think we were that good the year before. We scrimmaged a lot of time in the red zone. We smashed each other. Also, we did a better job scheme-wise in the red zone this year. We made our field goals in 2002. We missed a lot of field goals in 2001. At one point in time our kicker had made

24 field goals in a row. There were a lot of reasons we were better this year in the red zone. But the one reason we can control the red zone is the fact that we worked on it, we worked on it, and we worked on it. We worked on it and we studied the situations. That is the highest blitz area for the defense. We worked our offense like crazy to prepare our offense to pick up the blitz in the red zone.

We worked the heck out of the goal line situations. We always end practice with the *last play in the world*. We knew someday there would be a game where it would end with a fourth-and-one situation. It could be Ohio State going in to score, or it could be our defense that was put to the test where the outcome of the game would come down to one play. It was amazing how it worked this year. It came in game 14 in the Fiesta Bowl.

We worked on our two-minute drill. We worked on it every day in the spring and preseason. Then we worked on it at least once a week in the regular season. With the offenses today the two-minute offense is almost always going on. We work on the two-minute drill when we are ahead and when we are behind. It is situational learning. It is important to us.

I really believe you can find a quarterback in your building and you can find a quarterback who you can recruit and teach to be successful in two of those three areas. You can teach them to do those things. I hope we can recruit or find a quarterback that can make the big plays. That is the unknown. I know we can find a quarterback we can teach those things to. Being able to find a quarterback who can make the big play is something we have been able to do over the years.

I think the quarterback has more impact on your defense than any player you have. What he does when we have the ball has more emotional impact on your defense than any other player or coach on your team. You better make sure you work like crazy to have a quarterback that understands what you expect. Then you must help him prepare.

It is always a pleasure to be here. Earl Browning has the greatest clinic in the world. But as I have told him, he needs to learn to relax a little. Outside of that, I appreciate being here. Come visit us at Ohio State.

SECONDARY TECHNIQUES AND DRILLS

University of Notre Dame

You probably noticed in my introduction they had me going to and from a lot of places. If you coach long enough at the college and pro level, you will move a lot. When I moved to South Bend, that was my 10th move. If I am in one place more than three years, I get antsy and start looking for the moving van.

As we get older, we get bigger, grayer, or have more wrinkles. I've gotten grayer and have more wrinkles, but I have not gotten bigger. There are ways to assess the aging process. There are different phases that you go through. One indication that you are getting older is you can't remember people's names. After that, you forget to zip your pants up. The third thing is you forget to zip your pants down. I think I am in the area of forgetting to zip my pants up.

It is great to still be coaching. It is a pleasure to be back in Louisville. I have spent a lot of time here, and my wife and kids still love it here. I had some great years at the University of Louisville coaching with Howard Schnellenberger.

Today I want to talk about *secondary techniques and drills*. I also want to show you some of the things we did this year at Notre Dame. The first thing I want to do is show you the defensive goals chart we used at Notre Dame.

We have 12 goals on our *goal chart* at Notre Dame [Diagram 1]. You can see the places where we need to improve. We need to improve in our third-down conversion and three-plays-and-out area. We gave up some big pass plays this year, but we did not give up any bombs. The longest pass play we gave up this year was 57 yards. We definitely want to improve our sudden-change goal for next year. That is one area we are going to concentrate on in spring practice.

2002 DEFENSIVE GOALS	
1. Win	10-2
2. Allow 19 or Fewer Points	9 games
3. Shut Out 4th Quarter	7 games
4. 40% 3 Plays and Out	6 games
5. Stop 3rd Down Conversion (65%)	6 games
6. Get 3 Take Aways	8 games
7. No Run Over 20 Yards −3(23 or less)	7 games
8. No Pass Over 30 Yards	5 games
9. Allow 3.0 Yds. or Less /run	7 games
10. Allow 7 Yds. or Less/attempt	9 games
11. Score or Set Up 2 Scores	7 (2) − 5(1)
12. Sudden Change Stop	6 games

Diagram 1. Notre Dame goal chart

I am not going to spend a lot of time on philosophy, but it is necessary for any defense to have a *sound philosophy*. We will use a variety of coverages in the secondary with *zone* as our base coverage. We use pressure with man coverage to keep the offense off balance. We will disguise our coverages to complicate the quarterback's reads. To win we must have great effort on every play, swarm to the ball, and create turnovers. This will be our style of play.

This is what we emphasize with our defensive backs starting in the spring and carrying over to the fall. When the new staff first arrived at Notre Dame, we noticed they played almost exclusively man-to-man coverage. I told our defensive backs in our first meeting that in order to make interceptions, we had to face the quarterback. We had to give the quarterback different reads. If you do one thing all the time, the offense will get a fix on what you are doing and will exploit you.

The year before I got here, I watched Notre Dame play Tennessee. They played well through three quarters. In the fourth quarter that tight man-to-man defense made a mistake and Tennessee scored a touchdown. From that point on Notre Dame had to play catch-up and eventually lost the game.

We think we have a good chance to win if our guys have a *great attitude* and put forth a *great effort.* I tell them that their attitude will determine their effort and their effort will determine their attitude. If you have a player with great attitude, more than likely he will give you great effort. If you have a guy giving you great effort, then that is an indication of the type of attitude he has. I've never seen a player give great effort and have a bad attitude.

Our objectives as a defensive back are to *prevent the score, prevent the big play, get the football,* and *be tough.* We will not play a guy who is not aggressive and will not hit. We have to have players who can run and hit. I have used this adage my entire career. It is called the *seven P's.* That stands for *proper prior planning prevents piss poor performances.* We stress this to our players as they are preparing for practice or games.

As we coach our players, we have to instill in them some definite responsibilities. The first thing we have to have is *movement.* We must have players who can move. They must work to peak condition in order to strain on every play and break quickly and aggressively to the ball. I'll talk about that in detail later. The strain I refer to happens a lot in the backpedal movement. What the defensive back doesn't do in the backpedal technique is strain to keep the receiver from closing his cushion. The defensive back has to strain to keep the cushion so he can break on the receiver's route patterns.

The next phase of responsibility is *toughness.* The defensive back must be hard-nosed and aggressive. He must be the best defensive back he can possibly be. He has to have *concentration.* He has to know his *responsibility* and *execute on every play,* whether it is a pass or run. A defensive back must have *character.* When he is backed up against the wall, how does he respond? These guys have to be players you can depend on to fight. They are the ones you want in your foxhole.

There are some basic principles of secondary play by which we live. We have to have *great effort on every play.* They must have *proper rotation and pursuit to the football.* That is one way to avoid giving up the big play. We did an excellent job of not giving up the big play this year. You must keep the football inside and in front of the defense at all times. A defensive back has to always know where his help is. The defensive back lives by the creed: *In unity there is strength.* When a defensive back is pursuing the ball and misses a tackle, he wants to force the ball back to his help.

Defensive backs have to be *great tacklers.* We have tackling drills we use to work on different phases of tackling. We stress the *backward run.* That is the one technique that is extremely important to the defensive back. We have to teach great reaction to the football. Those are the things I am going to stress today.

The defensive back has to have *total understanding* of the coverage we are playing. There are a number of items he has to know about the coverage. He has to know stance, alignment, key, charge and responsibility, and techniques. In addition to the technical execution of the play, there are a number of variables on each play of which the defensive back must be aware. The down-and-distance, time left in the game or half, and the score, are just a few of the variables he has to consider.

The thing that we really had to stress this past year was *communication.* A lot of our defensive backs were quiet. When you play a lot of man-to-man, there is not a lot of communication required. We got better at it as the season went along, but to improve we must get much better next year. On every play there are calls that have to be made. I touched on this earlier, but attitude and effort will determine how the defensive back will perform.

To be a good defensive back, a player must have a sense of responsibility. He must want to be the very best player at his position and must work daily to improve. He has to make a first, second, and sometimes a third effort to be successful.

We always grade pursuit and finish in practice and game situations. Any loafing on a play will result in a minus for the player. That is the biggest grade the defensive back gets. It doesn't matter what you did on the play.

The next things I want to talk about are *run support*, *ball reaction*, and *backpedal*. The key thing in run support is to make sure each player knows his responsibility. We are always going to have a force man, secondary force man, cutback man, and a cutoff man. I have cover 2 drawn for my example and explanation [Diagram 2]. The force comes from the corner on this type of defense. The key thing is to make sure the corner is aggressive and restricts the running lane. We key a number of things in the secondary, depending on the scouting report and whom we are playing. We may key the ball, backs, or uncovered linemen.

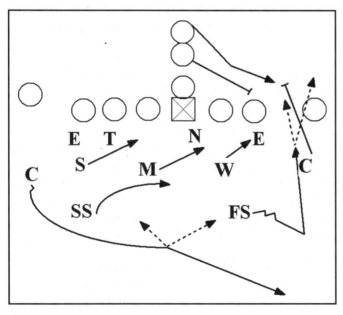

Diagram 2. Cover 2

The first thing the corner does is to *read his key*, whatever it may be. When he reads run, he immediately becomes aggressive and sprints inside.

The first thing he wants to do is beat the block of the receiver. If he can beat the receiver inside and still keep leverage on the football, then that is the path he takes. That may happen the first couple of times. However, after the defensive back beats the receiver inside a couple of times, the receiver will start to come down flat to make sure he gets to the defensive back. Regardless of how the defensive back takes on the block of the wide receiver, he wants to constrict the running lane as tight as he can. If the corner cannot constrict the running lane, he doesn't play.

The free safety is reading his key. As soon as he reads run, he shuffles to the outside. He must make sure the wide receiver is blocking on the corner and not releasing. When he sees the block of the receiver, he fills behind the corner. He is preparing to go inside or outside. If the corner is doing his job, the free safety will be filling inside.

The strong safety is the cutback man. I learned an important point in relation to this position when I was with the Minnesota Vikings. We tell him to run a banana route in his pursuit angle. He is filling behind the linebacker. If the linebacker gets knocked down, he has to replace the linebacker. If the ball continues to move outside, he curves his pursuit angle like a banana and runs to the alley. This helped us eliminate a lot of long runs. The longest run we gave up this past year was 37 yards.

The backside corner is the cutoff man. He will backpedal and revolve to the middle while he checks for the reverse. From the middle of the field he can go three different directions. He can come back to his position if the back reverses his field and tries to run the other end. He can fill up inside as the back is forced in by the corner. If the running back breaks containment, he can pursue across the field and make the tackle.

If the offense ran the football the other way, it would be the exact same pursuit. The left corner is the support, the strong safety is the secondary force, the free safety is the cutback man, and the right corner is the cutoff man.

The next thing we teach is *ball reaction*. Everyone who aligns in zone coverage has to see the quarterback. Everyone is keying the quarterback looking for the three-step drop. If the quarterback comes from under the center and is standing high and balanced in his retreat, we are going to play a three-step drop. If he has a backward lean in his retreat and is driving for depth, we are going to play a five- to seven-step drop. The key thing is to recognize the angle of the quarterback as to whether he is high or low in his retreat. If the defensive back reads the three-step drop, he freezes and keys the receiver.

As the defensive back reads the three-step drop, he looks at the quarterback's shoulder. If he opens his shoulder we feel he is going to throw the quick out or hitch. If he keeps them closed, we feel he is going to throw the slant route. Our backs did a good job of reacting to this last year. That gives the corner an indication of which angle he should drive. The only problem the defensive back has is the fade route. If the defensive back stops when the quarterback stops, the receiver continues to run. When the defensive back sees the fade coming he has to hit the receiver and turn and run with him.

If we are playing cover 2 or cover 3, the defensive backs are keying the quarterback. If the quarterback takes a five-step drop, the defensive backs are still reacting to the quarterback. If the receiver comes down and runs an out route, I don't want the defensive back to react to the route unless the quarterback is obviously looking in that direction.

We have to break before the quarterback throws the ball if we want to intercept it. I study quarterbacks and analyze their throwing motion. I try to give our safeties and corners a tip on how to react to the quarterback. Everything we do in cover 2 is based on reacting to the quarterback's release. We cannot intercept the ball or play great pass defense if we cannot get a break on the ball before the quarterback releases it. At the University of Louisville, we taught our defensive backs to break when the quarterback cocked the ball. A lot of the time as the quarterback drops, he will pat the ball immediately before throwing it. If the quarterback pats the ball and his shoulders are level, he is going to throw the ball in the 15-yard area. If his shoulders are tilted back, he is going to throw the ball deep. We practice and drill this with our defensive backs. If you break on the ball as the quarterback is throwing it, your chances of getting there are small.

If the corner reads the three-step drop, the pattern will be a five- to six-yard pattern. If he

doesn't get a three-step drop, he stays in his backpedal as long as he can to keep the receiver from closing the cushion. The receivers are trying to close the cushion and press the defensive back. After the receiver passes the five- to six- yard area, nothing is going to happen until he gets to the 10- to 12-yard area. We don't want to settle at 10 to 12 yards, but we are looking for a clue as to what the receiver might do. If the receiver passes 10 to 12 yards, he is not going to do anything until he gets to the 18-yard area. We have to depend on film work to reinforce that fact, but I think that will be the case most of the time.

The defensive back starts his *backpedal slow and relaxed*. After the receiver passes six yards, the defensive back has to increase the speed of his backpedal. When the receiver passes the 12-yard zone, the defensive back has to strain to keep his cushion while in the backpedal. That is when the corner has to really work hard to keep the receiver off him. When the receiver gets past 18 yards, it is time for the defensive back to open his hips and sprint deep with the receiver.

When we are in man-to-man coverage, we will read three keys on the receiver to determine when to react. We will *key the receiver's numbers, feet*, and *hips*. As the receiver explodes off the line of scrimmage, his numbers will be down. When he is in the move phase of his route his numbers will rise, he will chop his feet and his hips will sink. The defenders will plant and drive to the receiver.

When we begin to teach our defensive backs the *proper stance*, we will teach the basic way to get in the correct body position. Our defensive backs will align with a heal-toe relationship; their feet armpit-width apart. We have them put their hands flat on their thighs. We will ask them to bend their knees until their fingertips touch the bottom of their knee caps. After they have the proper knee bend, they will remove their hands from their knees and return them to the contour of their body. Their arms are bent in relation to the bend in their upper torso. They should not have to raise or lower their tail on their initial backward movement.

The proper stance is with their outside foot forward, and their feet are armpit-width apart with a toe-to-heal or toe-to-instep relationship. The defensive back will put the majority of his weight on his front foot. He is slightly cocked in because it is more comfortable when you look inside.

The first drill we use is a simple *backpedal drill* [DIAGRAM 3]. When we do this drill we move from the sideline out to the hash mark and back to the sidelines. The purpose of the drill is to develop proper backpedaling technique for the feet, hips, shoulders, and head. We start on the sideline and backpedal to the hash mark and sometimes to the middle of the field. We get into the proper stance and backpedal down the line. We are working on form in this drill. We want to pump our arms and keep our chin over our toes. Some people coach to keep the shoulders over the knees. It really doesn't matter because both positions are the same. The coaching points for this drill are to keep a narrow base, the feet close to the turf, the hips cocked in slightly shoulders low, and the head up.

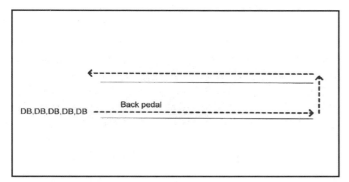

Diagram 3. Backpedal drill

These drills are the same ones I've done for a long time. I probably did them when I was here at the University of Louisville. If it is a good drill that teaches good technique, it doesn't get old and it works on all levels from junior high to the pros.

The *five-yard backpedal drill* is another excellent drill [Diagram 4]. The purpose of this drill is to develop good body position during the backpedal and improve reaction time. This is a full-speed backward drill in a five-yard area. Defenders put their toes on the line in a good stance and body position. On a command, the defenders backpedal five yards, plant their foot, and sprint forward to the line, then backpedal and plant their foot again, and sprint past the line. The coach wants to stress their chin over the toes, vigorous arm movement, leverage their feet, and their head up as they sprint forward. The coach needs to stand in a

position to see if their heads go back or comes up as they backpedal. Basically the head and hips are still and everything under them is moving. To keep their heads from going back, we coach them to keep their shoulders low.

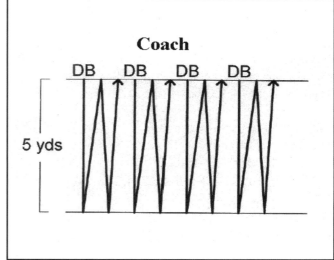

Diagram 4. Five-yard backpedal drill

One drill that we use to work on change of direction is called the *zigzag drill* [Diagram 5]. This drill teaches an ability to read and react to the quarterback's shoulders. It also develops the ability to rotate the hips and change direction quickly. We align four defenders five yards from the coach, side by side, and five yards apart. On a command or movement of a quarterback, the backs start there backpedal and drive off at a 45-degree angle on the movement of the quarterback's shoulder. On the quarterback's movement, they open their hips, push off their opposite foot, and elongate their stride as they change direction. We do three movements, plant, and sprint back past the line. You want to watch their eyes as they react to the quarterback's shoulders and eyes. You may want to throw the ball to one back as a signal for everyone to react back to the line.

If you want to put some variety into this drill, instead of bringing them back to the quarterback, have them speed turn as if they are running to cover a corner route. The key thing in this drill is their arm and head when they change direction. They have to stay low, throw their arm in the direction they are going, and get their head around. Wherever the head goes the body will follow.

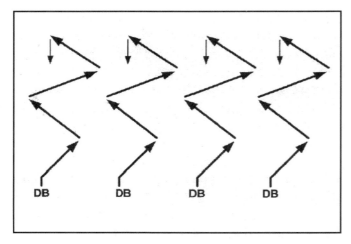

Diagram 5. Zigzag drill

This next drill puts a strain on the defensive backs and is called *backpedal and weave* [Diagram 6]. The backpedal is an age-old problem at every level of the game. When the defensive back gets into his backpedal, he wants to keep his cushion with the receiver. He has to maintain a vertical and horizontal cushion. If the defensive back starts out on the outside shoulder of the receiver, then that is the position he wants to maintain through out the route. If the receiver moves inside, the defensive back weaves inside to stay in the same position, while keeping his shoulders square. If the receiver moves outside, the defensive back weaves outside and keeps the same position. If a defensive back is in zone coverage and the ball is thrown deep, we expect the defensive back to turn into the ball. That means the defensive back is going to see the ball at the same time the receiver sees it.

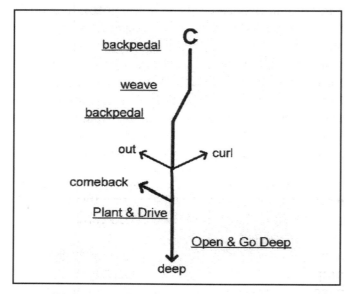

Diagram 6. Backpedal and weave drill

The purpose of this drill is to teach defensive backs to develop the ability to keep a lateral position on receivers. The defensive back aligns seven yards from the receiver. The defensive back will backpedal and weave on the receivers. He stays in his backpedal and covers all routes up to 18 yards. If the pattern goes past 18 yards, the back will open and go deep. Whether we are in man-to-man or zone, we key the quarterback through the three-step drop. The weave is a backpedal at an angle. If the receiver runs outside on the defensive back, the back turns his butt outside and backpedals on an angle until he gets his original position back. It is not a crossover step. When we weave we want to get width and depth at the same time. We can never lose our cushion. Any pattern run at less than 18 yards should still be in our backpedal and reacting back to the ball.

We want to keep a three-yard cushion. If the receiver gets too close to the defender, it is natural to open his hips to the receiver. That is not the way we teach it. We want to open to the ball or the quarterback. We don't want them to open to the receiver and then try to turn back to the ball. If a guy does that a couple of times, he is headed to the bench.

The defensive back aligns seven yards deep. He is keying his receiver, but watching the quarterback for the three-step drop. If the receiver comes off the line and quarterback shows a three-step drop, the defensive back must control his backpedal. The three-step pattern is going to be thrown at five to six yards, and caught around seven yards. If the defensive back is seven yards deep by alignment, he cannot retreat too deep and recover. We expect a collision at seven yards on a quick slant. It is not necessary for the defensive back to backpedal rapidly. He wants to be no deeper than nine yards. If the receiver tries to go deep, the defender has to cushion receiver.

The next drill is my favorite drill. If I could only do one drill this is the drill I would do. It is called the *stretcher drill* [Diagram 7]. This drill develops ball reaction and increases interception distances. Two defenders are aligned ten yards apart and ten yards away from the coach. The defenders backpedal and react to the shoulders of the coach. When the coach turns to throw to one of the defenders, that defender stops and prepares to catch the ball. The other defender has to break on the ball, intercept, and score. This forces the defenders to reach for the ball. We start in the middle of the field and work back deeper and wider. The second step is 15 yards deep and wider apart. We do the same thing at that distance and width. The third step is 20 yards deep with one defender on the hash mark and the other two yards inside the other hash mark. We do the same thing here.

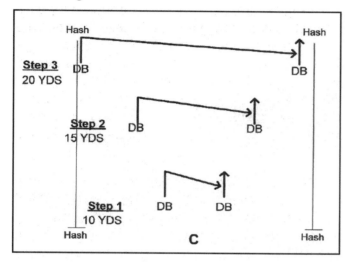

Diagram 7. Stretcher drill

When you start this drill you should probably designate one of the defenders as the receiver and the other as the defender. Later, have them react to your direction. When the coach looks at one of the defenders, he stops, and the other defender breaks on the ball. The defender has to break before the ball is thrown. I try to see who is breaking as I throw the ball. I sometimes have to look at the film to find out.

You can adjust the drill and put the defender out with one of them slightly deeper than the other. You do the same drill simulating the curl route. This makes the defender react up to intercept the ball. It is a good drill because it simulates game conditions.

This next drill helps your defenders with timing their jump and catching the deep balls at its highest point. It is called *deep ball drill* [Diagram 8]. It develops the defender's ability to maintain proper position on the receiver and body control. If you don't work on catching the deep ball, the receiver will out-jump the defender. It teaches the back to go after the ball at its highest point and intercept it. The corners align on the numbers five yards from the line of scrimmage. We align the safeties on the hash mark or in the middle. We go one at a time making each position do

the same thing. The coach is in the middle of the field. On a command, the defensive back will backpedal five yards, weave outside ten yards, turn, and sprint deep going for the ball. He will catch the ball at the highest point, call out, "Go," and sprint back to the line of scrimmage. This drill is a pitch-and-catch drill, but is essential if you want your defender to have any experience at catching the long ball. All interceptions are made at the highest point and must be returned to the line of scrimmage. Defenders must weave and turn inside, facing the quarterback and the ball, and drive deep to catch the ball. When I throw the ball I really stretch them on some throws.

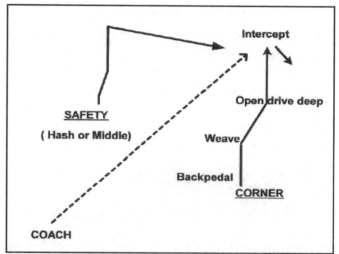

Diagram 8. Deep ball drill

I want to go to another phase with our defensive back plan. I want to talk about tackling. This is a basic *form tackling drill* [Diagram 9]. We want them to get into a proper fit position. Their heads should be up. We tell them to bite the ball. To bite the football the head has to be up. In this drill we align the tackler and ballcarrier in two vertical lines. The first back will tackle and the second back will carry the ball. In the first part of the drill, we put the tackler and ballcarrier into a proper fit. We place them together, give them a command, and let them drive with their legs. They are driving at a 45-degree angle.

In the second part of the drill, we increase the distance to five yards and do the same thing, except this time they have to move the five yards to make the contact. On the command, the ballcarrier will move forward at a 45-degree angle. The tackler will step dip and explode into the ballcarrier keeping his head up and his eyes open. Immediately upon contact the tackler wraps him up and grabs cloth. He will hit and lift upward and through the ballcarrier and drive him backward five yards. We tackle with the right shoulder and then with the left. The key is a spot at the bottom and between the numbers on the jersey.

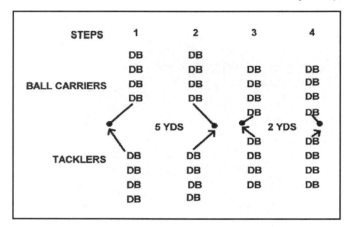

Diagram 9. Form tackling drill

The next drill is an *angle tackling drill* [Diagram 10]. We will align cones at the top and bottom of the numbers. The ballcarrier will align on the hash mark 20 yards from the tackler. The ballcarrier runs toward the cones. He may give the tackler a move to the inside or outside of the cones. The tackler runs to the ballcarrier from an inside-out angle. He takes away the cutback from the ballcarrier. He will never let the ballcarrier get him in a head-up position. He drives his head across the numbers of the ballcarrier, wraps him up, and drives him outside.

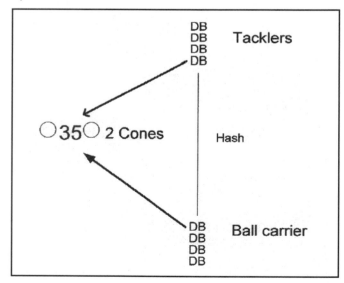

Diagram 10. Angle tackling drill

This next drill teaches open field tackling. It is called *catch-and-turn tackling drill* [Diagram 11]. The ball is thrown to a receiver who is facing the coach. He catches the ball, turns, and tries to elude the tackler. The tackler takes two backpedal steps and comes under control to make a sure, open field tackle. You can use different distances and angles while doing this drill. When teams throw the ball to a receiver, the most we want on the gain is where the receiver catches the ball.

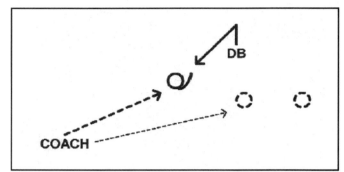

Diagram 11. Catch-and-turn tackling drill

In the *shuffle drill,* we teach foot movement and lateral movement [Diagram 12]. We use this drill with our man-coverage schemes. We want to develop quick reaction and get proper positions on receivers. We line our players up on the sideline and conduct the drill within a five-yard area where the sidelines intersect the yard lines. The designated receiver moves laterally and quickly back and forth within the five-yard area. On occasion the receiver makes a jab step upfield, then hustles back and continues to move laterally. The receiver makes two moves upfield. The defender mirrors the receiver by shuffling. Each time the receiver moves upfield, the defender moves his body in front of him. The defender has his hands behind his back and stays in position. We do this drill for six to eight seconds to complete each part of the drill.

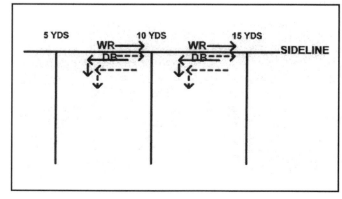

Diagram 12. Shuffle drill

The shuffle drill has four phases to it. Diagram 12 is phase one of the drill. Phase two is doing the same drill but allowing the defender to use his hands. The hands only come into play when the receiver moves upfield. We are looking for foot movement and hand placement.

Phase three of the shuffle drill is a press man-to-man, 1-on-1 type of drill. The receiver makes one quick move at the line of scrimmage. He releases upfield at full speed. The receiver tries to knock the defenders hands down and escape off the line as quickly as possible. We don't want the defender to reach for the receiver. He steps laterally, not forward, to make contact. He has to move his feet quickly. The defender uses his opposite hand when the receiver commits upfield. That helps him to open his hips in the proper way.

The *press cutoff drill* is another phase of this same drill [Diagram 13]. The receiver releases wide upfield. The defender sprints at an angle to junction the receiver downfield and runs with him. The defender places his outside shoulder in the receiver's chest.

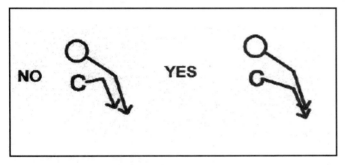

Diagram 13. Press cutoff drill

The defensive back has to know when and how to look for the ball. When we teach this phase of press coverage, we stress that the defender is either *in phase* or *out of phase* with the receiver. If the defensive back is in control of the receiver, he is *in phase*. If the defensive back is trying to catch up, we say he is *out of phase*. We put the receiver and defensive back on the numbers. The receiver is on the line of scrimmage and the defensive back is on the receiver's hip. The receiver runs a go route with the defensive back on his hip. When the ball is thrown, the receiver will look for the ball. At that point the defensive back opens his hips toward the quarterback, locates the ball, and makes a play on it. The defender uses his outside hand to feel the receiver. If the receiver starts to fade away from the hand, the defender works outside.

If the defensive back is out of phase, we teach a different technique. The defender has been beaten and has to catch up. The defensive back does not look back. He will sprint to catch up with the receiver. He will read the receiver's ear hole on his head gear. When the defensive back can see the receiver's eyes, he looks for the receiver's hands. When the receiver's hands go up, the defensive back takes his inside hand and forcefully hacks the receiver's outside arm. If you want to take the running out of this drill, you can pair up the defender and receiver and focus on ear hole, hands, and hack.

Let's watch some tape and see some of the things I have been talking about. Are there any questions you would like to ask? It has been a pleasure. I hope you got something out of my lecture. Since I was in Kentucky previously, the football has improved tremendously. I think that is due to all the hard work you guys are putting in. I think the football in Indiana and Kentucky has really improved. Thank you very much.

PRINCIPLES OF MAN AND ZONE COVERAGE

Indianapolis Colts

It is good to be here. The only reason I am in coaching today is because of the coaches I had growing up. They were great role models. I wanted to be just like those guys. I remember all my Pop Warner football coaches' names. Any time I go back to my home town, I look up my old coaches just to wish them well.

Coach Dungy sends his regards and said he enjoyed his days in Pittsburgh. He still likes to visit except when we have to come up to play the Steelers. I've been in Indianapolis for a year. Before that I was in Tampa. I coached at William and Mary for five years. Before that I was coaching in high school. In fact, the only reason I went into college coaching was because the school system I worked in wouldn't hire me as head coach at my old high school. They said I was too young.

What I am going to talk to you about are the *principles of man and zone coverage*. I'm going to point out the advantages and disadvantages of each. I want to share some of the thought processes that we go through on Monday and Tuesday as we prepare the game plan. We have to get our package ready to play for the upcoming game.

There is no magical coverage. We have a combination of coverages that we are going to use on Sunday that determines what we are going to play. I am here to serve you. If you have any questions, please don't be afraid to ask them. At the end if you want to go in another direction, just ask. I'm here for you.

When we get into our philosophy about whether to play man or zone, we want to know if we can stop the run on first and second down. We want to hold the offense to three yards or less on first and second down. On Monday and Tuesday that is our number one question. The fronts and the coverages have to be coordinated so we can accomplish what we are looking for. The second thing we want to know is if we can shut the passing game down and prevent the big play.

We evaluate ourselves to find out what kind of defense we are playing. The first thing we look at is the *number of points we gave up. On third and fourth down, is the defense giving the ball back to the offense, or are we allowing the opponent's offense to keep the ball?* The defense has to be able to get off the field. If we are playing good defense, we are forcing fumbles and interceptions and causing *turnovers.* We want to give the ball back to the offense. If you are doing those three things you are probably a good defense.

There are some definite advantages to playing *zone coverage.* When I talk about zone coverage, I am referring to *cover 2.* That keeps our linebackers in the box. There are easy adjustments to all kinds of formations and motions. Zone defense is good against shallow crossing patterns. Zone coverage helps us to evaluate the release of a receiver. It allows the defensive back to play press coverage and not worry about getting beat deep. Playing zone defense allows the defenders to see the quarterback. He is the ultimate key. We don't route read receivers. The defenders drop to a zone, read the quarterback, and break on the ball.

There are disadvantages in playing zone defense. There are holes in the zone defensive scheme. However, it has limited disguise against motion or slot formations.

In *man coverage,* there are some advantages. The defense matches their good defenders on the offenses' good receivers. We match up corner on receivers, safeties on tight ends, and linebackers on backs. Man coverage is good against the short passing game. Against the run, man coverage allows the defense to start with eight players in the box.

There some disadvantages if the defense plays man-to-man coverage. In some formations, the offense can force the defense to remove linebackers from the core of the defense. Adjustments to exotic formations are difficult to match up when the defense is in a man scheme. When a defense plays man coverage they lose some of their ability to disguise their coverage.

We play a lot of cover 2 in our secondary. It is a five-under and two- deep type of pass coverage. There is a four-man rush scheme with seven primary run defenders in the front. We have to do some things to help us in the cover 2 scheme because we are one gap short in our run responsibility.

We are a spot-drop team and we *key the quarterback* all the way. The reason we play cover 2 is that it is very good against the flat passing game. From the cover 2 scheme you can play the three-man route combination and be very sound in the defense. It is good against those kinds of routes but it is not great. When you play those route combinations, you have to be willing to give up small chunks of yards. You can stop the stop, the deep route, and the intermediate route, but you have to react back up to the short throw. This coverage is good against the pass on the two-man side.

When the defense plays cover 2, there are some things you have to give up. Cover 2 allows the defense to get only seven defenders in the box. This is not quarter coverage or rotation zone where the defense can cheat and get an extra man in the box. Cover 2 has to play with a seven-man box against the run. Our safeties are going to play pass and never the run.

The weakness of the defense is the quick slant pattern against a squat corner. We would like our guys to get a read off the receiver as he pushes upfield. He should see the three-step drop and be buzzing to the ball as the receiver runs the quick slant.

In the cover 2 defense there are vertical holes down the sideline. If a receiver gets an outside release and gets into the sideline, the sweet spot is about 23 yards down the sideline. If the quarterback and receiver can get the proper timing, then it becomes a 25-yard completion.

In this coverage we can only get seven men in the box. Since both safeties are going to be on the hash marks, they are not going to be able to get down into the box. That puts you one man short in the box against the run.

Our base alignments in the cover 2 defense are very standard. The defensive end is in a 6 technique head-up the tight end. He is a C gap player. The strongside defensive tackle is in a 3 technique. The nose tackle is in a cocked-nose position, which is a backside shade on the center. The backside defensive end is in a 5 technique.

Our corners alignments are one yard outside and four yards deep on the wide receiver [Diagram 1]. The corner takes an outside-leverage alignment on the receiver. They are flat players. The flat zone runs up to 12 yards deep and between the sideline and the numbers. He is expected to reroute receivers and get a hit on his wide receiver. Once he gets a reroute on the receiver he keeps his hands on the receiver and gets his head back on the quarterback. The corners are *mirror images* of one another.

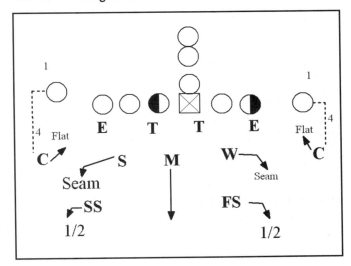

Diagram 1. Under defense cover 2

The corners constantly try to disguise what they are doing. They get up into a press position and back off. We set the depth at four yards because we cannot have contact with the receiver over five yards down the field.

If the number two receiver crosses the corners face, the corner hinges off his receiver and gets depth to his landmark. His landmark is 12 yards deep between the sideline and the numbers. If it is run, the receiver will lock on to him and try to block him. When that happens, the corner pushes the receiver off and keeps his outside leverage.

The Sam linebacker is head-up on the offensive tackle. He is a seam player. His zone runs up to 12 yards and is between the numbers and the hash marks. He wants to see the quarterback when he gets into his zone. The Will linebacker is aligned in a 3 technique to the weakside. He is the weakside seam player and plays just like the Sam linebacker.

The Mike linebacker aligns in the strongside A gap. He is the middle hook player. He is what we call a *deep run-through*. He is taking any vertical route coming down the middle of the field. It is his job to make the quarterback put air under the ball to throw it down the middle of the field. He is primarily looking for the tight end coming down the middle.

The strong and free safeties are aligned one yard outside the hash mark and 12 yards deep. They are half-field players. Their landmarks are two yards on top of the numbers. They drop slow as they start out. They key the quarterback, work away from him, and gain depth.

One of the weaknesses of the cover 2 defense is the holes in the defense. With this coverage we have to have a pass rush. The defender in the secondary can hold on to the receiver for only so long. The quarterback cannot be allowed to sit in the pocket and go from one side to the other and back again looking for receivers.

The quarterback can't have any more time than to look one side and go to his check downs. If the quarterback is looking to the left of our defense, we ask the Sam linebacker and corner to hold their landmarks. We want the safety to that side to get to the top of the numbers. The rest of the secondary we ask to cheat. We want them to get to the inner most part of their landmarks. They are squeezing their zone to the way the quarterback is looking. This helps to shrink some of the holes.

Most teams have a stripe down the middle of their helmet. We tell our defensive back to key the stripe. That lets us know where the quarterback is looking. We key the shoulders of the quarterback to time out our break and the angle we want to attack. We can tell them if the shoulders tilt back, the quarterback is going to throw the ball long. If he keeps the shoulders level, he is going to throw an intermediate or short route.

If the quarterback is looking at the defensive back, the back is not going to be able to tell if he is

looking inside or outside of him. He has to listen for calls coming form the other defenders. They are going to call, "in, in, in," or, "out, out, out." The quarterback cannot look one way and throw the ball somewhere else. We start looking for check downs.

If the offense goes to a slot formation, we stay in our cover 2 alignment and make adjustments to our alignments [Diagram 2]. The corner on the tight end side is two yards outside the tight end at the line of scrimmage. The opposite corner plays the same position and technique he played on the regular coverage. We stay in this set because we think we have the best of both worlds. The Sam linebacker goes out to cover the slot receiver. We lose him from the box, but we count the weak corner as in the box and we bring the strong safety down into the box.

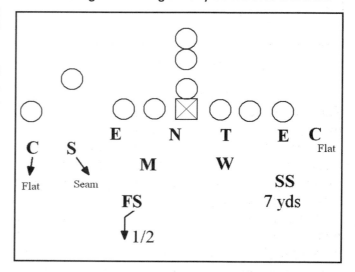

Diagram 2. Wide slot formation

This puts us back into our eight-man front scheme, but we are playing a variation of a cover 2 scheme. The strong safety is aligned at about seven yards and is flat-footed. He is not going to have to play many blocks in that position. He is run support for plays that are run at him and the cutback lane player on plays run away from him.

The offense can break the set and put the tailback wide as a third wide receiver to the tight end side [Diagram 3]. We move the cornerback out on him. Everyone plays the same cover 2 as we did on the first offensive set.

Everyone in the defense is on the move. We are moving back and forth and in and out as part of our disguise. We play a cover 3 rotation on occasion. We want to look like an eight-man front and man coverage. We try to disguise all of these defenses. The free safety is keying the tight end, wide receiver, and the quarterback. The tight end is going to tell him whether it is a run or pass.

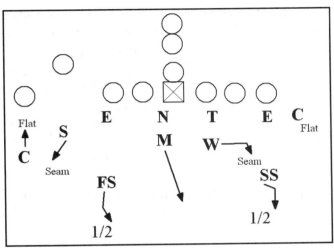

Diagram 3. Three wideouts

The tight end is going to take an outside release. The tight end knows we are playing a 6 technique and he doesn't want to go inside and get caught in all the traffic. The strong safety on pass is playing his normal coverage. If there is a strongside run, the strong safety is going to fill the backside A gap. He is the cutback player. If he sees the power play, which is the backside guard pulling, he goes across the ball and fits the next open gap that is the B gap to the strongside. We don't get enough reps for the strong safety as an in-the-box player. He can't read the guard pull and see all the things a linebacker might see on a consistent basis, but I believe he can learn how to play the technique we want him to.

To the slot side, we tell the Sam linebacker to split the difference between the slot receiver and the offensive tackle. He will never go any wider than his zone landmark. Since his zone landmark is the middle of the hash marks to the numbers, that is as wide as he will ever go. If the slot receiver is a wide receiver, the run read for the Sam linebacker is a little tougher. Wide receivers don't block linebacker so the wide receiver will bypass the linebacker on a run. The Sam linebacker doesn't have the advantage of the receiver coming down on him immediately to tell him it is run.

If the offense goes to a trips set, we walk the Will linebacker out [Diagram 4]. He plays the same

split rule as the Sam linebacker played on the wide slot. He is not going any wider than his zone landmark. His landmark is the middle of the hash marks to the numbers.

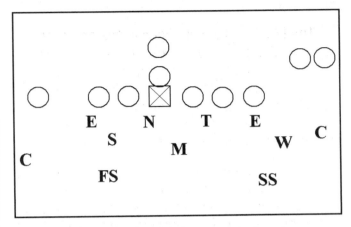

Diagram 4. Trips set

In cover 2 drill work, I do shuffle agility, turn-and-run agility, down the line, individual reroutes, and perimeter zone drops. In our individual reroute drill, we work on press, outside releases, and slant moves. These drills are my main staples. I call them my *EDD's*. That stands for *every day drills*. The reasons I came up with them is the amount of time you have to work on drills. We want to be fundamentally sound and play and do the fundamentals of football well.

The shuffle-down-the-line is a drill I use to help with the press or bump coverage. I want the defensive backs to shuffle down the line with their shoulders square to the line. I tell them the line is a cliff. If they set back off the line, they are stepping over the cliff. That is the same thing when we are playing press or bump coverage. I don't want them to drop their feet as they are shuffling down the line. If they do they are getting depth and width at the same time. I don't want them to do that. I want the defensive back to go flat down the line and I want to make the receive go east and west. If the defensive back drops his back foot, the receiver is going north and south.

The defensive back's hands should be inside and not flapping like a bird. I want them relaxed with their elbows underneath their arm pits. I want their hands inside the framework of their body. If they have to get a reroute, they will be able to punch up through a receiver's chest.

If the receiver takes a release, the defensive back has to turn and run with him. That is our next drill we do daily. The defensive back turns and runs to a designated point and changes directions. We use this drill because it is the second phase of cover 2. If the receiver gets an outside release, the defensive back has to turn and run to get a reroute on the receiver. The defensive back may get his reroute on the wide receiver, but he may have to turn and run to get to his landmark because the number two receiver is threatening his zone.

Down the line is the defensive back going down the line doing hip work. This work is used by our safeties more than our corner. It is a drill where players are flipping their hips from one side to the other. This drill is seen in the players' ability to get back to his zone drops, see the quarterback, and break on the ball. We speed the drill up as we go. The defensive backs are not going to be perfect. I would like to have *good, good, good*, but I will take *bad, bad, good*. The first one means is good alignment, good assignment, and good results. Bad, bad, good means a guy who is out of position, covering the wrong guy, but knocking the ball down.

What I can't stand is good, good, bad. That is a player who always lines up correctly, has great technique, but never finishes the play. I don't want that at all. I want them to know if they get themselves in trouble, what technique they can use to correct their mistake so they can finish the play and have good results.

When you do your reroute drills, make the defensive backs aware of being onsides. Make sure you have a ball in the drill, so your players don't line up offsides. In this drill we press the defender. If he takes an outside release, we want to shuffle punch and turn and run with him. The defensive back has to stay flat, get off the sideline, and back to his landmark. With an outside release by the wide receiver, you get an option route by the number two receiver. That means the number two receiver is pushing up the field and sitting down around the outside part of the numbers. The wide receiver is trying to occupy the corner by taking an outside release and tying the defensive back up. The defensive back has to get his head around, get his eyes back on the quarterback, and get back to his

landmark. If the quarterback looks at the defensive back, we want him to get depth to hold off the hole in the zone.

We work on the inside release because this is one of the weaknesses of the coverage. When we press this type of pattern, we want to work the upfield shoulder. We want to rip up and club up with our arms. We want to play the upfield shoulder and punch up with the upfield arm. We want to make the tackle with the low arm and strip the ball with the upper arm.

The reason we punch up on the ball instead of clubbing down is the way the receiver catches the ball. When the big receiver catches a ball, they pull the ball down to secure the catch. We want to do the opposite. As the receivers are pulling with the arms down, we want to punch up.

Big hits are not the thing we are looking for. We want interceptions. If we get the interception the offense gets the ball. If we make a big hit on a receiver, the offense takes that receiver out and puts another one in the game. That is a big crowd pleaser, but I want the interception.

The next coverage we are going to is the *man-free coverage*. In this coverage we have a post defender and a low-hole plugger. The low-hole plugger is our extra player in our concept. We have a four-man rush and we are playing with outside leverage. If we are playing a team that runs a lot of skinny posts, which we call a branch route, we adjust to an inside leverage in certain situations. If the ball is on the near hash mark and the receiver is six yards outside the numbers, we adjust our leverage to head-up to the inside. If the ball is in the middle of the field and the wide receiver's split is four yards outside the number, we will be into a head-up to inside alignment.

One of the strengths of the man-free coverage is a post defender. As far as I'm concerned, if I had a say in it, I would never play 0 man coverage again. I hate to put those guys out there with no help. If you are going to play 0 coverage, you better get the rush to the quarterback.

This coverage has a low-hole player. The three linebackers are responsible for the two backs in the backfield. They zone off on the backs and take them as they come out of the backfield. Of the three linebackers, one of them will be left free. He becomes the low-hole plugger. The low hole plugger helps jam any shallow crosses and patterns in the middle underneath.

This coverage gives you good match ups [Diagram 5]. It has corners on wide receivers. In the huddle we call *corners hang middle*. All that means is that the corners hang in the middle of the field. When the offense breaks the huddle, the corners locate their receivers and align on them. We play safeties on tight ends. Our alignments for the corners are one yard outside and 10 yards deep. The strong safety aligns three yards outside and five yards deep on the tight end. The free safety is 12 yards deep in the middle of the formation.

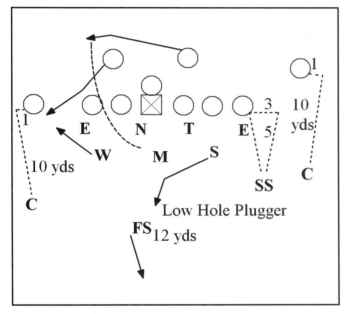

Diagram 5. Man-free coverage

The stuff we play in the pros is not as complicated as your stuff. I hope you believe me on that point. We don't have to play the option game. We don't have to put nine guys in the box to stop a running quarterback.

In the man-free concept we have an extra man to the tight end side. That gives us an eight-man front. This is an easy defense to get your run fits. All the linebackers and backs have to do is track their men and it should lead them into their run fits.

This coverage has some weaknesses like every other coverage. We think the weakness of this coverage is what we call bear pass. That is a pass that comes as an audible between the quarterback and the wide receiver. Everyone else is running a

running play. It is a two-man audible. The quarterback stands up and throws the ball to the wide receiver. It should not be a threat to the coverage, but the corner has to make an open field tackle. The other thing that can hurt this coverage is the inside pass route. They are patterns being run away from the corner and thrown quickly.

If we play the slot formation from the man-free coverage, our corners are on the same side [Diagram 6]. The corner playing the slot receiver will always be in a press position. The corner on the wide receiver is playing off. We do this so the defenders are not on the same level. If you get your defenders on the same level, they are easier to pick. The three linebackers are in the box playing a three-over-two concept on the running backs. The free linebacker is the low-hole plugger. The strong safety is three yards by five yards outside the tight end. The free safety plays in the middle of the formation splitting the two's and one's. He has to make sure the number two receiver can't get inside of him.

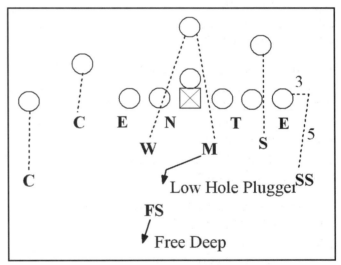

Diagram 6. Man-free slot

Against the trips set we put the strong safety on the third receiver instead of the Sam linebacker [Diagram 7]. The Sam linebacker takes the tight end.

If we call trips special, we are moving our safeties around to cover an H back in motion who creates a trips formation or an unbalanced set for our defense [Diagram 8]. If the offense starts out in a double formation with slot formation to the split end, we go to a trips special call. We want our safeties involved with this coverage. If the H back aligns in the right slot and goes in motion back toward the center, the strong safety takes the motion and gives a weak call to the linebackers. The strong safety comes back into the box with the H back and becomes an extra linebacker to the weakside.

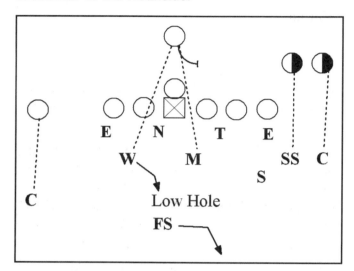

Diagram 7. Trips man free

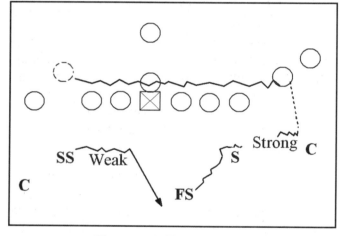

Diagram 8. Trips special

If he continues past the center, the free safety picks him up and gives a strong call to the linebacker. If the H back leaves the box, the safety calls, "I've got him." The weak and strong calls let the linebackers know they have help in the box. The *I've got him* call means the linebackers play a one-back fit instead of a two-back fit. The safeties exchange position as the H back goes across the formation.

Man drills are like zone drills. If you can't find the drills in your game tapes, you are doing the wrong

drills or you are teaching them poorly. The skills that show up only once in a while you need to eliminate. Work on the skills you use all the time. We teach individual breaks, bump-coverage footwork, transition drills, and 1-on-1 passing drills. We teach our bump-coverage footwork in three phases. We use what we call inch, quick-jam, and press-shuffle agility drills.

It is too hard to play bump coverage on a receiver if you don't get some kind of jam on him in the first four or five yards. The corner knows when he plays outside leverage, and a receiver gets away from him in the middle, he has a short and deep-hole player to help him. You can't stop everything. If we can win on our leverage side, that is good enough for me. I'm not going to fuss or cry about completions on the inside routes. If a receiver runs an out, deep out, or vertical route, I'm going to be upset at them.

The reason we are at 10 yards is to be able to play the three-step drop of the quarterback. Be careful using the backpedal so that you don't get your players making wasted movements. We are going to read through the three-step drop with vision on the quarterback. After the three-step read on the quarterback, the defender's eyes come back to the receiver. We punch and pedal, start slow, and increase as we go.

I want them to be comfortable in the backpedal without the receiver climbing all over him. It all comes too quickly at seven yards. That is why we are aligned at 10 yards. I want them to be able to come out of their backpedal and make a break on the ball. At 10 yards, after he makes the read on the three-step drop, he should be able to make the transition and come down hill. Now, he can make the play on a three-yard pattern. That pattern is going to be run at five yards and caught at seven. We are not dropping at all and should be able to make a play on that ball.

If the pass is completed, the defensive back needs to make sure the ball is caught in front of him. He has outside leverage and needs to make sure he can make a play on the ball.

That's all the time I have. It has been a real pleasure being here. Thank you very much.

TRANSITION DEFENSE

University of Florida

I once heard George Perles lecture and he said something that has remained with me through the years. He said, "If there was one defense that was the best then we would all be doing it." We all want to win. That is how we are judged in football. Everyone wants to have the best offense and the best defense.

I am not going to stand up here and talk a lot about defense. What you are doing on defense is probably what you should be doing on defense. What I want to do tonight is to give you some ideas that will make you a better football team. A lot of the times you go to football clinics and you hear speakers talk and you sit there thinking that you do not agree with what the speakers is saying. There is nothing wrong with that. This assures you of what you believe in. All that does is to make you feel that much better about what you are doing in your program. You may not believe everything I say here tonight, but that can make you believe more in what you are doing. I have learned one thing in coaching: *"It is not what you know; it is what you can make those players do."*

Having gone from the college ranks to the pros and then back to the college game, I can tell you what the game is all about. It is about getting those players to play tough. It is about getting those players to play your system as hard as they can play it. Once a coach can teach his system and get it across to the players, he has a chance to be successful. Once the players believe in the system and the coaches, they have a better chance to have a good program.

I spent over 12 hours getting here today. I had a lot of time to think about the things we need to do to get better at the University of Florida. Everyone is trying to get better. Coaches want to know what they can do to make their team better. You have the players that you have. It is that way in the NFL with free agencies. The pros lose players, and college teams lose players, and high schools lose players. The question is what can you do to get your players to buy into your system?

My topic is *transition defense*. I am going to do something that I have never done before. At the end of the lecture I am going to show some films that are negative. Sometimes you must figure out a way to make your players understand what you are talking about.

At this time of the year, everyone does a self-study of their offense, defense, and special teams. The reason you do this study is to find out how you can make your teams better. How can we make our defense better? What can we do to tailor our defense to our players? In my forth year in coaching I was fortunate enough to coach a great player. I was too dumb at the time not to realize that the player was the reason he was so good and not the fact that I was his coach. I kept thinking I was coaching his ass off and that was the reason he was so good.

The next year I went to another college and coached other players. But the guy I was coaching that year was not as good as the previous player. He did not make all of the plays. The point I am trying to make is this: *I think you must adjust your coaching.*

We went to the University of Florida last January 2002. Coach Spurrier had been there for 12 years and had won a lot of games. There were a lot of expectations when I took over as head coach. Do you know who had the toughest time adjusting to the new system, and to the new staff? From the beginning I let everyone know I could not be Steve Spurrier. I am Ron Zook. I could not be Steve Spurrier. That is just not me. The players adjusted to the new system. Sometimes the coaches have a hard time adjusting to a new system and to new coaches. We try not to make that a problem and we have to learn to adjust.

We always do a study on our defense. *We list all of the defenses and all of the coverages that we call.* If I am going into a game I want to go into the game with a lot more ammunition than I need. I want to have all of the bullets I can. That is not necessarily good. If the bullets are not shooting right you are not going to be very good.

Next we list the defensive consistency. Some teams use three yards to determine the consistency of a defense on a give play. Some teams use four yards to measure the consistency of a defense. You take every defense you call and go through the results. If the offense gained three yards or more the defense was not consistent. Again, the pros use four yards to measure the consistency. When you get down to your third-down defenses and you hold the offense to two yards or less then that is a consistent defense. List the defenses by down-and-distance. If you hold the offense to three yards or less, it is a consistent defense.

Next we look at all of the defenses that were scored on. You must be objective on this. "Why were we scored on?" *List our defenses and the coverages that were scored on.* We want to know why that defense was scored on. Sometimes it is because the defense was a bad call. You must understand that it is not always the players' fault. You must get the defense in the right situation. The offense may have had four wide receivers in the game and we were in our base defense. It is the coach's job to put players in position to be successful.

Next we take plays that gained over 20 yards against our defense and list them. Those are big plays to us. You may want to use 18 yards or 15 yards to determine the big plays. Some teams use 18 yards for a pass play and 15 yards for a running play. We just use 20 yards as a big play against us.

We list the defense and the coverage for the big plays. Why was the offense able to make the big play against our defense? We list the down-and-distance on each of those plays. We also list the players involved on that defense.

We break down where the ball starts and the percentage of times we are scored on. This is more for your players more than anything. We all know if the offense gets the ball backed up they have a lot less chance of scoring than they do if they get it on the 50-yard line. You may find that you need to work on your defense when you have a team backed up. We do a lot of *situation practice.* We scrimmage from the five-yard line coming out or from the five-yard line going in. We want to put them into different situations.

We chart the number of defenses we use over 10 times. You will be amazed what this will show. You will have some defenses that we have called a lot. But you check it out and see how many defenses you used over 10 times. A lot of the time we find out that we practice a certain defense, but we very seldom use it in a game. Think of all of the time it takes when you put in something new. We all do this. But the time we spend on this is important. Go back and look at the times you use those different defenses.

We all run the plays we are confident in when we get to key situations in a game. It is the same on defense. When it is third-and-one to go, we run the defense we are the most confident in. You have the most confidence in the defense you practice the most. It is the defense you play the most. In moving around from job to job, I have found that my favorite defense changes from job to job. Your team is different and the way teams play is different.

We keep track of sudden-change situations. What happens when the offense gets the ball in a sudden-change situation? We want to know what offense the opponents use when they get a sudden-change situation. They may throw the ball in second-and-short situations. We tell our defense to watch for the long ball when that happens. Again, we find that we practice a lot of time on defense that we do not play very much in games.

You will find out that a lot of big plays come from basic fundamentals. I am not telling you anything you do not know. But this will assure you that you are doing the right things. If you cannot get the fundamentals coached in the time period you are allotted then you are doing too much.

One thing I got from the NFL is the *big four.* Bill Arnsparger, who was the Athletic Director at Florida back when I was an assistant there, started the two-deep coverage and the rolled-up defense. He was the head coach at LSU at one time. He also coached in the

NFL at Miami, Washington, and San Diego of the NFL. Now he is back in San Diego coaching again. He said there was only one stat on defense that means anything. That is the *defense against the score*. He said all the rest of those stats do not make any difference. If the offense does not score, you have a good chance to win the game.

We talk to our team about the *big four*. *We are a blitzing team*. If you are going to be a blitzing team then you team must have a blitz attitude. When our guys blitz, we want them to go all out. There better be a puff of smoke coming out of the player as he makes his blitz. He must get to the area he is assigned to get to. That is a blitz attitude to us. The halfback may be 1-on-1, but that blitzing man is also 1-on-1 when he takes on the blocker on a blitz.

Next we talk about third-down defense. If we can win 67 percent of the third downs, we are going to win more games than we lose. We tell our players to play good third-down defense we must play good first- and second-down defense. There is nothing worse than getting into that third-and-three, four, or five to go. We must keep them out of the third-and-short yardage situations. Keep them in third-and-long. When it is third-and-long situation, a bell should go off in the head of the defensive men. We can blitz with a lot of confidence in those situations.

We want to play fast in the red zone. You must be good in the red zone. Where does the red zone start? To some teams it is the 20-yard line and for others it starts at the 18-yard line. When the ball gets down in that area they know what we are going to play. When the offense gets down to the 20-yard line we are only going to play one or two defenses. The defense must make a play in that area. They must be confident when the ball gets in that red zone.

The last of the big four is the two-minute situation. More games are lost in two-minute situations than in any other situation. When you get into those situations at the end of the half and at the end of the game, your players must have confidence. We only play a couple of defenses in those situations.

The difference between high school and college and the NFL is *margin of error*. In the NFL there is very little margin for error. You must dot the I's and cross the T's in the NFL. If you don't, they will find your mistakes and make you pay.

Next I want to talk about *off-season*. We break down our year like this. The first phase is *recruiting*. I know you do not have that in high school, but in college the players are ambassadors. They assist us in recruiting. The next phase is the *off-season*. That includes the weightlifting and the running. The next phase is *spring football*. Then we go to *summer conditioning and summer ball*. And the last phase is *the season*. That is how we break the year down.

We sit down and talk before each phase. We want to know what we want to accomplish in each phase of the program. Everyone wants to win, but we want to know how and why we are going to win.

We start with the phase of preparing to play a 14-game schedule. If we play in the SEC Championship, and then play in a bowl game, that gives us 14 games. Now, that is with a 12-game schedule. I think the colleges will go back to the 11-game schedule after this year.

We want to take the next step. If you are a team that was one or two plays away from winning the championship, what are you going to do to get to that next level? What are you going to do to put yourself into a situation where you can win the championship? What do you have to do? We have to make sure the players know what we are trying to get accomplished in that regard.

We must have the same chemistry and work habits that we had last year. Our work ethic is very good. It is the best I have been around at any level. There is a lot of competition for playing time at our place. We will have 42 players coming out of the tunnel in our first game that have never played in a game.

We must install our defensive package in the off-season. We must keep it polished once we install the defense. We are an eight-man front team. We may not be in the eight-man front all of the time. We are an eight-man front even out of a two-deep look.

Chasing the ball is a habit. People tell me I cannot coach the players at Florida like I coached in the NFL. I do not believe that. I coach the same today as I did when I coached in high school, in college, and in the NFL. Chase the ball. That is a habit. We want them to run to the huddle and we want them to practice the way they are going to play the game. We want that fast tempo. You do not have to be on the field all day. Teach in the classroom and coach on the field.

I feel you must have fun in football. Football is the hardest game there is. Every one of us has been knocked to our knees. The great thing about football is you have a chance to get back up. You must keep your eye on the bull's-eye.

There is no margin for error. If you give them an excuse they will take it. A reporter told me the other day that we were going to be very young next year. Who cares? So what if we are young. I am not going to use that as an excuse. We have a lot of players who do not have a lot of playing time. But they are going to get playing time really fast. As coaches we must lead the young players.

You must be demanding. I always coached the best players the hardest. Take the best player and make him perfect. In the NFL, not all of the players are great. There are some players in the NFL that are not all that good. But they have the ability to rise up to the level of that great player. Take that best player and coach him. If you love them, they will love you. If you expect the players to give you all they have, you must give them all you have. I tell the players I would prefer them to respect me 10 years from now than to like me now. If you can get your best player playing without a margin for error, the other players will rise to the occasion.

We want our players to know what to do and to play fast. The players hear me calling out, "Play fast, play fast," all of the time.

Doubt will defeat aggression. If you have doubt then you will not be aggressive. Bud Wilkinson once said, *"You cannot tell the difference between a player that is confused and a coward."* The players are not going to tell you they are a coward.

Emotion is the eraser for any screw-up. We want our players to play with emotion and to play fast. If you can play with emotion you cannot play fast. If you are not sure what you are doing you will not play with confidence. The best coaches I have been around are the ones who could give the players all they could handle and no more. They know when to stop and they know the difference in going beyond the player's

ability. When does it become too much for a player? Most of the time players understand what you have covered when they walk out of any meeting. But you put them into the game and it is another situation. When the crowd gets into the game the players do not remember all of the things you went over with them in the meetings. I believe the younger the players the less you give them. If they are worried about what to do they are not going to play very confident.

I think it is important for the players to know where you are coming from. Let them know your policy. We want our players on time for everything. That means meetings, practice, trips, and anything else that pertains to the team. We are all about going to class. We have to do that.

Everything we do is important. We treat it that way. It does not matter if it is stretching, meetings, or anything else. If the players are going to stretch, they should stretch. If they are talking and not really putting much into the stretching, we are going to get them up and go to work.

I think you must *practice smart.* I am not from the old school of beating the snot out of the players. The way things are today we must make sure we are getting our best players to the game. It does not do me any good to have my best player on the sideline in a cast.

We have *three types of practice.* When we are scrimmaging we have three ways of tackling the offensive man. First we have *tag off.* That means the defensive man must come under control in a good football position. His head is up, butt is down, and his knees bent. We do not just run by the ballcarrier and tag him. We are in a football position and tag him. We do everything except hit the ballcarrier.

Second we have what we call *thud.* We do not want anyone on the ground. When the ballcarrier comes through the line into the secondary we will tag off against them. But as they come through the line, we get into position and wrap-up and butt the ballcarrier.

The third tackling phase is the *live tackle.* I believe when you tag off it teaches better habits than you develop in live tackling. You do not teach the same good habits when you go live.

We teach our defense to stay away from our quarterbacks in practice. That is just one of the things we believe in. We want our players to stay off the ground when we are not going live. When we get players on the ground when we are going in thud mode, I tell them to get their feet moving or they would not be on the ground. If you make them stay off the ground, you will be a better technique football team. Make them move their feet.

We think the tempo of a game becomes a habit. If you want them to play fast you must practice fast. If you want them to play with tempo then you must practice tempo. "You play how you practice." You cannot talk a long time between plays in practice if you want them to develop a tempo.

I want to talk about the things we expect from our players. This is what we tell out player as far as what we expect of them.

We expect their best effort on and off the field. We expect their best effort all the time in their school work. What do you get? What do you expect from them?

We want them to ask questions. You have to look them in the eyes. You can tell if they are not sure about things. You know if they are not on the same page with you.

We tell the players not to be afraid to make mistakes. I have no problem with a player making a mistake. What I have a problem with is for the player to make the same mistake over and over. I do not like it when one player makes a mistake and the other players are not watching what is going on. There is no way you can give all of the players the same number of reps in practice. If a player makes the same mistake as the teammate in front of him, it means he is not paying attention.

We encourage our players to help each other. This helps the young players as well as the experienced players.

We set *goals* like most of you do. We have a few goals. I think it is important for everyone on the team to think in terms of those same goals. This does not mean you can't have personal goals. You need to have personal goals. My personal goal was to be the head football coach at the University of Florida. That was my goal when I got into coaching.

If everyone on your team is working for the same goal, all of the individual goals will take care of themselves. We want the same goal for everyone on our team. The players must understand this.

I taught biology in high school for two years. The one thing that schools do not do is to teach kids how to set goals. You must have goals but on the same token you want everyone on the same goal. The best opportunity to succeed and for everyone to reach their goal is for everyone to have a common goal.

We want our kids to stick together. To illustrate this point I give the kids a pencil. I take one of those pencils and break it. I take all of the pencil and put them together and I cannot break them. Let them see how strong the pencils are when they are put together. That is what you must do with the team. Have them stick together.

Football is the ultimate team sport. When I went to Miami of Ohio, we lost one game in 1975. We only lost one game that year. That was to Michigan State 14-13. We went 34-1-1 while I was there. Since I have been in coaching I have tried to get the same attitude that we had when I was on that Miami team. We were not great players but we had an attitude that we were not going to get beat. How do you develop that attitude? If you could tell people how to develop that attitude you could sell it. You would be a rich dude.

We ask our players how we can accomplish our goals. We can accomplish our goals because we have *adapted* the system to the players. You must adapt the offensive and defensive system to your players. This is true at any level. We can accomplish our goals because we have a great coaching staff. I am excited about our staff. We can accomplish our goals because we have good players. The players must believe this and they must understand this concept. I believe it in my heart.

Your team must be known for something. You can tell them what to do but you cannot do it for them. I do not believe in staying on the practice field a long time. But you can get three hours of work done in two hours. I do not just think this; I know it can be done. We want our players to complete every play. We want to finish. If you want them to do it in a game, you must do it in practice. We talked about going to the next level. It is not just going to happen.

All of our players want to be better players. As coaches we must find out who is willing to be a good player. Everyone wants to be better. But are they willing to be better. A lot of the players do not know what it is to work hard. How do you get them to work hard? That is what we must do as coaches.

We said we wanted to *set the tempo*. We must get them in and out of the huddle. If you want to talk to the players when you are scrimmaging, coach on the run. Run to the huddle with the players. Things are going to happen. We tell them to go to the next play just like we do in a game.

We tell our kids to forget a mistake and to go on. But how many times do coaches make mistakes and let it bother them. We have to practice what we preach and go on after we make a mistake. We want to finish the play. We want them to go all out until the play is over. We are constantly telling them to finish the play.

John Wooden, former UCLA basketball coach, gave us a lot of good ideas in coaching. No one will ever win as many games as that man did. I am going to go over some of these points very quickly.

- You are the only one that is going to know if you are completely prepared to play.

- Prepare one game at a time. The only way you can affect the future is by what you do today.

- Respect all of your opponents and fear none.

- Repetition is the law of learning and the key to consistency.

- People become stronger mentally and emotionally after adversity and tough times.

- Peace of mind and self-satisfaction is to know you have done your best and that your have done the best you can do.

- Challenge is what makes people grow to be the best they can be.

- How do you know if you are going far enough unless you have gone too far?

- If you are not living on the edge you are taking up space.

- Be more concerned for the team than for yourself.

- Every player has a role.

- No matter how good you are you should always try to get better.

- Your strength is how you handle criticism and praise.

Someone asked me what I wanted my players to be known for. This is what I would want my players to be known for. *I would want them to say they knew what to do and they were not confused.* If they know what to do they are not confused they are going to play fast. They are going to play with confidence and they are going to play with excitement. They are going to have fun. You will know if they are having fun or not. Nothing bad can happen if you have 11 guys flying to the football as fast as they can go. Run to the ball. It is a habit.

I want people to say that our football team is fundamentally sound. I want them to say our team plays with emotion. When I first took the job at Florida, I was asked by a sports writer at a press conference what I wanted the people to think about our team. This is what I told him. I want people to say our team walked out of the swamp and they were really having fun. If people walk out of your stadium and tell others that your team is having fun, chances are you are going to win more games than you are going to lose. This means they are playing fast and they are playing with emotion. They are playing with all they have. You are not going to win all of the games. It is impossible to win all the games. If they are having fun it gives them a chance to win. We want to eliminate doubt. It goes back to teaching them less.

The next point I want to discuss is *the question of playing man or zone defense.* If it is a defensive back, he must play with his eyes and he must know what he is keying. If he is playing zone, he must key the quarterback. If he is playing man coverage, he must keep his eyes on the receiver. If we are playing zone the quarterback is the person who is going to beat us. If we are playing man the receiver is the man that is going to beat us. When I am playing man coverage and the receiver comes downfield at me, what does the defensive back do? The first thing he does is to look at the quarterback. How do you break that habit? When we start out teaching the backs we do not even let them throw the football. We want the defender to get a position on the receiver. If I loose one step looking at the quarterback, that is three feet. I have to figure out how to make up that one step. In man coverage the man is going to beat me and I look at the man. In zone coverage the quarterback is going to beat me and I have to look at him.

We want to practice the techniques in proportion to the percentage of reps in a game. We want to practice the defense we are going to play in a game.

I think it is important for the defense to know the strengths and weaknesses of the defense. The more times an offense snaps the ball, the more chances they have to screw-up. As I said we are an eight-man front defense. You must know where you fit against the run. Everyone must know where they fit against the run. Everyone has an area and everyone must get there.

You must *believe* in your players. They are all you have. If that is all you have, you must find a way to make them think he is good enough to win with. If you don't it is your butt anyway. If he is all you have and if he is not good enough you must make him think he is good enough to win.

When the defense gets in the huddle they must know what the situation is. It is like driving a car on an icy road. You have to know there is ice on the road. You do not drive the same.

We must *communicate* with each other. You must think out loud. Talk! A play takes about six seconds to run. You end up playing about six minutes per game total. If you only play 10 games in a season, it comes out to 66 minutes. You work so hard to play that amount of time.

Alignment is also important. Get lined up. If they cannot get lined up you are doing too much. They must know their assignment. They must know the technique they are going to use on each play.

The job of the defense is to get the football back for the offense. Turnovers! Keep them out of the end zone and get the ball back for the offense.

I am going to do something I have never done before in a clinic. I am going to show you a film and I am going to point out the negative aspects of the game. We can talk about each of these situations as the come up in the film.

(Film)

I hope there was something that I said that made you feel better about what you believe about the game. If you are ever in Florida stop by and see us. We would love to have you. Thank you.

2003 COACH OF THE YEAR CLINIC MANUAL ORDER FORM

PRICES INCLUDE $5 FOR PRIORITY P & H PER MANUAL.
Make checks payable to: **Telecoach, Inc**

School P.O. or credit card requires a signature.
Telecoach, Inc. Tax ID #:61-0908034.
For add'l info call 502-425-2937 Fax: 502-425-0306

Mail to: Telecoach, Inc.
Attn: Earl Browning
PO Box 22185
Louisville, KY 40252

*Canadian and foreign orders: pay in US currency, and add $5.00 per manual for postal exchange.

Payment Method: _____Check _____ School P.O. _____ Master Card/Visa/Am.Ex./Discover

Credit Card No.: __/ __/ __/ __/ __/ __/ __/ __/ __/ __/ __/ __/ __/ __/ __

Exp. ___ ___/ ___ ___ Signature (required) _____

Quantity	CLINIC-YEAR	Unit Cost	$ Total Sale
_____	2003	$30.00	_____
_____	2002	$29.00	_____
_____	2001	$28.00	_____
_____	2000	$27.00	_____
_____	1999	$26.00	_____
_____	1998	$25.00	_____
_____	1997	$14.00	_____
_____	1996*2nd edition	$24.00	_____
_____	1995	$14.00	_____
_____	1994	$14.00	_____
_____	1993*2nd edition	$23.00	_____

<><><><><><><><><><><><><><>COACHING BY THE EXPERTS<><><><><><><><><><><><><><><>

Quantity		Unit Cost	$ Total Sale
_____	Coaching the Quarterback	$24.50	_____
_____	Coaching the 4-3 Defense	$21.43	_____
_____	Coaching Beyond the X's and O's	$21.50	_____
_____	Coaching the Offensive Line	$21.50	_____
_____	Coaching the Defensive Line	$21.50	_____
_____	Coaching the Secondary	$21.50	_____
_____	Coaching the Kicking Game	$21.50	_____
_____	INDIVIDUAL LECTURES (1969-1992)	$10.00	_____

View all lectures at: www.nikecoyfootball.com. Mail or e-mail name of lectures ordered.

Only KY schools include tax form 51A-126 or pay 6% sales tax. _____

TOTAL PAID _____

Mail To:
Name _____
School _____
Address _____
City _____ St_____ Zip_____ Plus_____